Understanding Cybersecurity

Understanding Cybersecurity

Emerging Governance and Strategy

Edited by
Gary Schaub Jr.

ROWMAN &
LITTLEFIELD
————— INTERNATIONAL

London • New York

Published by Rowman & Littlefield International, Ltd.
Unit A, Whitacre Mews, 26-34 Stannary Street, London SE11 4AB
www.rowmaninternational.com

Rowman & Littlefield International, Ltd. is an affiliate of Rowman & Littlefield

4501 Forbes Boulevard, Suite 200, Lanham, Maryland 20706, USA
With additional offices in Boulder, New York, Toronto (Canada), and Plymouth (UK)
www.rowman.com

British Library Cataloguing in Publication Data

A catalogue record for this book is available from the British Library

ISBN: HB 978-1-78660-679-2
      PB 978-1-78660-680-8

Library of Congress Cataloging-in-Publication Data

Names: Schaub, Gary, Jr., editor.
Title: Understanding cybersecurity: emerging governance and strategy /
   edited by Gary Schaub Jr.
Description: London; New York: Rowman & Littlefield International, Ltd., 2018. |
   Includes bibliographical references and index.
Identifiers: LCCN 2017046377 (print) | LCCN 2017058716 (ebook) |
   ISBN 9781786606815 (Electronic) | ISBN 9781786606792 (cloth : alk. paper) |
   ISBN 9781786606808 (pbk. : alk. paper)
Subjects: LCSH: Internet governance. | Computer networks—Security measures. |
   Internet—Security measures.
Classification: LCC TK5105.8854 (ebook) | LCC TK5105.8854 .U53 2018 (print) |
   DDC 384.3/34—dc23
LC record available at https://lccn.loc.gov/2017046377

♾™ The paper used in this publication meets the minimum requirements of American
National Standard for Information Sciences—Permanence of Paper for Printed Library
Materials, ANSI/NISO Z39.48-1992.

Printed in the United States of America

To My Mom and Dad

Thank you for your
immeasurable love and support

Contents

Preface

Over the past twenty-five years cyberspace has become the newest, most useful domain of productivity the world has ever known. This stems from the sheer ubiquity of the technology and its pervasive impact on modern life. However, along with this profound capability comes extreme vulnerability exacerbated by a growing dependency on everything cyberspace has to offer. This edited volume is dedicated to understanding cyberspace on a deeper level. Specifically, it explores the emerging governance structures for cybersecurity and the challenges associated with creating cyber strategies to cope with this powerful man-made domain.

Any publication is only as good as the profound ideas from the authors within it—ideas such as those represented here. The source for these ideas is *Strategic Studies Quarterly* (*SSQ*), the strategic journal of the U.S. Air Force, whose mission is to foster intellectual enrichment for national and international security professionals. *SSQ* provides a forum for critically examining, informing, and debating national security issues such as cybersecurity. We would like to thank all our contributing authors for their original sound judgments and for updating their arguments to make this edited volume a must-read publication for scholars interested in the future of cybersecurity. *SSQ* engaged authors from a plethora of organizations, including think tanks, research centers, and the most prestigious universities in the world. Their research met high peer review expectations and has expanded the intellectual prowess of academics and policy makers while influencing the national security debate. The result is a holistic approach to cyber that captures the essence of cyber governance and cyber strategy.

SSQ wishes to sincerely thank the volume editor, Dr. Gary Schaub Jr., for his proposal to create this project and for dedicating it to the Air University Foundation. His tireless efforts to manage all aspects of production, from updating the research to reviewing page proofs, were essential to this scholarly work and reflect a great sense of commitment to cybersecurity studies.

W. Michael Guillot, editor, *Strategic Studies Quarterly*

The Future of Things Cyber

Gen. Michael V. Hayden, USAF, Retired

Former Director, National Security Agency
Former Director, Central Intelligence Agency

Years ago, when I was an instructor for the Reserve Officer Training Corps (ROTC), the first unit of instruction for rising juniors dealt with communication skills. Near the beginning of the unit, I would quote Confucius to my new students: "The rectification of names is the most important business of government. If names are not correct, language will not be in accordance with the truth of things." The point had less to do with communicating than it did with thinking—thinking clearly. Clear communication begins with clear thinking. You have to be precise in your language and have the big ideas right if you are going to accomplish anything.

I am reminded of that lesson as I witness and participate in discussions about the future of things "cyber." Rarely has something been so important and so talked about with less clarity and less apparent understanding than this phenomenon. Do not get me wrong. There are genuine experts, and most of us know about patches, insider threats, worms, Trojans, WikiLeaks, and Stuxnet. But few of us (myself included) have created the broad structural framework within which to comfortably and confidently place these varied phenomena. And that matters. I have sat in very small group meetings in Washington, been briefed on an operational need and an operational solution, and been unable (along with my colleagues) to decide on a course of action because we lacked a clear picture of the long-term legal and policy implications of any decision we might make.

U.S. Cyber Command has been in existence for several years, and no one familiar with the command or its mission believes our current policy, law, or doctrine is adequate to our needs or our capabilities. Most disappointingly, the doctrinal, policy, and legal dilemmas we currently face remain unresolved even though they have been around for the better part of a decade. Now is the time to think about and force some issues that have been delayed too long.

This volume, therefore, could not be more timely as it surfaces questions, fosters debate, and builds understanding around a host of cyber questions. The issues are nearly limitless, and many others will emerge in these pages, but let me suggest a few that frequently come to the top of my own list.

How do we deal with the unprecedented? Part of our cyber policy problem is its newness, and our familiar experience in physical space does not easily transfer to cyberspace. Casually applying well-known concepts from physical space like deterrence, where attribution is assumed, to cyberspace, where attribution is frequently the problem, is a recipe for failure. And cyber education is difficult. In those small group policy meetings, the solitary cyber expert often sounds like "Rain Man" to the policy wonks in the room after the third or fourth sentence. As a result, no two policy makers seemed to leave the room with the same understanding of what it was they had discussed, approved, or disapproved. So how do we create senior leaders—military and civilian—who are "cyber smart enough"?

Is cyber really a domain? Like everyone else who is or has been in a U.S. military uniform, I think of cyber as a domain. It is now enshrined in doctrine: land, sea, air, space, cyber. It trips off the tongue, and frankly I have found the concept liberating when I think about operationalizing this domain. But the other domains are natural, created by God, and this one is the creation of man. Man can actually change this geography and anything that happens there actually creates a change in someone's physical space. There are those in the U.S. government who think treating cyber as an independent domain is just a device to cleverly mask serious unanswered questions of sovereignty when conducting cyber operations. They claim we have militarized a global commons. They want to be heard and satisfied before they support the full range of our cyber potential.

Privacy? When we plan for operations in a domain where adversary and friendly data coexist, we should be asking, "what constitutes a twenty-first-century definition of a reasonable expectation of privacy?" Google and Facebook know a lot more about most of us than we are comfortable sharing with the government. In a world where definitions of key concepts like transparency and secrecy seem to be shifting, what is the appropriate role of government and the Department of Defense? If we agree to limit government access to the web out of concerns over privacy, what degree of risk to our own security and that of the network are we prepared to accept? How do we articulate that risk to a skeptical public, and who should do it?

Do we really know the threat? Former director of national intelligence Mike McConnell frequently says that we are already "at war" in cyberspace. Richard Clarke even titled his cautionary book *Cyber War*. Although I generally avoid the "at war" terminology, I often talk about the inherent insecurity of the web; with the cost of admission so low and networks so vulnerable, why have we not had a true cyber Pearl Harbor? Is this harder to do than we think? Or are we just awaiting the inevitable?

What should we expect from the private sector? We all realize that most of the web things that we hold dear personally and as a nation reside or travel on commercial rather than government networks. So what motivates the private sector to optimize the defense of these networks? Some have observed that the free market has failed to provide an adequate level of security for the net since the true costs of insecurity are hidden or not understood. I agree. Now what: liability statutes that create the incentives and disincentives the market seems to be lacking? Do we consciously opt to depend on the private sector for security in a way we have not done in physical space for more than a century? Or do we opt for government intervention, including a broader Department of Defense (DoD) role to protect critical infrastructure beyond .mil to .gov to .com? The statutory responsibility for the latter falls to the Department of Homeland Security, but does it have the "horses" to accomplish this? Do we await catastrophe before calling for DoD intervention or do we move preemptively?

What is classified? Let me be clear: This stuff is overprotected. It is far easier to learn about physical threats from U.S. government agencies than it is to learn about cyber threats. In the popular culture, the availability of one hundred thousand applications for my smartphone is viewed as an unalloyed good. It is not—since each represents a potential vulnerability. But if we want to shift the popular culture, we need a broader flow of information to corporations and individuals to educate them on the threat. To do that, we need to recalibrate what is truly secret. Our most pressing need is clear policy, formed by shared consensus, shaped by informed discussion, and created by a common body of knowledge. With no common knowledge, no meaningful discussion, and no consensus, the policy vacuum continues. This will not be easy, and in the wake of WikiLeaks and Edward Snowden and other mass data breaches it will require courage, but it is essential and should itself be the subject of intense discussion. Who will step up to lead?

What constitutes the right of self-defense? How much do we want to allow private entities to defend themselves outside of their own perimeter? Indeed, what should Google appropriately do within its own network when under attack from the Chinese state? I have compared our entry into cyberspace to mankind's last great era of discovery—European colonization of the Western Hemisphere. During that period, large private corporations like the Hudson Bay Company and the East India Tea Company acted with many of the attributes of sovereignty. What of that experience is instructive today for contemplating the appropriate roles of giants like Google and Facebook? We probably do not want to outfit twenty-first-century cyber privateers with letters of marque and reprisal, but what should be the relationship between large corporations and the government when private networks on which the government depends are under sustained attack?

Is there a role for international law? It took a decade in the past century for states to arrive at a new Law of the Sea Convention, and that was a domain our species had had literally millennia of experience in. Then, as a powerful seafaring nation, we tilted toward maritime freedom rather than restraints. Regulating cyberspace entails even greater challenges. Indeed, as a powerful cyberfaring nation, how comfortable are we with regulation at all? After all, this domain launched by the DoD has largely been nurtured free of government regulation. Its strengths are its spontaneity, its creativity, its boundlessness. One of the best speeches given by an American official on macro net policy was by former secretary of state Clinton when she emphasized Internet freedom, not security or control or regulation. But there are moves afoot in international bodies to regulate the Internet, to give states more control over their domains, to Balkanize what up until now has been a relatively seamless global enterprise. How and when do we play?

Is cyber arms control possible? As a nation, we tend toward more freedom and less control, but—given their destructiveness, their relative ease of use, and the precedent their use sets—are distributed denial-of-service attacks ever justified? Should we work to create a global attitude toward them comparable to the existing view toward chemical or biological weapons? Should we hold states responsible if an attack is mounted from their physical space even if there is no evidence of complicity? And, are there any legitimate uses for botnets? If not, under what authority would anyone preemptively take them down? These are questions for which no precedent in law or policy (domestic or international) currently exists. If we want to establish precedent, as opposed to likely unenforceable treaty obligations, do we emphasize dialogue with like-minded nations, international institutions, or multinational information technology companies?

Is defense possible? At a recent conference, I was struck by a surprising question: "Would it be more effective to deal with recovery than with prevention?" In other words, is the web so skewed toward advantage for the attacker that we are reaching the point of diminishing returns for defending a network at the perimeter (or even beyond) and should now concentrate on how we respond to and recover from inevitable penetrations? This could mean more looking at our network for anomalous behavior than attempting to detect every incoming zero-day assault. It could mean concentrating more on what is going out rather than what is coming in. It could mean more focus on mitigating effects and operating while under attack rather than preventing attack. Several years ago, Mike McConnell and I met with a group of investors, and we were full-throated in our warnings about the cyber threat. One participant asked the question that was clearly on everyone's mind: "How much is this going to cost me?" At the time I chalked it up to not really understanding the threat, but in retrospect our questioner may have been on to something. At what point do we shift from additional investment in defense to more investment in response and recovery?

There are more questions that could be asked, many of them as fundamental as these. Most we have not yet answered or at least have not yet agreed on answers, and none of them are easy. How much do we really want to empower private enterprises to defend themselves? Do we want necessarily secretive organizations like National Security Agency (NSA) or Cyber Command going to the mats publicly over privacy issues? At what point does arguing for Internet security begin to legitimate China's attempts at control over Internet speech? Do we really want to get into a public debate that attempts to distinguish cyber espionage (which all countries pursue) from cyber war (something less common and more destructive)? Are there any cyber capabilities, real or potential, we are willing to give up in return for similar commitments from others?

Tough questions all, tougher (perhaps) but not unlike those our airpower ancestors faced nearly a century ago. As pioneer air warriors grappled with the unfamiliar, so must we. Until these and other questions like them are answered, we could be forced to live in the worst of all possible cyber worlds—routinely vulnerable to attack and self-restrained from bringing our own power to bear.

Chapter One

Internet Governance and National Security

Panayotis A. Yannakogeorgos

The debate over network protocols illustrates how standards can be politics by other means.

—Janet Abbate, *Inventing the Internet* (1999)

The organizing ethos of the Internet founders was that of a boundless space enabling everyone to connect with everything, everywhere. This governing principle did not reflect laws or national borders. Indeed, everyone was equal. A brave new world emerged where the meek are powerful enough to challenge the strong. Perhaps the best articulation of these sentiments is found in "A Declaration of Independence of Cyberspace." Addressing world governments and corporations online, John Perry Barlow proclaimed, "Your legal concepts of property, expression, identity, movement, and context do not apply to us. They are all based on matter, and there is no matter here."[1] Romanticized anarchic visions of the Internet came to be synonymized with cyberspace writ large. The dynamics of stakeholders involved with the inputs and processes that govern this global telecommunications experiment were not taken into account by the utopian vision that came to frame the policy questions of the early twenty-first century. Juxtapose this view with that of some Internet stakeholders who view the project as a "rational regime of access and flow of information, acknowledging that the network is not some renewable natural resource but a man-made structure that exists only owing to decades of infrastructure building at great cost to great companies, entities that believe they ultimately are entitled to a say."[2]

The sole purpose of cyberspace is to create effects in the real world, and the U.S. high-tech sector leads the world in innovating and developing hardware, software, and content services.[3] American companies provide technologies that allow more and better digital information to flow across borders, thereby

1

enhancing socioeconomic development worldwide. When markets and Internet connections are open, America's information technology (IT) companies shape the world and prosper. Leveraging the benefits of the Internet cannot occur, however, if confidence in networked digital information and communications technologies (ICTs) is lacking. In cyberspace, security is the cornerstone of the confidence that leads to openness and prosperity. While the most potent manifestation of cyberspace, the Internet, works seamlessly, the protocols and standards that allow computers to interoperate are what have permitted this technological wonder to catalyze innovation and prosperity globally. The power of the current Internet governance model strengthens the global power of the American example and facilitates democratization and development abroad by permitting the free flow of information to create economic growth and global innovation.[4] Today, this Internet is at risk from infrastructure and protocol design, development, and standardization by corporate entities of nondemocratic states.

Cybersecurity discussions largely focus on the conflict created by headline-grabbing exploits of ad hoc hacker networks or nation-state-inspired corporate espionage.[5] Malicious actors add to the conflict and are indeed exploiting vulnerabilities in information systems. But there is a different side of cyber conflict that presents a perhaps graver national security challenge: that is the "friendly" side of cyber conquest, as Martin Libicki once termed it.[6] The friendly side of cyber conquest of the Internet entails dominance of the technical and public policy issues that govern how the Internet operates. Current U.S. cybersecurity strategies do not adequately address the increasing activity of authoritarian states and their corporations within the technical bodies responsible for developing the protocols and standards on which current and next-generation digital networks function. But the issues related to governance of critical Internet resources (CIRs) and their impact on U.S. national security are often overlooked. Foreign efforts to alter the technical management of the Internet and the design of technical standards may undermine U.S. national interests in the long term. This chapter discusses the U.S. national security policy context and presents the concept of friendly conquest and the multistakeholder format of Internet governance, which allows for the free flow of information. There are many global challenges to the status quo, including the rise of alternative computer networks in cyberspace, that beg for recommendations to address those challenges.

INTERNET GOVERNANCE AND U.S. NATIONAL CYBER STRATEGY

Internet governance can be defined as a wide field including infrastructure, standardization, legal, sociocultural, economic, and development issues.

Within the context, this chapter focuses on the technical standards-setting bodies and protocols that do not elicit the same attention as more visible threats to national cybersecurity. In a human capital and resource-constrained environment, attention has focused on crime, espionage, and other forms of cyber conflict rather than on the issues related to governance of CIRs, development of technical standards, and design of new telecommunications equipment. In a domain that is already confusing to policy wonks, the complexity of Internet governance makes it even harder for policy makers to commit resources to a field that has no analogy in the physical world. In the nuclear age, there was no debate as to whether one could redesign the physical properties of uranium and apply them universally to eliminate the element's potential for weaponization. The underlying language of nuclear conflict was constrained by the laws of physics (e.g., nuclear fission, gravity). Physical limits in cyberspace exist as well by constraining information flows to the laws of physics—the wave-particle duality of radiation which, when modulated with bits, creates an information flow. However, the technical standards that permit information to flow across networks and appear within applications to create effects in the real world are bound only by the limits of human innovation and the politicized processes by which the standards are created and set. This affects the character of cyberspace. Its current form is free and open, but that does not necessarily mean it always will be. Understanding the strategic-level issues of Internet governance is thus just as critical as understanding the impact of vulnerabilities that threat actors may exploit to cause incidents of national security concern. In the national security context, the technical management of the Internet matters because it may allow authoritarian states to exert power and influence over the underlying infrastructure, thereby reshaping the operational environment.

Several current national strategies articulate nationwide responses to cyber threats.[7] They tend to focus on catastrophic national security incidents rather than on the battles within the organizations that set technical standards or manage the day-to-day operation of the Internet. American national strategies have consistently highlighted the importance of current multistakeholder forums for design and standardization of the technical standards via "collaborative development of consensus-based international standards for ICT ... a key part of preserving openness and interoperability, growing our digital economies, and moving our societies forward."[8] Furthermore, the challenges we face in international standards-setting bodies are recognized in that "in designing the next generation of these systems, we must advance the common interest by supporting the soundest technical standards and governance structures, rather than those that will simply enhance national prestige or political control."[9]

Security demands that the language of the Internet—the underlying technical standards and protocols—continue to sustain free-flowing information. If "code is law" in cyberspace, as some posit,[10] then the standards and protocols are the fabric of cyber reality that give code meaning. In policy circles, cyberspace is already considered the "invisible domain." Technical standards and protocols are thus "invisible" squared. However, these protocols define the character of the Internet and its underlying critical infrastructures. As noted elsewhere, "The underlying protocols to which software and hardware design conforms represent a more embedded and more invisible form of level architecture to constrain behavior, establish public policy.... [I]n this sense protocols have political agency—not a disembodied agency but one derived from protocol designers and implementers."[11] In the past, it was the United States that led the world in the development of protocols and standards. As a result, the values of freedom were embedded in the Internet's design and character, which incubated innovation that continues to spur socioeconomic development globally. Creating the Internet and maintaining the technical edge are two very different problems.

THE FRIENDLY SIDE OF CYBER CONFLICT

Looming battles in Internet standards and governance bodies will determine the future character of the Internet. The advanced deployment of IPv6 in Russia and China and development of new standards by near-peer-competitor countries are creating new technical standards and deploying them into the global marketplace, thus enabling friendly cyber conflict.

Friendly conquest occurs when a noncore operator of a system enters into partnership with a core operator in exchange for access to a desired information system. Cyber strategic theorist Martin Libicki notes,

> One who controls a system may let others access it so that they may enjoy its content, services and connections. With time, if such access is useful … users may find themselves not only growing dependent on it, but deepening their dependence on it by adopting standards and protocols for their own systems and making investments in order to better use the content, services or connections they enjoy.[12]

The core partner in such a coalition emerges to dominate noncore members who have come to depend on the service offered, though not without some vulnerability to the core partner's network. Fears exist "that the full dependence that pervades one's internal systems may leave one open for manipulation. ... The source of such vulnerability could range from one partner's general knowledge of how the infrastructure is secure, to privileged access to the infrastructure that can permit an attack to be boot-strapped more easily."[13]

Libicki operates with relational mechanisms to explain how coalitions leading to friendly conquest occur. Friendly conquest in cyberspace can be surmised as the willing participation of X in Y's information system. X willingly enters into a coalition with Y in cyberspace. Y's friendly conquest of X occurs when X becomes dependent on Y's system. This is not to say that X merely entering the coalition will cause the conquest. X's perceived need for access to Y's cyberspace (or inability to construct its own) causes it to willingly enter into a coalition with Y. X adopts Y's standards and protocols making up the information system architecture of Y's cyberspace in a way that allows it to interoperate within X's cyberspace. X adopts Y's cyberspace architecture and thus the necessary condition for Y's friendly conquest. It is a facilitating condition for X's hostile conquest. X might begin to use the standards and protocols of Y's cyberspace as a model for its own cyberspace. Since Y is an expert in its own standards and protocols, X's modeling of these standards in its own systems is another vulnerability, which can facilitate X's hostile conquest by Y. X does not have to be a friend. It can be a neutral or a possible future enemy of Y. There is utility in Y opening its cyberspace to X only if Y sees some benefit to itself, although Libicki does argue that Y will open its cyberspace regardless. Once friendly conquest is accomplished, Libicki argues, it can facilitate hostile conquest in cyberspace. Friendly conquest of X by Y may facilitate hostile conquest in cyberspace conducted by Y against X.

The Internet and its underlying technical infrastructure is a potent manifestation of how the United States, as core operator of an information system, extended friendly dominance over allies and adversaries alike through creation of the technology and setting the rules for its operation. The Internet relies on products designed and operated by U.S.-based entities such as the Domain Name System (DNS) and Internet Corporation for Assigned Names and Numbers (ICANN), Microsoft, and Cisco. Users around the world, such as Google and Facebook, have come to rely on services offered over this platform. The dominant position that U.S.-based entities currently have is not permanent. The Estonian-developed Skype is indicative that services may be non-U.S. in origin. Yet, even when an Internet-based service is created by foreign entities, most of the information flowing through the said application passes through hardware in the United States. When vulnerabilities are perceived, other nations may try to exit our information system to preserve their cyber sovereignty and expand their influence by attracting customers toward their own indigenous systems and away from the Internet.[14] Thus, our strategic advantage in cyberspace is not timeless and is being contested in varying degrees by near-peer competitors. Hence, we should understand their current responses to U.S. technological dominance to refine our cyber strategy within the context of friendly cyber conquest.

U.S. Air Force doctrine recognizes one aspect of friendly conquest: supply-side infrastructure vulnerabilities. "Many of the COTS [commercial off the shelf] technologies (hardware and software) the Air Force purchases are developed, manufactured, or have components manufactured by foreign countries. These manufacturers, vendors, service providers, and developers can be influenced by adversaries to provide altered products that have built-in vulnerabilities, such as modified chips."[15] Friendly conquest goes beyond adversaries merely being able to infiltrate the supply chain and create backdoors on servers of national security significance before they enter the United States.[16] The threat also comes from the emergence of new technologies in which the United States is not the core operator but may become dependent. With the focus on malicious cyberattacks, not enough attention is being paid to the soft underbelly of the cyber world—the technologies and standards that have allowed cyberspace to emerge from the electromagnetic spectrum.

China is making a great leap forward in terms of sowing the seeds for global friendly conquest in cyberspace. As reported by the U.S.–China Economic and Security Review Commission, "If current trends continue, China (combined with proxy interests) will effectively become the principal market driver in many sectors, including telecom, on the basis of consumption, production, and innovation."[17] U.S. reliance on China as a manufacturer of computer chips and other ICT hardware has allowed the potential for the introduction of intentional vulnerabilities and backdoors in the digital fabric of equipment used by U.S.-based entities, including the military. Extraordinarily low-priced Chinese-made computer hardware is a lucrative buy in Asia and the developing world.[18] Furthermore, Chinese entities, such as China Mobile, are on the leading edge of developing the standards of next-generation mobile 5G LTE networks within the International Telecommunications Union (ITU) IMT 2020 working group. According to the ITU, "The IMT-2020 standard is set to be the global communication network for the coming decades and is on track to be in place by 2020. The next step is to agree on what will be the detailed specifications for IMT-2020, a standard that will underpin the next generations of mobile broadband and IT connectivity."[19] In addition to the standards-setting bodies, Chinese telecommunication operators are preparing to deploy operational 5G networks within China.[20]

One example of how efforts at friendly conquest can make the United States vulnerable to cyber exploitation is demonstrated in China's failure at creating a telecommunication protocol as a result of the United States successfully blocking a Chinese effort to set wireless local area network (WLAN) authentication and privacy infrastructure (WAPI) protocol as an international wireless communication standard.[21] Despite what appeared to be a success, China went on to ban devices using the internationally accepted 802.11 Wi-Fi communication protocol standard just as it launched the WAPI standard domestically. The effect of this is that if mobile telecommunication equipment manufacturers wanted to have devices that could legally be sold in China, they had to produce equipment with the WAPI standards. Thus, Apple, Dell, and others began producing mobile phones with the Chinese WAPI standard on its chips.[22] This opens up the potential for control of standards within emerging markets, and also the potential for security risks being created with a Chinese standard now being commonplace on Wi-Fi telecommunications equipment. This could enable China to have a side channel into encrypted communications on those devices, allowing the Chinese government access to trusted communications if desired.

Such fears are not unfounded when put into the context of China's relationship with Microsoft. In 2003, China received access to the source code for Microsoft Windows in a partnership with Microsoft to cooperate on the discovery and resolution of Windows security issues. The China Information Technology Security Certification Center (CNITSEC) Source Code Review Lab, described as "the only national certification center in China to adopt the international GB/T 18336, the ISO 15408 standard to test, evaluate and certify information security products, systems and Web services," was the focal point of this collaboration.[23] Undeterred by International Organization of Standards (ISO) criteria, and unanticipated by many experts in the field, Chinese computer scientists reverse-engineered the code. This allowed them to develop malicious code, including viruses, Trojan horses, and backdoors, that exploited software vulnerabilities in the operating system. These efforts resulted in the shutting down of the U.S. Pacific Command Headquarters after a Chinese-based attack.[24] Chinese entities are also making great strides in developing core information systems upon which others will come to rely. Virtual reality (VR) technologies are one example of an emerging tool that could become as ubiquitous for social and commercial interactions as the Internet is today. Globally, people are increasingly using VR technology fused with the Internet to socially interact.[25] Experts have noted that

> any country that succeeds in dominating the VR market may also set the technical standards for the rest of the world, and may also own and operate the VR servers that give them unique access to information about future global financial transactions, transportation, shipping, and business communications that may rely on virtual worlds.

Global commerce is expected to "come to rely heavily on VR." Banking, transportation control, and communications are all types of global commerce occurring in a virtual reality.[26]

While current strategies do address the supply-chain risks posed by foreign manufacturing, the trend of China taking the lead in the protocols that will come to underlie VR and other technologies, as well as standard setting within international bodies, is a challenge that current cyber strategies insufficiently address. This may be due in part to the cultural differences in the relations between U.S.-headquartered multinational corporations (MNCs) and the U.S. government (USG) versus the MNCs in foreign countries that at times have very close relations to their own governments.

MULTISTAKEHOLDERS AND INTERNET GOVERNANCE

Business entities such as MNCs contribute to the formation of policies regulating international communications formally within the ITU and informally through the personal contributions of their employees within the ICANN, the Internet Engineering Task Force (IETF), and other organizations. Within the United States, telecommunications service providers (dating back to the era of electrical telegraph systems) were never part of a state-owned monopoly. This was not the case in the rest of the world.[27] British Telecom and Deutche Telekom, for example, were state-owned entities before being privatized in the 1990s. Granted, although there is no direct state control within the United States, telecommunications companies are regulated by the state. In international telecommunications negotiations, a state and its ICT firms have a symbiotic relationship.[28] This has been the case since the International Telegraph Union, predecessor of the ITU, began meeting in the mid-nineteenth century to regulate telegraphy policies.[29] Thus, the view in the developing world is that "at present, it is ... U.S. law which applies globally by default as most monopoly Internet companies are U.S.-based."[30]

If trade is a political activity, then firms are political actors. States can utilize firms to distribute or reward power to meet their own political objectives.[31] Since states and firms both cause effects on the behavior of the other, a dynamic bidirectional interaction exists between the state and the MNC.

Important policy tools that affect the behavior of MNCs include export controls, protectionism, and strategic trade policy. Export controls tend to have a political purpose since, as one expert notes, "they are designed to prevent rival states from gaining access to key resources and technologies," or to punish a state.[32] Firms manufacturing strategic goods rely on governments to adopt trade policies that will support the firm's competitive stance in the global market,[33] but states do place restrictions on what may be exported, even if it is to the detriment of a firm's competitiveness in foreign markets.[34] In the United States, the federal government lost the so-called encryption wars of the 1990s, when private industry protested policies prohibiting the export of strong encryption software for strategic reasons.[35]

In an effort to prevent criminals from communicating using unbreakable codes, some firms implement law enforcement intercept (LEI) mechanisms so that national security agencies can monitor suspected criminal and terrorist communications.[36] U.S. firms and persons associated with them, who develop, maintain, and revise the core standards and technological infrastructures, are stigmatized by such allegations that depict a rogue national security apparatus and private sector in collusion capturing all of the world's data. This does not reflect the fact that, unlike in authoritarian states, careful compliance with U.S. laws designed to protect user privacy maintains a separation between government and the private sector.[37] Media preferring headline-grabbing allegations decrease global trust in the American private sector and validate the narratives that the Internet governance mechanisms must be internationalized. Thus, the close relationship between governments and firms in the area of strategic trade policy affects both how firms operate and how governments counteract the misuse of cyberspace.[38]

The global perception that the U.S. government has de facto control of CIRs is largely shaped by other nations' experiences of the close relationship between telecommunications companies and their national governments. Uniquely, the U.S. government has never owned or operated any telecommunications companies. As the rest of the world shifted to the U.S. privatized telecom model, prior experience of government control of the sector did not leave their cognitive balance. These experiences cast a shadow of suspicion over the special agreement between the ICANN and the U.S. Department of Commerce (DoC), which created friction between the United States and the rest of the world.[39]

CRITICAL INTERNET RESOURCES
AND INFRASTRUCTURE

Technical management of the DNS, invented by the DoD and governed by it in its formative years, was assumed by the DoC in 1998 and subsequently evolved into its current nongovernmental multistakeholder model.[40] The description here will not delve into the tactical- and operational-level functioning of each organization that has a role in Internet governance.[41] It will instead offer a brief recap of the underlying technology and the organizations that have a role in setting the standards that allow for technical functioning of the Internet. It is thus the purpose of this section to provide an account of Internet governance as a source of national security concern. With discussions focusing on malicious activities, there has been little consideration to the implications of the peaceful work of designing and maintaining the Internet and the implications these activities have on U.S. interests.

CIRs "in the context of Internet governance usually refers to Internet unique logical resources rather than physical infrastructural components or virtual resources not exclusive to the Internet. CIRs must provide a technical requirement of global uniqueness requiring some central coordination: Internet address, DNS, Autonomous System Numbers."[42] Unlike the popular conception of a limitless Internet, the underlying address space is limited. Indeed, Internet protocol (IP) address space has nearly run out. Foreseeing this Internet protocol, engineers developed IPv6, which among other improvements increased the total number of potential IP addresses from 4,294,967,296 in IPv4 to 2^{128} in IPv6. It is recognized today that "deploying IPv6 is the only perennial way to ease pressure on the public IPv4 address pool."[43] As the world begins a transition from using IPv4 to IPv6 as the dominant communications protocol for the global Internet, the United States is not leading its deployment. Russia currently enjoys the greatest deployment in terms of market penetration, and China enjoys the greatest deployment in sheer numbers.[44] The consequences of delayed deployment are related to both Internet governance and the more traditional security threats. On the latter point, the National Institute for Standards notes that the "prevention of unauthorized access to IPv6 networks will likely be more difficult in the early years of IPv6 deployments."[45] Thus, competitor nations that have more experience in national-level deployments of IPv6 have greater technical understanding of its real-world operations. The Air Force NIPRNet has not entirely been enabled for IPv6. It has been noted that the plan is to use both IPv4 and IPv6 in parallel for the next 10–15 years.[46] As deployment of IPv6 as the backbone of the Internet continues, Russia and China may have the perceived legitimacy as IPv6 leads and take advantage of that opportunity to shift control of these scarce address spaces from the ICANN toward the control of an intergovernmental body, such as the United Nations.

THE ICANN AND THE CURRENT INTERNET
GOVERNANCE STRUCTURE

Because cyberspace is a man-made domain, infrastructure and standard-ization are critically important. Global bodies of computer scientists and engineers create the standards and rules on which the Internet—the most potent manifestation of cyberspace—operates. Indeed, many of these glo-bal bodies began as at the Defense Information Systems Agency (DISA), the Defense Advanced Research Projects Agency (DARPA), or other USG programs that were privatized in the mid-1990s. Thus, the development of the next-generation Internet does not have the United States as the prime mover.[47] Instead, standards and processes are being developed by Russian, Chinese, and other foreign scientists and engineers. Today's machines speak a form of the English language to each other. If U.S. scientific excel-lence continues its degenerative path, future networks may come to rely on machines speaking foreign languages. Furthermore, governance of the DNS and IP address allocation is being challenged to migrate from the current multistakeholder approach to an intergovernmental mechanism within the ITU. This is the friendly side of cyber conflict.

The DNS allows people to use Uniform Resource Locators (URLs) to com-municate with other machines on the Internet. Instead of having to type in the IP address of a website—a string of numbers—a person can type a natural language URL, such as www.af.mil, into a web browser to connect with the desired corresponding IP address. This makes the web user-friendly, and to the common user, might as well be the work of a wizard that allows informa-tion to be piped onto someone's computer. However, IP addresses are scarce, especially in IPv4. The processes for assigning scarce IP addresses and allow-ing the Internet to serve as a global platform are complex, both technically and, increasingly, politically.

The allocation of IPv4 address space to various registries is provided by ICANN via the Internet Assigned Numbers Authority (IANA).[48] Globally routable IP addresses reside in DNS databases on root zone databases that allow for the translation of URLs into IP addresses.[49] The top-level domain names, such as .com or .org, are maintained and updated by the ICANN, which was once under the DoC. After a transition of all Internet governance functions to ICANN in October 2016, ICANN continues to be the sole source of IP address allocation to specific DNSs and regional Internet registries to assure a uniform Internet experience for all. By governing and maintaining the DNS central root zone databases and backing them up on DNS servers worldwide, the ICANN assures that if a domain name is available, someone can buy it and link it with an IP address to create an online presence.[50] The structure for coordinating these names and addresses is indicated in figure 1.1.

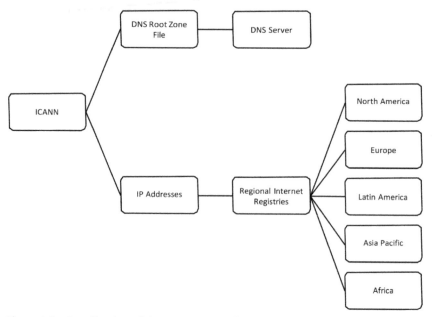

Figure 1.1   Coordination of the Internet's Naming System

INTERNET ENGINEERING TASK
FORCE: STEWARDS OF TCP/IP

The internationally standardized communications protocol stack, called Transmission Control Protocol and Internet Protocol (TCP/IP), allows for the flow of data packets and information across computer networks, including the Internet. TCP/IP is standardized by the International Organization of Standards for the Open Systems Interconnection (OSI) model as the basis of Internet networking. A brief description of how information is sent across networks is necessary to better understand the significance of TCP/IP. Data packets are the basic units of network traffic. They are the standard means of dividing information into smaller units when sending it over a network. A significant component of computer networks is the IP header, which contains information pertaining to the source and destination addresses. Machines require these strings of numbers to connect with other computers on the Internet or other networks.[51] All networked hardware must have a valid IP address to function on a network. Data packets are recreated by the receiving machine based on information within a header of each packet that tells the receiving computer how to recreate information from the packet data. Without internationally standardized protocols such as TCP/IP, there would be no assurance that packets could be read by a receiving machine.[52]

The most esoteric of all CIRs are the autonomous system numbers (ASNs). These numbers are used by network providers at "peering points" to allow information to flow from, say, Verizon to ATT, among other uses. Border gateway protocols are one aspect of ASNs.

Internet policy debates have proven the ineffectualness of multilateralism as the United States strives to lead and others fail to follow. American technological innovation in the development and maintenance of the Internet's backbone is unquestioned. But global efforts to promote regulatory reform, such as including institutions of global governance like the ITU as entities responsible for overseeing the ICANN, are a tense political issue closely linked with the national cybersecurity concerns of democratic and autocratic regimes alike. In sum, American "leadership" as first among equals has led to a succession of dead ends. We are witnessing countermoves by friends and competitors alike.

GLOBAL CHALLENGES TO THE STATUS QUO

Global information flowing through open elements of cyberspace, such as the Internet, is regulated by national and regional bodies coordinating their policies internationally. Standards that have been created for elements of cyberspace have required lengthy processes at various bodies, such as the International Organization for Standardization and ITU, to assure sufficient technical and political cooperation among nation-states. While U.S.-based entities have traditionally set the standards for Internet technology, China-based entities, such as the ZTE Corporation, are increasingly taking on roles within the ITU to draft important international standards that will shape the world's next-generation networks. This is not a recent development. As early as 2004, Chinese personnel working in senior ITU Telecommunication Standardization Sector positions began to discuss using the transition to IPv6 as a way to correct a perceived imbalance in address allocation between the United States and the developing world: "The early allocation of IPv4 addresses resulted in geographic imbalances and an excessive possession of the address space by early adopters. This situation was recognized and addressed by the Regional Internet Registries (RIR). ... Some developing countries have raised issues regarding IP address allocation. It is important to ensure that similar concerns do not arise with respect to IPv6."[53] This is indicative of a desire by some states to perhaps shift the governance of IPv6 address allocation into a global institution such as the ITU.

From the perspective of maintaining U.S. national interests, the current multistakeholder framework governing CIRs continues to be a good mechanism for regulating the day-to-day technical operations of the Internet. However, momentum related to Internet governance within the United Nations is gaining within political forums. Led by Russian and Chinese initiatives, competitors and partners alike have been working toward internationalizing the Internet's technical governance. China and Russia, along with India, South Africa, and Brazil, have led initiatives against U.S. dominance of the ICANN. These efforts have been in the works for nearly a decade.[54] As the DoD ARPANET experiment emerged to become a significant component of global socioeconomic development and governments increasingly came to realize its importance, the momentum for internationalizing its backbone, the ICANN, became greater. Recall that these pushes for internationalization are due in part to the perception of U.S. government control over ICANN via the DoC and the National Telecommunications and Information Administration (NTIA), shaped by the history of special relationships between state telecommunication corporations existing in other countries. The debates about the transition of all Internet governance functions from the NTIA to ICANN finally closed in October 2016 when Congress allowed for the contract for the IANA functions to lapse.

THE (POTENTIAL) TYRANNY OF THE INTERNATIONAL TELECOMMUNICATIONS UNION OVER CRITICAL INTERNET RESOURCES

One battleground for debates over internationalizing the ICANN was observed during preparations for the World Summit on the Information Society (WSIS),[55] when significant opposition to the current Internet governance began to emerge,[56] for instance, in March 2004 during a UN-hosted Global Forum on Internet Governance.[57] Brazilian delegate Maria Luiza Viotti claimed that Internet governance needed reform, since it is not inclusive of developing countries and instead appears to be under the ownership of one group of countries or stakeholders.[58] Lyndall Shope-Mafole, chair of South Africa's National Commission, spoke on similar lines, arguing that the legitimacy of the ICANN's processes, rather than its functioning, was of most concern for developing countries.[59] Thus, after rigorous talks, delegates concluded on the basis of concerns from the developing world that the ICANN required further reform. Throughout the WSIS process, and continuing in other forums discussing Internet governance and global cybersecurity, Brazil has continued to be a vocal proponent against the U.S. position in the ICANN. In 2011, India joined South Africa and Brazil in proposing to "operationalize the Tunis mandate" by

> bearing in mind the need for a transparent, democratic, and multilateral mechanism that enables all stakeholders to participate in their respective roles, to address the many cross-cutting international public policy issues that require attention and are not adequately addressed by current mechanisms and the

need for enhanced cooperation to enable governments, on an equal footing, to carry out their roles and responsibilities in international public policy issues pertaining to the Internet, India proposes the establishment of a new institutional mechanism in the United Nations for global Internet related policies, to be called the United Nations Committee for Internet-Related Policies (CIRP).[60]

The CIRP idea has gained momentum within the developing world as a counter to the current technical management of the Internet. Indeed, it echoes closely Chinese concerns voiced by the China Organizational Name Administration Center (CONAC) that "the U.S. government has the sovereign power to control the Internet resources. We therefore suggest making the computer security plan available for comment by all multistakeholders, for maintaining the security of cyberspace is not a mission only for the U.S. government, and it cannot be accomplished by any single nation."[61]

From Russia, then-prime minister Vladimir Putin stated,

> The International Telecommunication Union is one of the oldest international organisations; it's twice as old as the United Nations. Russia was one of its co-founders and intends to be an active member. We are thankful to you for the ideas that you have proposed for discussion. One of them is establishing international control over the Internet using the monitoring and supervisory capabilities of the International Telecommunication Union (ITU).[62]

Thus, the United States faces a significant challenge within the ITU from autocratic regimes leading the developing world to move control of CIRs toward a multilateral body. The underlying danger is a shift away from an Internet whose defining characteristic is the free flow of information toward a model in which the political agendas of nondemocracies attempt to exert control over the flow of information. Hence, the United States and like-minded nations must surge diplomatically to ensure the character of the Internet remains free from the political control of a multilateral institution.

This diplomatic struggle for control of the Internet has also been occurring within various other forums, like the UN Commission on Science and Technology for Development. Suggestions being made on the issue include the following:

- Establishment of an ad hoc working group under the Commission on Science and Technology for Development with a view to the development of an institutional design and road map to enhance cooperation on Internet-related public policy issues with the support of the Secretary-General,
- Creation of a more permanent committee on international public policy issues pertaining to the Internet within the United Nations system, possibly modeled on the Committee on Information, Communications and Computer Policy of the Organization for Economic Cooperation and Development,

- And more concretely, global policy questions should be addressed by an entity with global representation, such as the United Nations, and regional questions by entities with regional representation, such as the Council of Europe ... [and] the participation of relevant organizations in discussions on Internet governance at the quadrennial ITU Plenipotentiary Conference, and the public review process and Governmental Advisory Committee of ICANN.[63]

Such Internet public policy issues surfaced in December 2012 at the World Conference indicate that these ideas will resurface as part of the ITU effort to revise International Telecommunications Regulations (ITRs) to include governance of next-generation CIRs within the ITU's mandate and assume a greater role in Internet governance.[64] These proposals were mooted.

Making Internet governance open to intergovernmental processes could put U.S. national security at risk, given the potential for less-than-responsible state actors to take the current privatized laissez-faire approach to governing the Internet and have nation-states and their corporate entities take control of governing CIRs. This would not ensure DoD equities are protected in an environment where critical decisions on underlying technical standards and Internet operation would be left to national governments that are competing with the United States.

SHADOW "DNS" RISING

As described above, the CIRs that allow for universally resolvable URLs and global Internet communications are possible due to the root system that is managed by the ICANN and protocols designed, developed, and debated within the IETF (among other organizations). Although this allows for a free and open Internet to function, the standards and protocols that the ICANN uses to maintain the domain name registries can be used by individuals, ad hoc networks, and nation-states to design and deploy an alternative DNS that can either be independent of or "ride on top" of the Internet. A corporate LAN, such as ".company name" for internal company use, is an example of the first. When a group wishes to ride over the global DNS root but incorporates its own pseudo top-level domain, core operators of the pseudo domains can use specific software resources to resolve domains that are globally accessible within their alternative DNS. American audiences can experience what it is like to enter an alternative DNS universe via The Onion Router (TOR) network. Downloading the TOR package and navigating to websites one would prefer to visit anonymously (the typical use of TOR), one may point the TOR browser to websites on the ".onion" domain and mingle where the cyber underworld has started shifting the management of its business operations these days to avoid law enforcement and to add another layer of protection to its personas.[65]

Should significant usage of such shadow Internets occur, this could lead to the loss of confidence and utility of the Internet itself. The greatest risk comes when nation-states develop and deploy their own alternate DNSs for internal use, thereby separating themselves from the global Internet. This is different from controlling access points and actually develops country-level intranets that may or may not be connected to the global Internet.[66] The discussion below focuses on Russia and China as far as their successes in deploying potentially new intranets for in-country use. Other countries, such as Iran, are following suit.

U.S. involvement in *openly* promoting and organizing "digital activists" by "issuing up to $30 million in grant funding to increase open access to the Internet, support digital activists, and push back against Internet repression wherever it occurs in the fight for free flows of information, generates international friction that is counterproductive to promoting international cooperation on cybersecurity issues."[67] The "Internet Freedom Agenda" is one example of this phenomenon.[68] Such technology effectively allows citizen-activists to hack past government digital sentries to spread forbidden information. Other tools allow activists to don digital disguises and organize themselves into social movements designed to topple regimes. With the topic of "fake-news" and its potential impact on U.S. election results, it appears as if the Internet Freedom Agenda struck back.

An additional consequence has been the emergence of alternative national networks that essentially create alternate DNSs for in-country use, allowing for censorship of content and stifling the productivity of the current Internet topology. China is one country that has implemented this on a national scale, and Iran is closely following suit.[69] Others are sure to follow these attempts. The rise of a splintered Internet will certainly change the character of the current Internet, with negative consequences for freedom and prosperity worldwide. Those who wish the Internet to remain free and open will benefit, and draw a sharp, moral contrast with those wishing to control the master switch. Thus maintaining the current Internet governance model, while addressing legitimate concerns of friends and allies, will help assure the Internet continues to serve as a robust platform for human economic development.

CONCLUSION

Failure to pay attention to our vulnerabilities from Internet governance and friendly conquest may provide our adversaries with a strategic advantage in cyber conflict. Our own cyber-attack efforts will also become complicated as networks that are not based on protocols and standards developed by U.S.-based entities are deployed by our competitors. To aid how we conceive of cyberspace, as well as adjust to change within the cyber environment, there must be a broad dialogue on these issues. Despite the Internet's historic roots within the DoD, there has not been a well-organized effort to influence the development of technical standards and policies affecting Internet governance. Currently, the DoD has remained in a reactive mode, coordinating and commenting on the various global norms and standards being considered within the USG processes related to Internet governance. Because of this approach, the DoD and the USAF may be perceived as not having the legal expertise or technical reputation in Internet governance. The DoD, and the U.S. Air Force in particular, should exercise leadership and take a more active role in the development of IT infrastructure standards as it once did. Furthermore, it should more carefully document its role and provide metrics on its participation and position with Internet governance bodies. The air force should play a leading role within the DoD and the whole of government by explicitly focusing on a broader concept of friendly conquest that implicitly exists in policies, strategies, and doctrines. The 2012 World Telecommunications Conference in December 2012 may be the right place to commence this effort.

As the hardware and software on which the global Internet is based evolve and non-U.S. entities begin to invent new hardware, standards, and protocols, potentially taking market share away from U.S. entities, the U.S. position as core cyber infrastructure operator will diminish. The United States currently enjoys technological dominance through its position of developer and core provider of Internet services made possible by the ICANN and the top-level DNS. But our national cybersecurity strategies do not adequately address threats that may stem from other countries developing the protocols, standards, and technologies on which the next generation of networks will be based. The air force has a key role to play given the wealth of technical excellence that resides within its community of scientists and engineers. It cannot act alone, however, and the DoD will need to focus some of its already limited cyber resources toward Internet governance. Not doing so risks allowing foreign-designed technical standards and protocols to form the backbone of next-generation IT and potentially puts DoD operations at risk by reversing what is now an Internet characterized by the free flow of information on which the DoD depends. The USAF remains the leading U.S. military service impacting cyberspace, and thus its actions or inactions in Internet governance debates matter.

NOTES

1. John Perry Barlow, "A Declaration of *Independence* of Cyberspace" (February 8, 1996).

2. Tim Wu, *The Master Switch: The Rise and Fall of Information Empires* (New York: Alfred A. Knopf, 2010), p. 290.

3. Granted, for the most part, manufacturing does not occur within the United States, which presents the national security risk of supply-chain vulnerabilities. This is a subset of friendly conquest but remains beyond the scope of the argument here.

4. American values are a core national interest. *National Security Strategy* (Washington, DC: The White House, May 2010), p. 35.

5. See, e.g., Bryan Krekel, Patton Adam, and George Bakos, *Occupying the Information High Ground: Chinese Capabilities for Computer Network Operations and Cyber Espionage* (Washington, DC: U.S.–China Economic and Security Review Commission, March 27, 2012); and Dmitri Alperovitch, *Revealed: Operation Shady RAT*, McAfee White Paper (Santa Clara, CA: McAfee, 2011), http://www.mcafee.com/us/resources/white-papers/wp-operation-shady-rat.pdf.

6. Martin Libicki, *Conquest in Cyberspace* (New York: Cambridge University Press, 2007).

7. *National Strategy to Secure Cyberspace (NSSC)* (Washington, DC: The White House, February 2003); John Rollins and Anna C. Henning, *Comprehensive National Cybersecurity Initiative (CNCI)* (Washington, DC: Congressional Research Service, March 10, 2009; declassified in March 2010); the *International Strategy for Cyberspace* (Washington, DC: The White House, May 2011); and the *Department of Defense Strategy for Operating in Cyberspace* (Washington, DC: Department of Defense, July 2011) are to date the leading relevant directives on cybersecurity. Although the White House completed a cyberspace policy review in 2009, the primary suggestions in the review amount to existing policy recommendations already in the *NSSC* and declassified *CNCI*. After the White House *Cyberspace Policy Review*, several initiatives were either launched or announced by departments and agencies of the U.S. government. Declassification of the *CNCI* enabled the timely development of a framework for international partnerships consistent with a common cybersecurity policy. In 2011, the White House released the *International Strategy for Cyberspace*. Subtitled *Prosperity, Security, and Openness in a Networked World*, the document falls short of providing the solutions necessary to live up to its name. The simple fact is, without security there can be no prosperity or openness.

8. *International Strategy for Cyberspace*, p. 12.

9. *International Strategy for Cyberspace*, p. 15.

10. Lawrence Lessig, *Code: And Other Laws of Cyberspace, Version 2.0* (New York: Basic Books, 2006), p. 10.

11. Laura DeNardis, *Protocol Politics: The Globalization of Internet Governance* (Cambridge, MA: MIT Press 2009), p. 11.

12. Libicki, *Conquest in Cyberspace*, p. 12.

13. Libicki, *Conquest in Cyberspace*, p. 137.

14. The global positioning system (GPS) is one example where control of both the software and hardware is being contested. Although access to GPS is available without a fee for the basic service, friends and competitors alike have realized their dependence on this U.S. system makes them vulnerable. Russia is modernizing its GPS system, and the European Union and China are developing independent GPS systems of their own. The long time cycle from intent to implementation of these new systems is due to the immense financial costs of deploying a space network. Cyber time cycles may be shorter, given the lower costs associated with deploying a national computer network compared

with multiple high-tech satellites launched into space. For a more complete discussion of alternate GPS systems, see Lt. Col. Scott W. Beidleman, *GPS versus Galileo: Balancing for Position in Space* (Maxwell AFB, AL: Air University Press, 2006).

15. Air Force Doctrine Document (AFDD) 3-12, *Cyberspace Operations* (Maxwell AFB, AL: Curtis E. LeMay Center for Doctrine Development and Education, 2010), p. 4.

16. Bruce Rayner, "Ferreting Out the Fakes," *Electronic Engineering Times* (August 15, 2011), p. 24. See also John Markoff, "Computer Gear May Pose Trojan Horse Threat to Pentagon," *New York Times* (May 10, 2008), p. 12.

17. USCC Research Staff, *The National Security Implication of Investments and Products from the People's Republic of China in the Telecommunications Sector*, U.S.–China Economic and Security Review Commission Staff Report (Washington, DC: U.S.–China Economic and Security Review Commission, January 2011), p. 7, http://www.uscc.gov/RFP/2011/FINALREPORT_TheNationalSecurityImplicationsof InvestmentsandProductsfromThePRCinthe TelecommunicationsSector.pdf.

18. LCDR Achuthan Anand, *Information Technology: The Future Warfare Weapon* (New Delhi: Ocean Books, 2000), pp. 56–62.

19. "ITU Agrees on Key 5G Performance Requirements for IMT-2020," *International Telecommunication Union Press Release* (February 23, 2017), http://www.itu.int/en/mediacentre/Pages/2017-PR04.aspx.

20. "China Mobile Gets Nokia's 5G-Ready Airscale Base Station; Reveals Pre-5G/5G Landmarks with ZTE, Huawei," *Cellular News* (June 14, 2017), https://www.telegeography.com/products/commsupdate/articles/2017/06/14/china-mobile-gets-nokias-5g-ready-airscale-base-station-reveals-pre-5g5g-landmarks-with-zte-huawei/.

21. Grant Gross, "China Agrees to Drop WAPI Standard," *Computer World* (April 22, 2004), http://www.computerworld.com/article/2565021/mobile-wireless/china-agrees-to-drop-wapi-standard.html.

22. Ronald Deibert, *Black Code: Inside the Battle for Cyberspace* (Toronto: Signal Press, 2013), p. 79. See also "Apple iPhone 4S (GSM China/WAPI) 8, 16, 32, 64 GB Specs," *EveryiPhone.com* (July 3, 2017), http://www.everymac.com/systems/apple/iphone/specs/apple-iphone-4s-gsm-china-unicom-a1431-specs.html.

23. "China Information Technology Security Certification Center Source Code Review Lab Opened," *Microsoft News Center* (September 26, 2003), http://www.microsoft.com/presspass/press/2003/sep03/09-26gspchpr.mspx.

24. Barrington M. Barrett Jr., "Information Warfare: China's Response to U.S. Technological Advantages," *International Journal of Intelligence and Counterintelligence* 18, no. 4 (Winter 2005), p. 699.

25. Barrett, "Information Warfare."

26. Clay Wilson, *Avatars, Virtual Reality Technology, and the U.S. Military: Emerging Policy Issues* (Washington, DC: Congressional Research Service, April 2008), pp. 4, 12.

27. Anton A. Huurdeman, *The Worldwide History of Telecommunications* (Hoboken, NJ: John Wiley & Sons, 2003), pp. 91–146, 153–85. See also Jill Hills, *Telecommunications and Empire* (Champaign: University of Illinois Press, 2007), pp. 91–116.

28. Edward Comor, "Communication Technology and International Capitalism: The Case of DBS and US Foreign Policy," in Edward A. Comor, editor, *The Global Political Economy of Communication: Hegemony, Telecommunication and the Information Economy* (New York: St Martin's Press, 1994).

29. Jill Hills, *The Struggle for Control of Global Communications: The Formative Century* (Champaign: University of Illinois Press, 2002).

30. Parminder Jeet Singh, "India's Proposal Will Help Take the Web out of U.S. Control," *Hindu Online* (May 17, 2012), http://www.thehindu.com/opinion/op-ed/article3426292.ece.

31. Debora L. Spar, "National Policies and Domestic Politics," in Alan M. Rugman, editor, *The Oxford Handbook of International Business* (New York: Oxford University Press, 2008), p. 207.

32. Spar, "National Policies and Domestic Politics," p. 209.

33. Spar, "National Policies and Domestic Politics," p. 212.

34. Standard export restrictions are meant to prevent access, whereas sanctions or embargoes aim to act as punitive measures. Sanctions appear to have the greatest effects on firms. For example, firms in State I which imports from State A will be at a loss if State A subjects State I to a sanctions regime. However, firms that export from State A to State I will also be at a loss since they will suffer from a decline in sales and face the possibility of ties being severed with State I in the long term. Thus, as Spar notes, MNCs must remain aware of political developments within the countries in which they operate so as to not find themselves prohibited from accessing a market due to sanctions. Thus, export controls are one mechanism that can affect the behavior of firms and economies.

35. Richard C. Barth and Clint N. Smith, "International Regulation of Encryption: Technology Will Drive Policy, in Brian Kahin and Charles Nesson, editors, *Borders in Cyberspace: Information Policy and the Global Information Infrastructure* (Cambridge, MA: MIT Press 1998), pp. 283–99.

36. James Bamford, *The Shadow Factor: The Ultra-Secret NSA from 9/11 to the Eavesdropping on America* (New York: Doubleday, 2009). See also Claude Crépeau and Alain Slakmon, "Simple Backdoors for RSA Key Generation," in Marc Joy, editor, *CT-RSA'03: Proceedings of the 2003 RSA conference on the Cryptographers' Track* (Berlin: Springer-Verlag, 2003), pp. 403–16; and Benjamin J. Romano, "Microsoft Device Helps Police Pluck Evidence from Cyberscene of Crime," *Seattle Times* (April 29, 2008), http://seattletimes.nwsource.com/html/microsoft/2004379751_msftlaw29.html.

37. See the Foreign Intelligence Surveillance Act, the Electronic Communications and Privacy Act, and the Communications Assistance for Law Enforcement Act.

38. The crux of the argument made by those holding the opinion that states' sovereignty is at bay is that "the multinational corporation has broken free from its home economy and has become a powerful independent force determining both international and political affairs. [While] others [who] reject this argue that the multinational corporation remains a creature of its home economy." It follows that by the MNC breaking free from its home economy, the sovereignty and autonomy of states is compromised. Those that disagree with the above claim argue that the MNC has not become fully independent from the home country but remains "a creature of the home

country." Robert Gilpin, *Global Political Economy: Understanding the International Economic Order* (Princeton, NJ: Princeton University Press, 2001), pp. 278.

39. For a full exploration of this topic, see Panayotis A. Yannakogeorgos, "Cyberspace: The New Frontier and the Same Old Multilateralism" in Simon Reich, editor, *Global Norms, American Sponsorship and the Emerging Patterns of World Politics* (New York: Palgrave, 2010).

40. United States Department of Commerce, *Management of Internet Names and Addresses*, 63 Fed. Reg. 31741 (1998).

41. Harold Kwalwasser, "Internet Governance," in Franklin D. Kramer, Stuart H. Starr, and Larry K. Wentz, editors, *Cyber Power and National Security* (Washington, DC: NDU Press, 2009).

42. DeNardis, *Protocol Politics*, p. 11.

43. See, e.g., M. Ford, M. Boucadair, A. Durand, P. Levis, and P. Roberts, "Issues with IP Address Sharing," Internet Engineering Task Force, Request for Comments: 6269 (June 2011), http://www.hjp.at/doc/rfc/rfc6269.html.

44. Ingrid Marson, "China Launches Largest IPv6 Network," *CNET News* (December 29, 2004), http://news.cnet.com/China-launches-largest-IPv6-network/2100-1025_3-5506914.html.

45. Sheila Frankel, Richard Graveman, John Pearce, and Mark Rooks, *Guidelines for the Secure Deployment of IPv6: Recommendations of the National Institute of Standards and Technology* (Gaithersburg, MD: National Institute of Standards, December 2010).

46. Panayotis A. Yannakogeorgos, "The Rise of IPv6: Benefits and Costs of Transforming Military Cyberspace," *Air & Space Power Journal* 29, no. 2 (March–April 2015), p. 103. http://www.afspc.af.mil/news1/story.asp?id=123249968.

47. Indeed, one should recall that the World Wide Web, the commercial adaptation of the DARPAnet project, was a CERN (European Organization for Nuclear Research) initiative.

48. This agreement was renewed on July 2, 2012. See Internet Corporation for Assigned Names and Numbers, "ICANN Proposal to Perform IANA Functions Now Posted," (July 9, 2012), http://www.icann.org/en/news/announcements/announcement-2-09jul12-en.htm.

49. Robert E. Molyneux, *The Internet under the Hood: An Introduction to Network Technologies for Information Professionals* (Westport, CT: Libraries Unlimited, 2003), p. 86.

50. Internet Corporation for Assigned Names and Numbers, "Memorandum of Understanding Concerning the Technical Work of the Internet Assigned Numbers Authority," (March 1, 2000), http://www.icann.org/en/general/ietf-icann-mou-01mar00.htm.

51. Elihu Zimet and Edward Skoudis, "A Graphical Introduction to the Structural Elements of Cyberspace," in Kramer, Starr, and Wentz, editors, *Cyber Power and National Security*, pp. 91–112. See also Molyneux, *Internet under the Hood*, pp. 85–86.

52. Molyneux, *Internet under the Hood*, p. 27.

53. H. Zhao, "ITU and Internet Governance—Input to the 7th meeting of the ITU Council Working Group on WSIS, December 12–14, 2004," www.itu.int/ITU-T/tsb-director/itut-wsis/files/zhao-netgov02.doc.

54. For a comprehensive discussion of the dynamics of Internet politics as they relate to the perceptions by foreign countries that ICANN control is a cybersecurity for all, see Yannakogeorgos, "Cyberspace: The New Frontier."

55. The World Summit on the Information Society (WSIS) and its spin-off, the Internet Governance Forum (IGF), are the main venues where governments and all interested stakeholders debate the issues, determine the objectives, and determine principles surrounding the structure of the global information society. The first and second phases of the summit resulted in the *Geneva Declaration of Principles* and the *Tunis Plan of Action*, respectively.

56. The ITU is the main entity tasked with organizing the WSIS. The High-Level Summit Organizing Committee was formed to "coordinate the efforts of the United Nations family in the preparation, organization and holding of WSIS." It was made up of a representative of the UN secretary-general and the executive heads of relevant UN specialized agencies. Other UN entities were included as observers. The ITU secretary-general served as the chair of this committee. One of its important functions was to "ensure that the contributions of the actors participating in the various conferences were comprehensively merged with the contributions from preparatory committees and regional meetings in a consensus document that would serve as the basis for the *Declaration of Principles* and *Plan of Action* of the WSIS."

57. "UN ICT Task Force Global Forum on Internet Governance to be Held in March," *UN press release* (February 13, 2004), http://portal.unesco.org/ci/en/ev.php-URL_ID=14347&URL_DO=DO_PRINTPAGE&URL_SECTION=201.html.

58. "Global Internet Governance System Is Working but Needs to Be More Inclusive, UN Forum on Internet Governance Told," *UN press release* (March 26, 2004), http://www.un.org/News/Press/docs/2004/pi1568.doc.htm.

59. "Global Internet Governance System Is Working."

60. "Statement by Mr. Dushyant Singh, Member of Parliament, on Agenda Item 16—Information and Communication Technologies for Development, at the 66th Session of the United Nations General Assembly on October 26, 2011," http://content.ibnlive.in.com/article/21-May-2012documents/full-text-indias-un-proposal-to-control-the-internet-259971-53.html.

61. Yang Yu, "Chinese response to 'Further Notice of Inquiry on the Internet Assigned Numbers Authority Functions'," China Organizational Name Administration Center (CONAC), http://www.ntia.doc.gov/files/ntia/conac_response_to_fnoi.pdf. CONAC is a nonprofit organization established in 2008. With the authorization of the State Commission Office for Public Sector Reform (SCPSR) and the Ministry of Industry and Information Technology (MIIT), CONAC runs the registry for ".政务.cn" (Government Affairs) and ".公益.cn" (Public Interest). CONAC also actively participates in the global Internet community.

62. "Prime Minister Vladimir Putin meets with Secretary General of the International Telecommunication Union Hamadoun Toure," *Working Day* (June 15, 2011), http://premier.gov.ru/eng/events/news/15601/.

63. United Nations General Assembly Economic and Social Council, "Enhanced Cooperation on Public Policy Issues Pertaining to the Internet," Report of the Secretary-General (New York: United Nations, May 4, 2011), http://unctad.org/meetings/en/SessionalDocuments/a66d77_en.pdf.

64. Signed by 178 countries, the ITR is a global treaty applied around the world.

65. Disclaimer: This is for informational use only. Any action undertaken by the reader of this chapter on the .onion domain is at his or her own risk, and this author is not liable for any harm caused by or to the reader.

66. This is different from what Chris Demchak and Peter Dombrowski point to in "Rise of a Cybered Westphalian Age," *Strategic Studies Quarterly* 5, no. 1 (Spring 2011), where the focus on sovereignty of the Internet is on access points of incoming Tier 1 ISP connections into the country and maintaining government control of those.

67. United States Department of State, "Internet Freedom Fact Sheet" (February 15, 2011), https://2009-2017.state.gov/r/pa/prs/ps/2011/02/156623.htm.

68. Spencer Ackerman, "Does Obama's 'Net Freedom Agenda' Hurt the U.S.?" *Wired* (January 28, 2011), http://www.wired.com/dangerroom/2011/01/does-obamas-internet-freedom-agenda-hurt-the-u-s-without-helping-dissidents/.

69. Ye Tian, Ratan Dey, Yong Lui, and Keith W. Ross, "China's Internet: Topology Mapping and Geolocating," *INFOCOM: The Proceedings of the Institute of Electrical and Electronics Engineers* (2012), http://cis.poly.edu/~ratan/topologymappingchinainternetshort.pdf.

Chapter Two

Managing Decentralized Cyber Governance

The Responsibility to Troubleshoot

Mark Raymond

The cyber domain is widely acknowledged to be in the midst of a process of global rulemaking that includes an array of public and private actors from across the globe.[1] Many of these rules pertain, more or less directly, to issues of international security. Indeed, the question of cyber norms has been on the agenda of the First Committee of the UN General Assembly since 1998. Their work has made significant progress in the two most recent reports of its Group of Governmental Experts (GGE) on Developments in the Field of Information and Telecommunications in the Context of International Security.[2] The work of the GGE is vitally important; however, this state-centric process cannot be treated in isolation from the broader landscape of Internet governance and Internet policy—even though it concerns matters traditionally understood as the exclusive purview of states. Security and intelligence practitioners increasingly affect, and are affected by, decisions made about Internet governance and Internet policy in a variety of contexts at the global, regional, and even domestic levels. Many of these decision-making processes occur at least partially within the private rather than the public sphere.[3] Collectively, these processes of rulemaking entail the emergence of a broader cyber-regime complex alongside the narrow technical regime for Internet governance in an era characterized by the impending integration of the Internet and cyberspace with virtually every domain of human activity.[4] This process of regime complex formation is ongoing and remains contentious. Contention over Internet issues and the creation of this emerging cyber-regime complex is driven by a variety of factors, including the breadth of issues implicated (trade, security, human rights, etc.) and the diversity of participants in terms of actor type, interests, values, and views of legitimate procedures for rulemaking.[5]

Even the most optimistic projection for the nascent cyber-regime complex must acknowledge that, for the foreseeable future, most governance will remain decentralized. Decisions about policy, rules, and norms will be made by an extremely heterogeneous set of players that will often operate with a high degree of autonomy. Even where there are clear hierarchical authority relations between participants, the sheer complexity and pace of governance in this area will create autonomy in practice. Yet the shared global physical and logical resources crucial to the cyber domain mean that decisions made by these various parties may have implications for, and intended or unintended effects on, those outside their own jurisdictions. As a result, decisions made in one part of the cyber-regime complex can negatively impact the stability and interoperability of the network for others. The combination of the possibility of such effects and a highly decentralized regime complex exacerbates challenges of coordination and conflict resolution among an extremely diverse set of actors.

Since the various participants in the emerging global cyber-regime complex have distinct and at least partially incommensurate values and interests, policy coordination efforts are likely to remain limited. They will also be inhibited by the complexity of the subject matter. In such situations, one possible approach is to establish a shared commitment to "do no harm" or to refrain from taking steps that could negatively affect the stability or global interoperability of the cyber domain and the ability of the players to make use of it. Such an approach motivates recent calls for a norm of noninterference in what has been called the "public core" of the Internet.[6] Elimination of such cyber behavior is unlikely, in part because actors cannot agree completely (or even substantially) on the bounds of acceptable behavior. Accordingly, simple rules and norms of prohibition are unlikely to be sufficient for ensuring the viability of the cyber-regime complex. Further, a simple prohibition regime would likely be insufficient even in a world of angels. The reality of a massively complex, open global system built on the principle of "permissionless" innovation, combined with the law of unintended consequences, suggests the desirability of having previously agreed-upon means of responding when the activities of one group have negative implications (intended or not) for others.

This chapter argues that the capacity to effectively manage the set of challenges can be enhanced by cultivating a responsibility to troubleshoot (R2T).[7] First, it argues that the decentralized nature of the global cyber-regime complex combines with the shared logical resources and physical infrastructure of the Internet to produce both strategic opportunities and externalities that affect other parties. One solution to these problems would be to establish a prohibition regime. Next, it surveys other prohibition regimes employed to address international security threats. In doing so, it gives context to the common wisdom that prohibition is virtually impossible in the cyber domain and shows that elements of a proto-prohibition regime for the cyber domain are identifiable.[8] However, while prohibition may be worth pursuing, it is clearly insufficient. At least for the foreseeable future, mitigation and management processes will also be required. Accordingly, the third section explores options for an R2T as a core component of the global cyber-regime complex.

DECENTRALIZED GOVERNANCE OF A GLOBAL SYSTEM

While cyberspace is often understood as a global commons or even a pure public good, it is more accurately described as a set of nested "club" goods, since it is excludable and typically nonrivalous in consumption[9] and since decisions about cyberspace are taken in a myriad of separate institutional contexts arrayed in complex and variable authority relations.[10] At the most basic level, all Internet users are members of a single club: the club of global Internet users. Simultaneously, all users are also members of at least two other kinds of clubs—a club of Internet users in a particular state and a club of Internet users relying on a particular Internet service provider (ISP). Each of these clubs has different procedural rules for rulemaking and interpretation. National clubs of Internet users typically work according to the corresponding state's processes for legislation, regulation, and jurisprudence, though some states also have multistakeholder bodies governing some aspects of Internet policy. Clubs of users relying on a particular ISP are more commonly governed by contractual arrangements and terms of service, with civil law as a backdrop. Other notable clubs include those with special responsibility for core Internet technical functions, such as the Internet Corporation for Assigned Names and Numbers (ICANN) or the Internet Engineering Task Force (IETF).

As the Internet has become enmeshed with more and more aspects of economic, social, and political life, the narrow legacy Internet governance regime concerned with core technical functions such as the development of technical protocols and the management of Internet names and numbers has been drawn into a nascent global cyber-regime complex.[11] The result is that organizations with primary interests and responsibilities removed from the Internet and cyberspace are beginning to make decisions and to enact rules that can have significant unintended consequences for the stability and interoperability of the cyber domain. These actors include military and security agencies, antitrust regulators and consumer watchdogs, human-rights bodies, international trade bodies, and others.

These various entities and organizations nevertheless share the same physical infrastructure as well as globally harmonized standards and protocols for exchanging packets between the various independent networks that comprise the Internet and for resolving Internet domain names into Internet protocol (IP) address numbers. The combination of the end-to-end principle and the principle of permissionless innovation has been central to the rapid global spread of Internet access and to its economic potential; however, these principles have also enabled the actions and decisions of individual organizations to have far-ranging effects on the stability and interoperability of the broader global network.

Such effects are often unintended consequences of attempts to exercise control over Internet content in the service of various social, economic, and political policy objectives. Examples include a global YouTube outage caused by Pakistani attempts to block domestic access to video content deemed inappropriate on religious grounds, domain name seizures by American law enforcement agencies intended to enforce intellectual property laws, and ongoing European efforts to implement a "right to be forgotten" with respect to online search engines. These examples, and others, are indicative of what has been called "the turn to infrastructure in Internet governance."[12]

Cyber attacks, financially motivated cybercrime, and cyber espionage, whether conducted by states or firms, employ Internet infrastructure and mechanisms of technical Internet governance to accomplish unrelated objectives. Like content filtering and blocking measures, these activities can have negative unintended consequences for global Internet stability and interoperability. Some effects may be quite direct in nature. Manipulating the underlying technology and protocols may simply be done badly and cause technical problems. Given the low and rapidly falling barriers to entry in this field, significant cyber capabilities are likely to be acquired by a large number of public and private organizations with relatively low levels of expertise and sophistication; such novices may be particularly prone to execution errors. Other negative unintended effects on Internet stability and interoperability will be indirect in nature. The most likely pathways for ill effects include (1) attempts to "harden" networks to make them less susceptible to intrusion but sacrifice openness as a result, leading the network topology to more closely resemble a "cybered Westphalia"[13] and (2) escalating spirals of retaliation that cause episodic service interruptions and other collateral damage to third parties.

All of these diverse activities are enacted for reasons. Whether we evaluate these as good or bad reasons is beside the point of the argument being advanced here. The key point is that a large number of actors will be capable of forming their own views about the desirability of such forms of cyber conduct and also of *acting* on the basis of such views. It is this potential for autonomous action—which itself may have *further* unintended consequences—that makes these problems especially serious.

One approach to managing problems associated with unintended conse-quences in a decentralized governance environment would be to pursue pro-hibition of various forms of problematic cyber conduct. Grounds for such a ban might be rooted entirely in considerations of long-term consequences for Internet stability and interoperability, or they might also draw on complemen-tary justifications having to do with respect for state sovereignty or individ-ual human rights. Several bans on particular kinds of international conduct exist, and some have persisted for extended periods of time. What follows is a survey of several existing global prohibition regimes and the prospects for applying such an approach to cybersecurity governance.

PROHIBITION REGIMES AND INTERNATIONAL SECURITY GOVERNANCE

The common view of international politics—as a lawless Wild West in which sovereign states confront an anarchic system that compels them to act ruth-lessly or perish—is mistaken. Political scientist Tanisha M. Fazal, whose research focuses on the relationship between sovereignty and international law, has convincingly shown that—at least since 1945—the rate of "state death" has fallen sharply in response largely to changing norms of conquest.[14] While international norms, like all social rules, may sometimes be violated, the norm against acquiring territory by conquest appears to exert a significant constraining effect on state behavior to the point where many states in the international system, including several permanent Security Council members, appear to have ruled it out entirely as a policy option. International condem-nation of Russia's actions in Crimea demonstrates the continuing strength of the norm even as it requires acknowledgment that enforcement is imperfect.

Predation is hardly the only international conduct subject to prohibition. The extensive international relations literature documenting such regimes catalogs numerous cases of varying success.[15] Here the focus is on cases prohibiting conduct directly relevant to international security, to make three important points: (1) prohibition regimes are useful tools for achieving secur-ity policy objectives, (2) there are initial signs of a developing prohibition regime that captures multiple kinds of cyber conduct, and (3) even in a per-fect world, such a prohibition regime is insufficient to address the problems associated with decentralized governance of a shared global facility.

One prominent global prohibition regime bans gross violations of fun-damental human rights. An example is the ban on genocide codified in the Convention on the Prevention and Punishment of the Crime of Genocide (1948)—a prohibition that is also a *jus cogens* norm of international law under Article 53 of the Vienna Convention on the Law of Treaties.[16]

Similarly, the prohibition against torture is also such a norm of international law in addition to a treaty obligation under the Convention against Torture and Other Cruel, Inhuman or Degrading Treatment or Punishment (1984). In both cases, bans on particular forms of international conduct are framed in terms of these norms, which are binding on states regardless of their consent and which do not permit derogation. This latter quality of *jus cogens* norms substantially limits the varieties of special pleading open to states under the area of customary international law known as the law of state responsibility.[17]

Another class of internationally prohibited behaviors pertains to battlefield conduct. Wayne Sandholtz, a professor of international relations and law, has shown, for example, that wartime plunder has moved from a normal and expected part of war to prohibited behavior.[18] Similarly, political scientist Ward Thomas has argued that there is a relatively robust international norm against assassination.[19] There is also a ban on particular kinds of weapons. For example, biological and chemical weapons are subject to bans. The Biological Weapons Convention (1972) prohibits not only the use but also the production of this class of weapons,[20] though it lacks provisions for monitoring or inspection. In contrast, the Chemical Weapons Convention provides for extensive inspections in support of the associated taboo.[21] Bans have also been created for certain classes of conventional weapons. Examples include the ban on antipersonnel landmines[22] as well as the ban on cluster munitions.[23] In contrast, attempts to impose control on the international transfer of small arms and light weapons have been less successful.[24]

PROHIBITION IN THE CYBER DOMAIN

There are also signs of a developing global prohibition regime in the cyber domain. This proto-regime has at least three notable components. The first deals with promoting international cooperation on cybercrime. The Budapest Convention on Cybercrime commits state parties to harmonizing their domestic legal regimes with respect to computer crime. It also commits parties to good-faith cooperation in investigating and prosecuting such crimes across borders.[25] As such, it effectively seeks to deal with the problem of decentralized governance by negotiating common standards at the global level and leaving implementation to domestic authorities. While a useful step, it has been ratified by only forty-seven nations, primarily advanced industrial democracies.

The second component of the emerging cyber prohibition regime consists of work primarily by the UN GGE seeking to clarify the applicability of the law of armed conflict in the cyber domain. The group includes the governments of the United States, China, and Russia; it therefore reflects the preferences and understandings of key states. The 2015 report made several key advances. It expressed the belief that "voluntary, non-binding norms of responsible State behavior can reduce risks to international peace, security and stability." It further made several concrete recommendations for such norms. Finally, in a discussion of the application of international law to information and communications technologies (ICT), the GGE explicitly noted "established legal principles ... including, where applicable, the principles of humanity, necessity, proportionality and distinction."[26] American officials have indicated, though, that some states are thus far unwilling to make "more robust statements on how international law applies" in the cyber domain.[27] These efforts are preliminary, at best, and a great deal will depend on how these norms are implemented in concrete cases.

The final component of this proto-regime is the least developed. It involves the bilateral agreement between China and the United States regarding economic cyber espionage. In a September 2015 statement, the two governments indicated that "neither the U.S. nor the Chinese government will conduct or knowingly support cyber-enabled theft of intellectual property, including trade secrets or other confidential business information for commercial advantage." The agreement also provided for the establishment of additional government-to-government contacts for the review of cybercrime allegations.[28] Published reports have indicated that American firms continue to suffer intrusions originating in China that are said to be attributable to government-linked hackers.[29] Accordingly, it is important to be realistic about the likelihood of Chinese compliance; however, it may be that the value of the agreement is in publicly committing China to a norm from which its derogation can be criticized. International relations professor Daniel C. Thomas, whose research focuses on issues of European integration and international governance, has argued that the Helsinki Accords had this effect in committing the Soviet Union to human-rights norms and thereby helping to bring about the end of Communist rule.[30]

Thus, prohibition regimes are an important component of a global governance toolkit. There are good reasons to believe that some of the regimes discussed above have at least reduced the incidence and severity of particular kinds of undesirable conduct; however, these regimes vary in their comprehensiveness, formality, and effectiveness. In assessing the likely effectiveness of a cyber prohibition regime, a number of foreseeable problems arise pertaining both to whether other actors can be convinced to adopt a prohibition regime and whether a prohibition regime can be effectively implemented even if other actors are convinced of its utility and appropriateness.

Prohibition regimes are typically employed to deal with conduct that is widely agreed to be immoral or unethical. Thus, the degree of moral revulsion generated is an important determinant of whether actors will agree to them.

To the extent that some actors see different forms of cyber conduct as consistent with their identities or their substantive understandings of justice, they are unlikely to agree to prohibit such conduct. State conduct of economic cyber espionage provides an illustrative example. Some states and their populations may retain a more mercantilist understanding of what Australian constructivist scholar Christian Reus-Smit has called "the moral purpose of the state"[31] and thus believe aiding national firms counts (at least in the domestic arena) as praiseworthy state conduct. Such an argument is consistent with international security specialist Jacques Hymans's finding that leaders' perceptions of national identity are an important driver of state decisions regarding nuclear proliferation.[32]

Even if actors agree on what behaviors they want to prohibit, there may be other reasons a global prohibition regime lacks effectiveness. Political scientists Margaret Keck and Kathryn Sikkink have suggested that transnational advocacy networks are most successful in achieving their objectives when they are opposing conduct that entails physical harm to innocents and when that harm is the result of a short causal chain that easily connects the behavior with the resulting harm.[33] Given that many cyber harms accrue in the first instance to corporations rather than individuals (e.g., intellectual property or brand damage), it may be difficult to generate sufficient moral revulsion to support a broad regime prohibiting many forms of problematic cyber conduct. Further, many cyber harms typically involve highly complex and opaque causal chains that individual policy makers and voters are unlikely to understand in any depth.

Convincing others to support a prohibition regime dealing with particular forms of cyber conduct will also be more difficult to the extent that prohibiting such conduct will also undermine actors' attempts to achieve other valued goals. There are a variety of problems associated with dual-use technology. State security agencies, for example, may see particular forms of malicious code as critical to fulfilling their war-fighting and intelligence-gathering missions—even if they might agree that some uses of such technologies should be restricted.

Research also indicates that the presence of powerful champions on either side of an issue can affect the success or failure of advocacy efforts.[34] Such champions matter not only in terms of persuading other actors but also in determining which issues advocates decide to contest; further, champions may be organizations occupying positions of network centrality, in addition to individual norm entrepreneurs.[35] While the United States has attempted to champion a norm against economic cyber espionage, its efforts have been undermined by revelations about the activities of the American intelligence community. Most technology sector and civil-society organizations have focused on contesting privacy and other human-rights issues, whether or not in response to state surveillance online. Reluctance to publicly disclose data breaches to protect reputation and share value may well limit the willingness of other firms to champion prohibitions on many forms of problematic cyber conduct.

IMPLEMENTING CYBER PROHIBITION

Aside from challenges in securing political agreement on an expanded, robust cyber prohibition regime, there are two important aspects to address in implementing any such measures: the use of formal versus informal instruments and complications arising from monitoring and enforcement.

Most global prohibition regimes rely heavily on formal legal instruments that codify the proscribed behavior and obligations of various parties for monitoring, enforcing, and otherwise implementing the ban. However, considerable risks are associated with the use of hard-law instruments in this context; soft-law modalities may be more effective.[36] First, treaties and customary international law bind only states. Given the low barriers to entry and the key role of the private sector in the cyber domain, a hard-law global prohibition regime would not directly bind many of the relevant actors. Further, insofar as a hard-law instrument binds states to implement and enforce prohibitions within their own borders and to cooperate with other states in doing so, it could be expected to lead to a substantial number of requests under existing mutual legal-assistance treaties. Where mutual legal assistance is not effective, there may also be attempts to employ the law of state responsibility to pursue remedies. Such measures would place states in the difficult position of being responsible for the management of problem-solving on a global network that is expected to expand to several billion connected devices and on which it is often difficult to attribute particular conduct to specific actors. Even for advanced industrial democracies, it is questionable whether such arrangements are feasible; for emerging markets and developing states, the situation would be even more difficult.

A second reason to be skeptical of hard-law instruments for prohibiting problematic cyber conduct is that there are legitimacy risks associated with the codification of rules that are either unlikely to be obeyed or extremely difficult to enforce. Such rules risk becoming dead letters and serving as constant temptations for violators to argue that actors do not believe the proscribed conduct is actually inappropriate.

Finally, monitoring and enforcement present serious challenges for a global prohibition regime in the cyber domain, whether it is implemented via hard- or soft-law mechanisms. The issue presents clear enforcement problems among a large number of actors on an issue where attribution is generally difficult. Therefore, violations are both likely and difficult to prevent or punish. Access to the technology required to conduct such activities is already widespread and available from a large number of suppliers based in different countries. These technologies also typically have multiple purposes, further complicating efforts to curtail proliferation.

Despite these considerable challenges, soft-law prohibition norms are generally inexpensive to promote and can have substantial constraining effects on behavior when internalized. Accordingly, current prohibition efforts should be pursued with the realization that they will not provide sufficient tools to deal with problems arising from decentralized governance of a shared global facility. In particular, prohibition should be coupled with robust, institutionalized means of responding to intended and unintended disruptions to Internet stability and interoperability.

THE RESPONSIBILITY TO TROUBLESHOOT

The insufficiency of global prohibition norms to deal with problematic cyber conduct means that there will be an ongoing need for mechanisms to mitigate and manage such conduct when it does occur. While these mechanisms will naturally involve technology (improving hardware, software, and related technical standards), policy must also include attempts to address the social dimensions of such conduct or run the risk that bad actors will adapt and innovate, finding new ways to realize their goals. Measures should be aimed at reducing the frequency and severity of disruptive cyber conduct, fostering cooperation in repairing damage caused by misconduct, and preventing the escalation of such incidents into even more serious disputes or conflicts. Cultivating a responsibility to troubleshoot can enhance global capacity to manage challenges associated with decentralized cyber governance.

Coping with Unintended Consequences

The core challenge is to cope with negative effects on the stability or global interoperability of cyberspace. Since these kinds of effects are not typically intended outcomes, the remainder of this chapter emphasizes means for coping with unintended consequences rather than with intended effects. However, since determining intention is often difficult in practice, there is a strong argument for presuming any such negative effects to be unintended. If nothing else, publicly treating such events under a presumption that they are unintended serves two valuable purposes. First, it reduces the likelihood of hostility and escalation. Second, refusal to cooperate in resolving problems may provide prima facie evidence to third parties that the effect was intended (or at least welcomed) and demonstrate bad faith on the part of the responsible actor, thereby increasing reputational costs from engaging in such conduct.

Resolving these problems requires effective and reliable methods of quickly identifying and remedying the effects of malicious code and other means of disrupting cyberspace. These tasks are complicated not only by technical problems of diagnosis, attribution, and implementation but also increasingly by problems of jurisdiction in what Naval War College professors of strategy Chris C. Demchak and Peter Dombrowski have termed a cybered Westphalian age.[37] The decentralized nature of the international system and the cyber-regime complex create or exacerbate a host of problems in securing broad, reliable cooperation in responding to disruptions in the cyber domain. Aside from complications arising from domestic politics and international rivalries, these difficulties include differences in culture, institutions, specific domestic legal regimes, and basic capacity (infrastructure, skilled personnel, and financing).

Furthermore, it is not immediately obvious who should be responsible for *providing* such cooperation. Most Internet infrastructure is privately owned, and most jurisdictions have multiple large-network operators. Are such firms responsible, and if so, are they individually or collectively responsible? Further, a variety of actor types transmits information over these networks. In some cases, this information itself may be responsible for the disruption. What responsibility do over-the-top content providers, nontechnology firms acting as Internet consumers, state actors, civil-society groups, and private individuals bear? Computer emergency response teams (CERTs) typically assume responsibility for this level of cooperation and assistance as part of their mission statements,[38] but CERTs are highly varied in their capacity and in their scope of work.[39]

These difficulties will not be quickly or easily overcome. One useful step in doing so, however, would be to supplement prohibition efforts with the cultivation of a norm that all relevant actors must participate in good faith in efforts to resolve threats to the stability and interoperability of cyberspace. This requirement can be understood as an R2T. The underlying rationale for this suggestion is that norms shape behavior in a number of ways, for example by reducing the propensity of actors to engage in conduct that violates applicable norms and by shaping responses to violations by prompting criticism or sanctions.[40] Note, especially, that because they enable criticism and sanctioning behavior, norms can have significant and helpful effects even in cases where compliance falls substantially short.

The notion that even sovereign states have international responsibilities should not be controversial. The most basic of these—noninterference in the domestic affairs of other states—is foundational to the modern international system. Several other responsibilities are inherent to modern international law. These include the principle that treaties must be observed (*pacta sunt servanda*) and other *jus cogens* principles. The bodies of customary and conventional international law are also similarly binding on sovereign states. Among the latter, the UN Charter deserves special mention in creating responsibilities pertaining to the use of force and to compliance with measures authorized by the UN Security Council. The 2015 GGE report affirmed the applicability of the charter, in its entirety, in the cyber domain.[41]

As with any other field of social life, actors will sometimes fail to live up to their responsibilities. International law explicitly contemplates such situations. It does so in the first instance by making states responsible for their internationally wrongful acts, requiring them to provide apologies, damages, and other forms of restitution. Absent their willingness to do so, international law also authorizes wronged states to take certain self-help measures. Most importantly, even in exercising self-help, states have responsibilities to do so according to the terms of identifiable rules. As with rules of the road in many other areas of international politics, the law of state responsibility has taken important steps toward codification (and thus greater precision)[42] in the latter half of the twentieth century. This effort has, thus far, culminated in the publication of the International Law Commission's *Draft Articles on Responsibility of States for Internationally Wrongful Acts.*[43] While not yet formally adopted by states in the form of a treaty, the articles have been endorsed on multiple occasions by the UN General Assembly.

If anything, contemporary understandings of sovereignty are increasingly qualified by concomitant responsibilities. The "responsibility to protect" (R2P) is an important recent example.[44] Further, notions of international responsibility are increasingly extended to nonstate actors. The International Criminal Court recognizes individuals as bearing responsibility for certain kinds of grievous offenses even when undertaken in an official state capacity. Efforts to inculcate an ethos of corporate social responsibility, such as the UN Global Compact, also seek to create and uphold responsibilities for firms. It should not be controversial to extend notions of international responsibility, including an R2T, to various kinds of nonstate actors.

Relationship to Responsibility to Protect

The R2P is arguably the most significant addition to the body of international responsibilities since 1945. Rather than a single responsibility, it entails three related responsibilities arranged to ensure the greatest possible redundancy while reducing costs in terms of both sovereignty and enforcement. The primary obligation is that of the state to its own citizens, specifically, to protect them from genocide, war crimes, and crimes against humanity. This obligation includes not committing or inciting those acts against the state's own population, as well as protecting the population against the perpetration of such acts by third parties. The international community also has, in the first instance, the obligation to "encourage and assist" states in carrying out this obligation to their own citizens. In cases where states are unwilling or unable to fulfill the primary responsibility, R2P holds that the international community has a collective responsibility to provide such protection. It specifies that this is preferably done by peaceful means but that stronger measures are authorized if such means are impractical or unsuccessful.[45]

While the legal status of R2P is admittedly uncertain and the analogy between the R2P and any potential R2T is imperfect at best, surveying these shortcomings is instructive for effectively advocating and implementing an R2T. First, given the privatization of key Internet infrastructure, the limited capacity and expertise of many states with cyber operations, the low barriers to entry for the creation of significant cyber disruptions, and the difficulty of decisively attributing specific conduct to particular actors, allocation of an R2T exclusively to states would be unlikely to prove effective. In keeping with the avowedly multistakeholder nature of Internet governance, any R2T would need to be borne not only by states but also by firms and voluntarily by organizations with the means to contribute to ensuring its efficacy.

Second, the nature of the foundational responsibility in the two situations differs. The R2P is foremost an obligation of the state to its own citizens. In contrast, an R2T would be offered equally by states to citizens and noncitizens since it pertains in substance to the functioning of a global communications facility. Further, if the R2T is borne in part by nonstate actors, it cannot be owed on the basis of the relationship between state and citizen. The conception of the Internet as a governance system comprised of a set of nested clubs, as mentioned earlier, provides two distinct and nonmutually exclusive bases for grounding an R2T. On one hand, the obligation can be grounded in reciprocity: the responsibility of all clubs of Internet users to refrain from disruptive cyber conduct in return for the assurance that all other clubs will provide them the same consideration. This ground creates an obligation owed by groups to other groups. On the other hand, the obligation can also be grounded in the terms of membership for the most basic and universal club: the club of all global Internet users. This ground creates an obligation owed by members of a group to each other. Both routes are possible, and both can be pursued without contradiction since the substantive obligation is the same in both cases. Given the lack of a strong cosmopolitan ethos and the strength of more particularistic attachments in social life, the first basis may well prove more compelling overall, but the cosmopolitan basis resonates more clearly with the human-rights regime.

Third, the nature of the subsidiary collective responsibility also differs. The difficulty of attributing cyber conduct poses severe challenges for any efforts to implement collective action to intervene in the case of major cyber disruptions or extremely significant levels of other problematic cyber conduct such as large-scale economic cyber espionage. Taking steps that might include property damage or loss of life, at least with the collective authorization envisaged by the R2P, will likely demand the ability to demonstrate culpability in a public and convincing manner. At a more pragmatic level, inaccurately directed responses are unlikely to eliminate the undesired conduct and are further likely to prompt retaliation and loss of legitimacy. It is also doubtful whether there are any forms of cyber conduct sufficiently grave to satisfy the proportionality standards implicit in the R2P, which applies only in situations of genocide, war crimes, and crimes against humanity. Prior to reaching this level, such cases would almost certainly trigger other rules permitting a collective response, like the UN Charter provisions for self-defense and for the maintenance of international peace and security. The R2T is a means for addressing conduct of serious international concern that falls short of the extreme acts that trigger the R2P. Therefore, there is no need for the R2T to require (or authorize) more than the use of peaceful, cooperative means. The concept of a responsibility to troubleshoot cannot be a panacea to answer all problems arising from the cyber domain. To the extent that this responsibility is adopted, however, some problems can be made less severe and perhaps reduced in frequency. It is therefore a potentially important component of the broader cyber-regime complex currently in the process of formation.

The R2T proposed here is consistent with the recommendations of the 2015 Group of Governmental Experts. The GGE endorsed assistance for less-developed countries but also indicated that "capacity-building involves more than a transfer of knowledge and skills from developed to developing States, as all States can learn from each other about the threats that they face and effective responses to those threats." This speaks to a broad awareness that international cyber assistance is not simply a matter of development. Further, the group proposed several candidate norms that indicate general support for the notion that providing assistance is appropriate international behavior.[46] These candidate norms are discussed in more detail below. In general, the GGE recommendations are primarily focused on state actors and do not develop the notion that an R2T might also apply to nonstate actors. Further, given the preliminary state of international legal development in this area, the GGE merely expresses support for candidate norms. This is a sensible starting point but falls well short of a notion of responsibility.

Implementing the Responsibility to Troubleshoot

Several current and future options exist for implementing the R2T. As in many other areas of Internet and cyber governance, states have useful roles.

One such role pertains to information sharing. In general terms, this may involve sharing information on an ongoing basis to facilitate diffusion of best practices in cybersecurity. The GGE suggested, for example, that states should "encourage responsible reporting of ICT [information and communications technologies] vulnerabilities and share associated information on available remedies."[47] Information sharing may also involve more specific efforts in response to particular instances of problematic cyber conduct. This cooperation will often involve law enforcement agencies. In this vein, the GGE called for states to "consider how best to cooperate to exchange information, assist each other, prosecute terrorist or criminal use of ICTs, and implement other cooperative measures to address such threats."[48]

State involvement in implementing an R2T will need to go beyond information sharing to encompass a direct role in incident response. States are already significant network operators; their activities in this regard may have unintended effects on other parties. Further, as states play larger regulatory roles in the cyber domain, the number of channels through which state action can produce negative effects on Internet stability and interoperability is likely to grow. Finally, many states have created bodies to assist firms and individuals in dealing with cyber disruptions. These bodies may themselves produce unintended consequences for users outside the state's jurisdiction. In each of these cases, the state is itself the source of a kind of problematic cyber conduct. It is not unreasonable to suggest, therefore, that it bears a degree of responsibility to those affected by its actions. Even where the state is not the direct cause of cyber conduct that damages others, it may bear some responsibility under international law to states whose citizens are adversely affected.

The GGE took preliminary steps toward recognizing such responsibilities in proposing that states should "respond to appropriate requests for assistance by other States whose critical infrastructure is subject to malicious acts" and that they should "respond to appropriate requests to mitigate malicious activity aimed at the critical infrastructure of another State emanating from their territory."[49] While promising, these candidate norms are limited only to acts that target the critical infrastructure of other states, leaving most firms and citizens of other states relatively unprotected. In limiting the candidate norms to covering "malicious acts," the GGE also left unintended consequences (the primary problem discussed in this chapter) unaddressed. Further, there are numerous ambiguities in the phrasing. It is not clear, for example, what constitutes an "appropriate request" or even what is included under "critical infrastructure." Even if these candidate norms are ultimately accepted by most states, additional work remains to be done.

The work of mitigating and resolving problematic cyber conduct once it has begun is in large part dependent on technical competencies in engineering and computer science. But such work cannot occur effectively and reliably at the global level without proper governance and administrative structures to enable it. Over the last several years, Internet governance issues have become increasingly contested. Individual governments, including those of the United States, China, Russia, Brazil, and others, have initiated or increased efforts to exert influence over these issues. Incumbent entities including the ICANN, the IETF, and the Internet Society (ISOC) have also undertaken efforts to defend or expand their roles, and other players like the International Telecommunications Union (ITU), Organization for Economic Cooperation and Development (OECD), and World Economic Forum (WEF) have also sought enhanced roles. Of particular importance in implementing the R2T, however, are organizations dedicated to emergency response. CERTs, sometimes called computer security incident response teams (CSIRTs), can—and often do—play important roles in efforts to respond to cyber disruptions.

Since 1990, the Forum of Incident Response and Security Teams (FIRST) has provided a degree of coordination among these groups. Its membership is relatively global[50] but includes little representation in Africa and the Middle East. Further, members are disproportionately clustered in the developed world, and developing world members generally lack resources and expertise. FIRST has also undertaken efforts to coordinate with the International Organization for Standardization (ISO) and ITU to ensure lessons learned from computer security incidents are incorporated into efforts to revise and create technical standards. It is also currently in the process of developing a curriculum to ensure CSIRT training is consistent and of high quality. Individual members also organize and join special interest groups on a voluntary basis according to their interests.

The GGE explicitly recognized the importance of CSIRTs in its 2015 report. It called on states to "not conduct or knowingly support activity to harm the information systems of the authorized emergency response teams … of another State" and further indicated that states should "not use authorized emergency response teams to engage in malicious international activity."[51] These candidate norms suggest that there may be support for providing CSIRTs with a degree of protected status under international law.

Existing CSIRT programs and initiatives provide a solid foundation for implementing many parts of an R2T, especially if their trustworthiness and freedom to operate can be protected under international law, but in several important areas further development would be beneficial. First, expanding educational offerings will provide an important service to the global community. Second, additional work is needed in creating organizations in areas of the world where CSIRTs are less common. While FIRST cannot accomplish this alone, it can play an important advocacy and mobilization role alongside assistance from other Internet-community organizations and other stakeholders, including governments acting in their capacity as providers of and catalysts for development aid and capacity building. Third, the CSIRT community needs to engage in broader outreach to educate a wider array of organizations about its role and importance. Network operators, technology firms, universities, and some large financial institutions either have their own CSIRTs or are accustomed to working with them, but as the "Internet of Things" dramatically broadens the number of Internet-connected devices and objects, these concerns will become broadly relevant to firms both as producers and consumers. Ensuring that stakeholders are apprised of appropriate points of contact and available resources will facilitate timely, cooperative mitigation and remediation. These functions all parallel the requirement in R2P that actors assist each other in carrying out their primary responsibility. They are also consistent with other norms in the international system emphasizing the importance of providing capacity-building and technology transfer assistance to developing states.[52] Capacity in this sense includes not only technology itself but also knowledge about governance issues pertaining to ICTs.

The suggestions above deal with education, outreach, and capacity building. In addition, it would be helpful to increase and institutionalize CSIRT cooperation and coordination at a more operational level. One modest first step in this regard would be the establishment of a global clearinghouse system for notification of cyber disruptions and other problematic cyber conduct. Beyond notification, such a system could also perform a "handshaking" function, connecting parties experiencing issues with verified, trustworthy groups with the expertise and willingness to assist. Such a system could also help reduce duplication of effort. Finally, FIRST might play a role in developing and disseminating best practices. States and other stakeholders could play critical supporting roles in these endeavors, including by encouraging or requiring actors to make use of these mechanisms in responding to cyber disruptions rather than (or at least in addition to) employing private means of response.

Many forms of problematic cyber conduct revolve around access to sensitive information. Further, efforts to mitigate such conduct may bring CSIRT members and law enforcement officials into contact with the sensitive information of third parties, including those in other legal jurisdictions—for example, of individuals whose devices are part of illicit botnets. Accordingly, it is vital that efforts to implement an R2T are especially sensitive to compliance with human-rights protections and civil liberties, to prevent the inadvertent agglomeration of excessive powers by law enforcement and security agencies. The GGE recognized the importance of human rights, calling on states specifically to "respect Human Rights Council resolutions 20/8 and 26/13 ... as well as General Assembly Resolutions 68/167 and 69/106."[53] Each of these resolutions pertains to digital rights. This requirement of an R2T is

parallel to the Brazilian notion of a "responsibility while protecting" governing conduct of the international community in upholding the R2P.[54] Whereas
in implementing R2P the primary danger is to individuals' physical security,
in R2T the primary danger is to their privacy and digital rights. Accordingly,
a responsibility while troubleshooting (RWT) will reflect this difference.

Efforts to implement an R2T must also consider financing mechanisms.
Insufficient funding for work on Secure Sockets Layer (SSL) was revealed
to have played a role in the failure to identify and rectify the "Heartbleed"
flaw.[55] Only after the flaw was publicly revealed did major technology firms
agree to provide funding for the development of what had become a backbone of Internet commerce.[56] Financing mechanisms to implement the R2T
will need to take advantage of a variety of modalities, including private-sector
funding as well as public–private arrangements. However, there are reasons
to be wary of unorthodox funding streams and to preserve the notion of pub-
lic-sector financing (including at the global level) for some key functions.

While voluntary Internet-community efforts to fund and develop technology standards have been largely successful, these efforts may be prone to
market failures of the kind that afflicted SSL. Further, it is not immediately
obvious that SSL should need to rely on the private sector for funding, given
that governments are among its most important users. Government reliance
on SSL appears to be increasing. On June 8, 2015, a White House memo
announced the requirement that "all publicly accessible Federal websites
and web services only provide service through a secure connection" and
noted explicitly that "the strongest privacy and integrity protection currently
available for public web connections is Hypertext Transfer Protocol Secure
(HTTPS)," which may use SSL.[57] Setting aside questions about the wisdom
of designating a specific single encryption standard for government web
services, this public reliance on a particular technology raises the question
whether the public should play a role in funding the development and maintenance of that technology.

Regardless of questions about the proper roles for the public and private
sectors in financing efforts to deal with problematic cyber conduct, there is
a need to ensure that funders do not acquire undue influence over the implementation of R2T. Steps should be taken to implement arms-length arrangements that guard against the corruption or capture of such efforts in the
service either of profit or of national interest.

Fully developing and implementing an R2T, including a set of best practices for RWT, would require considerable consultation and care among a
diverse set of global stakeholders. The most recent GGE report provides
grounds to conclude that major governments may be receptive to some steps
in this direction. As international law expert Duncan Hollis has argued,
other parts of this agenda may also emerge from regional, bilateral, or even

unilateral steps.[58] It would likely also be possible for the technology industry and technical Internet governance bodies to make meaningful progress without including states; however, such scenarios must take into account the possibility that some states could block efforts in their own territory on national security or other grounds and that purely private efforts would likely underprovide services in the developing world.

CONCLUSION

That states have international responsibilities is beyond doubt, though the nature of those responsibilities continues to evolve. While the notion that nonstate actors have international responsibilities is more novel, it is nonetheless increasingly well established in international criminal law, international humanitarian law, corporate social responsibility, and in other issue areas. Nevertheless, there are multiple reasons to doubt the likelihood that efforts to ban problematic cyber conduct will succeed in the foreseeable future. At most, it may be plausible to generate support for a commitment to "do no harm" to the stability and interoperability of the Internet for others, even if some states are determined to exercise increasing surveillance powers and control over access to content within their own borders. Even if a global prohibition regime were adopted, there would be good reasons to ensure the existence of a robust set of institutionalized mechanisms for mitigating and remediating various kinds of intended and unintended disruptions to Internet stability and interoperability.

This chapter has explored possible modalities for, and challenges in implementing, a responsibility to troubleshoot. An R2T would need to apply to states, international organizations, and technology firms as well as large commercial Internet users and to relevant civil-society groups. The FIRST is well positioned for an expanded role; however, realizing this potential will require a great deal of assistance from other actors. Especially in its initial phases, the R2T should be embodied in hortatory soft-law instruments that permit greater flexibility and experimentation, that carry lower negotiating costs than formal hard-law instruments of international law, and that more easily enable the participation of nonstate actors.[59] The R2T should additionally be accompanied by an RWT that commits engaged parties to implementing best practices for the protection of sensitive data encountered in the process of mitigating and remediating threats to Internet stability and interoperability.

The creation of an R2T and an accompanying RWT will ultimately require a sustained advocacy campaign by a transnational network including government officials, international organization staff, corporate officers, and especially civil-society technologists and activists. Securing agreement on the desirability of social rules and successfully implementing them will no doubt be difficult. However, the alternative is not a scenario in which the cyber domain is entirely ungoverned by rules and in which actors have no responsibilities whatsoever. Cyberspace is already governed by a sprawling array of rules, implemented in a decentralized (and sometimes only partially overlapping) manner by a large number of public and private actors. Further, it is extremely likely that this emerging cyber-regime complex will continue to develop. New rules will be made to govern the cyber domain, some existing rules will fall into disuse, and others will be reinterpreted, changed, and applied in novel ways. The only question is the eventual trajectory of this rule system. Accordingly, it is not immediately clear that the development of an R2T is significantly less likely than other less desirable outcomes. Moreover, the likelihood of particular outcomes can be shaped by the exercise of agency. Since there is no guarantee that the future evolution of the cyber-regime complex will occur in a manner conducive to Internet stability and global interoperability, the R2T is an important hedge against the significant costs associated with cyber disruption in a context of highly decentralized governance.

NOTES

1. Laura DeNardis, *The Global War for Internet Governance* (New Haven, CT: Yale University Press, 2014); Mark Raymond and Laura DeNardis, "Multistakeholderism: Anatomy of an Inchoate Global Institution," *International Theory* 7, no. 3 (2015); and Madeline Carr, "Power Plays in Global Internet Governance," *Millennium: Journal of International Studies* 43, no. 2 (January 2015). See also Tim Maurer, "Cyber Norm Emergence at the United Nations—An Analysis of the Activities at the UN Regarding Cyber-security," *Discussion Paper 2011–11* (Cambridge, MA: Belfer Center for Science and International Affairs, September 2011), http://belfercenter.ksg.harvard.edu/files/maurer-cyber-norm-dp-2011-11-final.pdf.

2. United Nations (UN), Office for Disarmament Affairs, *Report of the Group of Governmental Experts (GGE) on Developments in the Field of Information and Telecommunications in the Context of International Security*, UN General Assembly (UNGA) A/68/98 (2013), https://documents-dds-ny.un.org/doc/UNDOC/GEN/N13/371/66/PDF/N1337166.pdf; and UNGA A/70/174 (2015), https://documents-dds-ny.un.org/doc/UNDOC/GEN/N15/228/35/PDF/N1522835.pdf. For scholarly assessments of the earlier iterations of the GGE, see Maurer, "Cyber Norm Emergence," and Eneken Tikk-Ringas, *Developments in the Field of Information and Telecommunication in the Context of International Security: Work of the UN First Committee, 1998–2012* (Geneva: ICT4Peace, 2012).

3. Mark Raymond, "Engaging Security and Intelligence Practitioners in the Emerging Cyber Regime Complex," *Cyber Defense Review* 1, no. 2 (Fall 2016).

4. Joseph S. Nye Jr., "The Regime Complex for Managing Global Cyber Activities," *Global Commission on Internet Governance Paper Series*, no. 1 (Waterloo, ON: Centre for International Governance Innovation, 2014), https://www.cigionline.org/sites/default/files/gcig_paper_no1.pdf.

5. Mark Raymond and Gordon Smith, editors, *Organized Chaos: Reimagining the Internet* (Waterloo, ON: Centre for International Governance Innovation, 2014); and Samantha Bradshaw, Laura DeNardis, Fen Osler Hampson, Eric Jardine, and Mark Raymond, "The Emergence of Contention in Global Internet Governance," *Global Commission on Internet Governance Paper Series*, no. 17 (Waterloo, ON: Centre for International Governance Innovation, 2015), https://www.cigionline.org/publications/emergence-of-contention-global-internet-governance.

6. Dennis Broeders, *The Public Core of the Internet: An International Agenda for Internet Governance* (Amsterdam: Amsterdam University Press, 2015), http://www.wrr.nl/fileadmin/en/publicaties/PDF-Rapporten/The_public_core_of_the_internet_Web.pdf.

7. Duncan Hollis, "An e-SOS for Cyberspace," *Harvard International Law Journal* 52, no. 2 (2011), http://www.harvardilj.org/2011/07/issue_52-2_hollis/. The concept of R2T is similar to what Hollis has called an "e-SOS" facility.

8. For such a view, see Lucas Kello, "The Meaning of the Cyber Revolution: Perils to Theory and Statecraft," *International Security* 38, no. 2 (2013), pp. 30–36.

9. Mark Raymond, "Puncturing the Myth of the Internet as a Commons," *Georgetown Journal of International Affairs* (2013), http://journal.georgetown.edu/wp-content/uploads/2015/07/gjia13005_Raymond-CYBER-III.pdf.

10. Raymond and DeNardis, "Multistakeholderism."

11. Nye, "Regime Complex."

12. Francesca Musiani, Derrick L. Cogburn, Laura DeNardis, and Nanette S. Levinson, editors, *The Turn to Infrastructure in Internet Governance* (New York: Palgrave, 2015).

13. Chris C. Demchak and Peter Dombrowski, "Rise of a Cybered Westphalian Age," *Strategic Studies Quarterly* 5, no. 1 (Spring 2011), http://www.au.af.mil/au/ssq/2011/spring/demchak-dombrowski.pdf.

14. Tanisha M. Fazal, *State Death: The Politics and Geography of Conquest, Occupation, and Annexation* (Princeton, NJ: Princeton University Press, 2007).

15. Ethan A. Nadelmann, "Global Prohibition Regimes: The Evolution of Norms in International Society," *International Organization* 44, no. 4 (1990). Global prohibition regimes date to the earliest stages of the constructivist turn in IR theory.

16. Jan Wouters and Sten Verhoeven, "The Prohibition of Genocide as a Norm of Jus Cogens and Its Implications for the Enforcement of the Law of Genocide," *International Criminal Law Review* 5 (2005), pp. 401–4. *Jus cogens* are fundamental principles of international law that are accepted by the international community of states as norms, from which no derogation is permitted.

17. United Nations, *Draft Articles on Responsibility of States for Internationally Wrongful Acts, with Commentaries*, (New York: United Nations, 2008), http://legal.un.org/ilc/texts/instruments/english/commentaries/9_6_2001.pdf.

18. Wayne Sandholtz, *Prohibiting Plunder: How Norms Change* (New York: Oxford University Press, 2007).

19. Ward Thomas, "Norms and Security: The Case of International Assassination," *International Security* 25, no. 1 (Summer 2000).

20. United Nations Office for Disarmament Affairs, The Biological Weapons Convention, April 10, 1972, http://disarmament.un.org/treaties/t/bwc/text.

21. Richard Price, "A Genealogy of the Chemical Weapons Taboo," *International Organization* 49, no. 1 (Winter 1995), http://dx.doi.org/10.1017/S0020818300001582.

22. Richard Price, "Reversing the Gun Sights: Transnational Civil Society Targets Land Mines," *International Organization* 52, no. 3 (Summer 1998), http://dx.doi.org/10.1162/002081898550671; and Adam Bower, "Norms without the Great Powers: International Law, Nested Social Structures, and the Ban on Antipersonnel Mines," *International Studies Review* 17, no. 3 (September 2015), http://dx.doi.org/10.1111/misr.12225.

23. Matthew Bolton and Thomas Nash, "The Role of Middle Power-NGO Coalitions in Global Policy: The Case of the Cluster Munitions Ban," *Global Policy* 1, no. 2 (May 2010); and Bonnie Docherty, "Breaking New Ground: The Convention on Cluster Munitions and the Evolution of International Humanitarian Law," *Human Rights Quarterly* 31, no. 4 (August 2009), http://muse.jhu.edu/article/363660.

24. R. Charli Carpenter, "Vetting the Advocacy Agenda: Network Centrality and the Paradox of Weapons Norms," *International Organization* 65, no. 1 (January 2011), http://dx.doi.org/10.1017/S0020818310000329.

25. Council of Europe, Budapest Convention on Cybercrime (2004), http://www.europarl.europa.eu/meetdocs/2014_2019/documents/libe/dv/7_conv_budapest_/7_conv_budapest_en.pdf.

26. UNGA A/70/174 (2015), http://daccess-dds-ny.un.org/doc/UNDOC/GEN/N15/228/35/PDF/N1522835.pdf?OpenElement. See especially pp. 7–8 and 13.

27. Michele Markoff, "Advancing Norms of Responsible State Behavior in Cyberspace," DipNote: US Department of State Official Blog (July 9, 2015), https://blogs.state.gov/stories/2015/07/09/advancing-norms-responsible-state-behavior-cyberspace.

28. Ellen Nakashima and Steven Mufson, "U.S., China Vow Not to Engage in Economic Cyberespionage," *Washington Post* (September 25, 2015), https://www.washingtonpost.com/national/us-china-vow-not-to-engage-in-economic-cyberespionage/2015/09/25/90e74b6a-63b9-11e5-8e9e-dce8a2a2a679_story.html.

29. Ellen Nakashima, "China Still Trying to Hack U.S. Firms Despite Xi's Vow to Refrain, Analysts Say," *Washington Post* (October 19, 2015), https://www.washingtonpost.com/world/national-security/china-still-trying-to-hack-us-firms-despite-xis-vow-to-refrain-analysts-say/2015/10/18/d9a923fe-75a8-11e5-b9c1-f03c48c96ac2_story.html.

30. Daniel C. Thomas, *The Helsinki Effect: International Norms, Human Rights, and the Demise of Communism* (Princeton, NJ: Princeton University Press, 2001).

31. Christian Reus-Smit, *The Moral Purpose of the State: Culture, Social Identity, and Institutional Rationality in International Relations* (Princeton, NJ: Princeton University Press, 1999).

32. Jacques E. C. Hymans, *The Psychology of Nuclear Proliferation: Identity, Emotions and Foreign Policy* (Cambridge, UK: Cambridge University Press, 2006).

33. Margaret E. Keck and Kathryn Sikkink, *Activists beyond Borders: Advocacy Networks in International Politics* (Ithaca, NY: Cornell University Press, 1998), p. 27.

34. Joshua W. Busby, *Moral Movements and Foreign Policy* (Cambridge, UK: Cambridge University Press, 2010).

35. Carpenter, "Vetting the Advocacy Agenda."

36. On the distinction between hard and soft law, see Kenneth W. Abbott and Duncan Snidal, "Hard and Soft Law in International Governance," *International Organization* 54, no. 3 (Summer 2000), http://dx.doi.org/10.1162/002081800551280.

37. Demchak and Dombrowski, "Rise of a Cybered Westphalian Age."

38. For example, see "FIRST Vision and Mission Statement," Forum of Incident Response and Security Teams (FIRST), accessed September 8, 2016, https://www.first.org/about/mission.

39. Mark Raymond, Aaron Shull, and Samantha Bradshaw, "Rule-Making for State Conduct in the Attribution of Cyber-Attacks," in Kang Choi, James Manicom, and Simon Palamar, editors, *Mutual Security in the Asia-Pacific: Roles for Australia, Canada and South Korea* (Waterloo, ON: Centre for International Governance Innovation, 2015).

40. These expectations are consistent with the constructivist literature in international relations. See, among many others, Emanuel Adler, "Seizing the Middle Ground: Constructivism in World Politics," *European Journal of International Relations* 3, no. 3 (September 1997); Martha Finnemore and Kathryn Sikkink, "Taking Stock: The Constructivist Research Program in International Relations and Comparative Politics," *Annual Review of Political Science* 4 (2001); and Alexander Wendt, *Social Theory of International Politics* (Cambridge, UK: Cambridge University Press, 1999).

41. UNGA A/70/174 (2015), p. 12.

42. Kenneth W. Abbott, Robert O. Keohane, Andrew Moravcsik, Anne-Marie Slaughter, and Duncan Snidal, "The Concept of Legalization," *International Organization* 54, 3 (Summer 2000), http://www.jstor.org/stable/2601339.

43. International Law Commission, *Draft Articles on Responsibility of States for Internationally Wrongful Acts*, 2001, http://legal.un.org/ilc/texts/instruments/english/commentaries/9_6_2001.pdf.

44. International Commission on Intervention and State Sovereignty, *The Responsibility to Protect* (Ottawa, ON: International Development Research Centre, 2001), http://responsibilitytoprotect.org/ICISS%20Report.pdf.

45. International Commission on Intervention and State Sovereignty, *The Responsibility to Protect.*

46. UNGA A/70/174 (2015), p. 11.

47. UNGA A/70/174 (2015), p. 8.

48. UNGA A/70/174 (2015), p. 8.

49. UNGA A/70/174 (2015), p. 11.

50. A complete list of FIRST members (accessed June 15, 2015) can be found at https://www.first.org/members/teams.

51. UNGA A/70/174 (2015), p. 11.

52. On "special and differential treatment," see Alexander Keck and Patrick Low, "Special and Differential Treatment in the WTO: Why, When and How?" *WTO*

Staff Working Paper No. ERSD-2004-03 (2004), http://papers.ssrn.com/sol3/papers.cfm?abstract_id=901629.

53. UNGA A/70/174 (2015), p. 11.

54. Conor Foley, "Welcome to Brazil's Version of 'Responsibility to Protect'," *The Guardian* (April 10, 2012), http://www.theguardian.com/commentisfree/cifamerica/2012/apr/10/diplomacy-brazilian-style.

55. James A. Lewis, "Heartbleed and the State of Cybersecurity," *American Foreign Policy Interests* 36, no. 5 (November 2014), http://dx.doi.org/10.1080/10803920.2014.969176.

56. . Jon Brodkin, "Tech Giants, Chastened by Heartbleed, Finally Agree to Fund OpenSSL," *ArsTechnica* (April 24, 2014), http://arstechnica.com/information-technology/2014/04/tech-giants-chastened-by-heartbleed-finally-agree-to-fund-openssl/.

57. Tony Scott, "Policy to Require Secure Connections across Federal Websites and Web Services" (Washington, DC: Executive Office of the President, Office of Management and Budget, June 8, 2015), https://www.whitehouse.gov/sites/default/files/omb/memoranda/2015/m-15-13.pdf.

58. Hollis, "An e-SOS for Cyberspace," p. 426.

59. Mark Raymond, "Renovating the Procedural Architecture of International Law," *Canadian Foreign Policy Journal* 19, no. 3 (2013), http://dx.doi.org/10.1080/11926422.2013.845580; Abbott and Snidal, "Hard and Soft Law."

Chapter Three

Tragedy of the Cyber Commons?

Roger Hurwitz and Gary Schaub Jr.

The concept of "the commons" has proved quite a fruitful one for many areas of policy analysis. In the realm of strategic and military matters, the idea entered the lexicon with Mahan's conception of the sea as "a wide common" whose control was critical for national power.[1] The idea reentered contemporary strategic discourse with historian Paul Kennedy's emphasis on "naval mastery" as the key for British hegemony[2] and political scientist Barry Posen's extension of the concept to the domains of outer space and airspace.[3] The concept of the "global commons" entered Department of Defense lexicon in 2004 to capture subsets of military domains over which state sovereignty has been abjured or cannot be asserted and that enable access to much of the globe, including international waters, international airspace, outer space, and cyberspace.[4] Because such ungoverned spaces and the resources they promise are precisely those that could engender conflict, states have negotiated treaties and understandings with regard to the seas, air space, and outer space.[5]

But what of cyberspace? Policymakers increasingly recognize the need for international agreements to regulate behaviors in this newest, man-made commons. One set of developments to regulate cyberspace stems from the assertion of sovereignty over it, with an increasing number of states attempting to control the content of Internet traffic entering their borders through filters at gateway points or through legal penalties against Internet service providers, domestic and foreign, for hosting or transmitting undesirable content, enabling monitoring by police and intelligence services through policy and technical means; and the creation of military services oriented toward the cyber domain.[6] Such solutions are effectively expropriations of a portion of the commons that reduce the availability and value of the resource for all other users.

Multinational efforts to regulate the commons of cyberspace without diminishing it have also made progress. The 2004 Budapest Convention on Cybercrime, which commits signatory states to harmonize their domestic laws toward cybercrime and to cooperate in good faith on cross-border investigation and prosecution, has been ratified by fifty-two states as of 2017.[7] Reports of the United Nations Group of Governmental Experts on Developments in the Field of Information and Telecommunications in the Context of International Security have provided a basis for states to agree to the "full applicability of international law to state behavior in cyberspace."[8] It has also affirmed five limiting norms and six good practices and positive duties.[9] Finally, the *Tallinn Manual on the International Law Applicable to Cyber Operations*, first produced under the auspices of the NATO Cooperative Cyber Defence Centre of Excellence in 2013 and updated in 2017, provides a "comprehensive analysis of how existing international law applies to cyber operations … ranging from peacetime legal regimes to the law of armed conflict."[10] Its "soft law" approach will likely facilitate clarification regarding how states should conduct themselves in the midst of a developing area without yet committing to formal treaties and conventions.[11]

These agreements together represent the emergence of a broader complex of norms and rules for the use of the man-made environment of cyberspace beyond the technical regime that governs the standards of the Internet.[12] Their development provides a basis for optimism that a governing regime can be developed, even if "a worldwide, comprehensive cybersecurity treaty is a pipe dream."[13] Nevertheless, this developing tapestry of norms, best practices, and international law is likely to be limited for the foreseeable future.

The limiting condition, we argue, is the very nature of cyberspace itself. We argue that while cyberspace can be usefully conceived of as a commons akin to air, sea, and outer space, it can also be seen as akin to an ecological commons whose benefits can be diminished by overexploitation by individual users and thus susceptible to the well-known "tragedy of the commons."[14] Whether the depletable resource that cyberspace provides is conceived of as communications, content, or trust, individual users rationally pursuing their own interests may degrade the domain for others, over time depleting the common resource for all. Three solutions are often proffered to provide essential governance of such common resources: centralized control and regulation of the resource, division of the resource through assignment of private property rights, and self-organization to govern the use of the resource.[15] Despite hopes among many that structures of effective self-governance will emerge in cyberspace, our analysis suggests that there are significant barriers that make this outcome unlikely.

In the next section, we discuss the multiple meanings of the "commons" as it applies to cyberspace. This includes cyber as a military domain, as an area of shared content, and as a depletable ecological resource. We elaborate on the latter and discuss communications and content as potential candidates for this common resource. We then give particular attention to the idea that trust is the key common pool resource of cyberspace and examine the implications of its depletion. The third section reviews the variables that previous research suggests facilitate self-organization and governance of common pool resources and evaluates them with regard to cyberspace. The final section draws conclusions from the analysis to suggest the likelihood that users of cyberspace will overcome significant barriers to their cooperation and provide self-governance that will enable the sustainment of public trust in cyberspace.

CONCEIVING OF THE CYBER COMMONS

Cyberspace produces benefits, whether directly through the provision of communications, content, or the network effects that they combine to form or indirectly through the reduction of transactions costs, increased scalability, and speed. Perhaps one of the primary sources of challenges—and opportunities—to developing international cooperation to sustain cyberspace as a resource is grasping the different conceptual meanings implied by the term *commons*. It has been used to characterize cyber as a strategic domain, a body of rights related to developing and sharing content, and a common pool resource. Each touches upon important aspects of cyberspace and provides differentiated means to frame key issues.

In many ways, cyberspace does not qualify as a "commons" at all.[16] According to Maj. Gen. Brett Williams, the director of operations, J3, U.S. Cyber Command, "cyberspace is simply the man-made domain created when we connect all of the computers, switches, routers, fiber optic cables, wireless devices, satellites and other components that allow us to move large amounts of data at very fast speeds."[17] Different parts of this infrastructure are owned by multiple parties—private and public, individual and collective—that perceive the benefits of connecting to the network in a standardized manner to outweigh the costs of such connectivity. The owners of these subsets of cyberspace infrastructure are subject to the legal authorities of the territory in which they are based and the incentive structures of the market in which they operate. Its users are akin to members of a nested series of clubs, defined by political jurisdictions and Internet service providers, that can partake of different levels and types of benefits (e.g., bandwidth and content) depending upon their membership conditions.[18] Furthermore, unlike natural environments that constitute the other domains of military action, cyberspace is ever-changing as servers are brought online, others are taken offline, and new forms of control, regulation, and technology are introduced. Focusing on the physical layer of cyberspace in this way leads to very different implications for policy, domestic and international law, safe operating procedures, individual rights, commercial use, national interests, and myriad other issues than conceiving it as a commons.

Conceiving cyberspace as a commons that is a subset of a domain in which action—military, political, economic, and social—occurs also has particular implications for strategy and policy. In this conception, it is an environment that permits the movement of men, materiel, goods, services, information, and so forth that facilitate activity at a distance. Thus, cyberspace gains its utility from the ability of its users to use it freely when they desire to communicate and transmit information as desired. From a strategic perspective, power derives from the ability of a party to manipulate cyberspace, to generate effects in, from, or through it—and the ability to disrupt or deny the ability of others to do the same.[19] Such actions include destroying or degrading computer and information systems and destroying, degrading, altering, and exfiltrating information from those systems to impact their operation (or that of other systems to which they are attached) and/or the decision-making context of other actors. Posen, following Mahan and Corbett,[20] characterizes this as obtaining "command of the commons," whereby the strategic actor "gets vastly more use out of the [commons] than do others; ... can credibly threaten to deny [its] use to others; and that others would lose a military contest for the commons if they attempted to deny them to the" strategic actor.[21] Dolman separates control from contestation: the former "provides the capacity to use the domain to create effects" while the latter is "the ability to block or deny access" to the domain.[22] As this suggests, the ability of all to utilize the commons and derive benefit from it is a peacetime phenomenon. But even then, shaping the environment for unilateral advantage, as opposed to simply enjoying its use, matters strategically. Indeed, Mahan argued that command of the maritime commons implied a vast infrastructure of political and economic influence that was the key to national power. Others have transposed this argument to the commons of the air and outer space,[23] and clearly a case could be made for cyber as well.[24]

A parallel conception of the "cyber commons" developed in the 1990s. It focused on the right to produce and share content developed and viewed the Internet as another venue in an already rich, lightly regulated, information and communications ecology. Endeavors like Wikipedia, the Creative Commons, MIT's free courseware, and the emergent blogosphere could create a second commons—one of content—that interacted with notions of freedom of mobility, global innovation for the Internet, and an evolving worldwide information sphere in which everyone could participate. Internet freedom advocates, such as Stanford Law professor Lawrence Lessig and others, ultimately grounded this conception of the cyber commons in the human right to access information and freedom of expression. The primary threats to be countered were those that restricted content with broad interpretations of copyright at the expense of fair use and enforced their views with state authority within a primarily domestic regulatory environment.[25]

At the international level, this vision of a cyber commons based upon content informs the policies of the United States and many of its allies and the positions they take with regard to international regulation of cyberspace. Most notable is the State Department's embrace of Internet freedom—the rights of cyber enablement of civic activism—but also significant is the emphasis on global interoperability, noninterference by states with packets passing through their territories, and decisions on Internet technology being made by technologists rather than by political authorities.[26] Its antithesis is the regulation of content as states pursue the security of themselves, their societies, and their identity against threat as diverse as Islamic terrorists, indigenous separatists, pornography, religious and political speech, and other content.[27] Indeed, the increasingly obvious use of cyber content by foreign powers to influence political discourse and elections has highlighted the strategic challenges of unregulated access and content—precisely among those states that have advocated it for all.[28]

A third conception of the cyberspace commons views it as a common pool resource that is susceptible to the "tragedy" of overuse, as individual consumers utilize more than their "fair share" and degrade the good, perhaps to the point of depletion. One key characteristic of common pool resources is that it tends to be difficult to limit or control access to the good. With ever-increasing access to cyberspace, the core of its content and communications capabilities are becoming less excludable. However, without concomitant increases in bandwidth, access exhibits rivalry in consumption—meaning that access by one precludes or reduces access for another. Indeed, as use increases, communications channels could become congested and the service enjoyed by all degraded.[29] This potential for congestion has been used by spammers and those that instigate distributed denial of service (DDoS) attacks to achieve their objectives. They have been compared to industrial polluters that benefit by creating costs that are borne by others, whether in the form of lack of access to a saturated network, additional costs to increase bandwidth, decreased speed to scan or filter content, and so forth.[30] This argument was more valid in the early days of public connectivity to the Internet and cyberspace, when network infrastructure and communications technology were nascent, or in places where these conditions still hold.[31] But as cyber infrastructure grows, conceiving of bandwidth as a depletable common pool resource is becoming less tenable—except when deliberately utilized to affect specific systems as part of a cyber attack.

Rather than focus on the issues arising from framing the capacity of physical infrastructure of cyberspace as a common pool resource, we turn attention toward the social aspect of cyberspace that has proven to be quite valuable: its ability to connect billions of people from every society on Earth.[32] From December 1995 through March 2017, Internet usage increased from sixteen million users to 3.739 billion—or from 0.4 percent of world population to 49.6 percent.[33] Perhaps the primary driver of this astounding growth is that cyberspace facilitates the development and deployment of network goods.

Network goods are products and services whose value increases with the number of people using the good or service.[34] This is because the good or service generates positive externalities (additional benefits that are not directly paid for) that are enjoyed by its users. The primary externality generated by network goods is an enhancement of the user's ability to interact and synchronize with other users.[35] As the population of users grows, standardization permits economies of scale in their interaction to reduce costs as well as an increase in utility and this, in turn, attracts further expansion of the user population.[36] Network goods create an ever-increasing virtuous cycle of benefits until they encounter a rival network good that is also entrenched—for instance, a different language or operating system.[37]

Trust in the ability of the network to deliver its benefits, we argue, is the ultimate common pool resource in cyberspace. Jacques Bus follows sociologist Nicolas Luhmann in explaining trust as "a mechanism that reduces complexity and enables people to cope with the high levels of uncertainty and complexity of (contemporary) life."[38] Trust in the reliability and minimal risks inherent in the system produces the positive externalities by ever-widening participation. This is consistent with findings by social scientists of strong positive correlations between public trust and economic growth.[39]

Public trust in cyberspace involves both confidence in the people and organizations that individuals deal with through digital technologies—including the institutions, laws, government, and the infrastructures of their society—as well as the trustworthiness of the technologies themselves. Public trust encourages individuals and organizations to access, and be accessed by, one another online, and that in turn enables the network effect of cyberspace. Trust is necessary because interaction with others online is not personal; it is opaque. Others might be anonymous or only partly identified and the context of interactions with them is distant, removed from first-hand knowledge, and potentially confusing. Trust can be buttressed by assumptions about others' concerns for reputation, commitments to roles, and by online mechanisms, like certificates and ratings, that can confirm claims made by others. Of late, however, trust in cyberspace may be strained by the publicity of various cyber threats, failure by organizations and governments to deter them, the compromise of online security mechanisms, and the widespread use of social media to systematically propagate falsehoods.[40] In addition, public trust suffers from many users' awareness that their online activities are being monitored, whether for commercial exploitation in the West or identification of political dissidents in authoritarian countries.

These abuses may lower or deplete public trust—that is, the aggregate willingness of users to go online—much like a renewable natural resource that can be overexploited. On this view, public trust can become rivalrous: trust betrayed by one user reduces the amount available for others, like a highway during rush hour. Continuing abuses against a diminishing public trust could lead to unsatisfactory provision of the online benefits that public trust enables. In concrete terms, individuals and organizations fearing cybercrime, invasions of privacy, unreliable information, and so forth would decrease their use of digital networks for economic transactions, information exchanges, and social interactions as their trust in the network diminishes.

But unlike the usual commons resources, such as forests and fisheries, public trust in cyberspace is not always a rival good. Like a highway after rush hour, it becomes less congested as the good is replenished. Mutually beneficial online interactions can sustain and renew public trust among individuals and organizations, relegating abuses to exceptions.[41] Consequently, there is little evidence of people exiting cyberspace or avoiding popular sites with controversial privacy policies. Still, in some democratic countries, relevant publics have demanded that service and search providers restrain tracking. Some governments have already responded with regulatory policies that will force adjustments by data aggregators and analysts. These actions can be read as instances of users defending the common pool resource by turning to existing authority for leadership and norm setting. They show that sustaining trust in cyberspace requires rules, transparent practices, accountability standards, and means of redress acceptable to users—in addition to security technologies. International efforts to achieve agreements to protect and sustain cyberspace will therefore need to take such concerns into account. That might not be a formidable challenge. Because cyber "apps" have become indispensable for so many users, they are likely to be reassured, at least momentarily, by small, facile steps by providers or regulators, including policy announcements, opt-out buttons, and new, if unintelligible, service agreements. Put another way, cyberspace is no longer a domain apart for its users, a place to visit at one's choosing, like a tourist resort, but has become part of the fabric of our lives.

Arguably, those whose activities deplete trust in cyberspace are not seeking to destroy the Internet—no more than peasants who allegedly overgrazed the commons wanted to degrade it. But these actors can pose different types of threats to it. On the one hand, there are would-be spammers, "hacktivists," cyber criminals, and terrorists. In popular imagination—and sometimes in their own—they adopt the traditional image of pirates, acting outside and beyond the laws of nations.[42] These groups are not seeking the demise of cyberspace, since that would put them "out of work," but some analysts believe that international cooperation to suppress such groups can be easily realized and comprise a first step toward more comprehensive agreements on cyberspace.

On the other hand, governments, online service providers, multinational corporations, and others—the so-called stakeholders—recognize the need for limits to sustain the commons of cyberspace, but will frequently flaunt them in the pursuit of individual interests. Even states that develop cyber weapons to damage cyber-based infrastructures and governments and spy on their online citizens value their own use of cyberspace while planning to constrain its use by others. The resulting ambivalence of many governments is perhaps best captured in a recent Chinese white paper. It celebrates the Internet for enabling economic and social development, and notes its use in propagandizing the public and in campaigns against provincial corruption, but stipulates that no organization or individual may produce, duplicate, announce, or disseminate information on the Internet having the following contents: being against the cardinal principles set forth in the Constitution; endangering state security, divulging state secrets, subverting state power, and jeopardizing national unification; damaging state honor and interests; instigating ethnic hatred or discrimination and jeopardizing ethnic unity; jeopardizing state religious policy and propagating heretical or superstitious ideas; spreading rumors and disrupting social order and stability; disseminating obscenity, pornography, gambling, violence, brutality, and terror or abetting crime; humiliating or slandering others and trespassing on the lawful rights and interests of others; and other contents forbidden by laws and administrative regulations.[43] Efforts to regulate content and enforce guidelines through methods such as deep packet inspections threaten the stability and sustainability of cyberspace by undermining trust in it.

Sophisticated actors who threaten public trust in cyberspace might foresee the adverse consequences of their acts. They might also calculate that whatever the damage they do, the depletion of public trust will be modest or the gains in using the Internet still so great that public trust and mutual accessibility will remain above some minimum threshold. Thus far, recent trends support that calculation. But will these trends be sustained absent some form of regulation?

GOVERNING THE CYBER COMMONS

Three solutions are often proffered to provide essential governance of such common resources: centralized control and regulation of the resource, division of the resource through assignment of private property rights, and self-organization of users to govern the use of the resource.[44] In many ways, each of these solutions is being pursued among governments, private corporations, technical experts, and individual users. As Laura DeNardis and Francesca Musiani argue, "Governance is collectively enacted by the design of technology, the policies of private companies, and the administrative functions of new global institutions like Internet Corporation for Assigned Names and Numbers (ICANN) and the Internet Engineering Task Force (IETF), as well as national laws and international agreements."[45] Can these entities organize themselves to provide effective governance over cyberspace's common pool resource of public trust?

The late political scientist Elinor Ostrom received the Nobel Prize in economics for determining cases and conditions where, in the absence of government control, users successfully self-organize for sustainable use of a commons.[46] She inductively derived a model of the conditions under which such cooperation would be more, or less, likely to obtain. Ostrom's model consists of ten variables that contribute to the construction of effective and self-enforced rules of use for a common pool resource in the absence of state authority.[47] These variables are (1) the size of the resource, (2) the number of users, (3) the ability of the resource to be extracted from its point of origin, (4) the importance of the resource to its users, (5) the productivity of the system that produces the resource, (6) the predictability of the system dynamics, (7) leadership, (8) norms and social capital, (9) shared knowledge among users, and (10) the rules under which users make collective decisions.

We draw on Ostrom in our discussion of these variables and their manifestation in cyberspace. Although somewhat crude, we follow Ostrom in indicating the tendencies of these variables on self-governance of cyberspace in terms of whether their values increase, decrease, or do not affect its likelihood of obtaining. In keeping with the observation that public trust in cyberspace depends on the trustworthiness of its hardware and software, as well as the behavior of their users, their properties are considered in evaluating the relevant variables.

Ostrom's discussion of the effects of these variables on the probability for self-organization is consistent with a rational actor model: the probability of self-organization increases the more its contribution to sustaining the common resource exceeds the costs of bringing agents to agreements and enforcing those agreements. Hence, the lower these costs, the greater the probability of self-organization. The assumption with regard to its process is that states would reach multilateral agreements to set rules and regulations for cyberspace and that they would either enforce these directly or empower an international agency to do so.

Size of Resource

Large resources with ill-defined boundaries discourage self-organization because of the high costs of defining the boundaries, monitoring use, and tracing the consequences of malfeasance.

The size of cyberspace, as measured by the several billion devices connected to the Internet, discourages defining its boundaries and monitoring behaviors in it. As a thought experiment, suppose "boundaries" for a trustworthy cyberspace were defined by a centrally maintained giant list of several billion verified safe devices, with "safe" designating malware-free or not having been involved in spying or other penetration operations. This list would require continual updating to accommodate devices being added to the Internet and recurrent verification of the safe devices, because anyone could be vulnerable to attack from a host spoofing a safe device. This approach would be very expensive and only partly effective in inspiring users' trust. Furthermore, some attacks are so stealthy as to be discovered only well after they have occurred, if at all.

Mapping boundaries and monitoring behavior can be more feasible, affordable, and convincing if national governments assume responsibility for the devices and users in their territories by certifying the machines and credentialing the users. Unilateral and multilateral means could then protect the defined national cyberspaces. Such means include implementations of "national firewalls" and the reduction of national portals, cyber passports for users, and assignment of consecutive Internet protocol (IP) addresses to specific territories. These steps would not stop all external attacks and exploits within a national cyberspace, but they would facilitate determining the origin of attacks and holding responsible authorities in the state where an attack originated.[48]

The resulting system would extend the principle of national sovereignty—the cornerstone of contemporary international relations—into cyberspace[49] and increase a state's control over its residents' online activities. Some states, including a few liberal democracies in the West, have already adopted or advocate some of these measures to deal with cybersecurity threats. Many governments, organizations, and individual users, however, will oppose full-blown development of the system for several reasons. First, it would sanction the fragmentation of the Internet into many an "internet in one country" with an attendant constriction of global communications. That process, already foreshadowed in China, Iran, and other authoritarian countries, would set back efforts to build a commons for discussion of items like climate change, scientific knowledge, and medical research on a global level. Second, multinational corporations and other agents of globalization, including economic managers in authoritarian countries, will consider this system an obstacle to a global economy in which businesses anywhere can have suppliers and customers everywhere. For them, a particularly threatening aspect of the projection of national sovereignty into cyberspace is the potential restriction in movement of information resources. Third, human rights advocates will oppose conceding the right to define a cyber attack to national governments, since their definitions can include a broad swath of content, as noted above in regard to China, as well as malicious code. Fourth, policy makers are likely to doubt whether governments will accept responsibility for cyber attacks originating in their territories under this system. These doubts can be grounded in current practices of government claiming ignorance of the attack origins or that they do not have the means to suppress all of them.

Finally, national boundaries in cyberspace are a way of dissecting the commons and privatizing the pieces. Because this commons is a network, its dismantling involves a loss of value. That is, the sum of the values of the parts will be less than the value of the original whole. The loss will be defined in different ways, but its anticipation will motivate broad resistance to the idea of national cyber borders. Nevertheless, the idea brings into relief questions about the character of the cyber commons: whether it is a thin communications overlay on, and ultimately reduced to, diverse geophysical entities and jurisdictions, or whether it provides sets of experiences—a mode of being— in which users might acquire new identities that transcend national identity. Jacques Bus considers the question, thankfully free of the usual panegyrics about the Internet flattening the world,

> Globalization, driven clearly by new [information and communications technologies] and the Web, creates understanding hence more trust through spreading information on history and reputation of societies, characteristics of societies and the lives of persons living in certain societies, and allowing easy worldwide communication. This may indeed lead to further erosion of the concept of "the human animal is best off at home." It may well lead to the need for a completely new view on societies and their cohesion and the role trust must play in this.[50]

Overall, the global reach of cyberspace mitigates against the probability that agreements on self-governance will emerge.

Number of Users

The more users of a common pool resource, the greater the transaction costs of getting them together and agreeing to change. Group size discourages self-organization, but its effect depends on the value of the other variables and the types of management tasks envisioned. The nearly four billion people who already access the Internet constitute the largest users group in human history. They should have opportunity to express their concerns in any international negotiations on the uses of cyberspace, since in many cases these are likely to be different from those of governments and other powerful stakeholders. For example, users in struggles against their own governments would certainly reject those governments' representation of their interests regarding anonymity, online tracking, and permitted content. On the other hand, recent world meetings on climate change and on cyberspace itself have demonstrated that processes that are open to groups claiming to represent the interests of individual citizens can rapidly become unmanageable, time-consuming, and unproductive. For that reason, an interpretation of national sovereignty, per which states rightfully represent their citizens' interests, is expedient if not just.

Unfortunately, even this stratagem will not reduce the relevant stakeholders to a manageable number. Negotiations will need to include representation from multiple stakeholders, including industrial sectors, especially information and communications technology (ICT), and international organizations, as well as the states. These groups can provide the technical knowledge to inform proposals as well as block implementation of any agreements reached without them. As Ostrom suggests,[51] the number of parties involved might not itself determine the difficulty in reaching an agreement. Rather when more parties are involved, especially when the issues are complex, there will be a greater number of competing claims that take time to reconcile, if they can be reconciled at all. Negotiations for the UN Convention on the Law of the Sea (UNCLOS), which regulates another commons, lasted a decade despite building on centuries of admiralty law and being more confined to issues of state sovereignty. There is much less legal tradition for cyber and, so far, no concerted efforts to harmonize state-level cyber laws. Thus, the very limited and regionally oriented Budapest Convention on Cybercrime has been slow in gaining adherence, with many of its signatories listing numerous reservations.[52] Perhaps some relief from these bleak prospects might be provided by cyberspace itself, in that aggregation of opinions, consultations, and negotiations can themselves now be conducted virtually as well as in person. By organizing information, lowering transaction costs, and speeding communications, cyber tools might permit decision making about their own futures.

Resource Unit Mobility

When resources are mobile, they are more difficult to bound and monitor. Therefore, Ostrom suggests that self-governance is less likely to occur than if the common pool resource is stationary, like a forest or a lake. Three types of mobility make effective and actionable monitoring of cyber devices difficult and costly. First, as already noted, the status of a device can change rapidly from "safe" to "compromised," frequently without the change being discovered until later, if at all. Second, over their course, wide-scale cyber attacks and exploitations will typically deploy different machines located at different IP addresses and geophysical locations. For example, during the massive July 2009 DDoS attack on U.S. government sites, 78,000–200,000 "zombie hosts" were utilized by the attacker.[53] Therefore, any monitoring or defense specific to an attack, like blockading potential sites, will probably involve multiple jurisdictions with consequent problems of coordination. Later investigations will be similarly complicated and attribution inevitably uncertain. As a result, parties to an agreement barring such attacks cannot rely on monitoring to verify that they are complying with the agreement or to identify violators. Third, the rise of mobile computing in the form of laptops, smartphones, and tablets has greatly increased the attack surface of cyberspace and the chore of any future monitoring program. The physical mobility of these devices also means they are exposed over their lifetimes to a variety of cyber threats and surveillance environments and to changes in their own security status. They will be more vulnerable than a machine tethered to a single server within an organization setting that has competent cybersecurity. They are more liable to penetration, theft of their information, and compromise. Once compromised, they can be turned into carriers for compromising networks to which they later connect, like corporate intranets.[54] Thus the ever-increasing mobility of cyber devices decreases the chances that agreements for self-governance will emerge.

Importance of Resource to Users

When the common pool resource is valued highly by its users, they have a greater incentive to monitor its use. Furthermore, if they recognize that value derives from its integration into other valued activities, then additional incentives exist to sustain it. Under such conditions, self-governance is more likely to emerge. An increasing amount of activity throughout the world involves the creation, collection, packaging, use, and distribution of information. The Internet and other parts of cyberspace are vital to these activities. Various government position papers on cybersecurity are clear in recognizing the economic, social, cultural, and scientific importance of cyberspace. In calling for the "creation of a global culture of cybersecurity," the UN General Assembly recognized that

> the increasing contribution made by networked information technologies to many of the essential functions of daily life, commerce and the provision of

goods and services, research, innovation and entrepreneurship, and to the free flow of information among individuals and organizations, Governments, business and civil society.[55]

Even authoritarian regimes in Iran, Egypt, and elsewhere, which confronted massive protests organized by cyber means, have hesitated to shut down the Internet in their countries because their economies depend upon it.

Governments and diplomats, however, have been less clear in recognizing how foundational public trust is for cyberspace. In calling for discussions of international norms for cyberspace, the UN group of governmental experts primarily focused on national security issues, including cybercrime and other cyber threats that are disruptive to government, economic, and social functions as well as the escalatory potential of misunderstandings in cyberspace to escalate to threaten international security.[56] Thus, although there are clear signs that the cyberspace and access to the Internet are highly valued, its impact on the probability of self-governance is leavened by a lack of focus on public trust in extant discussions.

Productivity of System

Perhaps the greatest deterrent to self-governance is the lack of need: "if [a resource] is already exhausted or very abundant, users will not see a need to manage for the future. Users need to observe some scarcity before they invest in self-organization."[57] Thus, the growing pervasiveness of cyberspace and the ever-increasing number of users investing their trust into its systems and one another suggests that there is no need to work to sustain public trust.

On the other hand, cybercrime, the incidence of attacks and exploits, the proliferation of malware, and threats to critical cyber infrastructure have increased. As threats to individual users become more sophisticated, evolving from unsolicited e-mails from Nigerian princes to legitimate software updates that have been hacked at the source to install ransomware,[58] and trust in the ability of larger stakeholders, such as Microsoft or governments, to take responsibility for preventing such threats is periodically shaken, questions arise as to the effectiveness of present security practices to sustain such trust.

These questions clearly motivate the various calls for international agreements on cyberspace behavior. They certainly motivated Microsoft's president and chief legal officer, Brad Smith, to call for a "Digital Geneva Convention" that would "commit governments to protecting civilians from nation-state attacks in times of peace," and commit "the tech sector" to "collective action that will make the internet a safer place, affirming a role as a neutral digital Switzerland that assists customers everywhere and retains the world's trust."[59] Jacques Bus notes that the possibility of states being behind many cyber threats "proves the urgency to come to international agreements on restraints in and defense against cyber attacks and for international cooperation to bring it under control."[60]

Having identified public trust as the depletable resource in cyberspace, Bus continues, "Public and private sector must work together at the international level to build a well-balanced infrastructure of technology and law/regulation that will give citizens trust to use the opportunities of the new digital world."[61] In a speech to the 2011 Munich Security Conference, British foreign minister William Hague made similar connections:

> We are working with the private sector, to ensure secure and resilient critical infrastructure and the strong skills base needed to seize the economic opportunities of cyber space, and to raise awareness of online threats among members of the public. But being global, cyber threats also call for a collective response. In Britain we believe that the time has come to start seeking international agreement about norms in cyberspace.[62]

Predictability of System Dynamics

There is a bias to accept the status quo in human decision making.[63] Perhaps Machiavelli said it best:

> there is nothing more difficult to execute, nor more dubious of success, nor more dangerous to administer, than to introduce new political orders. For the one who introduces them has as his enemies all those who profit from the old order, and he has only lukewarm defenders in those who might profit from the new order. This lukewarmness partly arises from fear of the adversaries who have the law on their side, and partly from the incredulity of men, who do not truly believe in new things unless they have actually had personal experience of them.[64]

It is easier to predict the consequences of continuing the minimal international regulation of cyberspace that exists today than the effect of various agreements to monitor and enforce some standards of behavior. With deterioration of public trust in cyberspace, the expansion of use—in terms of time spent, applications, and dependencies—will decelerate, and that will be accompanied by lower growth or drop in the incentives for development. Some users may have already reduced their use of public networks for critical data transmission; some organizations have reduced the number of access points or portals to themselves. These steps might grow toward widespread delinking and fragmentation—phenomena that devalue cyberspace.

Projecting the loss in value of a vulnerable cyberspace compared to a safe one is problematic because of different models for evaluating the socioeconomic value of cyber networks. However, it seems reasonable to suppose that as new users are drawn more from lower economic strata and less-developed countries, the economic value of the networks will increase at a lower rate than in earlier stages of their growth.[65] Such a trend has mixed implications for self-organization. First, providers will have little incentive to increase their investments in cybersecurity—especially if security costs are a linear function of the number of users. But inaction by the providers could put more pressure on governments to work for agreements that reduce threats. On the other hand, the trend also suggests that any exit of users will not initially diminish network value. So, until the situation is deemed intolerable and not just bad, governments, mindful of the costs of agreements, could resist pressure and delay self-organizing, despite their public calls for action.

Leadership

What can constitute leadership to organize self-governance in cyberspace? Theories of international relations suggest that cooperation is much more likely if a hegemonic leader—a stakeholder with both disproportional power over, and interests in, the issue—is willing to step forward and provide the resources necessary to absorb the transactions costs involved in coordinating the positions and interests of the others.[66]

Ever since the United States began developing "packet-switching technology and communications networks, starting with the 'ARPANET' network established by the Department of Defense's Advanced Research Projects Agency (DARPA) in the 1960s" and "later linked to other networks established by other government agencies, universities and research facilities," the United States has exercised hegemonic governance over the basic infrastructure of what has become the Internet.[67] It has also pursued policies informed by neoliberal theories of economics that have permeated Western policymaking since the 1970s to devolve the responsibilities of governance through privatization and internationalization.[68] While the contours of this devolution have been examined widely in the literature on Internet governance, it is clear that the United States no longer has the sole ability to govern its creation.[69]

In cyberspace, leadership is therefore lacking for productive, state-level negotiations—but not for want of actors that have had roles in organizing cyberspace. Most of it has taken place through the governance of Internet infrastructure and the setting of standards.[70] Over the past decade, the ICANN has provided competent, although frequently criticized, administration of domain allocations and oversight of registration. It has accommodated the spectacular growth of the Internet and accompanying commercial demands with a redesign of policies for top-level domains. While it has not been particularly open to the grassroots participation specified in its multistakeholder model, it has retained the confidence of service providers and the respect of most states, as evidenced by the United Nations' restraint from seeking involvement in administration of the Internet. But the ICANN is no norms entrepreneur and lacks the political skills, leverage, and power to reconcile competing interests among states over cyber behaviors and security. Additionally, it is seen by many states as a tool of U.S. policy.

The IETF has exercised leadership in Internet protocols, mostly as the endorser of standards. Its own history exemplifies self-organizing among stakeholders for management of a commons, but its amorphous decision-making process is an awkward model for negotiations on constraining human activities. In any case, it is unqualified to lead in such negotiations, its ambit is limited to the technical realm, its centrality in that realm has diminished as concerns now focus more on mobile computing apps and other layers beyond its purview, and its membership is still heavily American and European.[71]

The International Telecommunications Union (ITU), the UN agency responsible for ICT, has the ambition to lead policymaking and administration of cyberspace, and it led in organizing the World Summits on the Information Society (WSIS), which focused on soft issues: development-oriented uses of cyberspace, Internet governance, and bridging digital divides. Seen in the West as a tool for Russian and Chinese policy interests, it lacks the political credibility to assume leadership on hard issues like cyber espionage, information rights, and so forth. It probably also lacks the technological competence; the cybersecurity standards it developed and promoted in collaboration with the International Organization for Standardization (ISO) have proved expensive and unworkable.

Norms and Social Capital

If users share norms of reciprocity and sufficiently trust one another to keep agreements, they will face lower transaction costs in reaching agreements and monitoring. Continued economic globalization and the absence of major interstate wars could suggest that the major powers are developing adequate reciprocity structures and conflict avoidance mechanisms. Indeed, this assessment is supported by the fears expressed in the calls for cyber norms that misunderstandings about cyberspace behaviors could trigger unwanted conflicts. Nevertheless, the failure of negotiations on environmental regulations raises doubts that negotiations over cyberspace can fare any better, especially since the major powers have ideological differences regarding cyberspace, as great as the differences among economic interests that block resolutions of environmental issues.

Broadly speaking, the Russian and Chinese policy makers seek to extend the principle of national sovereignty to cyberspace by establishing a norm of

the state being the final arbiter of matters relating to cyberspace in its territory.[72] From a Western perspective, their motives are to control the ideational
space that cyber networks afford their populations and to prevent inquiry
into use of cyber by their governments or proxies for military campaigns,
political espionage, industrial espionage, and crime. Recall, however, that
the political traditions in Russia and China, even in the pre-Communist days,
empowered state authorities to decide what their citizens should think, and
that the principle of national sovereignty bars outsiders from interfering with
the exercise of that power. So an uncontrolled Internet can be politically
threatening and easily exploited by external rivals, in particular the United
States. Furthermore, Russia in particular has identified political and social
subversion through international communications as a key vulnerability for
themselves and others.[73] On this view, outsiders enabling dissent within
a country is no contribution to public debate; it is "information warfare"
conducted to weaken regimes to the point of greater accommodation with
the outsiders or even collapse. Already, in 2008, Russia, China, and other
members of the Shanghai Coordination Organization (SCO) have agreed
to outlaw supporting or hosting the dissemination of potentially disruptive
information.

In contrast, the United States and its NATO allies tend in their pronounce-
ments to view cyberspace as a central institution for a global economy, a
means for worldwide scientific and cultural exchange, a commons for political debate and development, and a social medium. Given this variety of
functions, there follows a multistakeholder model for control and defense of
cyberspace, with states being one type of stakeholder, along with nongovernmental organizations, service providers, ICT companies, critical infrastructure entities, corporate users, and individual users. But because cyberspace,
particularly the Internet, is prey to attacks and exploits by criminals, terrorists, and even states, by virtue of their authority and capabilities, states have
primary responsibility to provide the needed security without harming the
interests of other stakeholders. The diffusion of norms and treaties, such as
the Budapest Convention on Cybercrime, are instruments for fulfilling such
responsibility, as are the nurturing of a cybersecurity culture and capabilities
around the globe.[74]

This view, wedded to a decade-old vision of the Internet, ignores the demo-
graphic and technological changes that are remaking cyberspace and expectations for it: the change from hundreds of millions of users concentrated
in North America and Europe connected to the Internet through computers
to billions of users with the bulk in south and east Asia connected through
mobile devices and the rise of an Internet of things. As a result, practices
that might have once seemed in the interest of all are now controversial and

contested.[75] India, Brazil, and South Africa—leading voices on cyber issues among "nonaligned" countries—want these changes to be acknowledged as conceded major parts in any negotiations. They consequently favor transfer of authority away from technologically oriented agencies, reflecting the multistakeholder model, including ICANN and IETF, to a more policy-oriented agency, possibly under the United Nations, though not necessarily the ITU, that gives every state an equal voice.

Knowledge of the Resource and Its Users

The various calls for cyber rules reflect policy makers' knowledge that certain behaviors disrupt normal activities, sow public distrust, and threaten the sustainability of cyberspace. Their willingness to discuss issues beyond cybercrime acknowledges that those misbehaving may include their own governments and citizens. So, less time and money are needed to raise consciousness or convince skeptics that a problem exists and international cooperation can help solve it.

Choosing what to do requires more knowledge of the dependencies among various processes in cyberspace, particularly how the technological affordances affect social (agents') behaviors. The efforts at environmental regulation show that broad, comprehensive solutions will be opposed even when those who feel threatened by the proposal are offered side payments. So the problem space has to be decomposed with selection of some target whose proposed solution could gain traction, help reduce the overall level of cyber insecurity, and build confidence among the various agents, thus enabling pursuit of other targets. One frequent suggestion is that states cooperate to suppress cyber criminal gangs by denying their means to monetize their thefts. This suggestion understands (a) the gangs' dependency on particular banks and (b) that cybercrime serves as a development lab and testing ground for malware that might later be used by intelligence agencies in some states.[76] Less known is how strongly these agencies depend on the gangs and, therefore, the incentives their states need to cooperate on the proposal.

Collective Choice Rules

Participation in rulemaking is a key factor in establishing the legitimacy of those rules among those to whom they apply. It is the basis for democratic theory. The more people can see themselves as authors of the rules they are expected to follow, the more they will follow those rules. Yet multiple barriers exist to implement widely participatory forms of governance over the cyber commons. The first, perhaps, is the depth of knowledge required to understand the key issues involved beyond "how to get online" and "surf the

Internet." The greatest point of cyber vulnerability is the human user who enables exploitation of his or her system and those connected to it by not practicing good cyber hygiene: using decent passwords, not downloading unknown files from unknown sources, updating software when prompted or required, using virus-protection software, avoiding "click bait" hyperlinks to unknown websites, and so forth. Good cyber hygiene at the organizational and individual levels could blunt a considerable amount of computer crime and exploits, perhaps as much as 80 percent,[77] and yet most users are ignorant or inattentive to these practical issues. Second, many services require users trade their privacy for access, thus diluting notions of democratic participation free from potential exogenous consequences. Third, the number of users and the diffuseness of their representation would seem to preclude public participation in making rules. Finally, the global nature of cyberspace, encompassing populations with vast differences in language, culture, socioeconomic status, expectations, and so forth, reduces the chances of reaching agreement on even basic issues. Developing participatory systems to aggregate such disparate views presents an extraordinary challenge fraught with complications.[78] Absent such systems, users will be less able to see their rule following as part of a global interdependent effort to sustain cyberspace and therefore their own benefit from it.

Efforts to develop such mechanisms are afoot. The UN resolution for the "creation of a global culture of cybersecurity" anticipates that national cybersecurity efforts will have broad societal involvement, including that of the private sector, civil society, academia, and private individuals, but it is silent regarding rulemaking roles for nongovernmental actors. The public–private partnerships that have already emerged in Europe and North America appear focused on coordinating organization-level efforts and sharing information, without critiquing or innovating policies. But nongovernmental members, particularly by transnational corporations and nongovernmental organizations, for example Freedom House, should be encouraged to suggest rules. Many have experienced cyber attacks in a variety of legal and technological environments and probably know better than observers or governments what cyber laws and practices need to be harmonized across countries as part of international agreements.

The Internet Governance Forum (IGF), a consultative body established by the United Nations and based on a multistakeholder model, might also be used for public input into global-level conversations on rules for cyberspace. Its meetings have discussed cybersecurity issues but have so far deferred to national governments and specialized agencies for policy proposals. But the IGF could use cyber tools and techniques, such as online surveying and crowd sourcing, to collect and aggregate public opinion about rules and regulations needed in any future agreements.

CONCLUSIONS: SELF-GOVERNANCE
IN THE CYBER COMMONS?

Ostrom argued that most analyses of the governance of common pool resources placed too much reliance on presumptions: that individual users of common pool resources faced incentive structures wherein they benefited entirely from their consumption while the costs were borne by all other users. In such situations, free riding would prevail and common pool resources would face depletion unless the rate of replenishment outstripped that of consumption. Hence, the tragedy of the commons would prevail unless a central authority stepped in to manage the resource or the common resource was dissolved parceled out among its users, becoming excludable private property rather than shared.[79]

She argued that such conclusions were reasonable when reality corresponded closely with those presumptions. But, she argued, that conditions could deviate substantially from such presumptions and that each case of common pool resources ought to be examined empirically. Thus, Ostrom inductively derived the conditions that we considered throughout this chapter as those that affect the likelihood that the users of common pool resources would be able to coordinate its use among themselves and provide effective self-governance without the intrusion of the Leviathan or the dismemberment of the resource.

The values of the variables, summarized in table 3.1, do not favor self-organization in the cyber commons with regard to the resource of public trust. Conditions are not ripe for productive, enforceable agreements under which stakeholders, especially states, limit their trust-eroding cyber behaviors. As indicated by the positive values for the "importance of the resource" and "productivity of the system" variables, the widespread expressions of fear for the future of cyberspace has sparked interest in such agreements. However,

Table 3.1   Factors Affecting Self-Governance of Trust in Cyberspace

Variable	*Value*
Size of Resource	−
Number of Users	−
Resource Unit Mobility	−
Importance of Resource	+
Productivity of System	+
Predictability of System Dynamics	0
Leadership	0
Norms and Social Capital	−
Knowledge of Common Pool Resource	+
Collective Choice Rules	−

nothing beyond that should be expected until the values of some technological and other social variables change. Arguably, the pursuit now of a comprehensive global agreement or fall back to agreements among the "like-minded" will be counterproductive. It will likely deepen distrust among major cyber powers and discourage the sharing of useful knowledge of cyberspace.

As Ostrom observed, the tragedy of the commons is most likely to obtain when the common pool resource is distributed over a large population of users that act independently of one another, do not communicate with among themselves, pay no attention to the effects of their actions, and where changing the structure of their situation is costly.[80] Cyberspace as a commons of public trust seems to fit these conditions fairly well and therefore dampen hopes that the users will engage in cooperative endeavors to sustain it. It therefore seems that more effective paths to governance—state control and privatization—together offer a more effective mix of tools to ensure the reliability and safety of the technology that permits access to the network and increase the confidence in the people and organizations that individuals deal with through those technologies. Self-governance of the cyber commons is likely not forthcoming.

NOTES

This chapter is based upon Roger Hurwitz's "Depleted Trust in the Cyber Commons," published in *Strategic Studies Quarterly* 6, no. 3 (Fall 2012). Despite Roger's untimely passing, we believed that his insight into cyberspace as a common pool resource that could be depleted was important to include in our collection and that his original analysis could be further developed. We, of course, bear full responsibility for the changes in the argument.

1. Alfred Thayer Mahan, *The Influence of Sea Power Upon History: 1660–1783. Twelfth Edition* (Boston, MA: Little, Brown, 1890/1918), p. 25.

2. Paul M. Kennedy, *The Rise and Fall of British Naval Mastery* (London: Macmillan, 1983), p. 9.

3. Barry R. Posen, "Command of the Commons: The Military Foundation of U.S. Hegemony," *International Security* 28, no. 1 (Summer 2003), p. 8.

4. Chairman of the Joint Chiefs of Staff, *The National Military Strategy of the United States of America: A Strategy for Today, A Vision for Tomorrow* (Washington, DC: Department of Defense, 2005), p. 5, http://www.defense.gov/news/mar2005/d20050318nms.pdf.

5. For example, the *United Nations Convention on the Law of the Sea* (1982), the *Convention Relating to the Regulation of Aerial Navigation* (1919), and the *Treaty on Principles Governing the Activities of States in the Exploration and Use of Outer Space, including the Moon and Other Celestial Bodies* (1967).

6. Chris C. Demchak and Peter Dombroski, "Rise of a Cybered Westphalian Age," *Strategic Studies Quarterly* 5, no. 1 (Spring 2011).

7. "Chart of Signatures and Ratifications of Treaty 185: Convention on Cybercrime," http://www.coe.int/en/web/conventions/full-list/-conventions/treaty/185/signatures?p_auth=b333kCNV.

8. United Nations General Assembly Resolution. *Report of the Group of Governmental Experts on Developments in the Field of Information and Telecommunications in the Context of International Security*, A/68/98 (June 24, 2013), http://www.un.org/ga/search/view_doc.asp?symbol=A/68/98.

9. United Nations General Assembly Resolution. *Report of the Group of Governmental Experts on Developments in the Field of Information and Telecommunications in the Context of International Security*, A/70/174 (July 22, 2015), http://www.un.org/ga/search/view_doc.asp?symbol=A/70/174; and Henry Rõigas and Tomáš Minárik, "2015 UN GGE Report: Major Players Recommending Norms of Behaviour, Highlighting Aspects of International Law," *Incyder News* (August 31, 2015), https://ccdcoe.org/2015-un-gge-report-major-players-recom-mending-norms-behaviour-highlighting-aspects-international-l-0.html.

10. NATO Cooperative Cyber Defence Centre of Excellence, "Tallinn Manual 2.0 on the International Law Applicable to Cyber Operations," *Fact Sheet* (February 8, 2017), https://ccdcoe.org/sites/default/files/documents/CCDCOE_Tallinn_Manual_Onepager_web.pdf.

11. Bryan Druzin, "Why Does Soft Law Have Any Power Anyway?" *Asian Journal of International Law* 7, no. 2 (July 2017).

12. Panayotis A. Yannakogeorgos, "Internet Governance and National Security," *Strategic Studies Quarterly* 6, no. 3 (Fall 2012).

13. Adam Segal and Matthew Waxman, "Why a Cybersecurity Treaty Is a Pipe Dream," *Fareed Zakaria GPS*, October 27, 2011, http://globalpublicsquare.blogs.cnn.com/2011/10/27/why-a-cybersecurity-treaty-is-a-pipe-dream/.

14. Garrett Hardin, "Tragedy of the Commons," *Science* 162, no. 3589 (1968), pp. 1243–48.

15. Elinor Ostrom, *Governing the Commons: The Evolution of Institutions for Collective Action* (Cambridge, UK: Cambridge University Press, 1990).

16. Mark Raymond, "Puncturing the Myth of the Internet as a Commons," *Georgetown Journal of International Affairs* (2013–2014).

17. Brett Williams, "Cyberspace: What Is It, Where Is It, and Who Cares?" *Armed Forces Journal* (March 13, 2014), http://armedforcesjournal.com/cyberspace-what-is-it-where-is-it-and-who-cares/.

18. Raymond, "Puncturing the Myth of the Internet as a Commons," pp. 62–63.

19. Everett C. Dolman, *Pure Strategy: Power and Principle in the Space and Information Age* (London: Frank Cass, 2005), p. 21; and John B. Sheldon, "Toward a Theory of Cyber Power: Strategic Purpose in Peace and War," in Derek S. Reveron, editor, *Cyberspace and National Security: Threats, Opportunities, and Power in a Virtual World* (Washington, DC: Georgetown University Press, 2012), p. 207.

20. Julian S. Corbett, *Some Principals of Maritime Strategy* (Annapolis, MD: Naval Institute Press, 1911/1988), pp. 91–106.

21. Posen, "Command of the Commons," p. 8.

22. Everett C. Dolman, "New Frontiers, Old Realities," *Strategic Studies Quarterly* 6, no. 1 (Spring 2012), pp. 86–87.

23. Walter Boyne, *The Influence of Air Power Upon History* (Gretna, LA: Pelican, 2003); and Colin S. Gray, "The Influence of Space Power upon History," *Comparative Strategy* 15, no. 4 (1996).

24. Abraham Denmark and James Mulvenon, editors, *Contested Commons: The Future of American Power in a Multipolar World* (Washington, DC: Center for a New American Security, 2010).

25. Lawrence Lessig, *Code: And Other Laws of Cyberspace* (New York: Basic Books, 1999); Lawrence Lessig, *The Future of Ideas: The Fate of the Commons in a Connected World* (New York: Vintage, 2002); and Lawrence Lessig, *Code: And Other Laws of Cyberspace, Version 2.0*, 2nd revised edition (New York: Basic Books, 2006).

26. *International Strategy for Cyberspace: Prosperity, Security, and Openness in a Networked World* (Washington, DC: The White House, May 2011), http://www.whitehouse.gov/sites/default/files/rss_viewer/international_strategy_for_cyberspace.pdf. See also Secretary of State Hillary Clinton, "Remarks on Internet Freedom," (January 21, 2010), https://www.ft.com/content/f0c3bf8c-06bd-11df-b426-00144feabdc0?mhq5j=e3. The State Department's high-profile critique of foreign governments' politically motivated filtering led it to oppose the congressional antipiracy bills (SOPA and PIPA), which would have mandated commercially motivated filtering of foreign sites.

27. M. Dunn Cavelty, *Cyber-Security and Threat Politics: US Efforts to Secure the Information Age* (New York: Routledge, 2008); Ronald Deibert, John Palfrey, Rafal Rohozinski, and Jonathan Zittrain, editors, *Access Denied: The Practice and Policy of Global Internet Filtering* (Cambridge, MA: MIT Press, 2008); Ronald Deibert, John Palfrey, Rafal Rohozinski, and Jonathan Zittrain, editors, *Access Controlled: The Shaping of Power, Rights, and Rule in Cyberspace* (Cambridge, MA: MIT Press, 2010); and Ronald Deibert, John Palfrey, Rafal Rohozinski, and Jonathan Zittrain, editors, *Access Contested: Security, Identity, and Resistance in Asian Cyberspace* (Cambridge, MA: MIT Press, 2011).

28. Eric Lipton, David E. Sanger, and Scott Shane, "The Perfect Weapon: How Russian Cyberpower Invaded the U.S." *New York Times* (December 13, 2016); and Office of the Director of National Intelligence, *Assessing Russian Activities and Intentions in Recent US Elections. Intelligence Community Assessment 2017-01D* (Washington, DC: National Intelligence Council, January 6, 2017).

29. Charlotte Hess, "Untangling the Web: The Internet as a Commons," *Workshop in Political Theory and Analysis, Indiana University* (March 1996), p. 3, available at http://hdl.handle.net/10535/327; and Bob Braden, David Clark, Jon Crowcroft, Bruce Davie, Steve Deering, Deborah Estrin, Sally Floyd, Van Jacobsen, Greg Minshall, Craig Partidge, Larry Peterson, K. Ramakrishnan, Scott Shenker, John Wroclawski, and L. Zhang, "Recommendations on Queue Management and Congestion Avoidance in the Internet," *No. RFC 2309, Network Working Group, The Internet Society* (April 1998).

30. "Jo Twist, Web Guru Fights Info Pollution," *BBC News* (October 13, 2003), http://news.bbc.co.uk/2/hi/technology/3171376.stm.

31. Bernado A. Huberman and Lada A. Adamic, "Internet: Growth Dynamics of the World-Wide Web," *Nature* 401, no. 131 (September 9, 1999); and John Garrity,

"Getting Connected: The Internet and Its Role as a Global Public Good," *Georgetown Journal of International Affairs* 18, no. 1 (Winter/Spring 2017).

32. "World Internet Usage and Population Statistics, March 31, 2017—Update," *Internet World Stats* (update July 8, 2017), available at http://www.internetworldstats.com/stats.htm, accessed July 13, 2017.

33. "Internet Growth Statistics," *Internet World Stats* (updated May 25, 2017), available at http://www.internetworldstats.com/emarketing.htm.

34. Paul Klemperer, "Network Goods (Theory)," in Steven N. Durlauf and Lawrence E. Blume, editors, *The New Palgrave Dictionary of Economics, Second Edition* (Basingstoke, England: Palgrave, 2008).

35. Stanley J. Liebowitz and Stephen E. Margolis, "Network Effects and Externalities," in Peter Newman, editor, *The New Palgrave Dictionary of Economics and the Law* (London: Palgrave Macmillan, 1998).

36. Stanley J. Liebowitz and Stephen E. Margolis, "Network Externality: An Uncommon Tragedy," *Journal of Economic Perspectives* 8, no. 2 (Spring 1994).

37. Michael L. Katz and Carl Shapiro, "Systems Competition and Network Effects," *Journal of Economic Perspectives* 8, no. 2 (Spring 1994), p. 106.

38. Jacques Bus, "Societal Dependencies and Trust," in Hamadoun I. Touré and the Permanent Monitoring Panel on Information Security of the World Federation of Scientists, *The Quest for Cyber Peace* (Geneva: International Telecommunications Union, 2011), p. 18.

39. Bus, "Societal Dependencies and Trust," p. 19, citing Francis Fukuyama, *Trust: The Social Virtues and the Creation of Prosperity* (New York: Free Press, 1995); and Robert Putnam with Robert Leonardi and Raffaella Y. Nanetti, *Making Democracy Work: Civic Traditions in Modern Italy* (Princeton, NJ: Princeton University Press, 1993). For a negative example, see Anthony Padgen, "The Destruction of Trust and Its Economic Consequences in the Case of Eighteenth-Century Naples," in Diego Gambetta, editor, *Trust: Making and Breaking Cooperative Relations* (London: Basil Blackwell, 1988).

40. Jen Weedon, William Nuland, and Alex Stamos, *Information Operations and Facebook* (Menlo Park, CA: Facebook Security, April 27, 2017).

41. Mary Ann Eastlick, Sherry L. Lotz, and Patricia Warrington, "Understanding Online B-to-C Relationships: An Integrated Model of Privacy Concerns, Trust, and Commitment," *Journal of Business Research* 59, no. 8 (2006); and Han Li, Rathindra Sarathy, and Heng Xu, "Understanding Situational Online Information Disclosure as a Privacy Calculus," *Journal of Computer Information Systems* 51, no. 1 (2010).

42. Daniel Heller-Roazen, *The Enemy of All: Piracy and the Law of Nations* (Cambridge, MA: MIT Press, 2008).

43. Information Office of the State Council of the People's Republic of China, *The Internet in China* (June 8, 2010), available at http://www.china.org.cn/government/whitepaper/node_7093508.htm.

44. Ostrom, *Governing the Commons*.

45. Laura DeNardis and Francesca Musiani, "Governance by Infrastructure," in Francesca Musiani, Derrick L. Cogburn, Laura DeNardis, and Nanette S. Levinson, editors, *The Turn to Infrastructure in Internet Governance* (New York: Palgrave Macmillan, 2016), p. 3.

46. Ostrom, *Governing the Commons*; Elinor Ostrom, "A General Framework for Analyzing Sustainability of Social-Ecological Systems," *Science* 325, no. 5939 (July 24, 2009).

47. Ostrom, "A General Framework," p. 419.

48. A view of "state responsibility" is elaborated in the Russian draft for a "Convention on International Information Security," presented to the Second International Meeting of High-Level Officials Responsible for Security Matters, Ekaterinburg, Russia, September 22, 2011, http://2012.infoforum.ru/2012/files/konvencia-mib-en.doc. A problem with any plan that assigns responsibility to states for the cyber behaviors of their residents is that many states lack cybersecurity awareness, capacity, and computer forensic capabilities. This problem and the role for technologically advanced nations to help less advanced ones build such capacity are recognized in the U.S. International Strategy for Cyberspace and the United Nations General Assembly Resolution. *Creation of a Global Culture of Cybersecurity and Taking Stock of National Efforts to Protect Critical Information Infrastructures*, 64/211 (March 17, 2010), http://www.citizenlab.org/cybernorms/ares64211.pdf.

49. Demchak and Dombrowski, "Rise of a Cybered Westphalian Age," pp. 32–61.

50. Bus, "Societal Dependencies and Trust," p. 21.

51. Ostrom, *Governing the Commons*, p. 196.

52. Stein Schjølberg, "Wanted: A United Nations Cyberspace Treaty," in Andrew Nagorski, editor, *Global Cyber Deterrence: Views from China, the U.S., Russia, India, and Norway* (New York: EastWest Institute, 2010), p. 11.

53. Sin-seok Seo, Young J. Won, and James Won-Ki Hong, "Witnessing Distributed Denial-of-Service Traffic from an Attacker's Network," *Proceedings of the 7th International Conference on Network and Services Management* (2011), p. 242.

54. Ellen Nakashima and William Wan, "In China, Business Travelers Take Extreme Precautions to Avoid Cyber-Espionage," *Washington Post* (September 26, 2011); and Joel Brenner, *America the Vulnerable* (New York: Penguin Press, 2011), p. 61ff.

55. United Nations General Assembly Resolution 64/211.

56. United Nations General Assembly Resolution. *Group of Governmental Experts on Developments in the Field of Information and Telecommunications in the Context of International Security*, 65/201 (November 9, 2010), https://disarmament-library.un.org/UNODA/Library.nsf/1b0b0683e73e6da5852576e40054e901/d9d0a83c0f-2421d6852577e3005c4b5e/%24FILE/A%252065%2520405.pdf.

57. Ostrom, "A General Framework," p. 420.

58. "The WannaCry Ransomware Attack," Strategic Comments 23, no. 16 (May 2017); and Nicholas Weaver, "Thoughts on the NotPetya Ransomware Attack," *Lawfare* (June 28, 2017).

59. Brad Smith, "The Need for a Digital Geneva Convention—Microsoft on the Issues," *Microsoft* (February 14, 2017), available at https://blogs.microsoft.com/on-the-issues/2017/02/14/need-digital-geneva-convention/; and Brad Smith, "The Need for Urgent Collective Action to Keep People Safe Online: Lessons from Last Week's Cyberattack," *Microsoft* (May 14, 2017), available at https://blogs.microsoft.com/on-the-issues/2017/05/14/need-urgent-collective-action-keep-people-safe-online-lessons-last-weeks-cyberattack/.

60. Touré and the Permanent Monitoring Panel, *Quest for Cyber Peace*, p. 16.

61. Touré and the Permanent Monitoring Panel, *Quest for Cyber Peace*, p. 25.

62. Foreign Secretary William Hague, "Security and Freedom in the Cyber Age—Seeking the Rules of the Road," speech to the Munich Security Conference, February 4, 2011, http://www.fco.gov.uk/en/news/latest-news/?view=Speech&id=544853682.

63. William Samuelson and Richard Zeckhauser, "Status Quo Bias in Decision Making," *Journal of Risk and Uncertainty* 1, no. 1 (1988).

64. Niccolò Machiavelli (Peter Bondella, translator), *The Prince* (Oxford, England: Oxford University Press, 2005), p. 22.

65. According to the well-known Metcalfe's law, the value of a network is proportional to the number of cross-connections among its N users, that is N^2. The growth (or decline) in value with each user who joins (leaves) the network is proportional to 2N. The more extreme Leek's law equates network value with the number of distinct audiences that can be formed from the number of users, i.e., the number of subsets less the null set of N or 2N—1. So, the value of the network would incredibly double (or be halved) with each user joining (or leaving). A more reasonable evaluation, especially for large networks, assumes differential use by those in the network. Consistent with power laws (long-tail phenomena), usage is assumed to decline exponentially with delay in joining the network. Usage or transactions over the N users describes a hyperbole, with the first joiners the heaviest users. The cumulative benefit, hence value of the network, is then proportional to the area under the curve or natural log of N (lnN). The increase (decrease) in network value with each person joining (leaving) is significantly less than estimated by Metcalfe's law, and the change is decreasing rather than increasing. Thus, if the network provider's cost of acquiring an additional user is fixed, a point of diminishing returns on value will be reached.

66. Robert O. Keohane, *After Hegemony: Cooperation and Discord in the World Political Economy* (Princeton, NJ: Princeton University Press, 1984).

67. United States Department of Commerce, "Management of Internet Names and Addresses," (updated July 22, 2000), available at https://www.icann.org/resources/unthemed-pages/white-paper-2012-02-25-en.

68. Internet Governance Project, *The Future US Role in Internet Governance: 7 Points in Response to the U.S. Commerce Dept.'s "Statement of Principles"* (Atlanta: Georgia Institute of Technology, July 28, 2005), p. 2.

69. Jack Goldsmith and Tim Wu, *Who Controls the Internet? Illusions of a Borderless World* (Oxford, England: Oxford University Press, 2006); John Mathiason, *Internet Governance: The New Frontier of Global Institutions* (New York: Routledge, 2008); Lee A. Bygrave and John Bing, editors, *Internet Governance: Infrastructure and Institutions* (Oxford, England: Oxford University Press, 2009); Rolf H. Weber, *Shaping Internet Governance: Regulatory Challenges* (New York: Springer, 2009); Milton L. Mueller, *Networks and States: The Global Politics of Internet Governance* (Cambridge, MA: MIT Press, 2010); Marc Raboy, Normand Landry, and Jeremy Shtern, *Digital Solidarities, Communication Policy and Multi-stakeholder Global Governance: The Legacy of the World Summit on the Information Society* (New York: Peter Lang, 2010); Eric Brousseau, Meryem Marzouki, and Cécile Méadel, *Governance, Regulation, and Powers on the Internet* (Cambridge, UK: Cambridge University Press, 2012); Joanna Kulesza, *International*

Internet Law (New York: Routledge, 2012); and Laura DeNardis, *The Global War for Internet Governance* (New Haven, CT: Yale University Press, 2014).

70. Denardis and Musiani, "Governance by Infrastructure."

71. Thanks to Phillip Hallam-Baker for discussion of this point.

72. Keir Giles, "Russia's Public Stance on Cyberspace Issues," in Christian Czosseck, Rain Ottis, and Katharina Ziolkowski, editors, *4th International Conference on Cyber Conflict* (Tallinn: NATO Cooperative Cyber Defence Centre of Excellence, 2012); and DeNardis, *The Global War for Internet Governance.*

73. Indeed, the Chief of the General Staff of Russia, General Valeriy Gerasimov has emphasized the threat that "color revolutions" could pose to the Russian state and has appealed to Russia's strategic thinkers to develop ways to counter these threats. See Roger N. McDermott, "Does Russia Have a Gerasimov Doctrine?" *Parameters* 46, no. 1 (Spring 2016).

74. United Nations General Assembly Resolution 64/211.

75. Ronald Deibert and Rafal Rohozinski, "Contesting Cyberspace and the Coming Crisis of Authority," in Deibert, Palfrey, Rohozinski, and Zittrain, *Access Contested.*

76. Michael Schwirtz and Joseph Goldstein, "Russian Espionage Piggybacks on a Cybercriminal's Hacking," *New York Times* (March 12, 2017).

77. Brenner, *America the Vulnerable*, pp. 239–44; and Joel Brenner, personal communication with Roger Hurwitz, March 12, 2010.

78. James Bohman and William Rehg, editors, *Deliberative Democracy: Essays on Reason and Politics* (Cambridge, MA: MIT Press, 1997); and Archon Fung, "Varieties of Participation in Complex Governance," *Public Administration Review* 66, no. S1 (2006).

79. Ostrom, *Governing the Commons*, pp. 8–13.

80. Ostrom, *Governing the Commons*, p. 183.

Chapter Four

Rise of a Cybered Westphalian Age 2.0

Chris C. Demchak and Peter Dombrowski

No frontier lasts forever, and no freely occupied global commons extends endlessly where human societies are involved. Sooner or later, good fences are erected to make good neighbors, and so it must be with cyberspace. Today we are seeing the beginnings of the border-making process across the world's nations. From the Chinese intent to create their own controlled internal Internet, to increasingly controlled access to the Internet in less democratic states, to the rise of Internet filters and rules in Western democracies, states are establishing the bounds of their sovereign control in the virtual world in the name of security and economic sustainability. The topology of the Internet, like the prairie of the 1800s' American Midwest is about to be changed forever—rationally, conflictually, or collaterally—by the decisions of states.

In 2010, the crossing of the Rubicon into the age of cybered conflict[1] occurred with a surprisingly sophisticated, precisely targeted, and undoubtedly expensively produced worm in large industrial control systems. Its name was Stuxnet. As a malicious piece of software, it came as a surprise despite having floated around a year doing nothing but stealthily copying itself. The worm's target was the program controlling centrifuges in Iranian nuclear reprocessing plants.[2] Spread by infected USB thumb drives and the software in printer spoolers, it bypassed the Internet security controls in place against hackers and did not act maliciously until finding the precise computer DNA of Iranian nuclear reactors as Stuxnet's designers intended. While the worm infiltrated a wide variety of protections and Windows operating systems, the sophisticated Stuxnet authors demonstrated a new level of threat to cybersecurity. Despite early denials, the Iranian nuclear community ultimately admitted its plants were infected and its centrifuges unstable.

Stuxnet capped a two-year period in which the scope and complexity of national security challenges posed by cyberspace created a new level of insecurity.[3] From 2008 onward, a string of unsettling discoveries of massive theft of national data appeared via backdoors into otherwise secure national-level systems (e.g., GhostNet). Widespread stealthy infection of national systems occurred through sophisticated programs waiting to be connected to hidden remote servers, such as the Confiker worm and the wholesale copying of critical industrial technological advances by China. The age of vandals and burglars in cyberspace moved to the next level, resembling organized cyber mercenaries, cross-national pirates, and the undermining of nation-states on a massive cyber scale.[4] By 2017, the ransomware attacks, called WannaCry, seemed to combine elements of state-sponsored strategic attacks with criminality, a blend of messaging the international community with an effort to raise funds through blackmail.[5]

Until Stuxnet, however, it was not entirely clear if all the access points, malware, and rampant penetrations would lead to serious strategic harm. The consensus among states changed after Stuxnet. If such malicious software can take down whole energy systems at once, states have no choice but to respond if they are to protect their own governmental and military operations and uphold their responsibility to protect citizens and corporations.[6] The Stuxnet method and its success thus changed the notion of vulnerability across increasingly internetted societies and critical infrastructures. The days of cyber spying through software backdoors or betrayals by trusted insiders, vandalism, or even theft had suddenly evolved into the demonstrated ability to deliver a potentially killing blow without being anywhere near the target. Forcing nuclear centrifuges to oscillate out of control from an unknown and remote location suggests that future innovations might be able to destroy or disrupt other critical infrastructures upon which modern societies depend. As proof of concept as well as a model to be copied, the Stuxnet worm offers the possibility of distant enemies spending hundreds of staff hours and expertise to insert such applications throughout the nation—from oil pipelines to dam turbines to nuclear and fossil fuel energy plants to any other large-scale critical service controlled by computers. As the designers of Stuxnet demonstrated, being disconnected from the Internet will never again be a guarantee of security.[7] If any part of the plant, service, aircraft, or system is internally connected or if any electronic devices connect to the system from the outside, even if the device must be hand-carried, the system is vulnerable.[8]

Stuxnet is an exquisite example of the advantages afforded attackers in the current global cyberspace. Attackers freely choose the scale of their organization, the proximity of their targets, and the precision of their target group, all with near impunity. They may take all the time they need in capitalizing on these advantages and in using the Internet itself to collect more data on the intended targets. The ease of relatively risk-free conflict between adversaries within the global web is so apparent that even botnet gangs of criminals controlling secretly hacked personal computers fight among themselves technologically, often seeking to destroy and replace the other's malicious software. As shown by the denial of government and banking service in Estonia in 2007, wholesale assaults across physical borders can be deployed from one state to another by "patriotic hackers," while the originating state claims ignorance and inability to stop the assault.[9] By 2008 alone, the daily attacks on simply the U.S. ".gov" or ".mil" websites numbered in the millions.[10] Over the course of 2009, an unprecedented 75 percent of global companies across twenty-seven countries were the victims of cyber attack, with the average reported loss of $2 million.[11] By 2016, this average cost was $4 million, and $7 million in the United States.[12] In 2017, the value of such attacks ranges from 1 to 2 percent on average across the Westernized democracies.[13]

Today, protective measures in modern democratic states are often insufficient to repel the daily onslaught of attacks by state and nonstate actors, and the situation is worsening. Stuxnet's success ensured the rising perception of an all-source 24/7/360-degree national-level threat. In the future, a "son of Stuxnet" variant could also float for some time, seemingly harmless and unnoticed until triggered by a date, end-use, Internet signal, or an encounter with a specific kind of computer or program. At once, millions of computers might fail, suddenly try to send destroy commands to countless others, or even worse, suddenly replace true data with false in anything from aircraft to mass financial transactions. Even China recognizes an internal threat from its own vigorous development of cybered hacking talent inside the nation. While the intent had been to use the skills outwardly in "patriotic hacking," despite severe sanctions against hacking Chinese citizens, now Chinese authorities have to contend with their own very real internal cybered threats.[14] States under constant barrage cannot help but respond.

All states, in one way or another, will seek to control what they fear from the Internet—the lack of sovereign control over what comes through their borders. Thus, the transformation from frontier to regulated substrate across cyberspace has begun. While it is not recognized as such nor publicly endorsed by most democratic leaders, a cyberspace regulating process is happening, building the initial blocks of emergent national virtual fences. A new "cybered Westphalian age" is slowly emerging as state leaders organize to protect their citizens and economies individually and unwittingly initiate the path to borders in cyberspace. Not only are the major powers of China and the United States already demonstrating key elements of emerging cybered territorial sovereignty,[15] other nations are quickly beginning to show similar trends. From India to Sweden, nations are demanding control over what happens electronically in their territory, even if it is to or from the computers of their citizens.

This process may be meandering, but we argue it was inevitable given the international system of states and consistent with the history of state formation and consolidation. As cyberspace is profoundly man-made, no impossible barriers hinder the growth of national borders in cyberspace. They are possible technologically, comfortable psychologically, and manageable systemically and politically. Small steps in securing against threats will lead to further steps over time and, especially, in response to discoveries such as Stuxnet or its derivatives in the future.

In the process of border development, the singular marker of a new age of sovereignty and cybered conflict will come to be a normal part of the modern state's capacities: the national cyber commands or their security equivalents at the national level. To assure national safety in cyberspace, large, vulnerable states like the United States and China must anticipate and disrupt attacks far forward as well as repel a wide variety of threats. Otherwise, the mass attacks may spread too fast for effective defense. Just as militaries still exist in the modern age of mass weapons, they or their functional equivalents will also be sent to guard key national points in cyberspace. In so doing, they deepen national borders. This chapter argues that Stuxnet marks the official beginning of a new cyber-Westphalian world of virtual borders and national cyber commands as normal elements of modern cybered governments. Finally, we have seen these kinds of phenomena before in the old Westphalian world. Already, theories, international rules, institutions, and experiences exist to guide us as the new age fully matures.

THE "WESTPHALIAN" PROCESS

The Stuxnet worm marks a turning point into a new cybered conflict age in which states need to define territorial spaces of safety to reassure their citizens' safety and economic well-being. When it is widely accepted that critical systems can no longer be trusted if they are open to the web, political leaders will demand ways to eliminate the threats from entering their territory. The age of cybered conflict has begun, and it is natural for those hostile to any group to include cyber at key points in their plans, including debilitating entire systems. Equally expected, leaders of the threatened group will have to consider what responses keep critical functions secure. From water holes in the desert to river passages in the forest to mountain passes to central controlling nodes in the global web, conflict parties inevitably seek the critical gateways of the opposition to obtain advantage.

Frontiers are places of conflict between groups, historically lightly and poorly governed, less populated, and risky—places where value is extracted for little cost. When a frontier starts to become a commons,[16] productivity for all is imperiled by the grab-and-go nature of those using it. Those dependent on the frontier tend to form organizations to control their claim. Modern democracies are in essence complex aggregates of large-scale organizations. Their leaders routinely reach out to absorb uncertainties to control them, if possible, or push them away. The rising perception of a national-level threat means that all states, in one way or another, will reach out to control what they fear from the Internet—its frontier nature and the lack of sovereign control over what comes into their area of responsibility.

No freely occupied commons extends endlessly nor lasts forever where rising rapacious human populations are involved. It is normal for political leaders seeking relief from the interaction edges with other cultures or possible threats to look at reinforcing or installing borders. Being able to establish sovereign control is one hallmark of a functioning state. This need is true whether the border is enforced by passports for people, customs inspections for goods, or two-way filters for meta-tagged electronic bits. When states cannot protect their economic engines of growth and sustainability, the capacity of the state falls into question by those who control the resources under threat.[17]

Man's search for security has led to the formation of "fortress and badland" distinctions that marked territory for resource ownership for centuries, but until the 1648 Treaties of Münster and Osnabrücke (understood together as the Peace of Westphalia), borders did not stabilize over many generations. In this case, however, the Peace of Westphalia not only ended the Thirty Years' War in Europe but also heralded the emergence of the modern interstate system. After the Westphalian peace, the nation-state became the dominant form of social organization. As a result, leading states of the period helped codify and set about more or less enforcing a collectively agreed-upon set of rules, institutions, and norms by which they interacted with each other in international society.[18]

Particularly useful for international stability was the effect of the treaties in creating conditions supporting the gradual hardening of borders between and among states over the next 362 years. This process of settling on boundaries due to the mutual adjustments among states produced a concept of national territoriality that states could legitimately claim, and they could defend that territory against outside aggressors in just wars. With the rise of a general presumption of territoriality recognized by other external political leaders, modern states could stabilize internally and grow economically within those established, increasingly fixed borders.

Westphalia provided a demonstration or a proof of concept. Over time, the more established a state became and the fewer ungoverned internal areas or frontiers it allowed to continue, the stronger and less existentially vulnerable the nascent state became.[19] The significance of the Westphalian process for this chapter and its general argument is that the efforts of the modern state to cope with the emergence of the cybersphere is in many respects similar to the processes by which states became the dominant form of social organization within the international system. The ability of the state to provide stability and security within the increasingly unchallenged borders was necessary to internal development of social and economic progress. Without a form of Westphalian borders, conflicts previously at the boundaries easily spill over in both directions from opportunistic resource appropriations by actors within and without. The wide variety of authorities, powers, and capabilities over the last four hundred years accruing to the modern state become difficult to employ, redirect, or even limit. Just as the ability of modern bureaucratic states to corral resources productively drove other less successful organization forms from the scene internationally, their ability to provide internal certainty in their domestic territory gradually came to define what is today known as civil society in the Westernized world.[20]

Today the uncertainties, predatory and productive opportunism, legal and illegal resource conflicts, and changes to economic and social expectations reach directly into the domestic structures of the modern state. Just as before the Peace of Westphalia and its recognition of the systemic economic threats of insecurity within societies, states are beginning to grapple with the difficulties inherent in incorporating a new set of technologies into their citizens' community and individual interactions. The cybersphere has challenged the security of individuals and states themselves in ordinary systems considered essential to the critical functions of society. Increasingly, citizens are at the frontlines of the existential fight over stability in the wider society, and the responses from modern states have only now begun to crystallize.

The struggle to move these conflicts from the existential realm directly harming citizens to some more organized field of dispute has begun at least in discussions among allies and in international communities, but the process has been meandering.[21] Initially surprised by the reach of the predatory behaviors made possible by cyberspace's unfettered global reach, democratic governments have been slow to reinforce their monopoly of violence over external threats entering their nations and harming citizens. Laws emerged over the early 2000s focused on the internal symptoms rather than the external sources of the uncertainties, many focused on the individual citizen or commercial Internet service providers (ISPs). For example, in the United States, financial liability for the individual defrauded online in credit card usage limited the amount the citizen would lose.[22] In contrast, German law makes individual citizens responsible if they do not stop their personal computers from being taken over and used in massive spam or denial-of-services attacks.[23] Australia, however, enforces rules on the ISPs to keep the flow of malware to a minimum.[24]

Despite these efforts, organizations and governments have found their presence in cyberspace vulnerable to attempts to extract information, prevent access, and even to disable as happened with Stuxnet. By 2015, the number of attacks on federal agencies alone—leaving aside the much larger losses in the private sector—was said to jump 1,300 percent over ten years.[25] Governments, like the signatories to the Peace of Westphalia, are increasingly aware of the potential losses if hostile, curious, or just rapacious outside actors are able to reach easily and deeply inside their societies, into critical assets of families, banks, townships, airlines, or any of the myriad of critical systems sustaining the society. "It appears we can no longer see the Internet as a friendly shared resource and that strict boundaries will have to be put in place," said Bert Hubert, founder of Dutch-based software provider PowerDNS.com.[26] States, especially large, often cyber-targeted nations like the United States, are recognizing the need to respond. Their efforts to control are accumulating across the organizational and technological capabilities. The modern state intends to put in place a buffer, a bulwark, a way to buy the nation time to respond if attacked. In short, they are iterating toward national borders in cyberspace to relieve the pressure of the barrage of assaults.

PRACTICAL REINFORCEMENT—BORDERS DECREASE THE EASE OF CYBERED OFFENSE

Beyond the return to interstate protocols that are well understood, there is a practical aspect to cyber borders—they make it more difficult to cause harm. Making it necessary to get around borders physically forces larger organizations of people to arrange a physical entry to each nation under attack. Forcing attackers and criminals to move people rather than bytes means higher operational barriers to entry: more costs, more coordination efforts, and many more opportunities for any of these efforts to be noticed by national security monitoring organizations.[27] The border hurdles also can slow the pace of regrouping from failures or redirecting to capitalize on new information, as well as coordinating simultaneous target groups across borders.

Increasing the organizational difficulties for attackers also increases the loyalty challenge for bad actor organizations trying to control human agents at distance rather than merely reprogramming pawned computer networks. The job of attacking civil societies increases enormously when information must be verified *in situ* by informants who may or may not be trustworthy dispersed across monitored virtual borders. Borders reduce the advantages of scale, proximity, and precision an attacker has in pitching offensive surprises and level the playing field for the defending societies.[28] Some mass attacks that are possible today may, with borders, simply become impossible unless the organization is able to physically move large numbers of humans into each targeted country and coordinate rapidly around national borders or collaborating regional institutions. Borders raise skill, social, resource, and distance barriers for today's hackers and would-be attackers who lack exceptionally advanced skills.

VIRTUAL BORDERS—FEASIBLE, COMFORTABLE, AND MANAGEABLE

The slow development of a Westphalian-style accord parsing cybered sovereignty has every chance to proceed and eventually succeed. There are few natural dampeners to a neo-Westphalian process in the digital era. A cybered national border is technologically possible, psychologically comfortable, and systemically and politically manageable. Increasingly, the exceptionally skilled technologists are arguing for separation of critical systems to protect them from Internet predators and hostile actors. As a result, even if policy makers in each nation are inclined normatively to keep a fully open Internet, they will have few technical arguments to use in maintaining that position. Furthermore, borders are psychologically normal for citizens focused on continuing their access to Internet services safely. Users already expect some kind of government sanction against those who harm individuals via cyber means, and borders make historical and cultural sense for denizens of modern states.[29] Finally, a cyber border fits more easily with the institutional compromises and allocations of responsibilities already existing in the governance structures managing modern democracies.

First, the technology of cyberspace is man-made. It is not, as described by the early "cyber prophets" of the 1990s, an entirely new environment that operates outside human control, like tides or gravity.[30] Rather, as its base, the grid is a vast complex system of machines, software code and services, cables, accepted protocols for compatibility, graphical pictures for human eyes, input/output connections, and electrical supports. It operates precisely across narrow electronic bands but with such an amalgamation of redundancies, substitutions, workarounds, and quick go-to fixes that disruptions can be handled relatively well as long as everyone wants the system to work as planned.

However globally interconnected, cyberspace is dependent on preventing its internal need for precision being hijacked or massively disrupted by malicious or hostile actors. States are learning that everything about today's grid can be technologically regulated. There are many points of opportunity for the national government interested in controlling what eventually ends up being received on Internet desktops, laptops, mobile devices, or even independent appliances in homes and businesses. While connectivity is global—now increasingly found everywhere like land, air, sea, and even space—what is known as cyberspace *is* and *will* remain always man-made, -sustained, and -enabled. And, unlike the sea, land, air, or space, it can be unmade. Furthermore, land expanses, seas, air, and space quadrants do not exist only if information is flowing. Seeing a mountain does not automatically connect one individual to the next or even offer one useful clues about it, yet being on one node does connect individuals to others in this cybered underlayment, even if only with some hacking. Air masses are air masses, but strings of cyber bytes already have information in the way they connect from node to node in protocols. It would be as if a car could not continue on the freeway without broadcasting its VIN number, license, weight, and other data each time it approached an exit. If not approved to continue by the owner of that freeway node, the car would be forced off onto another road.

Today, some firm or agency runs and must maintain every single connection on the Internet. Even peer-to-peer (P2P) networks require a person to connect and maintain them. Some firm must develop the software to allow connections, and someone must also code the application allowing the exchanges of data, for good or ill. Today, the technological filtering occurs largely through private or semiprivate institutional intermediaries. Across the bulk of democratic and nondemocratic states, ISPs are finding that their ability to continue to provide services is increasingly dependent on providing filtering services determined by large, state-level authorities. There is no technological reason why these services cannot continue as regulated utilities, nor is there any reason why governments cannot control what runs into the nation from overseas cables or runs out of the nation to criminally harm citizens of other nations.

It is technologically possible for governments to require source tagging of bytes at some point to assure the passage of legally acceptable streams of data or applications or volumes of requests to curtail attacks on their soil or emanating from their soil illegally.[31] Changing the mix by social accord via government action changes the system as we access it, know it, and use it. If key cable junctions are broken, the Internet fails or slows to a crawl for whole nations. If the same cables are merely redirected through an extra set of computers that reject or delete unwanted patterns of data, then the Internet at the far end of the redirect will seem to be all that it was. Deleted material will simply never show up. With sufficient investment in leading-edge speed cables, inserted filtering servers, and capable transmission lines, it is possible to have a border that is not visibly intrusive to citizens and conceivably even faster than today. For example, while it is widely known that China controls its Internet, it is not widely known that this control rests on having only three main Internet gateways between its one-billion-plus population and the rest of the globe.[32] For the kinds of controls exerted by the Chinese government to go unnoticed by users is one piece of evidence that a border for every state, each with different security goals, is within technological reach, if not yet legally and formally sought.

Second, physical borders are known, accepted, and desired by citizens in modern civil societies, and that psychological comfort will be no different for the creation of borders in cyberspace. The relevant emphasis is on "borders," not on universal control of all cybered transactions occurring entirely within the boundaries of a democratic nation. Historically, citizens accepted borders as a security-enhancing necessity against external uncertainties undermining internally accepted rules of interaction. Without such limits, the collective sense of belonging is more easily undermined, as are the rules of civil behavior. Even a willingness to abide by norms of trust and nonthreatening behavior is tied to security, where collective rules can and cannot be enforced. To live in ungoverned societies is not only insecure, but it is also a psychologically palpable existential threat. As Joel Brenner explains,

> Constitutive rules define the structure of a given society, as well as the relationships that exist among the individuals that comprise that society; they also allocate essential tasks among the members of the society and ensure that these tasks are performed. Human societies have consisted of bounded systems situated in a delimited spatial area and composed of a defined populace (e.g., "the people of Rome," "the American public," and so on). These spatial and population constraints facilitate the operation of the constitutive rules: spatial and demographic isolation make it easier to socialize those who populate a society so that most accept and abide by its constitutive rules. They also make it easier to identify and suppress those who do not.[33]

Civil society deepens and strengthens when the expectation of modern liberal and universal social rule observance is justified routinely. Historically, the hostile or predatory deviations from actors outside the social jurisdiction of a modern state are exactly what citizens in their implicit social contract seek to avoid in according a territory their allegiance and legitimacy. Safety at home for the citizen in a highly digital society is a social-psychological need obliging the modern democratic state to act.[34]

Third, borders fit institutionally into the existing architecture of national systems management. Most nations make a distinction between the forces defending the borders from attack (militaries) and those protecting the individual citizens inside the nation from attack (police). This distinction is one of the direct outcomes of the rise of the modern state from the Westphalian Peace. But it is severely challenged by the unfettered character of the current global cyberspace topology. Today militaries, police, and intelligence organizations have been challenged both by the attacks and by the jurisdictional lack of clarity in obligations and ability to demand resources. Both state and nonstate competitors have used the interconnectivity inherent to the web to attack and disrupt operations and gather intelligence about capabilities and intentions across borders with impunity. This is especially true for the United States and other nations highly dependent on telecommunications for command and control; intelligence, surveillance, and reconnaissance; and the management of logistics. Moreover, many military and intelligence organizations have grasped the offensive possibilities of the cybersphere to reach past the borders of other states directly, in concept at least, into the homes of an opposing state's citizens. Across the military communities of the more modern states, information operations and strategic communications programs have been developed to influence adversaries and allies. Physical or "kinetic" attacks are now routinely facilitated by efforts to exploit enemy cyber vulnerabilities.[35]

Without the legitimating and bureaucratic clarity of a virtual border, for example, jurisdictional disputes in nations observing centuries of criminal versus national security civil society laws are hamstrung to respond. Stuxnet easily crossed borders as intended by its designers. If it were a nonstate actor, then the action is criminal, invoking the powers of police forces. If it were a state-level actor, then militaries would be involved. Today, it is not clear which groups were involved, in large part because the electronic trail of possible attribution moves readily across states, and states have no obligation to sanction bad behavior emanating outward from their territory. Nonetheless, a state's facilities were harmed, and many states are viewing that uncertainty and inability to lay blame and attribute the attack as unacceptable vulnerabilities.[36]

In principle, only from ungoverned or ungovernable territories do modern groups launch destructive missiles on neighboring nations without automatic interstate calls for sanctions. With physical borders, states that wish to be accepted internationally are obliged by law and custom to stop the attacking behavior of their residents or to allow the offended state to reach inside to stop it. Once the virtual limits of sovereign power can be demarcated in the global cybersphere, states ignoring or supporting massive denial-of-service attacks from their territories will be held internationally responsible. Domestic legal systems that today do not have internal laws criminalizing predatory cyber behavior affecting other states will have to initiate the kinds of internal controls already presumed in international policing. If they do not or if they actively promote the external attacks from their territory, just as in centuries of physical conflict, they will have to acknowledge the right of the attacked states to defend across borders if necessary. Distinguishing criminal laws and activity from national security missions and jurisdiction becomes enormously more manageable when the jurisdictional lines are drawn and recognized in a new cyber–Westphalian process.

Managing the bordered virtual sphere will also enable a third swathe of cyberspace to be identified as well—the ungoverned badlands equivalent to the very physical regions of failed or failing states. As civil society extends into cyberspace with rules of accepted behavior and reinforced by modern state institutions, it becomes easier to invoke the routine activities of international organizations to curb, if not cure, the disruptive activities of the failed-state portions of the international virtual globe. As a result, institutions will adapt and adjust while replicating the functional aspects of the current physical concords and rules of behavior to contain the harm by actors who deviate from the emerging virtual civil world. What is happening today in the slow civilizing of cyberspace, however scattered and seemingly unique, strongly depends on what individual governments see as either the threat or the leverage they have and the institutions they develop to act on those perceptions. For all, the beginnings of a need to control the sovereign, albeit digital, national territory are already present. None are controlling the harm, transmission, laws, or sanctions emerging on the sovereign territory of another state; rather, each is operating under the modern notion of monopoly of power on the territory already demarcated and looking to its own laws and control of actions on its territory, to include network connections.

EMERGENT VIRTUAL BORDERS

Indications of emergent borders within the cybersphere are appearing at many levels, making for a variety of models across the current extent of sovereignty the state presumes or seeks. China, for example, leads the authoritarian states with ubiquitous cyberspace regulation aimed at controlling information from outside and circulating inside its borders. In this "all points" model, the cyber border includes gateways for filtering information and the ability, in principle, to curtail the Internet connections between internal regions or between China and the rest of the world. It is a technological (limited gateways), institutional (regulated telecoms), and psychological (cyber self-censors and vigilantes) model operating on many levels at once.

China believes it is promoting stability and security within Chinese territory. "Whether we can cope with the Internet is a matter that affects the development of socialist culture, the security of information, and the stability of the state," President Hu of China said in 2007.[37] In the 1990s, the Chinese Communist Party recognized the power of unfettered access from/ to Chinese citizens and declared the Internet to be a fifth area of territoriality to be nationally secured. China thus built "Golden Shield," employing an estimated forty thousand Internet police who in 2009 shut down at least seven thousand websites, deleted 1.25 million pieces of information, and arrested 3,500 people, including 70 dissidents and bloggers now in jail. In addition to directly controlling the content, about thirty thousand netizens are employed part-time to intervene in online forum discussions and redirect conversations away from sensitive topics. The Chinese leadership routinely characterizes Westernized social media as subversive tools and sees U.S. diplomatic subversion in any U.S.-sponsored discussions of open Internet. Believing that state security and social stability are under attack, the Chinese government implemented a technologically sophisticated, heavily intelligence collection–driven second phase of the Golden Shield in 2010.[38]

Since at least 2012, Chinese senior political and corporate leaders have moved to an even more aggressive use of rising economic power with an admittedly wider agenda. A new narrative uses the rise of China as a future great or superpower to rationalize its right to question the existing international system.[39] Not only is China determined to ensure its own national sovereignty in cyberspace and in other sectors, but it overtly challenges the Western dominance of global Internet governance system. The apparent objective is to influence changes in cyberspace producing a structure more convenient—or at least less threatening—to Chinese national preferences.[40]

China has also been working on constructing its own Internet. With the China Next Generation Internet (CNGI), the limited number of Internet addresses expands massively by adding enough digits (IPv6[41]) to provide every single machine connecting to the Internet its own unique web address. This addressing protocol means every single web transaction can be tracked from the originating computer to any other, allowing for massive social surveillance especially when combined with advances in the raw computing speed and storage systems. Chinese investments in the techniques, tools, and talents—as well as start-up purchases and joint ventures—associated with big data analytics and artificial intelligence have massively increased in recent years. Ultimately, China intends to be able to record and individually track data in real time to individual computers.[42]

A surveillance-friendly addressing system is useful to the Chinese or any authoritarian government desiring to control its own borders without having to use proxies or agents to do their controlling. The so-called Great Firewall that Google declined to support in 2010 shifted responsibility to, and liability for, ISPs if a customer accessed forbidden sites or searched for banned topics.[43]

China justified these measures as essential for citizen safety against social disharmony, false information, fraud, piracy, and social ills such as pornography. These are common themes for political leaders and security specialist from states seeking to establish sovereign borders in cyberspace. In 2005, China announced an upgrade to the national text messaging filtering system with automatic police alerts when false information, reactionary remarks, or harmful activities such as fraud and scams are found in cell phone texts. In December 2005, the vice minister of the Ministry of Public Safety announced that the upgraded system's 2,800 surveillance centers had tracked 107,000 illegal cell phone text messages including approximately 33 percent associated with criminal fraud.[44] In the mid-2000s, Chinese citizens sent 218 billion text messages annually, so the 107,000 objectionable texts were not even a drop in the bucket. By 2010, however, the addition of supercomputers that can move trilobits per second provided advanced capabilities to filter cell phone text messages centrally. The police, using undisclosed criteria, create lists of prohibited terms that cell phone companies must use to scan all customer text messages. The cell phone companies were then required to automatically suspend the accounts and report the incidents to police if banned terms are found.

New technologies have enabled not only massive increases in the intrusive and comprehensive search mechanisms but also more punitive measures against those violating the restrictions. Chinese authorities have closed websites, especially those able to share files, and made it more difficult for citizens to establish their own sites.[45] The government has successfully gained control of the physical access of all web traffic in or out of China through three major gateways in Beijing, Shanghai, and Guangzhou.[46] Despite international disapproval, China's government used content controls to assert sovereignty over key aspects of its internal social space, to include any foreign technologies that are brought into China for commercial or even private uses. In 2017, a law—suspended in late 2016—requiring foreign companies working with large data to store all data on Chinese territory and submit their IT hardware and services for safety review was activated despite external pressures against it.[47]

Alternatively, several democratic nations, including Australia and Germany to some extent, have charted a "key firm" model of regulating large telecommunications firms, albeit loosely, with the goal of curbing malicious or thieving activity, not information flows. Other European democracies have enacted or are considering enacting Internet control measures to prevent theft or abuse of their citizens' personal information and property. Others, such as the United Kingdom, created overarching agencies to coordinate other state institutions regulating economic and social transactions across the Internet, but crucially not security organizations. One goal was to curb the theft of property and private data. More recently, however, European nations have demonstrated greater interest in implementing national security controls. In 2008, for example, Sweden passed legislation allowing its national police force's intelligence section to monitor all Internet traffic in and out of the country, whether by Swedish citizens or others. It was widely criticized by prominent privacy advocates, but the law withstood challenges as a central piece of antiterror legislation and is now considered noncontroversial.[48] The emerging model is still based on telecommunications firm capabilities but increasingly focused on security.

The path to a national border in cyberspace may not prove as difficult for EU nations as it would for other sectors because cyberspace policies are currently left largely to member states. Even European Union directives require the national authorities to enact implementing legislation. The level of security varies greatly across nations, and the larger nations such as the United Kingdom and France have not been waiting for an EU–wide solution to threats to their individual cyber resources or citizens.[49]

With or without the 2016 vote to leave the European Union ("Brexit"), the United Kingdom has steadily laid the foundation for a national border, sometimes for political reasons having little to do with cyberspace, such as a national identity card to curb illegal immigration. The rise of serious intrusions into sensitive government networks—at least three hundred over the course of 2009, for example[50]—pushed the United Kingdom to construct agencies and units under its Cabinet and attached to its intelligence community[51] with the specific missions of coordinating and informing the tools, tactics, and targets of cybersecurity across all governmental agencies.[52]

Current trends suggest the United Kingdom will be closely behind the United States over time as the elements of a national border in cyberspace are erected, in large part because the United Kingdom, as a close partner of the United States, is both more of a target and more informed about its vulnerabilities than other EU nations. The United Kingdom's separate, more American path to increasing cybersecurity may be accelerated following the Brexit vote to leave the European Union in 2016.[53] The singular marker of an emerging border, however, is the creation of a military organization—a cyber command—to protect the nation from the kinds of harm that historically only a peer state or neighbor could inflict. When a state establishes such a military organization in a public acknowledgement, it is declaring that the nation has territory to defend in the global cyber substrate and that the cyber threat poses a potentially existential threat. Creating such an organization identifies a national space that national leaders value and will protect using public resources including regulatory, law enforcement, and military capabilities. That the new cyber borders may not yet be recognized by other nations does not diminish the significance of this institutional declaration of sovereignty. Indeed, the mutual recognition of sovereignty was a key outcome of the long Westphalian state-building process.

The United States has itself laid the cornerstone necessary for a national cyber border by establishing the U.S. Cyber Command (USCYBERCOM). Presidents from George H. W. Bush to Donald Trump have stated and restated their intention to defend against, repel, or prevent whatever "threats" could come across its cyber border military capabilities and resources.[54] The establishment of CYBERCOM is important symbol of the emerging cyber–Westphalian international system. The "cyber command" model primarily rests on the use of national security institutions for cyber defense at and beyond a border.

CYBER COMMAND: THE U.S. MODEL

In the fall of 2010, the U.S. Cyber Command became operational after a year of institutional and legal preparation.[55] This institutional response to the rise of the cybered conflict age emerged to anchor a future cybered border for the whole nation. CYBERCOM's initial mission was to protect only military organizations from cyber attack, but as soon as a military unit existed to create a cyber safety wrapper around U.S. critical military assets, political statements emerged about creating the same protection for the whole nation.[56]

From the revolution in military affairs (RMA) to net-centric warfare, the United States has a history of providing new models for national-level security organizations, especially military organizations.[57] For the United States to announce a new national cyber command automatically provokes a new debate in the international military and legal communities.[58] Whether or not other nations need, want, or can afford to have a singular military unit focused on cybered conflict, their leaders, doctrine writers, and strategic thinkers will contemplate whether they themselves need such a unit when the remaining superpower signals how critical it is for national security.

Patterns of military emulation occurring since World War II are now recurring, with nation after nation developing some form of military or national security unit that looks and acts like a national cyber command, whether or not it initially bears that name. Already we have seen nations closely associated with the United States either mirroring it in creating their own cyber command or declaring an interest in having a unit that approximates the functions of U.S. Cyber Command. South Korea, for example, now has a military cyber command after enduring a massive assault in early July 2009.[59] Germany, whose senior ministers long opposed creating a military unit specifically for cyber, established a cyber command in April 2017.[60] In recent strategy decisions, the United Kingdom, while focused on the cyber protection of the entire society, has begun closer integration of its military cyber resources with its intelligence cyber resources in joint units under its relatively new Joint Forces Command.[61]

The U.S. model of a national cyber command has several distinctive elements that are shaping the emergence of cyber borders. First, the unit chosen by national leaders as their initial foray into strategic national security in cyberspace was a military command. They did not rely on or adapt a civilianized and national internal security agency built for disasters or crime such as the already established U.S. Department of Homeland Security (DHS). With the weight of U.S. resources to dedicate to a strategy of purely defensive mitigation from cascading surprise attacks, policy makers chose a natural experiment that clearly reinforced the idea that simply waiting for the attacks to hit and then mitigating the effects inside the physical borders is likely to be devastatingly insufficient. Militaries operate at the edges of nations in the modern state or deployed forward to prevent attacks. Choosing a military to be primus inter pares in national cybersecurity also reinforces the seriousness of the existential threat, as these institutions are historically the last resort of national survival. Creating U.S. Cyber Command redirected much of the global conversation about cybersecurity from merely blunting attacks after they arrive to repelling or disrupting the attacks before they cumulate into great harm. If cybersecurity is a mission involving military-like actions repelling attackers, then borders will have to be determined to guide when and where these actions can occur.[62]

Second, while the mission of the U.S. Cyber Command is fundamentally to protect U.S. military cybered interactions, the structure of the new command is dual hatted—the commander of the U.S. Cyber Command is also the director of the Department of Defense's (DoD's) premier signals intelligence agency, its National Security Agency (NSA). This unique design is clearly intended to blend operations to benefit simultaneously from what was traditionally considered offensive and defensive cybered operations and the collection of global intelligence. In cybered conflict, the offensive advantages of the attacker lie in relatively easily attained preemptive surprise using the intrinsic difficulty of predicting cascades in globally large-scale complex systems. The result is that a good defense requires the ability to successfully operate offensively, knowledgeably, and rapidly to preempt the preemptive attack, or at least anticipate it with sufficient time to prepare and mitigate its effects.

The peace versus war distinction has very little meaning operationally in the current frontier-like nature of global cyberspace where penetration tests to measure defenses would be offensive hacking if performed by adversaries. The U.S. Cyber Command model directly acknowledges the loss of this strategically and internationally accepted distinction by this dual-hatting structure.[63] In that Hobbesian choice, the blend of intelligence collection and analysis function with the ability to act offensively occurs in the internal deliberations of one man commanding both agencies' authorities by national laws but able to act quickly and knowledgeably across agency lines if necessary without the lag effects of disputes among authorities and organizational turf.[64]

That the cyber command can attack, defend, and collect information globally is an innovation critically important not only for the United States but also for the wider international community struggling to adapt its longstanding view of conflict and peace as distinct. While the concept of a Cold War or an international crisis is routinely understood and used in characterizing disagreements, war is distinguished from peace to clearly politically and psychologically guide international institutional actions, negotiations, and strategic expectations. Unfortunately, cyberspace by its dual-use nature and ubiquity can be hot, cold, warm, or turbulent in different parts of the world simultaneously. The U.S. institutional innovation made it clear that security rests on acknowledging the emerging reality of cyberspace and its spectrum of "cybered conflict" ranging from peace through war. This unit is meant to unify capabilities to detect, deter, and combat would-be attackers across a wide range of attack surfaces and avenues leading inside networks whether the nation is at peace or in war.

Put differently, the U.S. model suggests, rightly or wrongly, that the best way forward is to build upon existing intelligence and military organizations to secure the nation's cyber borders with a combination of offense, defense, and extensive intelligence collection.[65] For the majority of European democracies that have a great deal of difficulty in publicly and politically endorsing offensive measures in cyberspace, cybersecurity institutional adaptations have been incremental, mired in lengthy debates on civil liberties and economic consequences. The rapid implementation of the cyber command model by the United States broke the allies' collective cognitive logjam. Now, whether senior leaders agree in principal with the solution, they are discussing new organizations and responses for repelling a threat capable of existential damage; not just burglary or theft, but massive undermining of the economic health of the state. The developments of the Confiker worm, widening ravages of international cybercrime, and lastly the unsettling discovery of Stuxnet and its success in a critical infrastructure have sparked a strong new interest in the U.S. model, at least as an alternative.

More countries are accepting the need to consolidate state institutions to protect citizens and businesses from an extraordinarily complex set of lightning fast, unpredictable, and massive cyber threats. It occurred to every successful medieval leader that one needs moats, walls, watch towers, and guards, but also one must have rapid-reaction horse- and/or ship-mounted units to keep the worst attackers far from the capital. A national unit blending all those age-old functions in cyberspace becomes a logical consideration.[66] Within a year of constructing two distinct units for cybersecurity—one at the cabinet level—the change of British government in 2010 resulted in a stronger link between these units and budget increases for cyber. Furthermore, the next government declared cyber threats to be a top-tier national security issue.[67] By the latest UK cybersecurity strategy, not only were these links endorsed, the new National Cyber Security Centre is now explicitly a unit of the Government Communications Headquarters (GCHQ) with a mission to directly aid private companies under cyber attack when requested.[68]

In late 2008, France published the first defense white paper since 1994; the new strategy added the concept of whole nation security and elevated cybersecurity to one of four key national missions. The cyber mission was to create a military organization capable of guiding the other agencies in protecting the entire nation's national cyberspace. In the process, a small, formerly secretive unit has become its central and publicly discussed Agency for National Information Security (ANSSI). Over the course of the first year of existence, the organization helped research and justify legislation to allow further central control of defensive and, if necessary, offensive national cyber means. The ANSSI has continued to grow steadily and become a central locus of cybersecurity expertise for the French Government.[69] Other nations, especially those with limited cyber resources such as the Baltic States, are pushing to designate NATO as guarantor of their national cybersecurity, especially if cybered means accompany physical assaults to undermine the nation's resilience.[70]

Third, by designating U.S. Cyber Command as joint command rather than one separate from the four military services, its organization carries within it the seeds of its future elevation in importance for the nation. Already the command has been elevated from a sub- to a unified command equal to STRATCOM, its former superior headquarters.[71] As concepts for repelling attacks aimed beyond military forces at the heart of the United States have begun to coalesce politically, critical practical decisions will be made about where the tripwires are to be virtually drawn and maintained. The model does not make a small military unit that simply supports other government actors. Rather, its size, prominence, and position atop subordinate military service-only cyber commands reinforce the universality of the task to the whole nation. All the services are involved, and all of them are required to contribute to a coordinated national response to a major event involving U.S. military elements. Only a few threats—such as nuclear war and terrorism—have forced such rapid, unequivocally collective and ubiquitous responses beyond traditional physical domains of land, air, sea, and space.[72]

In 2011, a memorandum of agreement between the U.S. DoD and the DHS (the lead agency for national cyber defense for government agencies and critical infrastructure) formally initiated a process for the DoD to aid the DHS in the event of cyber-related catastrophes. The memorandum clearly invoked the direction of the support from the cyber-savvy DoD (read NSA and U.S. Cyber Command) to the cyber-responsible but overwhelmed DHS.[73] In this, another step is taken toward a national notion of a cyber territory to be defended, a virtual space involving the whole of the society. The terms of crossing over from border and outward duties for the military to inward, more domestic missions as a function of an anticipated cas extremis underscore both the importance and the need to have identified the border itself to regulate these agreements.

The *2015 DoD Cyber Strategy* added nationally significant cyber-economic events to the missions for which the U.S. Cyber Command is to be ready respond in defense of the nation.[74] While acting on this mission depends on orders from the president, the expansion reflects the past half decade of experience in a range of cyber conflicts with adversaries that range widely over the entire nation's "socio-technical-economic system" (STES) in their attacks. Defending the nation in cyberspace increasingly involves a more comprehensive whole-of-society approach, and cyber commands are inevitably going to be drawn into responding to what and who causes harm inside the old territorial borders.

Fourth, the offensive mission of any cyber command working for a democracy underscores the need for other democracies to establish their own borders in cyberspace to demand reciprocal noninterference in practice as well as de jure. The U.S. Cyber Command model leaves unanswered the question of bad actors operating from within one democracy operating outward to harm other democracies. This lack of clarification of the precise operational rules of engagement and reach continues to remain unresolved in part because of ongoing debate over legal authorities.

Leaving the debate open to discussion with allies and other democracies has allowed for parsing out the actions of allies, especially in NATO. For example, NATO's Center of Excellence on Cybersecurity is in Tallinn, Estonia[75]; its annual cyber conference has become one of the premier gatherings of cybersecurity government experts among Westernized nations. Furthermore, its researchers originated the concept of, and the Center hosted, the production of two volumes on cybersecurity and international law, entitled *Tallinn Manual* and *Tallinn Manual 2.0*.[76] Both have become seminal references for international and governmental lawyers among the Western nations and close allies in determining acceptable actions in cybered conflict, at least for now.

Increased experience will channel the next range of evolutionary steps, but there is an unspoken presumption, especially among senior NATO partners, that Western democracies are united in wanting security for everyone's cybered systems. Nonetheless, while the United States does not view its cyber command as threatening allies, that benign assessment is not universally shared. Many parties on the left in many European states are routinely concerned, with good historical reasons, about the concentration of power in government hands. For example, Germany has long preferred the deliberate dispersal of organizational interaction in security or data collection given its own history. This institutional separation, of course, defeats the close collaboration for response speed as the central concept for an organization such as U.S. Cyber Command, the United Kingdom's centralized cyber security operations center (CSOC)—later reborn as the National Cyber Security Centre under GCHQ—or even the French ANSSI.[77] This fear, however historically justified and currently endorsed, is more likely to view the U.S. development of a virtual border with skepticism and some concern with the extent that a military cyber command is attached. They are likely to be more interested in a border in cyberspace for their own nation to have the ability, if necessary, to constrain U.S. government actions in cybered preemption if they are anticipated to harm European citizens.[78]

At the end of the day, both friends and enemies will have greater incentives to demarcate in boundaries and defend in institutions their own national slice of cyberspace.[79] This is especially true with the rise of a singularly large-scale adversary—China—whose leadership rejects the global civil society values, and whose government has moved aggressively onto the international stage successfully promoting cyber sovereignty for itself and a large set of similarly minded more autocratic nations.[80] These nations account for the bulk of the state-sponsored and proxied cyber attacks undermining largely with impunity the economic and political security of the democratic civil societies whose leaders still formally oppose defensive borders in cyberspace. Creating U.S. Cyber Command is only one early mark of the transformation, but it further accelerates the state-level interest in acquiring greater control of the uncertainties of the rapidly declining cyberspace frontier. This transformation is not only natural for the new cybered conflict age, it may be desirable for global society and may prove essential for the future well-being of the minority of states in the coming largely autocratic and post-Western world that are consolidated democratic civil societies.

RESUSCITATION OF INTERNATIONAL RELATIONS THEORY AND HISTORY

With the establishment of borders in cyberspace, much of what we know about deterrence, wars, conflict, international norms, and security will make sense again as practical and historical guides to state actions and deliberations. With juridical borders enforced by technological means, also essential will be the means to monitor who is electronically crossing the line in the virtual sand and whether that passage of bytes is permitted by national law, either criminal, civil, or national security. These means will have to be maintained and adapted to emerging new threats. These mechanisms will be a combination of encryption (quantum and otherwise), unique machine/user identifiers centrally controlled, and local hardware-human "bio"-metrics. No more would the near Herculean task of tracking bad cyber actors on a massive scale hinder a normal civil society's desire for a functioning mechanism to deter that source of harm. A border in cyberspace necessarily presumes some form of verifiable and current originating data for everything trying to pass into the nation, from bytes to malware to phishing or mass assaults. The nature of connectivity and emergence of other states means that bad data coming from someplace will necessarily come from some territory of some state with overarching responsibility for allowing such transmissions to continue. No longer can a state claim it is not harboring those attacking every. mil or.gov addresses in the United States while encouraging their internal development of "patriotic" hacking skills and a blind eye to those who hack outward only.[81]

In the bordered future world of digitized states, hot wars—those involving kinetic destruction at the end of the peace–war cybered conflict spectrum—will inherently involve cyber operations and instruments in all phases of conflict. States will use cyber weapons while deploying state and nonstate proxies for influence operations taking advantage of the attribution problems well known for identifying the sources of attacks. Already the Russia–Ukraine war may be viewed as the first major cyber war because the Russian forces roam freely across this peace-war cybered conflict spectrum—at will smoothly flowing back and forth into kinetic actions using geo-locations in Ukrainian soldiers' cell phones to locate and bomb them and then into cyber attacks on electrical plants, newspapers, and Ukrainian civil society in general.[82]

Cross-border attacks will be regarded as such, even if largely cybered in their characteristics. With mutual recognition of cyber borders across the interstate system, if the sponsoring state refuses to stop the attacks or to allow the defending state to reach inside its territory to stop them, then the sponsoring state can be presumed to support them. Conditions much like the onset of war can then be said to exist. Cybered wars will include all the characteristics of wars in previous centuries such as heightening political tensions, collateral damage, revenge myths, and arms races.

With the rise of a national interest in protecting their own cyber turf, international norms will be negotiated state by state, region by region, coalition by coalition, and international regime by international regime. If current trends hold, China is set to become the global and autocratic "cyber hegemon," and avoiding "cyber vassalage" will—as it did throughout history—require democratic states to form a balancing "cyber alliance" to demonstrate collective cyber power in defensive resilience.[83] Cyberspace is man-made, and its contractual basis—its peer-or-pay characteristics—can be negotiated and controlled across borders just like food production and safety, trade subsidies and streams, banking reserves and credibility, and even whaling. Life on, around, and through the virtual borders will be as turbulent, semi-stable, and prone to smugglers, free riders, would-be upstarts, and annoyances as the physical borders are now in harbors, airports, land crossings, and maritime lines of control. According to then-British prime minister Gordon Brown, "Just as in the 19th century we had to secure the seas for our national safety and prosperity, and in the 20th century we had to secure the air, in the 21st century we also have to secure our position in cyberspace to give people and businesses the confidence they need to operate safely there."[84]

Many concerns of key nations will continue as well. For example, Germany will continue to demand for national cultural reasons to close its cyberspace to neo-Nazis and to track down smuggled P2P Internet sites that encourage attacks on brown-skinned people, just as Saudi Arabia will close off pictures of women in positions of power and disable P2P porn sites and silence internal dissidents. The Chinese bureaucracy will refuse to agree to international constraints on its national right to execute addicted online game fanatics who commit crimes, jail those who smuggled pictures of the Dalai Lama, or prevent citizens from reading some international news source. Tunisia and Libya will simply not talk about their internal controls and use surveillance and blocking technologies at will. Status quo pro ante will adapt to the emerging topology across the globally connected sociotechnical world.

The United States has already declared cyber threats to be at the top ranks of national security concerns, created a new major military unit, and moved along a multitude of fronts to shore up its own national ability to forestall destructive cybered cascades operating from cybered means. But normalcy also requires recognition of the international community's role in reducing interstate cybered threat just as borders may rise to protect a state. If attackers are limited by borders in the number of states they can attack at once using cybered means in their operations, they are forced to forage for weaker national structures or concentrate their resources on their main objectives. More states will be unaffected by mass attacks and will be able to develop essential internal and collective regional resilience to surprise attacks that the sheer complexity of cyberspace inevitably allows.[85]

Finally, the United Nations as an international forum was set up to negotiate between states, not nongovernmental stakeholders whose roles, responsibilities, and territories are not clearly and mutually accepted.[86] In the best of all possible futures, the UN agencies and commissions could provide mechanisms for nations to quietly and practically cooperate even if they publicly are at odds. When cyberspace becomes a more normalized international system for modern states, we might see cyber ambassadors at UN agencies or cyber attachés at embassies to physically and rapidly calm crises or to coordinate responses if cyber systems are under assault.[87] If the coming post-Western era continues the rules of conflict resolution and acceptable cybered civil society engagement that have been in place since the end of World War II, then what are considered normal and acceptable state behaviors in, through, and enabled by the cyberspace substrate are more likely to be collectively, not individually, developed and enforced. When states are cybered entities with sovereign boundaries and some measure of "robust cyber power" including both resilience and disruption capacities at the scale needed, they will be better able to represent and defend themselves in the face of cybered conflicts. Even with the rise of a cyber hegemon, a democratic and autocratic sea of allied and nonallied nations may be able to work out a relatively less predatory and chaotic era of cybered states and enforceable rule regimes as the globe continues its relentless digitization.

CONCLUSION

Soon, states' actions will delineate the formerly ungoverned or chaotic cybersphere by practice that will eventually lead to formal agreements. In the new cyber–Westphalian process, digital regions complete with borders, boundaries, and frontiers that are accepted by all states will inevitably emerge. The rising virtual mirroring of what has been painfully carved out in the concrete world is not all that undesirable for societal stability, economic returns, and international security in a conflictual cybered era. Individuals, a wide variety of social organizations, and, certainly, most forms of commerce thrive on order and regularity. In the material world, we know how to handle cross-border wars and attacks in ways that we struggle to handle cross-border cyber attacks masked by the density of modern Internet traffic. In the cybersphere, borders will emerge internally within nations as well as externally as commercial and personal security bulwarks against free riders and thieves. Once cyber borders have emerged, police and national laws will hold sway as they do today in the modern nation-state. In much the same way as they are handled in the physical world, attacks across borders will become state responsibilities, whether or not another state approves or guides the attacks.

As the process of constructing cyber borders progresses, the implications of pulling cyberspace back into the known world of updated international relations will be profound. Today, a rough consensus is emerging that something about the frontier nature of the web must be regulated, either by individual states or by enforceable international regimes. But until the last few years and the dramatic success of the Stuxnet attack, the debate was as much about an international regime as it was about a nation-by-nation response. The international regime approach, however, is fraught with time and attribution difficulties. Not only can such a regime take decades to build, enforcing it as the web stands today will require the very thing current topology of the web does not offer—a way to verify the identity of (and therefore sanction) the violator. The result is, wittingly or unwittingly, individual states have started down the path on their own toward controlling the way the web affects their citizens, organizations, and critical elements of the society. The transition of these states, the interstate system, and the topology of international power, of course, still lies ahead.

NOTES

1. *Cybered conflict* lies along a spectrum from peace to war. For clarity purposes, *cyber war* lies at the end of the spectrum where conflict fully within networks or blended with more kinetic means produces destruction and death. The term *cybered* is deliberately an adjective indicating it involves multispectrum elements beyond the narrow technological means entirely within a network. It is normally a component of the former. A cybered conflict is any conflict of national significance in which key events determining the path to the generally accepted outcome of the conflict could not have proceeded unless cyber means were nonsubstitutable and critically involved. Early in the development of the global cyberspace substrate, networks were not so widely distributed and one could discuss a *cyber conflict* that was hand-to-hand combat entirely within networks with no outside effects save the operation of the network. However, it was quickly realized that this was a rather unusual form of struggle and almost all the conflict was cybered with a host of socio-technical-economic effects at stake. Hence, the terms are distinctively and deliberately used in this chapter.

2. Nicolas Falliere, Liam O. Murchu, and Eric Chien, "W32.Stuxnet Dossier: Version 1.3," (2010), http//www.symantec.com/content/en/us/enterprise/media/security_response/whitepapers/w32_stuxnet_dossier.pdf.

3. Susan W. Brenner, "Distributed Security: Moving Away from Reactive Law Enforcement," *International Journal of Communications Law & Policy* 9 (December 2004).

4. For example, as the critical infrastructure of Westernized nations such as the United States has relentlessly moved online for automated 24/7 services with less labor or greater precision, the loss of a central server for the infrastructure of even small communities was more likely to prove devastating. In early 2010, a thief stole the one single computer running the automated system providing clean water for the town of Molalla, OR. Had the thief wanted to harm the citizens, taking over the computer remotely to disrupt or destroy the water filtration system would have been exceptionally easy. Even the apparently mistaken theft could have been worse had the

thief simply used the machine in situ to ruin the filtration system or poison it. "Theft in Molalla [Oregon] Reported to Department of Homeland Security: Computer Controlled Town's Water System," *KPTV Fox News Oregon* (March 26, 2010), http://www.kptv.com/story/14783428/stolen-computer-controlled-towns-water-system-3-26-2010.

5. Choe Sang-Hun, Paul Mozure, Nicole Perloth, and David Sanger, "Focus Turns to North Korea Sleeper Cells as Possible Culprits in Cyberattack," *New York Times* (May 16, 2017).

6. Isaac Porche, "Stuxnet Is the World's Problem," *Bulletin of the Atomic Scientists* (December 9, 2010).

7. David E. Sanger, "Iran Fights Strong Virus Attacking Computers," *New York Times* (September 25, 2010).

8. For a detailed account of Olympic Games, the cyber operation underlying Stuxnet see David E. Sanger, *Confront and Conceal: Obama's Secret Wars and Surprising Use of American Power* (New York: Crown, 2012).

9. Georgios Dementis, John F. Sarkesain, Thimas C. Wingfield, Goncalo Nuno Baptista Sousa, and James Brett Michael, "Integrating Legal and Policy Factors in Cyberpreparedness," *Computer* 43, no. 4 (2010), pp. 90–92.

10. Threats are considered so serious that cybersecurity officials are now expected to have training in known hacker methods. Bill Gertz, "Inside the Ring: Hacker Training," *Washington Post* (March 4, 2010).

11. Nigel Kendall, "Global Cyber Attacks on the Rise: 75 Per Cent of Companies Have Suffered a Cyber Attack, at an Average Cost of $2 Million, Says Symantec Security Survey," *Times* (London), (February 22, 2010).

12. Bill Laberis, "20 Eye-Opening Cybercrime Statistics," *Security Intelligence* (November 14, 2016).

13. See IDG, "2016 Global State of the Information Security Survey," *IDG Enterprise* (October 20, 2016), https://www.idgenterprise.com/resource/research/2016-global-state-of-information-security-survey/. See also the work and presentations of Melissa Hathaway and her team's Cyber-Readiness Index 2.0 for the comparative research both finding and building on these numbers. http://www.potomacinstitute.org/academic-centers/cyber-readiness-index.

14. Gillian Wong, "Chinese Police Shut Down Hacker Training Business," *Washington Post* (February 8, 2010).

15. For further details about this process and conceptual explanation, see Chris Demchak and Peter Dombrowski, "Cyber Westphalia: Asserting State Prerogatives in Cyberspace," *Georgetown Journal of International Affairs* (2014).

16. On the importance of the global commons, see Scott Jasper, *Securing Freedom in the Global Commons* (Stanford, CA: Stanford University Press, 2010).

17. Given human history, it does not much matter what precisely initiates the conflict; rather, it is the dependence of one or both parties on a pass, waterway, or global underlying sociotechnical system that determines the targeting on those items. Nomads had no fixed address, but they certainly had a sense of their rights to seasonal food crops and were willing to fight to exclude other groups to assure their own survival. Robert L. O'Connell, *Of Arms and Men: A History of War, Weapons, and Aggression* (London: Oxford University Press, 1989). See also Charles Tilly, *Coercion, Capital, and European States, AD 990–1992* (Malden, MA: Blackwell, 1992).

18. Stephen Krasner, "Shared Sovereignty: New Institutions for Collapsed and Failing Status," *International Security* 29, no. 2 (Fall 2004).

19. Charles Tilly, "Cities and States in Europe, 1000–1800," *Theory and Society* 18, no. 5 (1989).

20. Rajesh Tandon and Ranjita Mohanty, *Does Civil Society Matter? Governance in Contemporary India* (New York: Sage, 2003).

21. Joseph S. Nye Jr., *Cyber Power* (Cambridge, MA: Belfer Center for Science and International Affairs, 2010), http://belfercenter.ksg.harvard.edu/files/cyber-power.pdf.

22. Duncan B. Douglass, "An Examination of the Fraud Liability Shift in Consumer Card-Based Payment Systems," *Economic Perspectives* 33, no. 1 (1st quarter, 2009), pp. 43–49.

23. Ross Anderson, Rainer Böhme, Richard Clayton, and Tyler Moore, "Security Economics and European Policy," in Eric Johnson, editor, *Managing Information Risk and the Economics of Security* (New York: Springer, 2009), http://weis2008.econinfosec.org/papers/MooreSecurity.pdf.

24. David F. Lindsay, "Liability of ISPs for End-User Copyright Infringements," *Telecommunications Journal of Australia* 60, no. 2 (2010).

25. Suman Bhattacharyya, "Cyberattacks against the US Government Up 1,300% since 2006," *The Fiscal Times* (June 22, 2016), http://www.thefiscaltimes.com/2016/06/22/Cyberattacks-Against-US-Government-1300-2006.

26. Elinor Mills, "Web Traffic Redirected to China in Mystery Mix-Up," *CNET* (March 25, 2010).

27. This effect, according to John Mallery, research scientist at MIT, is a national cybersecurity means of increasing the "work factor" of the bad actor. The key strategic goal of cyber defense is to raise the work factors for attackers and to lower them for defenders. Work factors are conceptualized along dimensions of computational complexity, cost, cognitive difficulty, risk and uncertainty, cultural factors, and information differentials. See John C. Mallery, "Towards a Strategy for Cyber Defense" (presentation at the US Naval War College, Newport, RI, September 17, 2010).

28. For more details on the implications of cyber weapons for the scale, proximity, and precision of attacks, see Peter Dombrowski and Chris Demchak, "Cyber War, Cybered-Conflict and the Maritime Domain," *Naval War College Review* 67, no. 2 (Spring 2014), especially, pp. 83–87.

29. Douglas M. Gibler, "Bordering on Peace: Democracy, Territorial Issues, and Conflict," *International Studies Quarterly* 51, no. 3 (September 2007).

30. Narushige Shiode, "Toward the Construction of Cyber Cities with the Application of Unique Characteristics of Cyberspace," *Online Planning Journal* (1997), http://www.casa.ucl.ac.uk/planning/articles21/urban.htm.

31. On this point of curbing outward attacks, a functioning government controls the means of violence within its nation and that would include the means of enabling one of its citizens to attack another nation without governmental approval.

32. Kathrin Hille, "How China Polices the Internet," *Financial Times* online (July 17, 2009), https://www.ft.com/content/e716cfc6-71a1-11de-a821-00144feabdc0?mhq5j=e3.

33. Joel F. Brenner, "Why Isn't Cyberspace More Secure?" *Communications of the ACM* 53, no. 11 (November 2010), p. 2.

34. Paul Cornish, Rex Hughes, and David Livingstone, *Cyberspace and the National Security of the United Kingdom* (London: Chatham House, 2009).

35. Martin C. Libicki, *Cyberdeterrence and Cyberwar* (Washington, DC: RAND, 2009).

36. Pam Benson, "Computer Virus Stuxnet a 'Game Changer,' DHS Official Tells Senate," *CNN* (November 17, 2010), http://edition.cnn.com/2010/TECH/web/11/17/stuxnet.virus/index.html.

37. Michael Wines, Sharon LaFraniere, and Jonathan Ansfield, "China's Censors Tackle and Trip over the Internet," *New York Times* (April 8, 2010).

38. Ching Cheong, "Fighting the Digital War with the Great Firewall," *Straits Times* (April 5, 2010).

39. Xing Li and Timothy M Shaw, "'Same Bed, Different Dreams' and 'Riding Tiger' Dilemmas: China's Rise and International Relations/Political Economy," *Journal of Chinese Political Science* 19, no. 1 (2014).

40. Laura DeNardis, *The Global War for Internet Governance* (New Haven, CT: Yale University Press, 2014).

41. The Internet Society declared June 8, 2011 World IPv6 (Internet Protocol version 6) Day. "Google, Facebook and Yahoo Partner for World IPv6 Day," *Softpedia. com* (January 12, 2011), http://news.softpedia.com/news/Google-Facebook-and-Yahoo-Partner-for-World-IPv6-Day-177852.shtml.

42. Ben Worthen, "Internet Strategy: China's Next Generation Internet," *CIO.com* (July 15, 2006), http://www.cio.com/article/22985/Internet_Strategy_China_s_Next_Generation_Internet_.

43. Rebecca MacKinnon, "Commentary: Are China's Demands for Internet 'Self-discipline' Spreading to the West?" *McClatchy Report* (January 18, 2010), http://www.mcclatchydc.com/2010/01/18/82469/commentary-are-chinas-demands.html.

44. "China Keeping Closer Eye on Phone Text Messages," *New York Times* (December 6, 2005).

45. Sharon LaFraniere, "China to Scan Text Messages to Spot 'Unhealthy Content'," *New York Times* (January 20, 2010).

46. Wines, LaFraniere, and Ansfield, "China's Censors Tackle and Trip over the Internet."

47. Staff, "Foreign Firms Fret as China Implements New Cybersecurity Law," *Bloomberg News* (May 24, 2017).

48. Lucian Constantin, "Attack Hits Swedish Signals Intelligence Agency's Website," *Softpedia News* (November 6, 2009).

49. Michael Evans and Giles Whittell, "Cyberwar Declared as China hunts for the West's Intelligence Secrets," *Times* (London) (March 8, 2010).

50. Anthony Lloyd, "Britain Applies Military Thinking to the Growing Spectre of Cyberwar," *Times* (London) (March 8, 2010).

51. The Rt Hon Matt Hancock, Minister for the Cabinet Office, "The New National Cyber Security Centre Will Be the Authoritative Voice on Information Security in the

UK," *Government Communications Headquarters Press Release* (London: Cabinet Office, March 18, 2016).

52. The Rt Hon. Philip Hammond, *National Cyber Security Strategy 2016 to 2021* (London: Cabinet Office, November 1, 2016).

53. Kristan Stoddart, "UK Cyber Security and Critical National Infrastructure Protection," *International Affairs* 92, no. 5 (September 2016).

54. For an accessible historical account see, Fred Kaplan, *Dark Territory: The Secret History of Cyber War* (New York: Simon & Schuster, 2016). ·

55. Lance Whitney, "U.S. Cyber Command Prepped to Launch," *CNET News— Security* (March 23, 2010).

56. William J. Lynn, "Defending a New Domain: The Pentagon's Cyberstrategy," *Foreign Affairs* 89, no. 5 (September/October 2010).

57. Emily Goldman and Leslie Eliason, *The Diffusion of Military Technology and Ideas* (Stanford, CA: Stanford University Press, 2003).

58. Scott J. Shackelford, "From Nuclear War to Net War: Analogizing Cyber Attacks in International Law," *Berkeley Journal of International Law* 25 (May/June 2009).

59. "South Korea to Set Up Cyber Command Against North Korea—Two Years Earlier Than Planned," *Channel News Asia* (July 9, 2009).

60. Staff, "German Army Launches New Cyber Command," *Deutsche Welle* (April 1, 2017), http://www.dw.com/en/german-army-launches-new-cyber-command/a-38246517.

61. Richard J. Aldrich, *GCHQ: The Uncensored Story of Britain's Most Secret Intelligence Agency* (London: HarperCollins, 2010).

62. Ellen Nakashima, "Pentagon's Cyber Command Seeks Authority to Expand Its Battlefield," *Washington Post* (November 6, 2010).

63. U.S. laws enable "authorities" to draw legislative lines between offense (a military "Title 10" authority), defense (of military, "Title 18"; or of the wider government, a DHS mission), and the collection of national intelligence (a "Title 50" mission given the National Security Agency as primus inter pares electronic collector among other intelligence agencies).

64. This structural compromise was unusual for the United States, and it was hotly debated in the Congress before the first commander, General Keith B. Alexander, was confirmed as head of both agencies. Winning the debate were the need for a very wide intelligence view, a high level of skills, and the military ability to move quickly, as well as the character and expertise of the new commander himself. Ellen Nakashima, "Gen. Keith Alexander Confirmed to Head Cyber-command," *Washington Post* (May 11, 2010).

65. The post–World War II stovepipe separation of intelligence from operations is what prompted the creation of the U.S. cyber command as a dual-hatted entity, as the speed of cyber in both required closer cooperation without turf distinctions. There is one nation making a different decision—at least for now. Israel announced plans in 2015 to create a cyber command to be operational in 2018. Recently, in January 2017 it abandoned those plans to keep the existing unit structures—unit 8200 with the military intelligence mission and affiliation, and

the IDF Computer Service Directorate with the protection and counterattack missions. See Judah Gross, "Army Beefs Up Cyber-Defense Unit as It Gives Up Idea of Unified Cyber Command," *The Times of Israel* (May 14, 2017). It is possible that the small size of Israel may allow for the same close working arrangements without, as is needed in larger states, a unit combination to reinforce authorities and cooperation.

66. Even the loss of laptops, treated casually just years before, now engenders enormous legislative concern and recriminations against agencies even indirectly responsible for the cybersecurity of the nation as a whole, such as the GCHQ intelligence agency. " 'Cavalier' GCHQ Online Spy Centre Loses 35 Laptops—Centre Also Struggling to Keep Up with National Cyber Threats," *Computerworld UK* (March 12, 2010), http://archive.is/20120729004038/www.computerworlduk.com/news/it-business/19344/cavalier-gchq-online-spy-centre-loses-35-laptops/.

67. Richard Norton-Taylor, "National Security Strategy Says UK Is Under Threat of Cyber Attack," *Guardian* (October 18, 2010), https://www.theguardian.com/politics/2010/oct/18/national-security-strategy-cyber-attacks.

68. Philip Hammond, *National Cyber Security Strategy 2016 to 2021* (London: Her Majesty's Government, November 1, 2016).

69. See the website http://www.ssi.gouv.fr/site_rubrique97.html, hosted by ANSSI, which rather openly discusses its successes in strengthening cyber defenses.

70. "EU and US Join NATO Cyber Security Pact," *Computerworld UK* (November 10, 2010), http://www.computerworlduk.com/security/eu-and-us-join-nato-cyber-security-pact-3249914/.

71. Scott Maucione, "CYBERCOM's New Buying Power Now Closer to Reality," *Federal News Radio* (January 23, 2017), https://federalnewsradio.com/acquisition/2017/01/cybercoms-new-buying-power-now-closer-reality/. See also Mark Pomerleau, "Congress Set to Elevate CYBERCOM to Unified Combatant Command," *C4ISRNET* (December 1, 2016), http://www.c4isrnet.com/articles/congress-authorizes-elevating-cybercom-to-unified-combatant-command.

72. In contrast to common usage, we do not consider "cyberspace" to constitute a separate domain of warfare. For detailed explanation of this position, see Dombrowski and Demchak, "Cyber War, Cybered-Conflict and the Maritime Domain," especially, p. 75.

73. Cheryl Pellerin, "DOD, DHS Join Forces to Promote Cybersecurity," *American Forces Press Service* (October 13, 2010), http://archive.defense.gov/news/newsarticle.aspx?id=61264.

74. United States Department of Defense, *Cyber Strategy* (Washington, DC: Department of Defense, April 2015), https://www.defense.gov/Portals/1/features/2015/0415_cyber-strategy/Final_2015_DoD_CYBER_STRATEGY_for_web.pdf.

75. For further information, see the website of NATO's Cooperative Cyber Defence Centre of Excellence, https://ccdcoe.org/.

76. Michael N. Schmitt, editor, *Tallinn Manual 2.0 on the International Law Applicable to Cyber Operations, 2nd Edition* (Cambridge, UK: Cambridge University Press, 2017), https://ccdcoe.org/tallinn-manual.html.

77. Private conversation with senior civilian cybersecurity police official in Germany, October 2010.

78. Even the Chinese government has felt the need to have a cyber command equivalent and publicly announced its creation of a cyber warfare unit as a defensive measure in response to the provocative actions of the U.S. government in creating a cyber command. Tania Branigan, "Chinese Army to Target Cyber War Threat," *The Guardian* (July 22, 2010), https://www.theguardian.com/world/2010/jul/22/chinese-army-cyber-war-department.

79. "European Union Considers Stronger Cybersecurity, Stricter Penalties for Hackers," *The New New Internet (TNNI)* (October 1, 2010), http://blog.executivebiz.com/2010/10/european-union-considers-stronger-cybersecurity-stricter-penalties-for-hackers/.

80. One argument is that the democracies' pious insistence on having no borders in cyberspace and arrogant refusal to honor the Chinese demand that theirs at least be left alone was in part the instigator of the vigorous Chinese campaign to capture and change the international debate about sovereignty in cyberspace. See Chris C. Demchak, "Uncivil and Post-Western Cyber Westphalia: Changing Interstate Power Relations of the Cybered Age," *Cyber Defense Review* 1, no. 1 (Spring 2016).

81. John Markoff, David E. Sanger, and Thom Shanker, "Cyberwar: In Digital Combat, U.S. Finds No Easy Deterrent," *New York Times* (January 26, 2010).

82. The Russian military doctrine calls this "hybrid" warfare in which no declaration of war is needed and certainly no law of armed conflict is observed since the Russian state denies its military is involved irrespective of evidence produced internationally. We argue this is the true nature of conflict for the future—this blending of cyber into conflict between systems with and without actual and destruction. See Stephen Shenkland, "Russian Android Malware Tracked Ukrainian Military: Report," *CNET* (December 22, 2016), https://www.cnet.com/news/russian-android-malware-tracked-ukrainian-military-report/. See also Thomas Ricks, "Ukrainian Elder Statesman: How Russian Hybrid War Is Changing the World Order," *Foreign Policy* (March 21, 2017), http://foreignpolicy.com/2017/03/21/ukrainian-elder-statesman-how-russian-hybrid-war-is-changing-the-world-order/.

83. More precisely, the suggestion is for the consolidated democratic civil societies—demographically approaching nine hundred million—to form an operationally coherent "Cyber Resilience Alliance" to counter the exceptionally powerful scale of China as the rising, central, coherent single actor in the globally interconnected system. For more details, see Chris C. Demchak, testimony and panel on "China's Information Controls, Global Media Influence, and Cyber Warfare Strategy," U.S.–China Economic and Security Review Committee Hearing, Washington, DC, May 4, 2017.

84. Tom Espiner, "UK Launches Dedicated Cybersecurity Agency," *ZDNet UK* (June 25, 2009), http://www.zdnet.com/article/uk-launches-dedicated-cybersecurity-agency/.

85. The process of moving to better internal resilience is elaborated in a forthcoming book. The work argues for and outlines a security resilience strategy

involving both disruption and resilience via cybered institutional capacities developed and adapted at the national level. Chris C. Demchak, *Wars of Disruption and Resilience: Cybered Conflict, Power, and National Security* (Athens: University of Georgia Press, 2011).

86. Jaikumar Vijayan, "After Google-China Dust-Up, Cyberwar Emerges as a Threat," *Computerworld* (April 7, 2010), http://www.computerworld.com/s/article/9174558/After_Google_China_dust_up_cyberwar_emerges_as_a_threat.

87. Mark Raymond and Gordon Smith, *Organized Chaos: Reimagining the Internet* (Montreal: McGill-Queen's Press-MQUP, 2016).

Chapter Five

Blown to Bits

China's War in Cyberspace, August–September 2025

Christopher Bronk

Strategic theorists frequently lament that military planners are very effective at preparing for the last war, not the next one.[1] Planners today must cope with what conflict may look like in a new domain: cyberspace, the virtual and physical components of the global information infrastructure, what we may think of as a pre-noösphere.[2] This chapter projects a scenario of what a mostly, but not entirely, cyber conflict in East and Southeast Asia might look like in roughly a decade. One must hope the world's powers have learned that large-scale conventional war is an unfruitful undertaking that will disrupt our globalized international system in a manner where all lose. Of course, many of Europe's leaders believed a century ago that the menace of large-scale conventional war largely had become history.[3]

While it is the author's deepest and most sincere hope that no military conflict will come between China, Japan, India, the United States, or any other states of the Western Pacific and Asia, the massive interest in cyber conflict among these countries leads many to ponder such a struggle. We have come to recognize the Internet as a geopolitical domain for diplomacy and a potential space for conflict. In Asia, as almost nowhere else on the planet, the question of Internet sovereignty[4] is grafted onto the international system of states conceived in the time of de Groot and expanded in the crucible of hot and cold conflict during the nineteenth and twentieth centuries.

A STRATEGIC LENS FOR EAST ASIA

So what of state-centric conflict involving the Internet waged in Asia? Chinese officials sometimes speak of "our Internet," defining it not as an international cyberspace distinct of the political forces of the pre-Internet world, but rather a national infrastructure for digital communication and information dissemination. Discussion of international security in East Asia certainly considers a rising China.[5] "China's rapid rise generates new uncertainty and confusion about its status and role on the world stage."[6]

Boasting economic growth figures far in excess of the United States, Japan, or South Korea in the past decade and beyond, China's ascendancy has met with mixed responses in the Japanese and Korean populace.[7] Increased militarization in the region is a natural concern for both Tokyo and Seoul.[8] With Russia's place in the Far East considerably diminished since the breakup of the Soviet Union, China has begun to assert itself in a space largely filled by the United States after the Cold War.

In the Western Pacific, the United States has, for a variety of reasons, largely engaged in bilateral security agreements, exemplified by those with Japan and South Korea. U.S. efforts to establish a broad multilateral collective defense body in Asia on the model of NATO largely collapsed with the dissolution of the Southeast Asia Treaty Organization (SEATO) in 1977. Japan and South Korea participate, along with other U.S. allies, in multinational military exercises and diplomatic activities, but the pair has never been tied together by formal security agreement.[9] Although Japan, South Korea, and the United States have cooperated closely on diplomacy regarding North Korea's nuclear program through the six party talks, security collaboration remains largely mediated by the United States.

In East Asia, perhaps more than anywhere else on the globe, states matter.[10] One important yardstick is defense expenditures. Where the members of the Atlantic alliance have made deep and lasting cuts in military spending, from the Straits of Malacca to the Sea of Japan, demand remains strong for sophisticated weaponry despite the attendant high price tag. Potential flashpoints in East Asia are deeply frightening. The durability of American hegemony in the region is not assured, and the national politics contained by that hegemony must be considered.[11]

Admittedly, the chance of war with China still appears remote. However, the presence of tension combined with the general disinterest in moving from posturing to outright conflict may create avenues for dispute not seen previously in the international system. Asia continues to be economically globalized to an extremely high degree, but it is also a locale where state security politics figure so prominently on the international agenda. Further, it is one of the world's most digitally connected regions, yet paradoxically one where connections are filtered by government to varying degrees. How Asia's states and peoples disagree with one another will be deeply impacted by the confluence of these realities.

ASIA'S CYBER (IN)SECURITY PROBLEM

Cyberspace, which the U.S. Department of Defense (DoD) lists as its "fifth domain" of operations (after land, sea, air, and space), is an emergent area for international dialog and potential conflict. With the cyber attacks against Estonia in 2007 and those that accompanied the use of military force in Georgia the following year, cyber operations have become more clearly connected with the scope of options available in interstate conflict. Other attacks, against targets in Iran, Saudi Arabia, Ukraine, and elsewhere, suggest that the cyber attack is of growing utility in the repertoire of international conflict. How states behave with regard to the Internet appears to matter more and more within international affairs.[12] Google's decision to direct allegations of penetrations of its computer networks by individuals in China, coupled with Secretary of State Hillary Clinton's address on Internet freedom, sent a powerful message from Silicon Valley and Washington regarding the ideals held by the United States on the governance of cyberspace. The increasingly sharp tone of communications across the Pacific on how the Internet is to be governed and policed speaks to a new soft-power politics of the digital domain that rests between government and the information and communications technology (ICT) sector.[13]

But the international politics of cyberspace in East Asia are not the sum of the two largest powers in the region. Internet conflict may be a new area of international behavior falling somewhere between diplomacy and military action. While we may not have full-blown cyber war without war,[14] the cyber tool may be useful to governments and transnational organizations alike in voicing opinion without great cost. It may be a release valve for dissipating pressure, as may have been the case in 2001 when South Korean hackers protested the publication of a Japanese history textbook, which allegedly glossed over Japanese atrocities of the World War II, by launching a denial-of-service attack against Japan's Ministry of Education website. There are other examples. Chinese and Taiwanese cyber activists engaged in similar tactics when cross-straits relations reached low points in the 1990s. Also, North Korea is alleged to have launched its own computer network attacks against South Korean and U.S. government agencies, once again knocking their websites offline with the denial-of-service tactic.

To date, the cyber attacks in East Asia have been relatively benign. Web pages are defaced, allegations of espionage are leveled, and generally a status quo of sorts is maintained. No incident of infrastructure hacking, the sort of cyber-kinetic attack as was made against Iran's nuclear program or Ukraine's power grid, has been reported in the region. The threat politics of the cyber domain, however, do not stand still. Around the region, military resources are increasingly directed at cyber operations.[15] China, deeply impressed by U.S. information dominance in the 1991 Gulf War, has produced a considerable literature of strategic studies for cyber operations[16] while developing a national firewall system that shields the country from a considerable portion of web content.[17] The United States, too, has made strategic moves in cyberspace and is in the process of building a DoD cyber command that will manage the efforts of thousands of civilian and military "cyber warriors." Safe are assumptions that the United States' key allies in the region, chiefly Japan and Korea, will begin to collaborate more deeply on the cybersecurity issue. Already the head of the U.S. Federal Communications Commission and Japan's minister of communications have indicated the need to share.[18] Indeed, a growing chorus on the international scene is considering the need for enhanced collaboration and cooperation on the detection of vulnerabilities and responses to cyber incidents. Nonetheless, there is a degree of uncertainty as to whether cybersecurity will be an international issue in which neorealist or neoliberal theories prevail in Asia and beyond.[19] Such uncertainty drives the scenario offered here.

CONSIDERING STATE CYBER CONFLICT— THE CHINA SCENARIO

This chapter presents a scenario of conflict[20] between the People's Republic of China (PRC) and the United States and some of its allies one decade hence. While the goal is not to get bogged down on the particulars of why such a conflict would come to pass, the real point of interest is in thinking about how cyber war might supplant more traditional conflict and how cyber dimensions may alter warfare. To borrow from Alexander Vacca,[21] the U.S. armed services hold different views in vying for leadership on the cyber mission. The U.S. Navy, he argues, sees cyberspace as a contested commons, not unlike the seas, while the air force clings to Douhet's notions of airpower,[22] in which opponents will pound each other's cyber infrastructure in a manner akin to strategic bombing.

Imagined here is a conflict where the *information war*, a term rightly seen as overly broad by Martin Libicki,[23] but refined to its cyber component, it is as radical a construct to conflict as airpower was in naval warfare in 1941–1942. For the purposes of the scenario, I posit a conflict where China stands as the aggressor, although it is not hard to see a possible future in which China might see certain U.S. moves as provocative and even threatening. Consider a possible future where the United States refuses to service its debt to the PRC based on allegations of economic manipulation or as sour grapes over the Finlandization of Taiwan. Ponder, too, a world of the next decade where the

U.S.–India relationship continues to deepen, and the two countries warming relations and pooled sea power in the Indian Ocean leave China concerned about its access to petroleum sources and other raw materials in the Persian Gulf and Africa. Also suspend a bit of disbelief and think about a reunited Korea without U.S. troops and a Japan increasingly driven to counterbalance China's rise with substantially increased investment in its military, particularly its navy called by another name.

Of course, conflicts go from cool to hot at flash points, so for the purposes of this one, let us suppose that China, now firmly asserting itself over Taiwan as a quasi-autonomous region, faces the problems of city regions such as Shanghai, Guangzhou, and Hong Kong wishing for greater autonomy. Its large male population—a product of the one-child policy favoring birth of sons to daughters—restive and perhaps not as gainfully employed if the decades-long economic boom cools, sends Beijing looking for outside threats. The city-state of Singapore comes into focus as China's new other,[24] a sovereign entity Beijing wishes to bring inside the fold as it has Hong Kong, Macau, and Taipei. In a mostly digital rather than kinetic conflict, how might the PRC isolate the country sitting astride perhaps the globe's most important maritime choke point?

So let us imagine a late summer of 2025 in which the PRC has chosen to employ military force, largely in the cyber domain, to shift Singapore into its sphere and exert its influence monolithically over the Straits of Malacca. This is not the decision of a blindly angry dragon but rather the pragmatic move of a state needing to assert itself against a declining hegemon (the United States), a rising power (India), and an old foe (Japan) in adjusting the balance of power in East Asia.[25] With that preface, let us think of a war fought to conclusion, with a broader spectrum of tools, both military and economic, and with cyber war at its heart. What follows is a scenario, a sort of fiction, designed to push the boundaries of what our international system may look like in a decade. We commence with a cyber war about to begin in a networking lab somewhere in Northern Virginia.

LAYING THE FIELD OF BATTLE: A CLUE
OF CYBER WAR TO COME

If there were any advanced warning to be had of Chinese intent, it was to be found in cyberspace. For months, intelligence analysts at the National Security Agency (NSA) and information technology (IT) managers throughout the U.S. government handled an abnormally heavy load of probing activity on its new-generation quantum networks and legacy communication systems alike. There were numerous attempts to compromise all possible avenues to the Americans' Secret and Top Secret resources. Automated botnets consistently attempted to enter the classified computer networks of the DoD, the agencies of the intelligence community, and the systems of the United States' closest allies, as had been the case for two decades. Potential competitors and erstwhile allies alike read one another's mail whenever they had the chance. But in the days running up to the war, that activity spiked enormously.

Particularly alarming was a report from the Defense Information Systems Agency (DISA) in June 2025 of a piece of unknown computer code several bytes long, located crossing a high-to-low diode from a DoD Secret-level computer network to an unclassified host computer tracked down at an Army depot in Pennsylvania. Such an event was not at all unusual. DISA forensic specialists responded to dozens of code quarantine events of unauthorized data packets attempting to pass from unclassified to classified systems every day. Although alarms on the high-to-low passageway would occur,[26] in virtually every case the issue was some sort of false positive. Typically, there would be a software or hardware configuration error to be blamed.

Chasing down the latest high-low incident, the DoD computer emergency response team's (CERT's) first-line investigators grew curious about what they had found. The small piece of data, only 256 bytes long, appeared at first glance to be senseless jumble, perhaps a broken packet piece, banging aimlessly around the network. In quarantine, it was so innocuous that the initial case manager, a mid-level civilian, had ticked the box, "Move to dismiss" on the event report and expected the same from his subalterns. A contractor at DISA holding all-but-dissertation status in applied mathematics from Rutgers was the final name on the electronic form. Before checking himself off, the ostensibly failed number theorist decided to remove the code piece from tight quarantine and drop it onto the DISA training network. What occurred next put more than a dozen of the NSA's top mathematicians on a bus over to the nondescript DISA facility in Falls Church.

While exact details will likely be deeply classified for decades to come, assorted leaks and the information security rumor mill provide some hints as to exactly what transpired with this particular piece of unknown code. Transferred onto the disconnected training network—one which attempted to accurately simulate the convergence points of classified segmented networks and those in connection to the Internet—the code piece was observed engaging in some very peculiar behavior, in particular regarding interaction with other data on the network. It was able to reorient other pieces of code from basic applications typically found on straightforward implementations of widely used operating systems running on a variety of devices. Even more interesting was that it resisted all attempts to copy or archive it.

Watched closely, it appeared to be an intelligent software-assembling machine able to construct applications on an ad hoc basis, apparently without any outside control. Fascinating as this was to the assembled experts, even more interesting would be its sudden disappearance from the training network. After being the subject of sustained study for days, it simply vanished, never to be seen again. Some walked away from the experience claiming it to be an aberration, but to a number of DISA, DHS, and NSA participants in the forensic exercise, this odd digital artifact would do much to explain events that would come to pass in the immediate aftermath of China's commencement of electronic hostilities against the allies.

LIFTING THE ELECTRONIC VEIL

For China, network warfare had been identified as a key area of strategic development for decades. Witnessing the stunningly lopsided defeat visited upon Iraq in the 1991 Gulf War, People's Liberation Army (PLA) strategic theorists were awestruck by the U.S. military's incredible use of IT to direct the conflict and bring overwhelming force to critical points on the battlefield again and again.[27] Even more, the Chinese were deeply concerned by rumors that the Americans had blinded and spoofed Iraq's high command and systematically dismantled the country's air defense system by penetrating the national information grid. That set of events, followed by the NATO operations against Serbia in the late 1990s in which American information power once again made its presence felt,[28] gave the Chinese good reason to develop their digital forces.

By 2025, the PLA had fielded an impressive digital operations command of more than sixty thousand troops. Each of its seven military regions had a computer warfare regiment of more than four thousand soldiers. In addition, a full cyber warfare division had been established outside Shanghai that was reputed to solely focus on U.S. government and military networks. But the greatest asset held by the PRC in this area was its Information and Communications Operations Institute (ICOI), set up on a research park campus in suburban Beijing. While the operational formations in the army handled day-to-day operations and adhered to centralized tactics and operational guidelines, the ICOI was from where the big ideas on information operations emerged.

Reporting directly to the Central Military Commission but with links to the Chinese Academy of Sciences, the ICOI had at least fifteen thousand staff members and was essentially the national hackers lab. Little was known about the institute until the defection of a high-level employee with a PhD in artificial intelligence who had studied abroad for several years before returning to the PRC. Walking into the Australian consulate in Tokyo in July 2020, ostensibly to renew his tourist visa, the graying software engineer passed a letter to a vice-consul that would begin his journey to Canberra and eventually the United States.

While the defector was not a high-level operative of China's cyber warfare center, as those individuals were likely prohibited from engaging in overseas travel, he was the first member of its staff to find his way to the offices of a foreign intelligence service. Thorough interrogation revealed his decision to leave his home country for good came on the heels of a divorce, largely precipitated by his own deeply closeted involvement with the Falun Gong movement. The Australians were only too happy to have the defector, whom they gave the pseudonym Wan Lu. After securing permanent asylum, Dr. Lu began to divulge voluminous information about his former employer. A theoretician steeped in formal logic who toiled in machine learning, Lu offered up the major areas of attention at the ICOI. He was able to pass along the institute's reading list, which in and of itself, was an important piece of intelligence. At the outbreak of the conflict, Lu was in Canberra, where he had been set up in a research fellowship at the Australian National University, only a few miles from the U.S. Embassy. There he stayed until the second day of the war. Certainly, the defector was of immense value to the allied cyber warfare research community pooling on the campuses of several research universities around the United States.

COMPUTER KRIEG

Many a pundit and strategic theorist had wondered what shape unrestrained information warfare might take. The opening hours of China's virtual war with the United States and its allies over Singapore would confirm many of the worst suspicions of that crowd. Chinese forces were quite clearly working inside the decision loop of the allied forces. Preliminary moves by the PLA in the information space indicated that it could do much damage to enemy communication and computing resources, but a series of hints would reveal that China also likely had compromised, at least to a degree, the encryption mechanisms used to secure U.S. and allied military and diplomatic communications. At times, Beijing most probably held the capacity to have a fairly complete information picture even of very high-level, classified systems, although the reverse was also likely true.

From the outset of the conflict, PLA cyber warfare efforts were disruptive activities, highly visible to allied political and military leaders. They preceded formal hostilities, which would be marked by the sinking of a Singaporean guided missile frigate in the South China Sea on September 5. The cyber attack had a rolling start, rather than being a bolt from the blue. When the PRC did finally choose to make use of kinetic options, the cyber war was already well underway.

For the American and Japanese leadership, in particular, there was enormous trouble in employing even rudimentary information technologies effectively during the first days of the war. Personal computers, radio networks, satellite receivers, control systems, and battlefield communication hardware failed, often making it impossible for allied commanders to share intelligence and conduct joint planning. Only a few dedicated, high-end, satellite-based communication channels were able to connect American field commanders in Japan and Hawaii with the Pentagon. But even these links were vulnerable, with the PLAAF's antisatellite missile attacks on September 6 producing enormous damage to U.S. telecom satellite coverage over the Pacific.

Although Guam was the sole location of an electromagnetic strike by the Chinese, and an effective one at that, the PRC was reluctant to repeatedly use strategic missiles to short out the information grid of its enemies in the same way for fear of provoking a nuclear response from the Americans. Rather than fry the allies' systems with electromagnetic pulse (EMP) weapons, the Chinese launched attacks via the global fiber network. Often the weapon of choice was sophisticated botnets, in which legions of zombie computers and mobile devices were employed to "gang up" on unclassified government and private systems and bring them to a screeching halt in crushing denial-of-service attacks. This was especially true on Singapore, where all forms of voice and data communication, save its little-used but still operable POTS—plain old telephone service—were disrupted. Government and private networks alike collapsed in hours under withering and complex attack.

Although the Americans, Japanese, and Singaporeans had highly secure classified systems, of greater operational value to their militaries on a day-to-day basis were the general-duty, unclassified networks employed for routing supply information, passing low-level internal communications, or simply informing lower formations of their duties and responsibilities. It was at this level that the PLA displayed mastery in the operational art of cyber warfare. Although unclassified, when aggregated, the information passing across these networks provided highly useful intelligence to the Chinese on U.S. dispositions and strategy. PLA intelligence could paint a very detailed picture of enemy movements from tracking information on cargo operations and reporting on demand for fuel and other basic supplies throughout the theater. With access to many corporate databases and networks as well, the PLA could use its information or disrupt its resources to sow chaos across the targeted countries.

Despite Google's noisy departure from (and quiet return to) China years before, many multinational corporations had unified information systems directly linked to subsidiaries in China. Those networks served as a backdoor into finance, energy, telecommunications, and defense firms alike. It took the NSA and Justice Department weeks to cut these linkages completely, largely through isolation of all fiber-optic cables to the Chinese mainland.

Attempts to mobilize conventional forces were hampered by denial-of-service attacks against systems thought impregnable to such attack. One episode at Iwakuni, the main U.S. Navy and Marine Corps air station in Japan, spoke to the PLA's enormous skill in knocking all manner of systems offline inside the allied militaries. Reporters from one news outlet documented it through their description of an incident on the first day of the shooting war. Hanging around with a maintenance team to research a piece on morale in the military, the American journalists scored an inside scoop on one of the biggest stories of the war. Their story painted a stark picture, which remained censored for weeks.

> Although no bombs fell on Iwakuni while we were there, the Chinese attack was felt nonetheless. [Lieutenant] Colonel Sutherland [chief operational officer for Marine Aircraft Group 12] had spent most of the morning receiving reports from the men and women who armed, fueled, and fixed the fighter aircraft on the base that their diagnostic equipment, RFID readers, and other digital tools simply were not working. The system that monitored logistics across the base had failed. Several tanker trucks had to be gotten out of mothballs just to get jet fuel flowing. The devices that transferred flight plans from the planning office to the aircraft themselves all failed. Across the base, things that typically functioned for years without a hitch suddenly broke down.
>
> "Everybody's coming to me with a problem that I've never seen in my 18 years with the Corps," Sutherland was overheard to say at one point. "Nothing's working!" The frustration on the base was enormous. While Iwakuni's Marines and Sailors struggled to get their jets airworthy, reports filtered in, largely via radio, of the attack on the carrier Carl Vinson in the Straits of Malacca. Fearful of air raids on Japan, the pilots and mechanics put in a tremendous effort to get their planes in the sky, but that would not happen until late in the afternoon. With the loss of electronic tools, clearing each fighter for takeoff became a drawn-out manual process in which nothing seemed trustworthy at first glance.

In Washington, the president and National Security Council (NSC) were astounded at the enormous gaps in connectivity with U.S. forces around the globe as well as the number of failed links with traditional allies in NATO and elsewhere. The vaunted White House Communications Agency, always able to connect the president with anyone, anywhere, anytime, had enormous difficulty in placing a simple phone call to the Japanese prime minister. The connectivity crisis threw into disarray contingency plans requiring key leaders to evacuate Washington and take up positions outside the city. With communications in disarray, no one on the NSC was willing to pack up and head to Mount Weather or some other bunker dozens or hundreds of miles away. Plans for continuity of government, involving mass movements of the federal bureaucracy and leadership, were largely put on hold with only the president pro tempore actually leaving town before dawn on the second day of the shooting war.

One line known to be functioning was the DoD hotline to Ministry of National Defense headquarters in Beijing. Several attempts to complete a call were made during the opening hours of conflict. Although nobody on the NSC knew exactly what they would say to the Chinese if they decided to pick up, there was a great sense of urgency that any and all attempts should be made in getting a dialog underway. Still in stunned disbelief, American political and military leaders desperately wanted to ask their Chinese counterparts, "What the hell are you doing?"

False information was also being injected into the allies' information systems. The breakdown of Pacific Command's (PACOM) logistical system underscored the level of confusion produced by the PLA's ability to place errant data at the time and place of its choosing. Supplies failed to show up where requested. The problem went beyond the military itself. Both Federal Express and UPS were forced to shut down operations for more than a week as their information systems piled up packages almost everywhere except where they belonged.

For defense planners at the Pentagon, it was hard enough to know what U.S. forces were doing, let alone the enemy. There was good reason to believe that misinformation, mostly in the form of e-mail, was traversing allied networks. Ships at sea in the Pacific encountered all manner of navigation and datalink issues, a problem later found to involve a Trojan horse delivered to ships transiting the port at Changi, Singapore, when they hooked up to the base fiber network to perform the high-bandwidth data upload/download that was for all practical purposes impossible to do at sea via low-bandwidth satellite systems. Several warships at Pearl Harbor were found to have severe data corruption issues thanks to this Trojan, often dramatically impacting the function of their command and control systems. The carrier *Stennis*, outfitting for departure from Everett, Washington, was severely affected, but navy officials decided to beef up her IT complement and attempt to make fixes while under way.

On Hawaii, PACOM's headquarters at Fort Shafter quickly found itself overwhelmed with data security issues. When PACOM was able to submit its initial want list to the secretary of defense and joint chiefs, it requested numbers of IT security and forensic staff outnumbering by several times the actual number on the government payroll. Heavily dependent on war rooms filled with standard commercial off-the-shelf desktop and laptop computers, staff work ground largely to a halt. No exercise at the war college could prepare the majors, commanders, captains, and colonels for the wholesale disruption of their tools. Disconnected from the DoD's global information grid, nearly all of PACOM's IT was, for several days, so much junk.

U.S. RESPONSE

While disruptions to the American network infrastructure were visibly apparent throughout the early days of the conflict, solid estimates regarding the amount of information tapped by the PLA's network penetration activities remain hard to find. The NSA, DHS, DISA, CIA, State, the Department of Justice, and a host of other bureaus and offices pulled together every asset they had to revalidate the trustworthiness of each and every critical national security network in a manner fitting postdisaster hospital triage. There were simply not enough people to be thrown at the problem of auditing systems and taking the comprehensive measures needed to secure them for operation under the conditions of high-intensity information warfare.

Initial reports to the NSC in the opening days were bleak, with many in the cyber-intelligence and security divisions unable to see much light at the end of the tunnel. Commitment of large numbers of staff from industry and the alumni of government-sponsored information security education programs brought additional talent to the problem, but in cyberspace the PRC was dominating the struggle. Time and again, systems thought to be clean and ready for operation would begin exhibiting suspect behavior assumed to have been remedied. This need to revisit systems again and again drained resources and tapped expertise at a frightening pace. Many an administrator or software code auditor would spend weeks at their posts, working to answer why for every backdoor or siphon found, another would simply pop up somewhere else or reappear exactly where it had been removed before.

With the application of top theoretical talent from several American universities, responses began to emerge to the attack. Under the leadership of CalTech computer scientist Jules Adams, an outside working group took a broad view of the massive effort underway and began putting together ideas on the newly discovered attack techniques and patterns. For the country's brightest minds in computing, math, and a host of related fields, the challenge was to begin deciphering exactly how the PLA was employing tiny pieces of code, as located by the DISA investigators in June, so effectively. How could strings of text barely long enough to fill two lines on a piece of paper be so effective in serving as the catalyst for disrupting networks and passing data to proxy computers accessible to the Chinese?

The answer would come from a pair of digital imaging experts at the University of Rochester. Investigators had been stymied by confining their thinking on size of the malicious code at work. They were puzzled by the capacity of this data, dubbed nanocode, to seamlessly move from system to system, building and destroying at will, morphing, disappearing, and reappearing without rhyme or reason. Early speculation had hit on some good points, including that the code was interacting in some way with the core structures of the systems upon which it resided. But this did not explain the capacity for the malicious code sections to operate so uniquely. The New Yorkers hit on the answer when they began playing with power.

An electrical engineer by training, Prof. Goran Filipowicz first raised the question of whether the nanocode was receiving instructions facilitated by constants at the physical level. His collaborator, Tony Ikeda, a researcher on high-efficiency, low-energy imaging, had worked for years on systems that harnessed high-speed processing to construct low-bandwidth camera technology systems. He built cameras that had few pixels but took many, many pictures to create a single still image very quickly. Ikeda postulated that the nanocode was conducting this sort of framing to actually function as if it were many times larger and, even more interestingly, pass tiny amounts of data hidden in the noise of the electrical interactions on each microprocessor.

They believed the PLA had created the capacity to employ "sub-bits," pieces of noise residing in noise but able to independently communicate simple instructions and sequences. China's cyber attack, rather than an organic cellular process, was more akin to one employing subpieces of DNA. Bioinformaticians from the University of Washington in Seattle and the University of Toronto were the next to run with Ikeda and Filipowicz's work. Operating out of a hastily constructed super lab on the campus of Carnegie Mellon University staffed with hundreds of researchers and managed by the RAND Corporation out of its Pittsburgh office, the bioinformatics team began producing evidence that the nanocode under study was obviously receiving instructions from intelligent outside sources—human beings—but also taking leads from a broad set of environmental phenomena particular to the signatures, settings, and architecture of each affected network. While the engineering behind the PLA's network operations was no doubt brilliant, leaders at the Pentagon were not interested in discussions on theoretical topics. They wanted results, especially the person at the top of the list, air force general Marybeth Kline, head of U.S. Cyber Command.

Under immense pressure to get results out of the nation's computing brain trust, General Kline, a PhD in linguistics, had decamped from her headquarters at Fort Meade, which had long served as home to the NSA. Working closely with CalTech's Adams, Kline chose to spend much of her time managing the researchers, although with frequent trips back to the NSA operations center at Fort Meade. While those visits were typically immensely depressing, they kept the four star focused and on task. She would return to the revitalized rustbelt city with a new sense of urgency that was palpable to the academics, military staffers, and contractors alike. Several days after arriving and taking over the offices of the president of the University of Pittsburgh, a portrait of Lt. Gen. Leslie Groves, legendary director of the Pentagon construction and the Manhattan Project, appeared on the wall over her desk. Results were needed, soon.

Progress was made, but it would be weeks before the assembled group would make important discoveries in wireless device cross-pollution and deep sleeper malicious code segments, which would turn the tide in the defensive battle for control of America's cyber infrastructure. During that period, many lives would be lost due to technologies failing to function as they were intended throughout the theater of operations and beyond. Although widespread attacks on the U.S. national critical infrastructure were few—including an incident where most of the electronic medical records of the Veterans Administration simply became irrecoverably corrupted—the PLA did not shut out the lights from Tacoma to Tampa. (The electrical grid on Singapore was crashed on the first day of attacks and stayed that way until after cessation of hostilities.)

Kline's leadership was of enormous value in overseeing the push to put systems right, but her focus on defense had not come without price. Cyber Command's attention on the defensive effort had translated to minimal activity in going after China's network infrastructure. While the air force's 67th Network Warfare Wing at Lackland AFB would lead the charge against the Chinese information infrastructure, it began by running stale, one-dimensional options from its playbook. Employing predictable tactics and devoid of high-level strategic input, Cyber Command's main offensive formation was also quick to reach out into academia and the private sector, commissioning every computer science graduate student in the state of Texas of U.S. citizenship (and some not) into the National Guard by order of the governor.

Enlisting the hacker community was a job largely handled by the FBI. NSA analysts drew up a short list of freelancers, misfits, and virtuosos and passed it off to the Justice Department within days of the outbreak of hostilities. Intimidating federal agents showing up at doorsteps across the country further bolstered the ranks of the U.S. cyber forces. Of course with the hackers, the choice was often depicted as either service or jail time. Few failed to cooperate, and although no one was actually indicted through this unusual recruiting process, stories did make the rounds of mock detention preceding a first stab at what would eventually lead to above-board, gainful employment as freelancers. Although it would take more than a month to actually string together a formal organization of this rabble, the most brilliant among this category of new public servants had an impact on the war in cyberspace almost immediately. War did not end, but rather was mitigated.

CYBER WAR'S ROLE IN THE TRANS-ASIA WAR

China's initial foray into cyber war was not at all what many experts in the field had prognosticated for years. No electronic Pearl Harbor or Waterloo had occurred, and other than a few flickers here and there, the U.S. power grid held up surprisingly well. It appears the Chinese Central Military Commission had made a calculated decision to leave much of the infrastructure up and running in the nations it had decided to wage war upon, although there is a strong counterargument that the PRC's cyber forces were largely checked in knocking out infrastructure by more than twenty years of concerted effort in building more secure systems. Whatever the case, China's electronic forces were able to massively disrupt vital communications around the world during the opening days of the conflict. What is more, they were able to exert a persistent influence in this arena, continuing to bring down systems thought to have received a clean bill of health.

Harder to ascertain was the capacity of the PRC to draw information from the networks of the allies throughout the duration of the war. Losing trust in much of the digital infrastructure at their command, American and allied commanders often preferred to arrive at decisions by conference. Authority for decision making largely devolved to commanders in the field, many of whom believed that was how it was supposed to be anyway. Despite a long-standing dependence on IT in the execution of global command and control, U.S. admirals and generals quickly fell back upon the initiative of their subordinates and the relationships they had developed in decades of training with foreign counterparts. Thanks to Beijing's great skill in busting and breaking into allied computer networks, there was no way for White House planners to burn the midnight oil around broad tables, sifting through intelligence and selecting targets. In the end, that was probably a net plus for the allies.

The conflict of 2025 ended with puzzling results. After inflicting considerable damage upon one another, the protagonists simply ramped back from intensive cyber operations to station keeping. Singapore retained its independence, and a naval standoff between U.S. and Chinese carrier forces never met with conclusive end. Submarines were sunk and cruise missiles dispatched, but no bombs fell on Honolulu or Hong Kong. General war was avoided, principally thanks to a high degree of risk aversion on both sides. After approximately fifty-five days, the Sino-Asian conflict ended without treaty, agreement, or even much in the way of international communication.

REFLECTION ON A CONFLICT THAT WASN'T

Although scenarios are generated, mostly by Hollywood, of a cybergeddon in which machines run amok and shadowy hackers turn society on itself, the reality is that exploitation of technological information systems, whether telegraphic taps and intercepts or radio jamming, has been a part of conflict since being incorporated into warfare. Two centuries ago, Napoleon Bonaparte opined, "The battlefield is a scene of constant chaos. The winner will be the one who controls that chaos, both his own and the enemies'." The cyber dimension, which renders all but firsthand sight to be converted into ones and zeros, will no doubt advantage those able to master it and disadvantage those who fail to do so.

For more than a decade, China's military theoreticians have pondered the role of information technology on warfare.[29] Doubtless, China's military officers see IT as a great leveler and force multiplier, as have Americans who spent the past decade celebrating an IT-infused revolution in military affairs.[30] In the future, whenever two relatively well-equipped and trained nation-states face off in armed conflict, the cyber dimension will no doubt be important. This chapter ties together some anecdotes of a war unfought by the two most powerful nations on Earth. Such epic struggles are fortunately rare in human history, but one must wonder how the Davids of our day will employ cyber weapons to bring down their Goliaths.

The major question of the scenario outlined here is, "Can a forceful political objective be achieved by cyber arms alone?" Did cyber attack bring Iran to the negotiating table on a nuclear agreement?[31] To what degree malware can substitute for missiles will be decided by national governments and transnational groups in the coming years. It is clear terror organizations tend to favor real crash and bang with the attendant casualties over virtual means of inflicting damage. However, countries with much to lose by initiating kinetic actions and likely to be punished with sanctions and censure might choose the digital weapon more frequently.

In the aftermath of the Stuxnet attack on Iran, countries concerned with cyber vulnerability should prepare for the rapid mobilization of digital infrastructure remedy and repair resources. In a major cyber event, the problem set will likely be large, and the quantity of qualified talent and time available will be grossly insufficient. Steps can and should be taken in the United States to consider how to ramp up capacity for pulling together academia, industry, and government resources to meet a major contingency. Civil defense in the cyber domain must be considered a necessity.

We have not yet seen how the digital information dimension will impact conflict. While a decade ago we hoped to lift the fog of war with Internet computing, it now seems likely that new space has been created for contested perception. The digital tools for command and control have been met by countermeasure and so on. Most likely, cyber conflict will be an "always on" engagement, even if international policy is enacted to forbid it. Sweating and bleeding will blur in this realm of conflict, as it may reside across a span of intensities from low to high. The only certainty in cyber conflict is that conflict there will not unfold in the ways we may expect.

NOTES

1. John Aquilla and David Ronfeldt, *In Athena's Camp: Preparing for Conflict in the Information Age* (Santa Monica, CA: RAND, 1997).

2. Pierre Teilhard de Chardin, *The Phenomenon of Man* (New York: Harper Perennial, 1955/2002).

3. Michael Bordo, Alan Taylor, and Jeffrey Williamson, editors, *Globalization in Historical Perspective* (Chicago, IL: University of Chicago Press, 2003).

4. Timothy S. Wu, "Cyberspace Sovereignty? The Internet and the International System," *Harvard Journal of Law and Technology* 10, no. 3 (Summer 1997).

5. Christopher Coker, *The Improbable War: China, the United States and the Continuing Logic of Great Power Conflict* (Oxford: Oxford University Press, 2015); Jin Kai, *Rising China in a Changing World: Power Transitions and Global Leadership* (New York: Springer, 2016); and Graham T. Allison, *Destined for War: Can America and China Escape Thucydides's Trap?* (Boston, MA: Houghton Mifflin Harcourt, 2017).

6. Xiaoyu Pu, "Controversial Identity of a Rising China," *The Chinese Journal of International Politics* 10, no. 2 (2017).

7. "Strategic Jousting between China and America: Testing the Waters," *The Economist* (July 29, 2010).

8. Thomas J. Christensen, "Chinese Realpolitik: Reading Beijing's World View," *Foreign Affairs* 75, no. 5 (September/October 1996); Lee Chung-Min, "China's Rise, Asia's Dilemma," *The National Interest* 81 (Fall 2005).

9. Victor D. Cha, *Alignment despite Antagonism: The United States-Korea-Japan Security Triangle* (Stanford, CA: Stanford University Press, 1999).

10. Gilbert Rozman, *Northeast Asia's Stunted Regionalism: Bilateral Distrust in the Shadow of Globalization* (Cambridge, UK: Cambridge University Press, 2004).

11. Duncan Snidal, "The Limits of Hegemonic Stability Theory," *International Organization* 39, no. 4 (Autumn 1985).

12. Mary McEvoy Manjikian, "From Global Village to Virtual Battlespace: The Colonizing of the Internet and the Extension of Realpolitik," *International Studies Quarterly* 54, no. 2 (June 2010).

13. Cameron Ortis and Paul Evans, "The Internet and Asia-Pacific Security: Old Conflicts and New Behaviour," *Pacific Review* 16, no. 4 (2003).

14. Bruce Schneier, "Remarks," First Worldwide Cybersecurity Summit, Dallas, TX (May 4, 2010).

15. Myriam Dunn Cavelty, *Cyber-Security and Threat Politics: US Efforts to Secure the Information Age* (New York: Routledge, 2008).

16. Chris C. Demchak, "Key Trends across a Maturing Cyberspace affecting US and China Future Influences in a Rising deeply Cybered, Conflictual, and Post-Western World," Testimony before Hearing on China's Information Controls, Global Media Influence, and Cyber Warfare Strategy, U.S.–China Economic and Security Review Commission, Washington, DC (May 4, 2017), https://www.uscc.gov/sites/default/files/Chris%20Demchak%20May%204th%202017%20USCC%20testimony.pdf; and Yuezhi Zhao, "China and Cybersecurity: Espionage, Strategy, and Politics in the Digital Domain. Edited by Jon R. Lindsay, Tai Ming Cheung, and Derek S. Reveron," *Pacific Affairs* 89, no. 4 (2016).

17. Jinying Li, "China: The Techno-Politics of the Wall," in Ramon Lobato and James Meese, editors, *Geoblocking and Global Video Culture* (Amsterdam: Institute of Network Cultures, 2016).

18. Kristi Govella, "Cyber Security: A New Frontier for the U.S.–Japan Alliance," Berkeley APEC Study Center (May 12, 2010), http://bascresearch.blogspot.com/2010/05/cyber-security-new-frontier-for-us.html.

19. Ronald Diebert and Rafal Rohozinski, "Risking Security: Policies and Paradoxes of Cyberspace Security," *International Political Sociology* 4, no. 1 (March 2010).

20. Iver Neumann and Erik Overland, "International Relations and Policy Planning: The Method of Perspectivist Scenario Building," *International Studies Perspectives* 5, no. 3 (2004).

21. W. Alexander Vacca, "Cultural Constraints on Cyber Warfare: The Ongoing United States Air Force Experience," 51st Conference of the International Studies Association, New Orleans, LA (February 17–20, 2010).

22. Giulio Douhet, *Command of the Air* (Washington, DC: Office of Air Force History, US Government Printing Office, 1983).

23. Martin Libicki, *Conquest in Cyberspace* (Cambridge, UK: Cambridge University Press, 2007).

24. Iver B. Neumann, "Self and Other in International Relations," *European Journal of International Relations* 2, no. 2 (June 1996).

25. William R. Thompson, *On Global War* (Columbia: University of South Carolina Press, 1988).

26. This essay assumes that air gapping of classified and unclassified networks largely continues, but with the possibility for some bridging between them.

27. Wang Pufeng, "The Challenge of Information Warfare," *China Military Science* (Spring 1995).

28. Julian Borger, "Pentagon Kept the Lid on Cyberwar in Kosovo," *The Guardian* (November 9, 1999).

29. Toshi Yoshihara, *Chinese Information Warfare: A Phantom Menace or Emerging Threat?* (Carlisle, PA: Strategic Studies Institute, 2001).

30. See Pufeng, "Challenge of Information Warfare."

31. Sue Halpern, "US Cyber Weapons: Our 'Demon Pinball,'" *The New York Review of Books* (September 29, 2016).

Chapter Six

Nuclear Lessons for Cybersecurity?

Joseph S. Nye Jr.

Identifying "revolutions in military affairs" is arbitrary, but some inflection points in technological change are larger than others: for example, the gunpowder revolution in early modern Europe, the industrial revolution of the nineteenth century, the second industrial revolution of the early twentieth century, and the nuclear revolution in the middle of the last century.[1] In this century, we can add the information revolution that has produced today's extremely rapid growth of cyberspace. Earlier revolutions in information technology, such as Gutenberg's printing press, also had profound political effects, but the current revolution can be traced to Moore's law and the thousand-fold decrease in the costs of computing power that occurred in the last quarter of the twentieth century.

Political leaders and analysts are only beginning to come to terms with this transformative technology. Until now, the issue of cybersecurity has largely been the domain of computer experts and specialists. When the Internet was created forty years ago, this small community was like a virtual village of people who knew each other, and they designed an open system with little attention to security. While the Internet is not new, the commercial web is less than two decades old, and it has exploded from a few million users in the early 1990s to some two billion users today. This burgeoning interdependence has created great opportunities and great vulnerabilities, which strategists do not yet fully comprehend. As Gen Michael Hayden, former director of the CIA says, "Rarely has something been so important and so talked about with less clarity and less apparent understanding [than cyber security]. ... I have sat in *very* small group meetings in Washington ... unable (along with my colleagues) to decide on a course of action because we lacked a clear picture of the long-term legal and policy implications of *any* decision we might make."[2]

Governments learn slowly from knowledge, study, and experience, and learning occurs internationally when new knowledge gradually redefines the content of national interests and leads to new policies.[3] For example, the United States and the Soviet Union took decades to learn how to adapt and respond to the prior revolution in military affairs—nuclear technology after 1945. As we try to make sense of our halting responses to the current cyber revolution, are there any lessons we can learn from our responses to the prior technological transformation? In comparison to the nuclear revolution in military affairs, strategic studies of the cyber domain are chronologically equivalent to 1960 but conceptually more equivalent to 1950. Analysts are still not clear about the lessons of offense, defense, deterrence, escalation, norms, arms control, or how they fit together into a national strategy. After a short overview of the problem of cybersecurity in the next section, I will suggest several general lessons and then discuss a number of international lessons that can be learned from the nuclear experience. While the two technologies are vastly different, as I will argue below, there are nonetheless useful comparisons one can make of the ways in which governments learn to respond to technological revolutions.

CYBERSPACE IN PERSPECTIVE

Cyber is a prefix standing for computer and electromagnetic spectrum–related activities. The cyber domain includes the Internet of networked computers but also intranets, cellular technologies, fiber-optic cables, and space-based communications. Cyberspace has a physical infrastructure layer that follows the economic laws of rival resources and the political laws of sovereign jurisdiction and control. This aspect of the Internet is not a traditional "commons." It also has a virtual or informational layer with increasing economic returns to scale and political practices that make jurisdictional control difficult. Attacks from the informational realm, where costs are low, can be launched against the physical domain, where resources are scarce and expensive. Conversely, control of the physical layer can have both territorial and extraterritorial effects on the informational layer. Cyber power can produce preferred outcomes *within* cyberspace or in other domains *outside* cyberspace. By analogy, sea power refers to the use of resources in the oceans domain to win naval battles on the oceans, but it also includes the ability to use the oceans to influence battles, commerce, and opinions on land. Likewise, the same analogy can be applied to airpower.

  The cyber domain is a complex man-made environment. Unlike atoms, human adversaries are purposeful and intelligent. Mountains and oceans are hard to move, but portions of cyberspace can be turned on and off by throwing a switch. It is cheaper and quicker to move electrons across the globe than to move large ships long distances through the friction of salt water. The costs of developing multiple carrier task forces and submarine fleets create enormous barriers to entry and make it possible to speak of American naval dominance. In contrast, the barriers to entry in the cyber domain are so low that nonstate actors and small states can play significant roles at low cost.

The Future of Power describes diffusion of power away from governments as one of the great power shifts of this century.[4] Cyberspace is a perfect example of this broader trend. The largest powers are unlikely to be able to dominate this domain as much as they have others like sea, air, or space. While they have greater resources, they also have greater vulnerabilities, and at this stage in the development of the technology, offense dominates defense in cyberspace. The United States, Russia, Britain, France, and China have greater capacity than other state and nonstate actors, but it makes little sense to speak of dominance in cyberspace. If anything, dependence on complex cyber systems for support of military and economic activities creates new vulnerabilities in large states that can be exploited by nonstate actors. Four decades ago, the Pentagon created the Internet, and today, by most accounts, the United States remains the leading country in both its military and societal use. At the same time, however, because of greater dependence on networked computers and communication, the United States is more vulnerable to attack than many other countries, and the cyber domain has become a major source of insecurity.[5]

The term *cyber attack* covers a wide variety of actions ranging from simple probes, to defacing websites, to denial of service, to espionage and destruction.[6] Similarly, the term *cyber war* is used very loosely for a wide range of behaviors. In this, it reflects dictionary definitions of war that range from armed conflict to any hostile contention (e.g., "war between the sexes" or "war on poverty"). At the other extreme, some use a very narrow definition of cyber war as a "bloodless war" among states that consists only of conflict in the virtual layer of cyberspace. But this avoids important issues of the interconnection of the physical and virtual layers of cyberspace discussed above. A more useful definition of *cyber war* is, hostile actions in cyberspace that have effects that amplify or are equivalent to major kinetic violence.

In the physical world, governments have a near monopoly on large-scale use of force, the defender has an intimate knowledge of the terrain, and attacks end because of attrition or exhaustion. Both resources and mobility are costly. In the virtual world, actors are diverse, sometimes anonymous, physical distance is immaterial, and offense is often cheap. Because the Internet was designed for ease of use rather than security, the offense currently has the advantage over the defense. This might not remain the case in the long term as technology evolves, including efforts at "reengineering" some systems for greater security, but it remains the case at this stage. The larger party has limited ability to disarm or destroy the enemy, occupy territory, or effectively use counterforce strategies. Cyber war, although only incipient at this stage, is the most dramatic of the potential threats. Major states with elaborate technical and human resources could, in principle, create massive disruption as well as physical destruction through cyber attacks on military as well as civilian targets. Responses to cyber war include a form of interstate deterrence (though different from classical nuclear deterrence), offensive capabilities, and designs for network and infrastructure resilience if deterrence fails. At some point in the future, it may be possible to reinforce these steps with certain rudimentary norms, but the world is at an early stage in such a process.

If one treats hacktivism as mostly a disruptive nuisance at this stage, there remain four major categories of cyber threats to national security, each with a different time horizon and different (in principle) solutions: cyber war and economic espionage are largely associated with states, and cybercrime and cyberterrorism are mostly associated with nonstate actors. For the United States, at the present time, the highest costs come from espionage and crime, but over the next decade or so, war and terrorism may become greater threats than they are today. Moreover, as alliances and tactics evolve among different actors, the categories may increasingly overlap. In the view of ADM Mike McConnell, "Sooner or later, terror groups will achieve cyber-sophistication. It's like nuclear proliferation, only far easier."[7] We are only just beginning to see glimpses of cyber war—for instance, as an adjunct in some conventional attacks, in the denial-of-service attacks that accompanied the conventional war in Georgia in 2008, or the recent sabotage of Iranian centrifuges by the Stuxnet worm. Deputy Defense Secretary William Lynn has described the evolution of cyber attacks from exploitation, to disruption of networks, to destruction of physical facilities. He argues that while states have the greatest capabilities, nonstate actors are more likely to initiate a catastrophic attack.[8] A "cyber 9/11" may be more likely than the often-mentioned "cyber Pearl Harbor."

LEARNING FROM ONE REVOLUTION TO ANOTHER?

Can the nuclear revolution in military affairs seven decades ago teach us anything about the current cyber transformation? At first glance, the answer seems to be no. The differences between the technologies are just too great. The National Research Council cites differences in the threshold for action and attribution—nuclear explosions are unambiguous, while cyber intrusions that plant logic bombs in the infrastructure may go unnoticed for long periods before being used and, even then, can be difficult to trace.[9] Even more dramatic is the sheer destructiveness of nuclear technology. Unlike nuclear, cyber does not pose an existential threat. As Martin Libicki points out, destruction or disconnection of cyber systems could return us to the economy of the 1990s—a huge loss of GDP—but a major nuclear war could return us to the Stone Age.[10] In that and other dimensions, comparisons of cyber with biological and chemical weaponry might be more apt.

Moreover, cyber destruction can be disaggregated, and small doses of destruction can be administered over time. While there are many degrees of nuclear destruction, all are above a dramatic threshold or firebreak. In addition, while there is an overlap of civilian and military nuclear technology, nuclear originated in war, and the differences in its use are clearer than in cyber where the web has burgeoned in the civilian sector. For example, the "dot mil" domain name is only a small part of the Internet, and 90 percent of military telephone and Internet communications travel over civilian networks. Finally, because of the commercial predominance and low costs, the barriers to entry to cyber are much lower for nonstate actors. While nuclear terrorism is a serious concern, the barriers for nonstate actors gaining access to nuclear materials remain steep; renting a botnet to wreak destruction on the Internet is both easy and cheap.

It would be a mistake, however, to neglect the past, so long as we remember that metaphors and analogies are always imperfect.[11] In words often attributed to Mark Twain, "history never repeats itself, but sometimes it rhymes." There are some important nuclear-cyber strategic rhymes, such as the superiority of offense over defense, the potential use of weapons for both tactical and strategic purposes, the possibility of first- and second-use scenarios, the possibility of creating automated responses when time is short, the likelihood of unintended consequences and cascading effects when a technology is new and poorly understood, and the belief that new weapons are "equalizers" that allow smaller actors to compete directly but asymmetrically with a larger state.[12]

Even more important than these technical and political similarities is the learning experience as governments and private actors try to understand a transformative technology—and adopt strategies to cope with it. While government reports warning about computer and Internet vulnerability date back to 1991 and the Pentagon recently released a new strategy, few observers would argue that the country has developed an adequate national strategy for cybersecurity. It is worth examining the uneven and halting history of nuclear learning to alert us to some of the pitfalls and opportunities ahead in the cyber domain. Ernest May once described U.S. defense policy and the development of nuclear strategy in the first half-decade following World War II as "chaotic."[13] He would likely apply the same term to the situation in cyberspace today.

SOME GENERAL LESSONS

Expect continuing technological change to complicate early efforts at strategy. At the beginning, both fissile materials and atomic bombs were assumed to be scarce, and it was considered wasteful to use atomic bombs against any but countervalue targets—that is, cities. Bernard Brodie and others concluded in the important 1946 book *The Absolute Weapon* that superiority in numbers would not guarantee strategic superiority, deterrence of war was the only rational military policy, and ensuring survival of the retaliatory arsenal was crucial.[14] These postulates of "finite" or "existential" deterrence persisted throughout the Cold War and serve as the basis for the nuclear strategies of countries such as France and China to this day. In the bipolar competition of the Cold War, however, the strategy of finite deterrence was challenged by the development of the hydrogen bomb in the early 1950s. Destructive power was no longer scarce but now unlimited. While hydrogen bombs could lead to explosions counted in the tens of megatons, their real revolutionary effect was to permit miniaturization, which allowed multiple weapons to pack huge destructive power into the nose cones of another technological surprise—intercontinental ballistic missiles—which shortened response times to less than an hour. This burgeoning explosive power produced great concern about the vulnerability of limited arsenals, an enormous increase in the number of weapons, diminished prospects for active defenses, and the development of elaborate counterforce war-fighting strategies.

Both superpowers had to confront the "usability paradox." If the weapons could not be used, they could not deter. The United States and the USSR were locked in a positive-sum game that involved avoiding nuclear war, but simultaneously they were locked in a zero-sum game of political competition. In the game of political chicken, perceptions of credibility became crucial. Some prospect of usability had to be introduced into doctrine, and for decades strategists wrestled with issues of counterforce targeting, exploring strategic defense technology, and the issues of perception that disparities in large numbers might create for extended deterrence. Elaborate war-fighting schemes and escalation ladders were invented by a nuclear priesthood of experts who specialized in arcane and abstract formulas. In 1976, Paul Nitze and the Committee on the Present Danger expressed alarm about American weakness when the United States possessed tens of thousands of weapons, and in 1979, even Henry Kissinger predicted that because of American nuclear weakness, Soviet risk-taking "must exponentially increase."[15] In fact, the opposite proved to be the case. While politicians and strategists assailed the idea of mutual assured destruction as an immoral and dangerous strategy, "mutually assured destruction" (MAD) turned out to be a fact, not a policy. As McGeorge Bundy noted in his final work, when it came to the Cuban missile crisis, existential deterrence worked, and a few Soviet bombs created deterrence despite an overwhelming American superiority in numbers.[16]

Looking at today's cyber domain, interdependence and vulnerability are twin facts that are likely to persist, but we should expect further technological change to complicate early strategies. ARPANET was created in 1969, and the domain name system and the first viruses date back to 1983; however, as noted above, the mass use and commercial development of cyberspace date only from the invention of the World Wide Web in 1989 and widely available browsers in the mid-1990s.[17] As one expert put it, "As recently as the mid-1990s, the Internet was still essentially a research tool and the plaything of a few."[18] In other words, the massive vulnerabilities that have created the security problems we face today are less than two decades old and are likely to increase. While some experts talk about reducing vulnerability by reengineering the Internet to make attribution of attack easier, this will take time. Even more important, it will not close all vectors of attack.

Early strategies focused on the network: improving code, computer hygiene, addressing issues of attribution, and maintaining air gaps for the most sensitive systems. These steps remain important components of a strategy, but they are far from sufficient. In some ways, the invention and explosion in the usage of the web is analogous to the hydrogen revolution in the nuclear era. By leading society and the economy to a vast dependence on networked communications, it created enormous vulnerabilities that could be exploited not only through the Internet but also through supply chains, devices to bridge air gaps, human agents, and manipulation of social networks.[19] With the development of mobility, cloud computing, and the importance of a limited number of large providers, the issues of vulnerability may change again. Given such technological volatility, a cybersecurity strategy will have to be multifaceted and capable of continual adaptation. It should increase the ratio of work that an attacker must do compared to that of a defender and include redundancy and resilience to allow graceful degradation of complex systems so that inevitable failures are not catastrophic.[20] Strategists need to be alert to the fact that today's solutions may not suffice tomorrow.

Strategy for a New Technology Will Lack Adequate Empirical Content

Since Nagasaki, no one has seen a nuclear weapon used in war. As Alain Enthoven, one of Robert McNamara's "whiz kids" of the early 1960s, retorted during a Pentagon argument about war plans, "General, I have fought just as many nuclear wars as you have."[21] With little empirical grounding, it was difficult to set limits or test strategic formulations. Elaborate constructs and prevailing political fashion led to expensive conclusions based on abstract formulas and relatively little evidence. Fred Kaplan described the environment thusly,

> The method of mathematical calculation, driven mainly from the theory of economics that they had all studied, gave the strategists of the new age a handle on the colossally destructive power of the weapons they found in their midst. But over the years the method became a catechism. ... The precise calculations and the cool, comfortable vocabulary were coming all too commonly to be grasped not merely as tools of desperation but as genuine reflections of the nature of nuclear war.[22]

In the absence of empirical evidence, these nuclear theologians were able to spend vast resources on their hypothetical scenarios.

Cyber has the advantage that with widespread attacks by hackers, criminals, and spies, there is more cumulative evidence of a variety of attack mechanisms and of the strengths and weaknesses of various responses to such attacks. It helps that cyber destruction can be disaggregated in a way that nuclear cannot. But at the same time, no one has yet seen a cyber war, in the strict sense of the word, as defined above. Denial-of-service attacks in Estonia and Georgia and industrial sabotage such as Stuxnet in Iran give some inklings of the auxiliary use of cyber attacks, but they do not test the full set of actions and reactions in a cyber war between states. The U.S. government has conducted a number of war games and simulations and is developing a cyber test range, but the problems of unintended consequences and cascading effects have not been experienced. The problems of escalation as well as the implications for the important doctrines of discrimination and proportionality under the Law of Armed Conflict remain unknown.

New Technologies Raise New Issues in Civil–Military Relations

Different parts of complex institutions like governments learn different lessons at different paces, and new technologies set off competition among bureaucracies. At the beginning of the nuclear era, political leaders developed institutions to maintain civilian control over the new technology, creating an Atomic Energy Agency separate from the military as a means of ensuring civilian control. Congress established a Joint Atomic Energy Committee. But gaps still developed in the relationship between civilians and the military. Operational control of deployed nuclear weapons came under the Strategic Air Command (SAC), which had its own traditions, standard operating procedures, and a strong leader, Curtis LeMay. In 1957, LeMay told Robert Sprague, the deputy director of the civilian Gaither Committee that was investigating the vulnerability of American nuclear forces, that he was not too concerned because "if I see that the Russians are amassing their planes for an attack, I'm going to knock the sh-t out of them before they take off the ground." Sprague was thunderstruck and replied, "But General LeMay, that is not national policy," to which LeMay replied, "I don't care. It's my policy. That's what I'm going to do."[23] In 1960, when President Eisenhower ordered the development of a single integrated operational plan (SIOP-62), SAC produced a plan for a massive strike with 2,164 megatons that targeted China as well as the Soviet Union because of "the Sino-Soviet Bloc."[24] The limited nuclear options that civilian strategists theorized about as part of a bargaining process would not have looked very limited from the point of view of the Soviet bargaining partner—not to mention China.

While Cyber Command is still new and has very different leadership from the old SAC, cybersecurity does present some similar problems of relating civilian control to military operations. Time is even shorter. Rather than the thirty minutes of nuclear warning and possible launch under attack, today there would be three hundred milliseconds between a computer detecting that it was about to be attacked by hostile malware and a preemptive response to disarm the attack. This requires not only advanced knowledge of malware being developed in potentially hostile systems but also an automated response. What happens to the human factor in the decision loop? Obviously, there is no time to go up the chain of command, much less convene a deputies' meeting at the White House. For active defense to be effective, authority will have to be delegated under carefully thought-out rules of engagement developed in advance. Moreover, there are important questions about when active defense shades into retaliation or offense. As the head of Cyber Command has testified, such legal authorities and rules still remain to be fully resolved.[25]

Civilian Uses Will Complicate Effective National Security Strategies

Nuclear energy was first harnessed for military purposes, but it was quickly seen as having important civilian uses as well. In the early days of the development of nuclear energy, it was claimed that electricity would become "too cheap to meter" and cars would be fueled for a year by an atomic pellet the size of a vitamin pill.[26] The engineers' optimism about their new technology was reinforced by a political desire to promote the civilian uses of nuclear energy. Fearful that antiwar and antinuclear movements would delegitimize nuclear weapons and thus reduce their deterrent value, the Eisenhower administration promoted an Atoms for Peace program that offered to assist in the promotion of nuclear energy worldwide. Other countries joined in. The

net effect was to create a powerful domestic and transnational lobby for promotion of nuclear energy that helped provide India with the materials needed
for its nuclear explosion in 1974 and justified the French sale of a reprocessing plant to Pakistan and a German sale of enrichment technology to Brazil
in the mid-1970s.

The Atomic Energy Commission and the Joint Atomic Energy Committee
had been created to assure civilian control of nuclear technology, but over
time both institutions became examples of regulatory capture by powerful
commercial interests—more interested in promotion than regulation and
security. Late in the Ford administration, both institutions were disbanded.
However, after the oil crisis of 1974, it became an article of faith that nuclear
would be the energy of the future, that uranium would be scarce, and thus
widespread use of plutonium and breeder reactors would be necessary. When
the Carter administration, following the recommendations of the nongovernmental Ford-Mitre Report,[27] tried to slow the development of this plutonium
economy in 1977, it ran into a buzz saw of reaction not only overseas but also
from the nuclear industry and its congressional allies at home.

As mentioned earlier, the civilian sector plays an even larger role in the
cyber domain, and this enormously complicates the problem of developing
a national security strategy. The Internet has become a much more significant contributor to GDP than nuclear energy ever was. The private sector is
more than a constraint on policy; it is at the heart of the activity that policy
is designed to protect. Risk is inevitable, and redundancy and resilience
after attack must be built into a strategy. Most of the Internet and its infrastructure belong to the private sector, and the government has only modest
levers to use. Proposals to create a central agency in the executive branch
and a joint committee on cybersecurity in Congress might be useful, but one
should be alert to the dangers of regulatory capture and the development
of a cyber "iron triangle" of executive branch, congressional, and industry
partners.

From a security perspective, there is a misalignment of economic incentives in the cyber domain.[28] Firms have an incentive to provide for their
own security up to a point, but competitive pricing of products limits that
point. Moreover, firms have a financial incentive not to disclose intrusions
that could undercut public confidence in their products and stock prices. A
McAfee white paper notes, "The public (and very often the industry) understanding of this significant national security threat is largely minimal due
to the very limited number of voluntary disclosures by victims of intrusion
activity."[29] The result is a paucity of reliable data and an underinvestment in
security from the national perspective. Moreover, laws designed to ensure
competition restrict cooperation among private firms, and the difficulty of
ascertaining liability in complex software limits the role of the insurance

market. Public–private partnerships are limited by different perspectives and mistrust. As one participant at a recent cybersecurity conference concluded, something bad will have to happen before markets begin to reprice security.[30]

INTERNATIONAL COOPERATION LESSONS

Learning Can Lead to Concurrence in Beliefs without Cooperation

Governments act in accordance with their national interests, but they can change how they define their interests, both through adjusting their behavior to changes in the structure of a situation as well as through transnational and international contacts and cooperation. In the nuclear domain, the initial learning led to concurrence of beliefs before it led to contacts and cooperation. The first effort at arms control, the Baruch Plan of 1946, was rejected out of hand by the Soviet Union as a ploy to preserve the American monopoly, and the early learning was unilateral on both sides.

As we have seen, much of what passed for nuclear knowledge in the early days was abstraction based on assumptions about rational actors, which made it difficult for new information to alter prior beliefs. Yet gradually, both sides became increasingly aware of the unprecedented destructive power of nuclear weapons through weapons tests and modeling, particularly after the invention of the hydrogen bomb. As Winston Churchill put it in 1955, "The atomic bomb, with all its terrors, did not carry us outside the scope of human control," but with the H-bomb, "the entire foundation of human affairs was revolutionized."[31] In his memorable phrase, "safety will be the sturdy child of terror." On the other side of the Iron Curtain, Nikita Khrushchev recalled, "When I was appointed First Secretary of the Central Committee and learned all the facts about nuclear power I couldn't sleep for several days. Then I became convinced that we could never possibly use these weapons, and I was able to sleep again. But all the same we must be prepared."[32] These parallel lessons were learned independently. It was not until 1985 that Ronald Reagan and Mikhail Gorbachev finally declared jointly that "a nuclear war cannot be won and must never be fought." That crucial nuclear taboo has existed for nearly seven decades and was well ensconced before it was jointly pronounced.

A second area where concurrence in beliefs developed was in the command and control of weapons and the dangers of escalation as the two governments accumulated experience of false alarms and accidents. A third area related to the spread of nuclear weapons. Both the United States and the Soviet Union gradually realized that sharing nuclear technology and expecting that exports could remain purely peaceful was implausible. A fourth area of common knowledge concerned the volatility of the arms race and the expenses and risks that it entailed. These views developed independently and in parallel, and it was more than two decades before they led to formal cooperation. Perfect concurrence of beliefs would lead to harmony, which is very rare in world politics. Cooperation in the nuclear area responded to both some concurrence of beliefs as well as actual and anticipated discord.[33]

By its very nature, the interconnected cyber domain requires a degree of cooperation and governments becoming aware of this situation. Some analysts see cyberspace as analogous to the ungoverned Wild West, but unlike the early days of the nuclear domain, cyberspace has a number of areas of private and public governance. Certain technical standards related to Internet protocol are set (or not) by consensus among engineers involved in the nongovernmental Internet Engineering Task Force (IETF), and the domain name system is managed by the Internet Corporation for Assigned Names and Numbers (ICANN). The United Nations and the International Telecommunications Union (ITU) have tried to promulgate some general norms, though with limited success. National governments control copyright and intellectual property laws and try to manage problems of security, espionage, and crime within national policies. Though some cooperative frameworks exist, such as the European Convention on Cyber Crime, they remain weak, and states still focus on the zero-sum rather than positive-sum aspect of these games. At the same time, a degree of independent learning may be occurring on some of these issues. For example, Russia and China have refused to sign the Convention on Cyber Crime and have hidden behind plausible deniability as they have encouraged intrusions by "patriotic hackers." Their attitudes may change, however, if costs exceed benefits. For example, "Russian cyber-criminals no longer follow hands-off rules when it comes to motherland targets, and Russian authorities are beginning to drop the laissez-faire policy."[34] And China is independently experiencing increased costs from cybercrime. As in the nuclear domain, independent learning may pave the way for active cooperation later.

Learning Is Often Lumpy and Discontinuous

Large groups and organizations often learn by crises and major events that serve as metaphors for organizing and dramatizing diverse sets of experiences. The Berlin crises and particularly the Cuban missile crisis of the early 1960s played such a role. Having come close to the precipice of war, both Kennedy and Khrushchev drew lessons about cooperation. It was shortly after the Cuban missile crisis that Kennedy gave his American University speech that laid the basis for the atmospheric test ban discussions.

Of course, crises are not the only way to learn. The experience of playing iterated games of prisoner's dilemma in situations with a long shadow of the future may lead players to learn the value of cooperation in maximizing their payoffs over time.[35] Early steps in cooperation in the nuclear domain encouraged later steps, without requiring a change in the competitive nature of the overall relationship. These governmental steps were reinforced by informal "Track Two" dialogues such as the Pugwash Conferences.

Thus far, there have been no major crises in the cyber domain, though the denial-of-service attacks on Estonia and Georgia and the Stuxnet attack on Iran give hints of what might come. As mentioned earlier, some experts think that markets will not price security properly in the private sector until there is some form of visible crisis. But other forms of learning can occur. For example in the area of industrial espionage, China has had few incentives to restrict its behavior because the benefits far exceed the costs. Spying is as old as human history and does not violate any explicit provisions of international law. Nevertheless, at times governments have established rules of the road for limiting espionage and engaged in patterns of tit for tat retaliation to create an incentive for cooperation. While it is difficult to envisage enforceable treaties in which governments agree not to engage in espionage, it is plausible to imagine a process of iterations (tit for tat), which develops rules of the road that could limit damage in practical terms. To avoid "defection lock-in," which leads to unwanted escalation, it helps to engage in discussions that can develop common perceptions about redlines, if not fully agreed norms, as gradually developed in the nuclear domain after the Cuban missile crisis.[36] Discussion helps to provide a broader context (a "shadow of the future") for specific differences, and it is interesting to note that China and the United States have begun to discuss cyber issues in the context of their broad annual Strategic and Economic Dialogue, as well as in informal Track Two settings.

Learning Occurs at Different Rates in Different Issues of a New Domain

While the U.S.-Soviet political and ideological competition limited their cooperation in some areas, awareness of nuclear destructiveness led them to avoid war with each other and to develop what Zbigniew Brzezinski called "a code of conduct of reciprocal behavior guiding the competition, lessening the danger that it could become lethal."[37] These basic rules of prudence included no direct fighting, no nuclear use, and communication during crisis. More specifically, it meant the division of Germany and respect for spheres of influence in Europe in the 1950s and early 1960s and a compromise on Cuba.

On the issue of command and control, concerns about crisis management and accidents led to the hotline, as well as the Accidents Measures and Incidents at Sea meetings of the early 1970s. Similarly, on the issue of nonproliferation the two sides discovered a common interest and began to cooperate in the mid-1960s, well before the bilateral arms control agreements about issues of arms race stability in the 1970s. Unlike the view that says nothing is settled in a deal until everything is settled, nuclear learning and agreements proceeded at different rates in different areas.

The cyber domain is likely to be analogous. As we have seen, there are already some agreements and institutions that relate to the basic functioning of the Internet, such as technical standards as well as names and addresses, and there is the beginning of a normative framework for cybercrime. But it is likely to take longer before there are agreements on contentious issues such as cyber intrusions for purposes like espionage and preparing the battlefield. Nevertheless, the inability to envisage an overall agreement need not prevent progress on subissues. Indeed, the best prospects for success may involve disaggregating the term *attacks* into specific actions that could be addressed separately.

Involve the Military in International Contacts

As mentioned above, the military can be under civilian control but still have an independent operational culture of its own. By its nature and function, it is charged with entertaining worst-case assumptions. It does not necessarily learn the same lessons at the same rate as its civilian counterparts. Early in the strategic arms limitation talks (SALT), Soviet military leaders complained about the American habit of discussing sensitive military information in front of civilian members of the Soviet delegation. The practice had the effect of broadening communication within the Soviet side. At the same time, Soviet military leaders had little understanding of American institutions or the role of Congress and how that would affect nuclear issues. Their involvement in arms talks helped to produce a more sophisticated generation of younger leaders. As Foreign Minister Andrei Gromyko put it, "It's hard to discuss the subject with the military, but the more contact they have with the Americans, the easier it will be to turn our soldiers into something more than just martinets."[38]

In the cyber domain, the Chinese People's Liberation Army (PLA) plays a major role in recruitment, training, and operations. China today provides more opportunities for PLA generals to have international contacts than was true for Soviet officers during the Cold War, but those contacts are still limited. Moreover, while political control over the Chinese military is strong, operational control is weak, as shown by a number of recent incidents.

Indeed, seven of the nine members of the Standing Military Commission wear uniforms, and there is no National Security Council or equivalent to coordinate operational details across the government. The lessons from the nuclear era would suggest the importance of involving PLA officers in discussions of cyber cooperation.

Deterrence Is Complex and Involves More Than Just Retaliation

Early views of deterrence in the nuclear era were relatively simple and relied on massive retaliation to a nuclear attack. Retaliation remained at the core of deterrence throughout the Cold War, but as strategists confronted the usability dilemma and the problems of extended deterrence, their theories of deterrence became more complex. While a second-strike capability and mutual assured destruction may have been enough to prevent attacks on the homeland, they were never credible for issues at the low end of the spectrum of interests. Somewhere between these extremes lay extended deterrence of attacks against allies and defense of vulnerable positions such as Berlin. Nuclear deterrence was supplemented by other measures, such as forward basing of conventional forces, declaratory policy, changes of alert levels, and force movements.

Many analysts argue that deterrence does not work in cyberspace because of the problem of attribution, but that is also too simple. Interstate deterrence through entanglement and denial still exists even when there is inadequate attribution. Even when the source of an attack can be successfully disguised under a "false flag," other governments may find themselves sufficiently entangled in symmetrically interdependent relationships that a major attack would be counterproductive—witness the reluctance of the Chinese government to dump dollars to punish the United States after it sold arms to Taiwan in 2010.[39] Unlike the single strand of military interdependence that linked the United States and the Soviet Union during the Cold War, the United States, China, and other countries are entangled in multiple networks. China, for example, would itself lose from an attack that severely damaged the American economy, and vice versa.

In addition, an unknown attacker may be deterred by denial. If firewalls are strong or the prospect of a self-enforcing response ("an electric fence") seems possible, attack becomes less attractive. Offensive capabilities for immediate response can create an active defense that can serve as a deterrent even when the identity of the attacker is not fully known. Futility can also help deter an unknown attacker. If the target is well protected or redundancy and resilience allow quick recovery, the risk-to-benefit ratio in attack is diminished.[40] Moreover, attribution does not have to be perfect, and to the extent that false flags are imperfect and rumors of the source of an attack are widely deemed credible (though not probative in a court of law), reputational damage to an attacker's soft power may contribute to deterrence. Finally, a reputation for offensive capability and a declaratory policy that keeps open the means of retaliation can help to reinforce deterrence. Of course, nonstate actors are harder to deter, and improved defenses such as preemption and human intelligence become important in such cases. But among states, nuclear deterrence was more complex than it first looked, and that is doubly true of deterrence in the cyber domain.

Begin Arms Control with Positive-Sum Games Related to Third Parties

Although the United States and the Soviet Union developed some tacit rules of the road about prudent behavior early on, direct negotiation and agreements concerning arms race stability or force structure did not occur until the third decade of the nuclear era. Early efforts at comprehensive arms control like the Baruch Plan were total nonstarters. And even the eventual SALT agreements were of limited value in controlling numbers of weapons and involved elaborate verification procedures that themselves sometimes became issues of contention. The first formal agreement was the Limited Test Ban Treaty, where detection of atmospheric tests was easily verifiable and it could be considered largely an environmental treaty. The second major agreement was the Non-Proliferation Treaty of 1968, which was aimed at limiting the spread of nuclear weapons to third parties. Both these agreements involved positive-sum games.

In the cyber domain, the global nature of the Internet requires international cooperation. Some people call for cyber arms control negotiations and formal treaties, but differences in cultural norms and the impossibility of verification make such treaties difficult to negotiate or implement. Such efforts could actually reduce national security if asymmetrical implementation put legalistic cultures like the United States at a disadvantage compared to societies with a higher degree of government corruption. At the same time, it is not too early to explore international talks and cooperation. The most promising early areas for international cooperation are not bilateral conflicts, but problems posed by third parties such as criminals and terrorists.

For more than a decade, Russia has sought a treaty for broad international oversight of the Internet and "information security" banning deception or the embedding of malicious code or circuitry that could be activated in the event of war. But Americans have argued that arms control measures banning offense can damage defense against current attacks and would be impossible to verify or enforce. And declaratory statements of "no first use" might have restraining effects on legalistic cultures like the United States while having less effect on states with closed societies. Moreover, the United States has resisted agreements that could legitimize authoritarian governments' censorship of the Internet. Cultural differences present a difficulty in reaching any broad agreements on regulating content on the Internet. The United States has called for the creation of "norms of behavior among states" that "encourage respect for the global networked commons," but as Jack Goldsmith has argued, "Even if we could stop all cyber attacks from our soil, we wouldn't want to. On the private side, hacktivism can be a tool of liberation. On the public side, the best defense of critical computer systems is sometimes a good offense."[41] From the American point of view, Twitter and YouTube are matters of personal freedom; seen from Beijing or Tehran, they are instruments of attack. Trying to limit all intrusions would be impossible, but on the spectrum of attacks ranging from soft hacktivism to hard implanting of logic bombs in SCADA (supervisory control and data acquisition) systems, one could start with cybercrime and cyberterrorism involving nonstate third parties where major states would have an interest in limiting damage by agreeing to cooperate on forensics and controls. States might start with acceptance of responsibility for attacks that traverse their territory and a duty to cooperate on forensics, information, and remedial measures.[42] At some later points, it is possible that such cooperation could spread to state activities at the hard end of the spectrum, as it did in the nuclear domain.

CONCLUSION

Historical analogies are always dangerous if taken too literally, and the differences between nuclear and cyber technologies are great. The cyber domain is new and dynamic, but so was nuclear technology at its inception. It may help to put the problems of designing a strategy for cybersecurity into perspective, particularly the aspect of cooperation among states, if we realize how long and difficult it was to develop a nuclear strategy, much less international nuclear cooperation. Nuclear learning was slow, halting, and incomplete. The intensity of the ideological and political competition in the U.S.–Soviet relationship was much greater than that between the United States and Russia or the United States and China today. There were far fewer positive strands of interdependence in the relationship. Yet the intensity of the zero-sum game did not prevent the development of rules of the road and cooperative agreements that helped to preserve the concurrent positive-sum game.

That is the good news. The bad news is that cyber technology gives much more power to nonstate actors than does nuclear technology, and the threats such actors pose are likely to increase. The transnational, multiactor games of the cyber domain pose a new set of questions about the meaning of national security. Some of the most important security responses must be national and unilateral, focused on hygiene, redundancy, and resilience. It is likely, however, that major governments will gradually discover that cooperation against the insecurity created by nonstate actors will require greater priority in attention. The world is a long distance from such a response at this stage in the development of cyber technology. But such responses did not occur until we approached the third decade of the nuclear era. With the World Wide Web only two decades old, may we be approaching an analogous point in the political trajectory of cybersecurity?

NOTES

1. Oddly, Max Boot does not list the nuclear revolution. See his *War Made New: Technology, Warfare and the Course of History, 1500 to Today* (New York: Gotham Books, 2006).

2. Michael V. Hayden, "The Future of Things Cyber," *Strategic Studies Quarterly* 5, no. 1 (Spring 2011), p. 3.

3. A pioneering work on this question is Lloyd Etheredge, *Can Governments Learn?* (Elmsford, NY: Pergamon Press, 1985).

4. Joseph S. Nye Jr., *The Future of Power* (New York: Public Affairs Press, 2011), chap. 5.

5. This point is emphasized by Richard A. Clarke and Robert Knake in *Cyberwar* (New York: HarperCollins, 2009).

6. For skeptical views that cyber war is overhyped, see Michael Hirsh, "Here There Be Dragons," *National Journal* 23 (July 2011), pp. 32–37.

7. McConnell quoted in Nathan Gardels, "Cyberwar: Former Intelligence Chief Says China Aims at America's Soft Underbelly," *New Perspectives Quarterly* 27, no. 2 (Spring 2010), p. 16.

8. Deputy Secretary of Defense William Lynn, remarks at 28th Annual International Workshop on Global Security, Paris, France, June 16, 2011, http://www.defense.gov/Speeches/Speech.aspx?SpeechID=1586.

9. William Owens, Kenneth Dam, and Herbert Lin, editors, *Technology, Policy, Law and Ethics Regarding U.S. Acquisition and Use of Cyberattack Capabilities* (Washington, DC: National Academies Press, 2009), p. 294.

10. Martin C. Libicki, "Cyberwar as a Confidence Game," *Strategic Studies Quarterly* 5, no. 1 (Spring 2011), p. 136. See also Martin C. Libicki, *Cyberdeterrence and Cyberwar* (Santa Monica, CA: RAND, 2009), p. 136.

11. Richard Neustadt and Ernest May, *Thinking in Time: The Uses of History for Decision-Makers* (New York: Free Press, 1986).

12. Owens, Dam, and Lin, *Technology, Policy, Law and Ethics*, pp. 295–96.

13. Ernest May, "Cold War and Defense," in Keith Neilson and Ronald G. Haycock, editors, *The Cold War and Defense* (New York: Praeger, 1990), p. 54. I am indebted to Phillip Zelikow for bringing this to my attention.

14. Fred Kaplan, *The Wizards of Armageddon* (New York: Simon & Schuster, 1983), p. 30.

15. Kissinger quoted in Robert Jervis, *The Meaning of the Nuclear Revolution* (Ithaca, NY: Cornell University Press, 1989), p. 102.

16. McGeorge Bundy, *Danger and Survival: Choices about the Bomb in the First 50 Years* (New York: Vintage, 1990).

17. Stuart Starr, "Toward a Preliminary Theory of Cyberpower," in Franklin Kramer, Stuart Starr, and Larry Wentz, editors, *Cyberpower and National Security* (Washington, DC: NDU Press, 2009), pp. 82–86.

18. Joel Brenner, *America the Vulnerable* (New York: Penguin Press, 2011), p. 15.

19. On supply chain vulnerability, see Scott Charney and Eric Werner, *Cyber Supply Chain Risk Management: Toward a Global Vision of Transparency and Trust* (Redmond, WA: Microsoft Corporation, July 25, 2011), http://www.microsoft.com/download/en/details.aspx?id=26826.

20. I am indebted to John Mallery of MIT's Computer Science and Artificial Intelligence Laboratory (CSAIL) for his work on these points.

21. Kaplan, *Wizards of Armageddon*, p. 254.

22. Kaplan, *Wizards of Armageddon*, p. 391.

23. Kaplan, *Wizards of Armageddon*, p. 134.

24. Kaplan, *Wizards of Armageddon*, p. 269.

25. Gen Keith Alexander, quoted in "US Lacks People, Authorities to Face Cyber Attack," *Associated Press* (March 16, 2011).

26. Brian Balogh, *Chain Reaction: Expert Debate and Public Participation in American Commercial Nuclear Power, 1945–1975* (Cambridge, UK: Cambridge University Press, 1991), p. 31.

27. The Nuclear Energy Policy Study Group, *Nuclear Power: Issues and Choices* (Ford-Mitre Report) (Cambridge, MA: Ballinger, 1977).

28. See Brenner, *America the Vulnerable*.

29. Dmitri Alperovitch, "Revealed: Operation Shady RAT," McAfee White Paper 1.1 (2011), p. 3, http://www.mcafee.com/us/resources/white-papers/wp-operation-shady-rat.pdf.

30. Jason Pontin, remarks at plenary panel, EastWest Institute Cybersecurity Summit, London (June 2, 2011).

31. Churchill quoted in Michael Mandelbaum, *The Nuclear Revolution* (Cambridge, UK: Cambridge University Press, 1981), p. 3.

32. Khrushchev quoted in Jervis, *Meaning of the Nuclear Revolution*, p. 20.

33. I am indebted to Robert O. Keohane for this point.

34. Joseph Menn, "Moscow Gets Tough on Cybercrime," *Financial Times* (March 22, 2010).

35. See Robert Axelrod, *The Evolution of Cooperation* (New York: Basic Books, 1984).

36. For a description of the gradual evolution of such learning in the nuclear area, see Joseph S. Nye Jr., "Nuclear Learning and U.S.-Soviet Security Regimes," *International Organization* 41, no. 3 (Summer 1987). See also Graham Allison, "Primitive Rules of Prudence: Foundations of Peaceful Competition" in Graham Allison, William

Ury, and Bruce Allyn, editors, *Windows of Opportunity: From Cold War to Peaceful Competition in U.S.-Soviet Relations* (Cambridge, MA: Ballinger, 1989).

37. Zbigniew Brzezinski, *Game Plan* (Boston, MA: Atheneum, 1986), p. 244.

38. Arkady Shevchenko, *Breaking with Moscow* (New York: Ballantine, 1985), pp. 270–71. See also Raymond Garthoff, "Negotiating SALT," *Wilson Quarterly* (Autumn 1977), p. 79.

39. For details, see Nye, *Future of Power*, chap. 3.

40. I am indebted to the unpublished writings of Jeff Cooper on these points.

41. Jack Goldsmith, "Can We Stop the Global Cyber Arms Race," *Washington Post* (February 1, 2010).

42. See, e.g., Eneken Tikk, "Ten Rules for Cyber Security," *Survival* 53, no. 3 (June–July 2011), pp. 119–32.

Chapter Seven

Escalation Dynamics and Conflict Termination in Cyberspace

Herbert Lin

U.S. national security planners have become concerned in recent years that this country might become engaged in various kinds of conflict in cyberspace. Such engagement could entail the United States as the target of hostile cyber operations, the initiator of cyber operations against adversaries, or some combination of the two.

To date, most serious analytical work related to cyber conflict focuses primarily on the initial transition from a preconflict environment to that of conflict. Little work has been done on three key issues: (1) how the initial stages of conflict in cyberspace might evolve or escalate (and what might be done to prevent or deter such escalation), (2) how cyber conflict at any given level might be deescalated or terminated (and what might be done to facilitate de-escalation or termination), and (3) how cyber conflict might escalate into kinetic conflict (and what might be done to prevent kinetic escalation). Each of these issues is important to policy makers, both in preparing for and managing a crisis. Before beginning that discussion, it is instructive to consider some relevant terminology and concepts.

TERMINOLOGY AND BASIC CONCEPTS

The term *offensive cyber operations* as used here refers collectively to actions taken against an adversary's computer systems or networks that harm the adversary's interests. In general, an offensive cyber operation gains access to an adversary's computer system or network and takes advantage of a vulnerability in that system or network to deliver a payload. In a noncyber analogy, *access* might be any available path for reaching a file in a file cabinet.

A *vulnerability* might be an easy-to-pick lock on the file cabinet—and note that ease of picking the lock is irrelevant to an Earth-bound intruder if the file cabinet is located on the International Space Station where access to the file cabinet would be difficult. The *payload* describes what is to be done once the intruder has picked the lock. For example, the intruder can destroy the papers inside, alter some of the information on those papers, or change the signature on selected documents.

Access is "easy" when a path to the target can be found without much difficulty; a computer connected to the Internet may well be such a target. Access is "difficult" when finding a path to the target is possible only at great effort or may not be possible for any practical purposes. An example of such a target may be the onboard avionics of an enemy fighter plane, which is not likely to be connected to the Internet for the foreseeable future. In general, access to an adversary's important and sensitive computer systems or networks should be expected to be difficult. Furthermore, access paths to a target may be intermittent—a submarine's on-board administrative local area network would necessarily be disconnected from the Internet while underwater at sea but might be connected while in port. If the administrative network is ever connected to the on-board operational network (controlling weapons and propulsion) at sea, an effective access path may be present for an adversary.

A *vulnerability* is a security weakness in the system or network that is introduced by accident (by some party that has a legitimate reason to access the system) or on purpose (by a would-be intruder). An accidentally introduced weakness (a "security bug") may open the door for opportunistic use of the vulnerability by an adversary. Many vulnerabilities are widely publicized after they are discovered and may be used by anyone with moderate technical skills until a patch can be disseminated and installed.[1] Adversaries with the time and resources may also discover unintentional defects that they protect as valuable secrets—also known as *zero-day vulnerabilities*.[2] A deliberately introduced vulnerability occurs because the intruder takes an action to create one where one did not previously exist. For example, an intruder might deceive a legitimate user of the targeted system or network to disable a security feature (e.g., reveal a password). Both kinds of vulnerability are useful to intruders as long as the weaknesses introduced remain unaddressed.

Payload is the term used to describe the things that can be done once a vulnerability has been exploited. For example, once a software agent (such as a virus) has entered a given computer, it can be programmed to do many things—reproduce and retransmit itself, destroy files on the system, or alter files. Payloads can have multiple capabilities when inserted into an adversary system or network—that is, they can be programmed to do more than one thing. The timing of these actions can also be varied.

Depending on the intent of the intruder, an offensive cyber operation can be classified as cyber attack or cyber exploitation. *Cyber attack* is the use of deliberate actions related to information technology (IT)—perhaps over an extended period of time—to alter, disrupt, deceive, degrade, or destroy adversary computer systems or networks or the data and/or programs resident in or transiting these systems or networks.[3] Such effects on adversary systems and networks may also have indirect effects on entities coupled to or reliant on them. A cyber attack seeks to cause adversary computer systems and networks to be unavailable or untrustworthy and therefore less useful to the adversary. Because so many different kinds of cyber attack are possible, the term *cyber attack* should be understood as a statement about a methodology for action—and that alone—rather than as a statement about the scale of the effect of that action. *Cyber exploitation* is the use of deliberate IT-related actions—perhaps over an extended period of time—to support the goals and missions of the party conducting the exploitation, usually for the purpose of obtaining information resident on or transiting through an adversary's computer system or network. Cyber exploitations do not seek to disturb the normal functioning of a computer system or network from the user's point of view—indeed, the best cyber exploitation is one that goes undetected.

The similarity between these two concepts and the exploitation channel are the most important characteristics of offensive cyber operations. *Cyber attack* and *cyber exploitation* are very similar from a technical point of view. They use the same access paths and take advantage of the same vulnerabilities; the only difference is the payload they carry. These similarities often mean that the targeted party may not be able to distinguish easily between cyber exploitation and cyber attack—a fact that may result in that party's making incorrect or misinformed decisions. The primary technical requirement of cyber exploitation is that delivery and execution of its payload be accomplished quietly and undetectably. Secrecy is often far less important when cyber attack is the mission, because in many cases the effects of the attack will be immediately apparent to the target. All exploitation operations require a channel for reporting the information they collect. If the channel happens to be two-way, payloads can be remotely updated. Thus, the functionality of the operation may be different today than it was yesterday—most significantly, it may be an exploitation payload today and an attack payload tomorrow. In some cases, the initial payload consists of nothing more than a mechanism for scanning the system to determine its technical characteristics and an update mechanism to retrieve the best packages to further the compromise.

ATTRIBUTION

Attribution is the task of identifying the party that should be held politically responsible for an offensive cyber operation.[4] *Technical attribution* is the ability to associate an attack with a responsible party through technical means based on information made available by the cyber operation itself—that is, technical attribution is based on clues available at the scene (or scenes) of the operation. *All-source attribution* is a process that integrates information from all sources, not just technical sources at the scene of the attack, to arrive at a judgment (rather than a definitive and certain proof) concerning the identity of the intruder.

As a general rule, attribution is a difficult matter. It is made more difficult as more of the following factors are present:

- The techniques used have never been seen before, so the investigator is unable to link them to other parties that have used similar techniques in the past.
- The intruder leaves no forensic clues and makes no technical mistakes (i.e., tradecraft is error-free).
- The intruder maintains perfect operational security, so there are no other sources of intelligence (e.g., SIGINT, HUMINT).
- The motivations for conducting the operation are unknown, or the operation occurs during a time when political circumstances do not suggest conflict or adversarial relations to associate a known party's demands or interests with a possible perpetrator.
- The intrusion requires a rapid response that prevents a thorough investigation, raising the likelihood of a mistaken attribution.

If most or all of these factors are present, then attribution is virtually impossible. On the other hand, it is rare that *all* of these factors are present. One might thus reasonably conclude that although technical attribution is indeed difficult, all-source attribution is sometimes possible. Solving the problem of attribution is not as hopeless as is often portrayed.

THE NEED FOR INTELLIGENCE SUPPORT

Offensive cyber operations against a given system require detailed knowledge about both access paths to and vulnerabilities in the targeted system. The amount of detail should not be underestimated—in principle, it may involve very "small" details such as

- the specific processor model (and even the serial number of the processor) in use on the system;

- the operating system in use, down to the level of specific version, the build number in use, and the history of security patches applied to it;
- IP addresses of Internet-connected computers;
- specific versions of systems administrator tools used;
- the security configuration of the operating system (e.g., whether certain services are turned on or off, or what antivirus programs are running); and
- the physical configuration of the hardware involved (e.g., what peripherals or computers are physically attached).

Note that none of these items of intelligence is easily available from satellite or aerial reconnaissance. As a general rule, a scarcity of intelligence regarding possible targets means that any offensive cyber operation launched against them can only be a "broad-spectrum" and a relatively indiscriminate or blunt attack. Such an attack might be analogous to the Allied strategic bombing attacks of World War II that targeted national infrastructure on the grounds that such infrastructure supported the war effort of the Axis. Substantial amounts of intelligence information about targets and paths to those targets are required if the operation is intended as a very precise one directed at a particular system. Conversely, a lack of such information will result in large uncertainties about the direct and indirect effects of an operation and make it difficult to develop accurate estimates of likely collateral damage.

ACTIVE DEFENSE

Defensive measures in cybersecurity seek to frustrate offensive operations taken against systems or networks. Passive defensive measures, such as hardening systems against penetration, facilitating recovery in the event of a successful offensive operation, making security more usable and ubiquitous, and educating users to behave properly in a threat environment, are important elements of a strong defensive posture.[5] Nevertheless, for the defense to be successful, these measures must succeed every time an adversary attacks. The offensive operation need only succeed once, and an adversary who pays no penalty for a failed operation can continue with follow-on operations until it succeeds or chooses to stop. This places a heavy and asymmetric burden on a defensive posture that employs only passive defense.

If passive defense is insufficient to ensure security, what other approaches might help to strengthen one's defensive posture? One possibility is to eliminate or degrade an adversary's ability to successfully conduct offensive cyber operations. In that case, the operation is ultimately less successful than it might otherwise have been because the defender has been able to neutralize the operation in progress or perhaps even before it was launched.

A second possibility is to impose other costs on the adversary, and such a strategy is based on two premises. First, imposition of these costs reduces the adversary's willingness and/or ability to initiate or to continue an offensive operation. Second, knowledge that an operation will prove costly to one adversary deters others from attempting to conduct similar operations—and advance knowledge of such a possibility may deter the original adversary from conducting the offensive operation in the first place. There are many options for imposing costs on an adversary, including economic penalties such as sanctions, diplomatic penalties such as breaking of diplomatic relations, and even kinetic military actions such as cruise missile strikes. In-kind military action—a counteroffensive cyber operation—is also a possibility.

Both of these possible reactions—neutralization of an adversary's offensive operation and imposition of costs to the adversary for the operation—are often captured under the rubric of *active defense*. But note well—the attempt to impose costs on an adversary that conducts offensive cyber operations might well be seen by that adversary as an offensive act itself. This may be especially true in the fog of cyber conflict, where who is actually doing what may be uncertain.

EVOLVING OR ESCALATING CONFLICT

The phenomenon of escalation is a change in the level of conflict (where level is defined in terms of scope, intensity, or both) from a lower (perhaps nonexistent) to a higher level. Escalation is a fundamentally interactive concept in which actions by one party trigger other actions by another party to the conflict. Of particular concern is a chain reaction in which these actions feed off one another, thus raising the level of conflict to a level not initially contemplated by any party to the conflict. Escalation can occur through a number of mechanisms that may or may not be operative simultaneously in any instance.[6] It includes four basic types: deliberate, inadvertent, accidental, and catalytic.

Deliberate escalation is carried out with specific purposes in mind. For example, a party may deliberately escalate a conflict from some initial level (which may be zero) to gain advantage, to preempt, to avoid defeat, to signal an adversary about its own intentions and motivations, or to penalize an adversary for some previous action. Offensive cyber operations—specifically, cyber attacks—are one of many possible military options for deliberate escalation.

Inadvertent escalation occurs when one party deliberately takes actions that it does not believe are escalatory but which are interpreted as escalatory by another party to the conflict. Such misinterpretation may occur because of incomplete information, lack of shared reference frames, or one party's thresholds or "lines in the sand" of which other parties are not aware. Communicating to an adversary the nature of any such thresholds regarding activity in cyberspace may be particularly problematic, even under normal peacetime circumstances.

For example, Nation A does X, expecting Nation B to do Y in response. But in fact, Nation B unexpectedly does Z, where Z is a much more escalatory action than Y. Or Nation A may do X, expecting it to be seen as a minor action intended only to show mild displeasure and that Nation B will do Y in response, where Y is also a relatively mild action. However, due to a variety of circumstances, Nation B sees X as a major escalatory action and responds accordingly with Z, an action that is much more significant than Y. Nation A perceives Z as being way out of proportion and, in turn, escalates accordingly.

Accidental escalation occurs when some operational action has direct effects that are unintended by those who ordered them. A weapon may go astray to hit the wrong target; rules of engagement are sometimes unclear; a unit may take unauthorized actions; or a high-level command decision may not be received properly by all relevant units. It is especially relevant here that there is often greater uncertainty of outcome due to a lack of adequate intelligence on various targets when certain kinds of offensive cyber operations are employed.

Catalytic escalation occurs when some third party succeeds in provoking two parties to engage in conflict. For example, Party C takes action against Party A that is not traced to Party C and appears to come from Party B. Party A reacts against Party B, which then believes it is the target of an unprovoked action by Party A. The inherent anonymity of cyber operations may make "false-flag" operations easier to undertake in cyberspace than with kinetic operations.

Through such mechanisms, the escalatory dynamics of conflict show how a conflict, once started, might evolve. Of interest are issues such as what activities or events might set a cyber conflict into motion, what the responses to those activities or events might be, how each side might observe and understand those responses, whether responses would necessarily be "in-kind," or how different kinds of states might respond differently.

Theories of escalation dynamics have been elaborated in the nuclear domain. But the deep and profound differences between the nuclear and cyber domains suggest that any theory of escalation dynamics in the latter would require far more than small perturbations in nuclear escalation dynamics theories, though such theories might be useful points of departure for developing new ones applicable to cyberspace. Some of these differences include the greater uncertainties in attribution of cyber actors, the broad proliferation of significant capabilities for cyber operations to a multitude of states and a variety of nonstate actors as well, and the inherent ambiguities of cyber operations compared to the very distinct threshold of nuclear weapons explosions.

To suggest some of the difficulties involved, consider the following scenarios:

- Nation Blue may believe it has been attacked deliberately by Nation Red, even though Red has not done so. Indeed, because of the ongoing nature of various attack-like activities (e.g., hacking and other intrusions) against the computer systems and networks of most nations, Blue's conclusion that its computer systems are being attacked is certainly true. Attribution of such an attack is a different matter, and because hard evidence for attribution is difficult to obtain, Blue's government may make inferences about the likelihood of Red's involvement by giving more weight to a general understanding of Red's policy and posture toward it than might be warranted by the specific facts and circumstances of the situation. Evidence that appears to confirm Red's involvement will be easy to find, whether or not Red is actually involved. If Red is a technologically sophisticated nation (such as the United States), the lack of "fingerprints" specific to Red can easily be attributed to its technological superiority in conducting such attacks.
- An active defense of its systems and networks undertaken by Nation Red against Nation Blue could have significant political consequences. For example, even if Red had technical evidence that was incontrovertible (and it never is) pointing to Blue's government, Blue could still deny that it had launched such an attack—and in the court of world opinion, its denial could carry some credibility when weighed against Red's past assertions regarding similar issues. That is, Red's cyber attacks (counter–cyber attacks, to be precise) undertaken under the rubric of active defense may not be perceived as innocent acts of self-defense, even if they are. The result could be a flurry of charges and countercharges that would further muddy the waters and escalate the level of political tension and mistrust.
- The point at which a software agent for cyber attack is introduced or planted on an adversary's computer system or network is, in general, different from the point at which it is activated and begins to do damage. Blue (the nation being attacked) may well regard the hostile action as beginning at the moment Red's agent is planted, whereas Red may believe the hostile action begins only when the agent is activated.

- During periods of crisis or tension when military action may be more likely, it is entirely plausible that Blue would increase the intensity of security scans it conducts on its critical systems and networks. More intense security scans often reveal offensive software agents implanted long before the onset of crisis and that may have been overlooked in ordinary scans, and yet discovery of these agents may well prompt fears that an attack is pending.
- The direct damage from a cyber attack is often invisible to outsiders. Without CNN images of smoking holes in the ground or troops on the move, an outside observer must weigh competing claims without tangible evidence one way or the other. Under such circumstances, the reputations of the different parties in the eyes of each other are likely to play a much larger political role.
- Nation Red plants software agents in some of Nation Blue's critical networks to collect intelligence information. These agents are designed to be reprogrammable in place—that is, Red can update its agents with new capabilities. During a time of crisis, Blue's authorities discover some of these agents and learn that they have been present for a while, that they are sending back very sensitive information to Red, and that their capabilities can be changed on a moment's notice. Even if no harmful action has yet been taken, it is entirely possible that Blue would see itself as the target of Red's cyber attack.

What follows are some speculations on some of the factors that might influence the evolution of a cyber conflict (see textbox 7.1).

CRISIS STABILITY

Where kinetic weapons are involved, crisis stability refers to that condition in which neither side has incentives to attack first. Crisis stability is especially important for nuclear weapons, where the existence of an invulnerable submarine-based nuclear missile force controlled by Nation Blue means that Nation Red could not escape retaliation no matter how devastating a first strike it could launch. In terms of cyber weapons, there is no conceivable way for one nation to eliminate or even significantly degrade the cyber-attack capability of another.[7] But the question remains whether a second-strike cyber-attack capability is the enabling condition for crisis stability in cyberspace.

A related question is that of incentives for preemption. Preemptive attacks by Red against Blue are undertaken to prevent (or at least blunt) an impending attack by Blue on Red. If Blue is planning a cyber attack on Red, a

---

Textbox 7.1 Questions about Escalatory Dynamics of Cyber Conflict between Nation-States

---

Crisis Stability

- What is the analog of crisis stability in cyber conflict?
- What are the incentives for preemptive cyber attack?

Escalation Control and Management

- How can intentions be signaled to an adversary in conflict?
- How can cyber conflict between nations be limited to conflict in cyberspace?
- What thresholds of "line-crossing" activity might be created in cyberspace, and how might these be communicated to an adversary?
- How should cyber attack be scoped and targeted so that it does not lead an adversary to escalate a conflict into kinetic conflict?
- How can a modestly scoped cyber attack conducted by a government be differentiated from the background cyber attacks that are going on all of the time?
- How can the scale and scope of a commensurate response be ascertained?
- What confidence-building measures might actually reassure an adversary about a lack of hostile intent?

Complications Introduced by Patriotic Hackers

- How can "freelance" activities on the part of patriotic hackers be handled?

Incentives for Self-Restraint in Escalation

- What are the incentives for self-restraint in escalating cyber conflict?

Termination of Cyber Conflict

- What does it mean to terminate a cyber conflict?

Necessary Capabilities for Escalation Management

- How can national authorities exercise effective command and control of cyber forces in a rapidly evolving conflict environment?
- What is the scope and nature of national capabilities (e.g., technological, command and control, law enforcement/legal capabilities) needed to implement any approach to escalation management and conflict termination in cyberspace?
- How can each side obtain realistic assessments of one's own or an adversary's cyber state and condition (e.g., heavily or lightly damaged)?
- How might other resources/capabilities available to the United States be used to manage escalation of conflict in cyberspace?

preemptive cyber attack on Blue cannot do much to destroy Blue's attack capability; at best, Red's preemptive attack on Blue might tie up Blue's personnel skilled in cyber operations. On the other hand, it is hard to imagine circumstances in which Red would realize that Blue were planning an attack, as preparations for launching a cyber attack are likely to be invisible for the most part.

A second relevant scenario is one in which Blue is planning a kinetic attack on Red. Intelligence information, such as photographs of troop movements, indicates preparations for such an attack. Under these circumstances, Red might well choose to launch a preemptive cyber attack with the intent of delaying and disrupting Blue's preparations for its own.

SIGNALING INTENTIONS IN CYBER CONFLICT

Nothing in the set of options above is specific to cyber conflict—such issues have been an important part of crisis management for a long time. But managing such issues may well be more difficult for cyber conflict than for other kinds of conflict. One reason is the constant background of cyber-attack activity. Reports arrive constantly of cyber attacks of one kind or another on U.S. computer systems and networks, and the vast majority of these attacks do not have the significance of a serious cyber attack launched by a party determined to do harm to the United States. Indeed, the intent underlying a given cyber attack may not have a military or a strategic character at all. Organized crime may launch a cyber attack for profit-making purposes. A teenage hacking club may launch a cyber attack out of curiosity or for vandalism purposes.

Thus, if one nation wishes to send a signal to its cyber adversary, how is the latter to recognize that signal? Overtly taking credit for such an attack goes only so far, especially given uncertain communications in times of tension or war and the near certainty of less-than-responsible behavior on the part of one or both sides.

A dearth of historical experience with the use of serious offensive cyber operations further complicates efforts at understanding what an adversary might hope to gain by launching a cyber attack. In the absence of direct contact with those conducting such operations—sometimes even in the presence of such contact—determining intent is likely to be difficult and may rest heavily on inferences made on the basis of whatever attribution is possible. Thus, attempts to send signals to an adversary through limited and constrained military actions—problematic even in kinetic warfare—are likely to be even more problematic when cyber attacks are involved.

DETERMINING THE IMPACT AND
MAGNITUDE OF CYBER RESPONSE

If an adversary conducts a cyber attack against the United States, the first questions for U.S. decision makers will relate to impact and magnitude. Such knowledge is necessary to inform an appropriate response. If, for example, the United States wishes to make a commensurate response, it needs to know what parameters of the incoming attack would characterize a commensurate response.

In many kinds of cyber attack, the magnitude of the impact of the first attack will be uncertain at first and may remain so for a considerable period of time. Decision makers may then be caught between two challenges—a policy need to respond quickly and the technical fact that it may be necessary to wait until more information about impact and damage can be obtained. These tensions are especially challenging in the context of active defense and active threat neutralization.

Decision makers often feel intense pressure to "do something" immediately after the onset of a crisis, and sometimes such pressure is warranted by the facts and circumstances of the situation. On the other hand, the lack of immediate information may prompt decision makers to take a worst-case view of the attack and, thus, to assume that the worst that might happen was indeed what actually happened. Such a situation has obvious potential for inappropriate and unintended escalation or kinetic response.

TRANSPARENCY AND CONFIDENCE-
BUILDING MEASURES

Where kinetic weapons are concerned, transparency and confidence-building measures such as adherence to mutually agreed "rules of the road" for naval ships at sea, prenotification of large troop movements, and noninterference with national technical means of verification have been used to promote stability and mutual understanding about a potential adversary's intent.

Translating traditional transparency and confidence-building measures into cyberspace presents many problems. For example, generating forces in preparation for offensive cyber operations can be done essentially behind closed doors and with a small footprint, so evidence suggesting impending hostile action will never be evident, except with advance public notice. Thus, there is no reasonable analog for "notification of movement or massing of forces." Because the success of offensive cyber operations is largely dependent on stealth and deception, reassurances of Nation Blue regarding the benign nature of any cyber activity observed, assuming it can be seen and attributed, ring hollow to any parties that have a competitive or politically tense relationship with Blue. Traditional kinetic operations—those military operations on land, sea, and air—are easily distinguishable from most nonmilitary movements. By contrast, it is often difficult to distinguish between military and nonmilitary cyber operations, particularly between cyber attack and cyber exploitation. During a crisis, Blue may consider collecting intelligence on Red as stabilizing and thus lower the likelihood of mistaken escalation. Red may well interpret this as Blue preparing the battlefield as a prelude to attack.

These comments are not meant to suggest that all transparency or confidence-building measures for cyberspace are futile—only that applying traditional measures to cyberspace will be difficult, and new forms of conduct and behavior may be needed to promote transparency and build confidence.

Catalytic Cyber Conflict

Catalytic conflict as mentioned earlier refers to the phenomenon in which a third party instigates or seeks to escalate conflict between two other parties. These could be nation-states or subnational organizations such as terrorist groups. To increase confidence in the success of initiating a catalytic war, the instigator might attack both parties, seeking to fool each into thinking the other was responsible.

Because high-confidence attribution of cyber attacks under all circumstances is highly problematic, an instigator would find it relatively easy to deceive each party about the instigator's identity; thus, a double-sided catalytic attack may be plausible. Also, if a state of tension already exists between the two parties involved, leaders in each nation will be predisposed toward thinking the worst about the other, making them less likely to exercise due diligence in carefully attributing an attack. An instigator might consequently choose just such a time to conduct a catalytic cyber attack.

COMPLICATIONS INTRODUCED
BY PATRIOTIC HACKERS

When traditional kinetic military operations are involved, it is generally presumed that the forces involved engage in armed conflict only at the direction of the cognizant government, only by its authorized military agents, and specifically, not by private groups or individuals. That is, governments maintain their armed forces to participate in armed conflict under the government's direction.

But in the Internet era, it is necessary to consider that nonstate actors may become involved in conflict. During times of conflict (or even tension) with another nation, some citizens may be motivated to support their country's war effort or political stance by taking direct action in cyberspace. Such hacktivists or patriotic hackers are private citizens with some skills in the use of cyber-attack weapons, and they may well launch cyber attacks on the adversary nation on their own initiative, that is, without the blessing and not under the direction or control of the government of that nation.

A number of incidents of privately undertaken cyber attacks have been well publicized. For example, immediately after the start of the second intifada in Israel in late September 2000, Palestinian and Israeli hackers conducted a variety of cyber attacks on each other's national web presence on the Internet.[8]

Following the 2001 incident between the United States and China in which a U.S. EP-3 reconnaissance aircraft collided with a Chinese F-8 interceptor, both Chinese and American hackers attacked the web presence of the other nation. In both cases, attacks were mostly aimed at website defacement and denial of service.[9] In the wake of the May 1999 bombing by the United States of the Chinese embassy in Belgrade, the U.S. National Infrastructure Protection Center issued an advisory (NIPC Advisory 99-007) noting "multiple reports of recent hacking and cyber activity directed at U.S. government computer networks, in response to the accidental bombing of the Chinese embassy in Belgrade … Reported activity include[d] replacing official web pages with protest material and offensive language, posting similar language in chat rooms and news groups, and denial of service email attacks."[10] American hackers have been known to attack jihadist websites. For example, an American was reported by *Wired* magazine to have hijacked www.alneda. com, a widely used website for jihadist recruitment.[11] His motive for doing so was said to be a decision made after the September 11 attacks: "I was going to use every skill I had to screw up the terrorists' communication in any way I could." Additionally, Russian hackers are generally reported to have been responsible for the cyber attacks on Estonia in 2007 and Georgia in 2008.[12]

Patrick Allen and Chris Demchak generalize from experiences such as these to predict that future conflicts between nations may involve spontaneous attack action in cyberspace by "patriots" on each side. Also, rapid escalation of these actions will occur to a broad range of targets on the other side. Because hacktivists are interested in making a statement, they will simply attack sites until they find vulnerable ones. Sympathetic individuals from other nations will become involved to support the primary antagonists.[13]

The actions of these patriotic hackers may greatly complicate escalation management. Such actions may be seen by an adversary as being performed under the direction, blessing, tacit concurrence, or tolerance of the state and therefore are likely to be factored into the adversary's assessment of the state's motives and intent. The state's efforts to suppress patriotic hackers may be seen as insincere and are likely to be at least partially unsuccessful as well. In a worst-case scenario, actions of patriotic hackers during times of tension may be seen as an officially sanctioned cyber first strike, even if they have not acted with government approval or under government direction.

Yet another complication involving patriotic hackers is the possibility that they might be directed by, inspired by, or tolerated by their government but in ways in which the government's hand is not easily visible. Under such circumstances, hostile acts with damaging consequences could continue to occur with corresponding benefits to the nation responsible despite official denials. At the very least, the possibility that patriotic hackers may be operating could act as a plausible cover for government-sponsored cyber attacks, even if there were in fact no patriotic hackers doing anything.

INCENTIVES FOR SELF-RESTRAINT IN ESCALATION

One set of incentives is based on concerns about an adversary's response to escalation. Understanding this set of incentives is necessarily based on a sense of what kinds of offensive cyber actions—whether cyber attack or cyber exploitation—might be mistaken for cyber attack and might lead to what kinds of adversary responses, either in cyberspace or in physical space. In this regard, an essential difference between cyber attack and the use of a nuclear, chemical, biological, or space weapon is readily apparent—the initial use of any nuclear, chemical, biological, or space weapon, regardless of how it is used, would constitute an escalation of a conflict under almost any circumstances. By contrast, whether a given cyber attack, or conventional kinetic attack for that matter, would be regarded as an escalation depends on the nature of the operation—the nature of the target(s), their geographical locations, or their strategic significance.

A second set of incentives is based on concerns about blowback—the possibility that a cyber attack launched by Nation Blue against Nation Red's computers might somehow affect Blue's computers at a later time. Understanding the likelihood of blowback will require a complex mix of technical insight and intelligence information.

DE-ESCALATION AND CONFLICT TERMINATION

Conflict termination presumes the existence of an ongoing conflict to which the participants desire an end. It requires several elements, including:

- a reliable and trustworthy mechanism that can be used by the involved parties to negotiate the terms of an agreement to terminate a conflict,
- a clear understanding on all sides about what the terms of any agreement require each side to do,

- assurance that all parties to an agreement will adhere to the terms of any such agreement, and
- capabilities for each party that can ensure all entities taking action on behalf of that party adhere to the terms of any such agreement.

In the cyber environment, these elements may be problematic. National leaders and their representatives will almost certainly be communicating with each other through electronic channels, the reliability of which may be questionable in certain kinds of cyber conflict. A cease-fire agreement in cyberspace presumes each side can know that the other has stopped hostile activity in cyberspace. However, ambiguity and technical limitations create problems. Nation Blue may conduct cyber exploitations seeking to verify that Nation Red is standing down in cyberspace. Red may interpret these operations as prelude to Blue's continuing an attack campaign against it. Patriotic hackers of Blue may press onward against Red even though both Red and Blue have themselves agreed to a cyber cease-fire. During conflict, there is no reason to assume the cessation of continuing cyber operations conducted by others who are not part of the conflict (e.g., criminals). In some cases, ongoing offensive operations by these third parties may be mistakenly attributed to Red or Blue. The two nations may differ in their interpretation of key concepts. What activities constitute an "attack" in cyberspace, or what evidence should be used to determine if an attack is occurring? Differing interpretations and inadequate technical capabilities may impede understanding. For kinetic military forces, a variety of technical means (e.g., photoreconnaissance aircraft and satellites, ocean-scale sonar arrays) are capable of monitoring movements of military personnel and equipment. Most importantly, these means operate from outside territory controlled by an adversary and provide information that is generally regarded as reliable. But because the footprint of cyber forces is so small, movement of adversary forces can take place without signatures that can be externally observed.

Based on precedents in kinetic conflict, it is plausible that nations seeking a cease-fire in a cyber conflict would ask for the deactivation of these hostile agents. To comply with such a request (not an unreasonable one in the context of a cease-fire), these nations will need to maintain cyber "demining" capabilities regarding the offensive software and/or hardware agents they implant into adversary systems, networks, and infrastructure. For example, they will need to keep track of where these agents are implanted or be able to communicate with them to disarm them—a capability that may rule out offensive agents that operate in a fully autonomous manner.

Each party will naturally have concerns about its adversary's commitment to adhere to the terms of a cyber cease-fire, especially in the aftermath of a conflict. On what basis would Blue's government believe a claim by Red that it was indeed complying with the terms of a cease-fire? How much would

Red tell Blue about system and network penetrations it had made, knowing such information might be used to prosecute an attack or defend more effectively against Red? The availability of effective ways to address the issues described above is almost certainly one aspect of being able to manage conflict termination in cyberspace.

Analysts sometimes raise the issue of how the United States might deter escalation when it has more at stake in cyberspace than its adversaries. The first point to consider is that deterrence of cyber attack does not necessarily entail a threat to respond through cyberspace against an adversary's cyber assets, and when noncyber threats against an adversary's noncyber assets are considered, the calculus of deterrence may well be different. For example, kinetic weapons can, in principle, be employed against valuable physical military targets. Although the threshold for such a response may well be higher, an adversary would still have to consider the possibility of a noncyber response to any attack. Consistent with this point, U.S. policy makers have always noted that the United States reserves the right to respond appropriately in a time, place, and manner of its own choosing. In addition, concerns over blowback may deter an adversary. If an adversary's interests are entangled with those of the United States, it may be deterred from taking actions that might harm U.S. interests because of concerns that one ultimate effect of such actions would be to harm the adversary's interests. For example, a nation that is owed a great deal of money by the United States might well be unlikely to conduct an attack that undermines its financial stability.

Lastly, many analysts note that deterrence is a psychological phenomenon and that threats of retaliation must be focused on assets that an adversary holds dear and values highly. In principle, what an adversary—or more precisely, an adversary decision maker—holds dear can span a wide range, from personal to national (e.g., tools of national power). In the category of personal assets are financial entities (e.g., a leader's bank accounts could be drained), reputation (e.g., a scandal in a policy maker's past might be revealed), and close friends and relatives (e.g., the interests of such individuals could be compromised). Such assets are not typically considered in a traditional military context—but nontraditional approaches to deterrence may well be needed to deal with the nontraditional threats that cyber attacks pose.

The approaches described above may be most useful in deterring hostile cyber operations intended to achieve large-scale effects. They are unlikely to be useful in deterring operations intended to achieve smaller effects, because smaller effects by definition do not cause maximum pain for either side. Put differently, the argument that the United States has more at risk in cyberspace than its adversaries is simply not relevant when the amount of damage that can be done (by definition) is small.

KINETIC ESCALATION

Issues of escalation and conflict termination in cyberspace are complicated by the fact there may be cross-domain linkages. Although conflict might, in principle, be limited to hostile operations in cyberspace alone, there is no reason this is necessarily so, and policy makers must contemplate the possibility that conflict in cyberspace might spill over into physical space, and might even lead to kinetic actions.

For example, if national command authorities decide to retaliate in response to a cyber attack, an important question is whether retaliation must be based on a "tit-for-tat" response. Assuming the perpetrator of a cyber attack is known to be a hostile nation, there is no reason in principle the retaliation could not be a kinetic attack against the interests of that hostile nation. Allowing a kinetic response to a cyber attack expands the range of options available to the victim. An extreme case is, in the event of a cyber attack of sufficient scale and duration that it threatens the nation's ability to function as a modern society, the attacked nation might choose to respond with kinetic force. On the other hand, the use of kinetic operations during an ostensibly cyber-only conflict is an important threshold. Nations involved in a cyber-only conflict may have an interest in refraining from a kinetic response—for example, they may believe kinetic operations would be too provocative and might result in an undesired escalation of the conflict.

In addition, the logic of offensive cyber operations suggests that such operations are likely to be most successful when the initiator of these operations has the time to gather intelligence on likely targets—such intelligence gathering is obviously time-limited once overt kinetic conflict breaks out.

If understanding the dynamics of cyber-only conflict is difficult, understanding the dynamics of cyber conflict when kinetic operations may be involved is doubly so. To the extent national decision makers have incentives to refrain from conducting offensive operations that might induce a strong kinetic reaction, the obvious approach would be to conduct cyber attacks that are in some sense smaller, modest in result, targeted selectively against less provocative targets, and perhaps more reversible. The similarity of such an approach to escalation control in other kinds of conflict is not accidental, and it has all of the corresponding complexities and uncertainties.

In keeping a cyber conflict from escalating into physical space, it is important to think about "lines in the sand" beyond which one side warns another not to cross. For example, it is reported that during the first Gulf War, the United States regarded Iraqi use of chemical weapons against U.S. forces as one such threshold of unacceptable activity, one that might well provoke the use of U.S. nuclear weapons against Iraq. When only traditional kinetic forces are involved, lines in the sand might be the use of certain weapons, attacks on or damage to certain targets, movement or placement of armed forces beyond certain geographical lines, and so on. Cyber analogs to these thresholds are hard to construct. Describing a class of cyber weapon whose mere use would be wholly unacceptable is hard to imagine, since there are no real cyber analogs to true weapons of mass destruction (WMD) where even a single use of a WMD qualitatively changes the landscape of kinetic conflict. And in cyberspace, what is the analog of a geographical border beyond which cyber weapons may not be placed?

Perhaps the most promising analog is the notion of specific targets that might be placed off limits—cyber attacks on such targets could, in principle, be deemed unacceptable. One class of off-limits targets might be cyber assets associated with truly critical infrastructure, such as the bulk power grid or the banking and financial system. But as any bank executive will confirm, some of these targets are under attack quite frequently—so attacks that do not cause large amounts of damage or loss probably should *not* qualify as crossing the threshold of unacceptability. There is also the question of being able to assign *political* responsibility to some perpetrator for the conduct of a successful large-scale attack on some off-limits target—a question whose answer may be in doubt, given the difficulties of rapid attribution of a cyber attack. Finally, one might well ask how a cyber asset would be positively identified as being associated with the bulk power grid or the banking and financial system. Would we provide a computer-readable identification tag on every such computer? Such a tag might make these targets obvious to other parties wishing to do us harm.

Even presuming that specific thresholds could be identified, such information would need to be communicated clearly to an adversary. Such communication is difficult even in scenarios of traditional military conflict, and all of these difficulties obtain in the cyber context. But it is worth observing that because cyber conflict is fundamentally based on deception, persuading an adversary to believe any U.S. statement about what is off-limits may be particularly challenging.

THE POLITICAL SIDE OF ESCALATION

Despite the focus of the discussion above on escalation dynamics from a primarily military standpoint, escalation dynamics inevitably have a political and psychological component that must not be overlooked. For example, the discussion of active defense above pointed out that U.S. cyber attacks undertaken under the rubric of active defense may not be perceived by others as innocent acts of self-defense, even if they are intended as such. While both sides in most conflicts claim they are acting in self-defense, cyber conflicts are a particularly messy domain in which to air and judge such claims.

Another possible misperception may arise from intelligence-collection activities that might involve cyber-attack techniques. The discussion above noted the problems of misperceiving exploitation as a prelude to continuing cyber operations during a cease-fire. But the problem is broader than that—during conflict or in the tense times that often precede conflict, the needs for current intelligence on the adversary are particularly acute. Knowing what the adversary is doing and the scope and nature of its future intentions are very important to decision makers, and the need to collect such intelligence will almost certainly result in greater pressures to use the entire array of available intelligence-gathering techniques—including techniques of cyber exploitation. If the adversary is unable to distinguish between an offensive operation for exploitation and one for attack—an outcome that seems all too likely—a cyber exploitation may run the risk of being perceived as part of an imminent attack, even if this is not the intent of decision makers.

Finally, it seems likely that escalation issues would play out differently if the other nation(s) involved are or are not near-peer competitors. Escalation to physical conflict is less of a concern to the United States if the nation has weak conventional forces and/or is a nonnuclear state. But a nation with nuclear weapons, or even strong conventional forces in a position to inflict significant damage on U.S. allies, is another matter entirely. Relationships with such states may well need to be explicitly managed, paying special attention to how escalation may be viewed, managed, and controlled, and most importantly, how miscalculation, misperception, or outright error may affect an adversary's response.

Dynamics such as these suggest that factors other than the ones dictated by military or legal necessity play important roles in escalation dynamics, if only because they can strongly affect the perceptions of decision makers on either side.

THE FUTURE OF ESCALATION DYNAMICS

The issues of escalation dynamics, conflict termination, and cross-domain linkages in cyberspace play out against a rapidly changing technological, policy, and geopolitical environment. The substrate of cyberspace—computing and communications technology—is characterized by change on a timescale much shorter than the planning horizon for traditional military acquisitions and planning. Upgrades notwithstanding, major weapons platforms are expected to serve for decades, while the IT environment changes rapidly in a few years. The growing use of cloud computing is a further—and potentially disruptive—change in possible computing platforms and may require new concepts for assigning responsibility for cyber operations. Mobile computing may present opportunities for determining device location as well as being the enabling technology for many new users of cyberspace. IT will be increasingly embedded, ubiquitous, and connected within all elements of modern society, potentially increasing vulnerabilities to all manner of societal functions. The result is that operational concepts for escalation management must take into account a rapidly evolving set of targets and offensive and defensive capabilities.

In most traditional domains of conflict, U.S. military doctrine has been based on the establishing dominance—that state in which friendly forces have maximum freedom of action and adversary forces have minimal freedom of action. But in the cyber domain, this presumption is not sustainable—and senior U.S. military leaders are beginning to speak publicly about this point.[14] Much of the traditional U.S. approach to escalation control is based on the ability of friendly forces to establish dominance at any level of conflict on the premise that an adversary would not choose to escalate if, at the higher level of conflict, it could not hope to prevail.

Nation-states are increasingly concerned about the risks inherent in involvement in cyberspace. Even apart from the protection of critical national infrastructure and military assets, various nations express deepening worries about traditional criminal activity in cyberspace, protection of intellectual property, and increased connectedness for political movements that may pose a threat to government interests and stability.

Nonstate actors are increasingly important players in cyberspace. Multinational corporations and organized crime syndicates, for example, all have some nontrivial capability to conduct offensive operations in cyberspace to further their interests, and even small groups of individuals can have a large impact by exploiting certain characteristics of cyberspace (e.g., WikiLeaks).

Although existing theories of escalation dynamics and conflict termination may serve as useful points of departure, what is understood very poorly today is how these theories may apply in cyberspace. In the future, finding ways to manage cyber conflict will be even more intellectually challenging than it was for traditional conflict.

NOTES

1. The lag time between dissemination of a security fix to the public and its installation on a specific computer system may be considerable, and it is not always due to unawareness on the part of the system administrator. It sometimes happens that the installation of a fix will cause an application running on the

system to cease working, and administrators may have to weigh the potential benefit of installing a security fix against the potential cost of rendering a critical application nonfunctional. Adversaries take advantage of this lag time to exploit vulnerabilities.

2. A *zero-day attack* is a previously unseen attack on a previously unknown vulnerability. The term refers to the fact that the vulnerability has been known to the defender for zero days. (The adversary has usually known of the attack for a much longer time.) The most dangerous is a zero-day attack on a remotely accessible service that runs by default on all versions of a widely used operating system distribution. This type of remotely accessible zero-day attack on services appears to be occurring less frequently. In response, a shift in focus to the client side has occurred, resulting in many recent zero-day attacks on client-side applications. For data and analysis of zero-day attack trends, see Daniel Geer, "Measuring Security," (undated), http://geer.tinho.net/measuringsecurity.tutorialv2.pdf.

3. An adversary computer or network may not necessarily be owned and operated by the adversary—it may simply support or be used by the adversary.

4. For purposes of this chapter, the term *attribution* is used to refer to the identification of the party to which political responsibility should be assigned for the cyber operations that harm the interests of the target. This qualifier is necessary because the entity "responsible" can also be the machine(s) involved in the operation or the specific human beings who took specific actions (at a keyboard) to launch the operation. One of these other meanings may be more relevant, depending on the purposes for which attribution is sought. For more discussion of this point, see David D. Clark and Susan Landau, "Untangling Attribution," *National Security Journal 2*, no. 2 (March 16, 2011), http://harvardnsj.org/2011/03/untangling-attribution-2/, as well as William Owens, Kenneth Dam, and Herbert Lin, *Technology, Policy, Law, and Ethics Regarding U.S. Acquisition and Use of Cyberattack Capabilities* (Washington, DC: National Academies Press, 2009), chap. 2.

5. The broad topic of how to improve passive cyber defenses and enhance resilience of U.S. computer systems and networks is addressed in a variety of National Research Council (NRC) reports on this topic: *Computers at Risk,* 1991; *Information Technology for Counterterrorism,* 2003; *Cybersecurity Today and Tomorrow: Pay Now or Pay Later,* 2002; *Realizing the Potential of C4I: Fundamental Challenges,* 1998; *Trust in Cyberspace,* 1999; and *Toward a Safer and More Secure Cyberspace,* 2007, all authored by the NRC and published by National Academies Press, Washington, DC. Other important reports include President's Information Technology Advisory Committee, *Cyber Security: A Crisis of Prioritization* (Washington, DC: National Coordination Office for Information Technology Research and Development, February 2005); and Commission on Cyber Security for the 44th Presidency, *Securing Cyberspace for the 44th Presidency* (Washington, DC: Center for Strategic and International Studies, 2008).

6. This taxonomy is based mostly on Forrest E. Morgan, Karl P. Mueller, Evan S. Medeiros, Kevin L. Pollpeter, and Roger Cliff, *Dangerous Thresholds: Managing Escalation in the 21st Century* (Santa Monica, CA: RAND, 2008). Though the RAND discussion is silent on escalation in cyberspace *per se.*

7. Even in the case of a nuclear EMP attack directed against electronic equipment in another nation, there is no reason to assume that all of that nation's cyber-attack capabilities are necessarily resident within its boundaries. Because cyber attacks can originate from anywhere, some cyber-attack capabilities may have been deployed in other nations—indeed, some attack agents may already have been clandestinely deployed in U.S. systems.

8. "Cyberwar Also Rages in Mideast," *Associated Press* (October 26, 2000), http://www.wired.com/politics/law/news/2000/10/39766.

9. Michelle Delio, "A Chinese Call to Hack U.S.," *Wired* (April 11, 2001), http://www.wired.com/news/politics/0,1283,42982,00.html.

10. Available at http://www.merit.edu/mail.archives/netsec/1999-05/msg00013.html.

11. Patrick Di Justo, "How Al-Qaida Site Was Hijacked," *Wired* (August 10, 2002), http://www.wired.com/culture/lifestyle/news/2002/08/54455.

12. "Expert: Cyber-Attacks on Georgia Websites Tied to Mob, Russian Government," *Los Angeles Times* (August 13, 2008), http://latimesblogs.latimes.com/technology/2008/08/experts-debate.html.

13. Adapted largely from Patrick D. Allen and Chris C. Demchak, "The Palestinian-Israel: Cyberwar," *Military Review* 83, no. 2 (March–April 2003), pp. 52–59.

14. For example, RADM William Leigher, deputy commander of the U.S. Navy Cyber Command, was recently quoted as saying that "Unlike the physical domain, achieving dominance [in the cyber domain] may be impossible." Amber Corrin, "Dominance in Cyberspace Might Not Be Possible," *Defense Systems* (January 27, 2011), http://defensesystems.com/articles/2011/01/27/afcea-west-cyber-warfare-panel.aspx.

Chapter Eight

The Specter of Nonobvious Warfare

Martin C. Libicki

Innovations, both technological and organizational, over the last few decades have created a potential for nonobvious warfare,[1] in which the identity of the warring side and even the very fact of warfare are completely ambiguous.

The Stuxnet computer worm is a noteworthy example. This worm is believed to have infiltrated Iran's Natanz centrifuge facility, causing equipment to destroy itself over a period of weeks and leading to the premature retirement of 10 percent of Iran's uranium enrichment capability. Within several months of the worm's public disclosure (September 2010), Western intelligence sources announced that the earliest date Iran could build a bomb had been pushed back several years—and, indeed, the inventory of working centrifuges plateaued for two years before rising in mid-2012. With sanctions biting, and too little progress made on developing a nuclear arsenal, Iran agreed to halt its program in 2015. Until the worm was discovered and dissected, the Iranians were uncertain why their equipment wore out so fast. Indeed, when confronted publicly with the possibility, they first denied any such attack had happened, only to reverse themselves obliquely two months later.

Although nonobvious warfare can be epitomized by cyber warfare,[2] states can attack one another in many ways without the victim being certain exactly who did it or even what was done. Some, like electronic warfare (against nonmilitary targets) and space warfare, have yet to materialize in any strategically significant way. Others, such as naval/land mining or sabotage, have long historical antecedents. What they share is ambiguity. A short list of warfare types that *could* plausibly be conducted in a nonobvious manner include the following:

- cyber warfare;
- space warfare;

- electronic warfare;
- drone warfare;
- sabotage, special operations, assassins, and mines;
- proxy attacks;
- weapons of mass destruction; and
- intelligence support to combat operations.

The best example of nonobvious warfare—now termed *gray zone conflict*—can be found in Russia's behavior in Crimea and Eastern Ukraine since early 2014. Crimea, for instance, was captured by "little green men"—Russian soldiers without identifying insignia, thereby allowing the patina of deniability over the operation. Eastern Ukraine's capture was a more long-term process involving local insurgents aided by Russian units whose existence was denied even after several soldiers were captured in Ukraine. Russia's efforts throughout this conflict included various forms of cyber war (DDOS attacks, the attempted hijacking of Ukrainian election machinery, several takedowns within Ukraine's power grid), information operations (fake news, official lies, and other propaganda), militarized cyber espionage (Android malware that provided targeting location for Ukrainian artillery batteries), electronic warfare (against cell phone systems), and the sabotage of information infrastructures (via wire cutters). Granted, Russia's intervention may be all too obvious in Kiev. Yet, it may be nonobvious enough to provide a fig leaf allowing countries to hide so as to avoid confronting Russia outright for its aggression.

Nonobvious warfare stands starkly in contrast to, say, a tank invasion across the German-Polish border, an event unlikely to spur questions such as "Whose tanks are those ... and why are they here?" By contrast, the *uses* of nonobvious warfare are limited. It is quite difficult to take over the capital of another country anonymously (proxies may do so but at that point often cease being proxies and evolve to dependents or even independents). Defensive warfare is almost always carried out by whoever owns what is being defended. Even coercion requires self-identification *if* the "me" in the point—"don't tread on me"—is to be adequately conveyed. But there are some types of warfare that can be satisfactorily or even more advantageously carried out if there is doubt about who did what. Again, Stuxnet provides an example. Retarding the Iranian nuclear program benefitted Israel, whether or not anyone knows for certain whether Israel (or anyone else) did it. Furthermore, if the purpose of warfare is to change minds in the victim's capital, uncertainty may focus subsequent reflection on what such an attack says about the security and (reduced) power of the victim rather than on the malevolence of the undetermined attacker.

Accordingly, this chapter explores the topic in several steps. The first is to develop a sense of what it means to be nonobvious. The second is to delineate several forms of warfare that may, under some circumstances, be nonobvious and why. The third is to speculate on how states (and nonstate actors) might use nonobvious warfare. The fourth is to speculate on how victimized states can respond to the threat of nonobvious warfare.

WHEN IS WARFARE NONOBVIOUS?

Ambiguity is the heart of nonobviousness. If the victim is unsure of who carried out an operation, it may hesitate to respond in the same way as if it were certain. Alternatively, the rest of the world might have doubts even if the victim is certain, leaving the victim wary of responding as it might have if *others* were very sure of matters.

Nonobviousness is enhanced if the events in question can themselves be questioned. Some could be accidents or utter mysteries, for example, the unexplained failure of a satellite. Others could be crimes, such as bank robberies by politically inclined groups, or acts of espionage—many events labeled as cyber attacks are really attempts to steal information. Nevertheless, some nonobvious warfare incidents would clearly be acts of war if they were obvious—in which case, the key ambiguity is the actor not the act.

Some forms of warfare are nonobvious because the relationship between the attacker and a state is unclear. For instance, to what extent is Hezbollah or the insurgents of eastern Ukraine, working for their own ends, and to what extent are they a puppet manipulated by Tehran or Moscow? In some cases, the perpetrators may be state employees who are not necessarily, or at least not provably, working under the command and control of the state itself. Does the fact that someone close to the Russian political structure claimed credit for having organized attacks on Estonian institutions in Russia mean it was an attack by Russia?[3] Pakistan's ISI intelligence agency has been accused of shielding Taliban warlords; so, is Pakistan at war with Afghanistan? If both questions can be answered "yes," then these are two examples of nonobvious warfare.

Finally, many forms of nonobvious warfare present no personal risk to war fighters—which it would have to, almost by definition, since the capture or identification of the perpetrator may make the source of the attack obvious. But one cannot conclude that *states* that employ such war fighters are off the hook just because their war fighters are. A no-fingerprints approach to warfare may be a logical next step after a no-footprints approach, but the two are still quite different.

Nonobviousness is not an absolute, and the actionable response threshold for the victimized state will vary greatly. The primary criterion is how confidently the victim feels a particular state carried out an attack—if, indeed, what happened really *was* an attack. This perceived likelihood is almost always going to be nonzero. Few states truly believe that no other state wants to harm them. Even what later prove to be accidents (e.g., the explosion in the USS *Maine*) are often blamed on other states (e.g., Spain). If there is a crisis (e.g., Spain's attempt to quell a Cuban insurgency), the tendency to believe that any harmful and unusual occurrence was an attack will be that much higher.

So the attacker who would strike with impunity must ask whether or not the confidence with which the victim believes that it carried out the attack is likely to be greater or less than the confidence that the victim requires to respond to the attack. Everything depends on what the threshold of response is, and there may be many types of responses. Evidence sufficient to gain a criminal conviction in a U.S. court "beyond reasonable doubt" is rarely the issue, although similarly high levels of confidence may, in fact, be required before the victim decides to go to war. On the other hand, mere suspicion may suffice to curtail active or disapprove of prospective cooperative arrangements such as mutual military exercises, joint research, or network peering relationships. With some forms of nonobvious warfare, the target may be uncertain of state sponsorship but may convince itself that such a state has to shoulder some blame if it reasonably could have detected and stopped or hindered such an attack and refused to do so.

Exactly how the target state acquires the confidence that another specific state carried out an attack will also vary, but one cannot go very far wrong by considering means, motives, and opportunity. Opportunity—in the form of some traceable delivery vehicle—often best distinguishes obvious from nonobvious warfare. But opportunity is only one leg of the stool. Consider, for example, how the United States would react to the detonation of a so-called suitcase nuclear weapon circa, say, 1962. The suitcase would be incinerated, leaving little forensic evidence. But at that time, only three other states had the *means* to carry out a nuclear attack, and of those three, only one, the USSR, had a *motive* to do so. In such circumstances, the lack of a visible delivery vehicle would have little dented U.S. confidence in the belief that the USSR had done it. Similarly, for many types of nonobvious warfare, such as attacks on spacecraft, the list of suspects would be fairly short since the number of space-faring nations is limited (although, in that case, the victim must also credibly distinguish accidents from attacks).

TYPES OF NONOBVIOUS WARFARE

What makes various forms of nonobvious warfare, in fact, nonobvious? We examine them individually.

Cyber Warfare

Hackers can sit anywhere and attack systems around the world, disrupting their functioning, corrupting the information they hold and the algorithms they run, and, as Stuxnet showed, even breaking machines by feeding them harmful commands from hacked systems. Attribution is particularly difficult for a cyber attack. The ones and zeroes that constitute the attack do not bear the physical residues of their operators (especially if these ones and zeroes were copied from others' tools). Successfully attacked systems, almost by definition, cannot distinguish an attack from completely benign inputs at the time (with a distributed denial-of-service attack, it is volume, not content, that matters; the attacking bytes generally come from "innocent" machines that have been tricked into spamming the victim). Forensic methods such as tracing the attack back to its sources can be easily frustrated by bouncing the attack through enough portals, using the services of an innocent machine, or jumping on a third-party Wi-Fi connection. States wanting to guess who attacked them find they must rely on means and motive. Means offer only a little help for an unsophisticated attack, since over a hundred countries have investigated offensive cyber war and the list of hackers includes organized crime groups, nonstate actors, and individuals. It is generally believed that only a state could have pulled off a sophisticated attack such as Stuxnet, with its four zero-day exploits and two stolen certificates. Iran may have figured, once it realized that it *had* been attacked, only Israel and the United States would have both the reason and the talent to carry out such an attack. But it is not entirely impossible that either Russia or China may have wanted to retard Iran's rush to nuclear weapons.

No one yet knows whether cyber attacks carried out in a nonobvious manner will prove advantageous to those who carry them out. It is by no means clear that Russia's (or Russian) attacks on Estonia or Georgia did it that much good. If Israel attacked Iran in cyberspace, what looks like success may be viewed as the beginning of a new set of military operations, or, alternatively, a very special case that no one else can or need duplicate.

Space Warfare

Satellites normally lose capability from time to time in the depths and darkness of space. An attack on a satellite without the attack vehicle being discovered may come close to the perfect crime. States may want to know what happened, but deorbiting a satellite may not necessarily be something the satellite was designed to do, may be rendered impossible by the nature of the attack, and will require the expenditure of a substantial amount of fuel. Although postrecovery analysis would likely indicate what happened, it still may not answer who did it. That noted, getting away with satellite murder presents difficulties. The United States has the capability to find every sufficiently large ground-based missile launch and tracks space objects supposedly the size of wrenches (the exact details are undoubtedly classified). Because it has a fairly good idea what every satellite is supposed to be doing, those otherwise employed necessarily get noticed, but the advent of microsats, nanosats, and picosats may complicate detection by subtraction in years to come. Ground-based systems might blind satellites, but the satellites have to be looking at whatever it is that is doing the blinding (hence, indicating where the laser is coming from). The number of states that can buy a launch is much larger than the few that can launch objects into space.

Electronic Warfare

As our wired world becomes increasing wireless, the potential for electronic jamming grows apace. Small generic radiating devices surreptitiously emplaced or scattered about can block GPS signals (at least for commercial receivers) and wreak havoc with communications, ranging from cell phone and emergency communications to machine controllers. Such devices can sometimes be quite difficult to find but not hard to characterize (deliberate jamming is unlikely to be confused with natural causes or accidents for very long). Using generic devices can frustrate trace-back, but the real trick in anonymity is to not get caught emplacing such devices. Once the devices start operating, their lifespan is limited, either because they are discovered or because their batteries die.

Drones

Under some relatively narrow set of circumstances, an attack by drones may be carried out without firm attribution. The requirements are many. The drone has to avoid crashing (or must be recovered if it does); otherwise, there is a fair chance of tracing even a generic drone back to its last buyer. The targeted country either has to have relatively poor radar coverage or abut territory or oceans where there is no radar coverage. If the drone comes from the ocean, the list of possible attackers can be limited to those with ships in the area at the time. The drone itself has to be fairly generic—so that its profile at a distance is consistent with the inventory of many different countries—or else stealthy. Finally, the possibility that a drone attack can be a nonobvious attack by the United States must await the development of attack drones by countries *other than* the United States—failing that, any such drone will be assumed to be American. For states on the outs with the United States, the combination of motive and means may suffice.

Special Operators, Saboteurs, and Assassins

As with drones, the key to maintaining anonymity in special operations is to avoid getting caught. Ironically, the ability to carry out *many* special operations without getting caught requires so much organizational and professional skill that the number of countries capable of doing this is few—making accusations that much more credible. Hence, perfection may be its own undoing, unless the attacker shows considerable restraint. This category includes mine-laying by stealthy conveyance (e.g., submarines), which gives it a historic resonance, if nothing else, but also contemporary resonance, as in the mysterious—and disputed—damage to an Irish vessel primed to run Gaza's blockade.[4]

Proxy Attacks

This broad category includes terrorists, insurgents, militias, and privateers. Attribution becomes difficult because it generally requires the perpetrators be caught (or use a recognizable modus operandi) but mostly because it requires tying the perpetrator to a major actor. In practice, however, the link between insurgent groups and states really is ambiguous, and not necessarily by design; empowering individuals with organization, ideology, and weaponry tends to make them believe that their goals are important in and of themselves. The Vietcong, for instance, may have been established and sustained by North Vietnam but had somewhat different priorities.[5] Africa provides a more apropos case in which various countries that sponsored insurgencies against their neighbors managed to find themselves under siege by insurgents of their own, similarly backed.

Attacks Using Weapons of Mass Destruction

The so-called suitcase bomb of the Cold War era has been joined by the use of biological and chemical agents—of which there are many types—all of which offer, at least in theory, a method of killing people without a state necessarily getting caught doing it. Because weapons of mass destruction, as a general rule, are relatively small, their use may not require forcible insertion, and modern electronics allow them to be detonated remotely. However, such attacks are considered particularly heinous, and nearly every state has signed one or more international treaties against doing so. For that reason, more such attacks may well be traced to their ultimate source than a similarly stealthy attack by high explosives. Granted, infectious agents, particularly those that may yet be invented by DNA recombination techniques, can be delivered in a very stealthy manner. But unless a state's own citizens are somehow immune to their effects, it is unclear what that state would gain from using them or, if used in a "doomsday machine" mode, why a state would want to be nonobvious about the matter.

Intelligence Support to Combat Operations

Although technically not warfare, a state with a sophisticated stand-off intelligence collection and processing/distribution mechanism can provide data that can be a great help for its friends. If the assistance is not directly intercepted and its distribution is limited, then others would have difficulty discerning the origin for certain (although states may suspect that opponents punching over their weight may have gotten some help, only a handful of countries could and would supply it). Unlike other forms of nonobvious warfare, helping out with information is not particularly heinous, and denials—or at least "neither confirm nor deny"—are par for the course in the intelligence world. Nevertheless, the supplying state may not want to show its hand in the conflict lest it be accused of being a belligerent or if it has a rival that can then justify *its own* assistance to the other side.

It merits repetition that unless the attack looks like a complete accident—and the target is completely credulous—there is no such thing as a completely unattributable attack. Every state has its enemies or untrustworthy friends, and if anything untoward happens, the usual suspects will be trotted out for examination. Conversely, plausible deniability matters only if the victimized state really does need something close to judicial proof to take action or is relieved that the authorship of the attack is not so obvious that its unwillingness to respond is not seen as cowardice. Perpetrators do not have to be caught red-handed to suffer reprisal in the hands of those who can put means, motives, and opportunity together to form a sufficiently robust basis for action.

THE USES OF NONOBVIOUS WARFARE

If is often easier to state what *cannot* be done with nonobvious warfare. Its inapplicability for conquest and specific coercion has already been noted. Furthermore, any purpose that requires a sustained series of attacks cannot use a nonobvious warfare technique if the probability of ascription for each attack is nonzero and the probability of ascribing one event is at least somewhat independent of the probability of ascribing another; patterns may be easier to attribute than solitary events. These criteria, strictly speaking, would rule out space warfare, electronic warfare, drones, and special operations, but there are degrees of obviousness and a varied context-related tolerance among countries for calling it out. So these are not absolutes—although in practice any nonobviousness that relies on the difficulty of distinguishing accident from attack cannot easily survive repetition. A campaign of cyber warfare may also cease being nonobvious after repetition, but there are fewer constraints on proxy warfare—where attribution has to be inferred rather than discovered—and intelligence support to warfare.

So what *can* be done with nonobvious warfare? One use is general coercion or dissuasion. Instead of signaling, "if you do this we will do that," the signal is, "if you do this then bad things will happen to you." Because the act of signaling itself may implicate the attacker, it helps if the signals come from someone else. Others may be willing to help if there are multiple states with a common interest, such as Vietnam, Indonesia, and the Philippines all opposing Chinese bumptiousness in the South China Sea. These others may also be coreligionists or co-ideologues (e.g., "disrespect our religion and bad things happen to you"). The use of nonobvious warfare for compulsion is trickier to pull off insofar as it is easier for disparate entities to agree on what can be condemned than to agree on what should be done.

Another fairly obvious use is sabotage, à la Stuxnet, carried out to deny its target some capability. The difficulty is that sabotage is rather pointless unless it takes place on a very large scale or is somehow associated with an operation (if it is a combat operation, the target might assume that the saboteurs work for the combatants). Even if the damage is permanent, states can generally recover. The attack on the Iranian centrifuges made sense because of the strong desire felt by some countries to hobble Iran's nuclear program and buy time. Another rationale for sabotage is to push a target past a nearby tipping point, even if this tends to be visible only in retrospect. Otherwise, the consequences of carrying out what could be an act of war may outweigh the gains, even if getting caught is unlikely.

An untraceable attack of sufficient magnitude may also weaken the target prefatory to an armed attack or at least so distract the target that it cannot assign the resources, such as sensors, in-place weapons, or management attention, required to foresee and prepare for what turns out to be an imminent overt attack. Clearly, if an attack does come, the precursor will cease being a nonobvious attack in retrospect (unless the target has multiple eager enemies, each looking for signs of weakness, in which case, what looks obvious may still be wrong). The advantages of starting in a nonobvious mode are twofold. First, if the initial attack were obvious, the target might countermove in ways that make the attack harder to pull off. It may know where to point its defenses, so to speak; it could rally others to pressure the attacker; or it could even counterattack. Second, if the attack falls short of its objectives, the attacker may cancel the overt attack and remain obscure in hopes of eluding punishment.

Correspondingly, a nonobvious attack may be a test to see if the particular technique works, what the target's defenses are, and where improvements should be sought. However, it would be an expensive test if the target itself should learn something about its vulnerabilities and thereby have cause to work them and evidence on how to do so.

Nonobvious operations can also help win the wars of third parties. Such help can be nonobvious either if the *fact* of help is not obvious or if the *source* of help could be any of several countries or entities such as insurgent or mercenary groups. This raises the question of why such a state would want not to leave fingerprints. One reason is that the attacks take place in a country other than the one that wanted help (e.g., Syria attacks Iraq, and the United States attacks targets in Syria), thereby becoming an act of war in its own right and an excuse for the attacked country to call on *its* friends to help (e.g., attack Iraq). More likely, however, the assistance supports operations within the state under attack, either by another state or by insurgents, so these factors do not come into play. What *does* matter, however, is the appearance of commitment and how it prevents assuming a commitment to pursue victory or lose face. Intervening and then withdrawing prematurely raises doubts about the state's seriousness of purpose and even trustworthiness, even if such a state never made an explicit commitment to stay the course.

Nonobvious warfare can also be carried out for narrative effect. Normally, in warfare, the attacker and the target are both part of the narrative, and unless the attacker actions are totally baseless, the contest over narratives is likely to be two-handed with each side's fans supporting their own side. However, if the attacker is unknown, or at least unclear, then the focus of the story is necessarily on the target, and the theme is likely to focus on why the target was attacked—and may well dwell on what the target did that merited the attack or why the target could not secure itself. That, in fact, may be the attacker's motive: to create a crisis of confidence in the target state, either weakening it outright, creating fissures in its body politic, or at least making it more amenable to concession.

Finally, if an attacker can persuade the target that it was hit by a third party, it may catalyze conflict that will be to the attacker's advantage. A nonobvious Taiwanese cyber attack on the United States during a crisis with China, for instance, might put the United States at odds with China and thus more likely to support Taiwan. An attacker that instigates a war between two former trading partners could force both to purchase from the remaining relevant neutral, the attacker. Of course, if attribution follows, the attacker will have made one enemy it did not need and perhaps a second enemy as well—the country that the attacker hoped would be fingered.

THE TARGET'S RESPONSE OPTIONS

In some cases, ambiguity works to the target's advantage by giving it an excuse to avoid responding; it can claim uncertainty about who perpetrated the attack or what, in fact, was done. Not knowing helps the targeted nation ward off popular calls to fight and redeem its honor. In some cases, the attacker itself may not necessarily think the worse of the target's honor if no response ensues; in other cases, it will convince that itself the target knew but was lying to avoid a confrontation. Consider, analogously, the phantom Israeli nuclear arsenal. Once other powerful Middle Eastern states acknowledge that Israel has nuclear arms, they must answer as to why they do not. No polity is fooled, but neither must it be taunted by the prospect why they, themselves do not.

Mostly, though, targets would simply want such attacks to stop—but how? Defense is clearly an option and one that would logically assume greater importance the less it can lean on not hitting back because it is unsure about who committed the offense. Another option is to help create pressure from the world community to end the possession of the requisite attack technology, but most of these cannot be effectively banned. Cyber weapons are largely the obverse of system vulnerabilities, the attack code is trivial to hide, and many of the underlying technologies of offense are required for cyber defense. Electronic jamming is inherent in the ability to generate radio frequency energy. Intelligence support for third parties is identical to intelligence support for military operations in general. The weapons of sabotage, special operations, and insurgencies are small arms. Conversely, weapons of mass destruction and land mines (but not naval mines) are already banned by treaty. The only weapons not covered by treaties that could conceivably be banned are antisatellite weapons and drones; both have legitimate (overt) military purposes. More broadly, it is how such weapons are used rather than the weapons themselves that determines the characteristics of nonobvious warfare.

A variant on the second approach is to develop a global consensus that the covert use of warfare is far more heinous than its overt use. Thus, if such weapons *are* used—something that may not always be apparent—the world community would support efforts to pressure potential users into allowing investigations that would clarify which state was at fault. After all, most forms of warfare are universally held to be crimes if carried out by those outside the military; thus, even the accused state should have an interest in finding and rooting out its dangerous criminals, assuming it would wish to shift the blame. Where states use proxies and such acts *are* crimes, they may be pressured to cooperate with international police investigations. Russia has stubbornly refused to prosecute or extradite its cyber criminals who are careful to prey only on foreigners. Satisfaction for the aggrieved party, however, assumes police actions can establish reasonable levels of certainty.

More problematically, the closer the trail of investigation comes to the doors of military or intelligence establishments, the greater the reluctance of states to allow matters to proceed. Such reluctance would not be unfounded—if purported acts of nonobvious warfare allow investigators to peer into covert operations, states may go to great lengths to interpret the need for evidence in ways that would also allow them to uncover the secrets of their rivals.

The last recourse is for victimized states and their allies to respond to suspected warring states as if certain they did it. In doing so, they must factor in how certain *others* are that the accusation is correct and, to some extent, whether the purported attacking state believes it is guilty. Many nonobvious warfare techniques can be carried out by rogue elements. As noted, some responses, such as chilling relations between the target and the purported attacker, do not require anything close to conclusive proof; mere uneasiness suffices. Other responses, such as retaliation, normally require high levels of confidence. In the end, the victimized state has to weigh the risks associated with false negatives (doing nothing in the face of aggression) and false positives (retaliating against the innocent). Note further that "plausible deniability" is hardly an absolute in this case. Unless the victimized state can only respond through the court system—and states cannot go on trial, only their leaders—the balance between responding and not responding may tip well before the confidence meter hits 100 percent. A relatively pacifist state surrounded on all sides by friends (e.g., Belgium) and embraced by alliances may want near certainty and may not react even then; an anxious, well-armed state surrounded on all sides by potential adversaries (e.g., Israel) may be less fussy.

Or the victim could retaliate by using nonobvious warfare itself. Ostensibly, the mutual commitment of both sides to modulate their responses to one another might limit the potential for open and, hence, more destructive warfare—as long as both sides are careful not to reveal themselves. This may create a set of strange incentives wherein both sides' nonobvious warfare communities take pains not to reveal the activities of their counterparts lest power and influence on both sides shift to communities whose warfare methods are quite obvious. Conversely, the perception that it is acceptable to escalate in a nonobvious manner rather than call out the other side may allow the destructive cost of nonobvious warfare to rise to its limits. If matters then become obvious, the warfare level that forms the foundation for the next set of threats starts at the much higher level.

ASSESSMENT AND CONCLUSIONS

Would the spread of nonobvious warfare be a good thing? Even if wielded solely in pursuit of good aims, such techniques corrode both military values and diplomatic norms. Nonobvious warfare, almost by definition, has to be the work of small teams that must isolate themselves from the larger community, much like intelligence operatives, lest word of their adventures leaks out. The efforts of the small nonobvious warfare teams would leave the mass of the national security establishment quite uncertain about what exactly was going on and who exactly was behind all the activity (only some of which would appear to be accidents).

Nonobvious warfare is also a poor fit for democratic states and a far better fit for authoritarian or failing states in which the intelligence community has become decoupled from its legitimate governance structure. States with long-term reputations to manage are likely to see the downside from having to lie about their warfare activities when so confronted.

Universal or even wide adoption of nonobvious warfare would likely yield a more suspicious world. Once attacks are shaped to look like accidents, many accidents will start to smell like attacks. Nations would react (even more than they do now) to suspicions rather than actual substance; attackers might be credited/blamed for far more than they actually merit. In too many countries, *anything* that seems askew is blamed on the United States (or Israel) and their ubiquitous and omnipotent intelligence agencies. Part of their polities' maturity entails improvements in their ability to distinguish fact from fantasy; evidence that such fantasy had a kernel of truth behind it would hardly facilitate the maturation process. Indeed, under crisis circumstances, it is conceivable a conflict could start even though the accused did nothing.

And of course, a crisis could start when a state used such techniques thinking it would never be caught—and was.

NOTES

1. The term *nonobvious* had an earlier manifestation in Jeff Jonas's data-mining product, Non-Obvious Relationship Analysis.

2. *Warfare*, used here, comprises operations carried out for political ends by states aimed at the destruction, corruption, or significant disruption of assets or interests associated with other states using means that are generally considered illegal if not done by states. Our discussion is limited to states, because nonstate actors do not always have return addresses or even always unambiguous identities, and individuals therein can be subject to legal actions in ways that states cannot be.

3. Sergei Markov, a state Duma deputy from the pro-Kremlin Unified Russia Party, claimed, "About the cyberattack on Estonia … don't worry, that attack was carried out by my assistant. I won't tell you his name, because then he might not be able to get visas." "Behind the Estonia Cyberattacks," *Radio Free Europe/Radio Liberty* (March

6, 2009), http://www.rferl.org/content/Behind_The_Estonia_Cyberattacks/1505613. html.

4. Robert Mackey, "Irish Flotilla Activists Show Damage to Their Boat," *The Lede: Blogging the News* (July 1, 2011), http://thelede.blogs.nytimes.com/2011/07/ 01/what-flotilla-activists-videos-look-like/.

5. Which came to near naught after the original ranks were greatly reduced in the 1968 Tet offensive.

Chapter Nine

Act and Actor Attribution in Cyberspace

A Proposed Analytic Framework

Eric F. Mejia

Technical Sergeant Joe Pesek rolled out of bed shortly after 0600 to get breakfast at the Noncommissioned Officers' NCO club. He was assigned to the 5th Bomber Group and had arranged to meet his friends for golf after breakfast. The course in Honolulu was beautiful, and there was no better way to spend a lazy Sunday morning. Waiting for the bus, he admired the beautiful blue sky flecked with distant aircraft. Seeing this many aircraft meant a carrier must be coming into port. Joe wasn't alarmed until the first plane pulled up low over Hickam Airfield with machine guns chattering. The clearly visible rising sun of Imperial Japan on the wings told the story—Japan had attacked Pearl Harbor.[1] The following day, December 8, 1941, the United States and Japan declared war against each other.

Seventy years later, Air Force Major Shelly Johnson rolled out of bed looking forward to another day of leave in Honolulu. Taking out her smartphone, she tried to scan a check into her account so that she would have extra spending money. Despite several attempts, the check failed to deposit. Frustrated, she used her tablet to access the bank's website; however, the homepage refused to load. She finished breakfast and tried again without luck. Irritated, she gave up and got into her car to enjoy her day of leave. A few days later she read the headline: "Major Banks Hit with Biggest Cyberattacks in History."[2] The article explained how several of the largest banks, including her own, had been the victim of a cyber attack. The Islamist group Izz ad-Din al-Qassam Cyber Fighters claimed responsibility for the attacks; however, researchers were divided about whether they were responsible. Senator Joe Lieberman claimed the attacks were actually conducted by Iran in response to U.S. economic sanctions. The article provided more questions than answers. Major Johnson wondered who actually

185

conducted the attack. Could it even be considered an attack, and if so, what was attacked: the customers, the individual banks, the U.S. economy? Who would respond, and how?

These two scenarios highlight the critical importance of attribution. In the case of Pearl Harbor, there was a hostile armed attack directly attributable to a known state actor. These facts established the proper response—war—and the proper responder: the military. In the second scenario, the act and actor were uncertain; consequently the proper response and responder were equally uncertain. *Actor attribution* is concerned with determining who is responsible for a hostile cyber act. *Act attribution* is concerned with determining the relevant characteristics, or attributes, of the hostile cyber act, typically the severity of the act. Both are necessary to determine the appropriate response to an act of cyber hostility, and both help frame which organization should be the primary responder. An analytic framework incorporating both act and actor attribution helps delineate responsibility for hostile cyber acts and determine the appropriate response. This chapter examines the definition and importance of cyber attribution and proposes such an analytic framework for considering act and actor attribution. It briefly examines two high-profile cyber attacks, and concludes with recommendations to address the problems associated with cyber attribution.

DEFINING ATTRIBUTION

The Basic Legal Framework

It is clear, at least from the U.S. perspective, that cyberspace is not a "law-free" zone and that established principles of international law apply.[3] The legal framework for use of force by states is contained in the *Charter of the United Nations*, which generally prohibits states from using force against another state. As specified in Article 2(4), "All Members shall refrain in their international relations from the threat or use of force against the territorial integrity or political independence of any state, or in any other manner incon-sistent with the Purposes of the United Nations."[4] The charter recognizes two exceptions. First, Article 42 permits use of force if authorized by the UN Security Council. Second, and more important for our analysis, Article 51 permits use of force in self-defense against an armed attack, stating that "nothing in the present Charter shall impair the inherent right of individual or collective self-defence if an armed attack occurs against a Member of the United Nations."[5] These articles did not originally apply to the conduct of nonstate actors. However, international law has developed so that states may use force in self-defense against another state for acts of nonstate actors attributed to it.[6] A state may also use defensive force directly against nonstate actors if the host state is unable or unwilling to prevent armed attacks from emanating within its territory.[7]

Finally, the use of force is bounded by the law of armed conflict (LOAC), including the concepts of distinction, necessity, and proportionality. Applying the LOAC to hostile cyber acts may cause unnecessary concern among lawyers and unnecessary hesitancy among commanders. This is because responding to a hostile cyber act will likely involve targeting dual-use objects and because of the perceived increased risk of "knock-on," or unexpected collateral damage.

Dual-use objects may serve both a military and civilian function. The typical example is a bridge, which is equally useful for conveying both military and civilian vehicles. Similarly, most hostile cyber acts will transit civilian cyber infrastructure, including computing systems, data storage systems, and telecommunication lines. Further, malicious cyber code may be prepositioned on civilian cyber infrastructure. Despite the fact that these are clearly dual-use objects, the LOAC often permits them to be targeted. Addressing the issue involves applying Article 52(2) of the Protocol additional to the Geneva Conventions (GPI) to the facts.[8] Although the United States has not ratified the GPI, it recognizes Article 52(2) as binding customary international law. Article 52(2) sets out a two-part test for analyzing whether an object is an appropriate military target. The first issue is one of *distinction*—is the object a legitimate military objective? Article 52(2) limits attacks to objects whose "nature, location, purpose or use make an effective contribution to military action." In the case of hostile cyber acts, cyber infrastructure may be a legitimate military objective if it is used to conduct a hostile cyber act or if malicious code is prepositioned on it in anticipation of a future hostile use. In either case, the use of the object may make it a legitimate military objective and therefore appropriately targetable. The second issue is one of *necessity*. Does the total or partial destruction or neutralization of the object, in the circumstances ruling at the time, offer a definite military advantage? In the case of an ongoing hostile cyber act or prepositioned malicious code, this is a fairly low hurdle to overcome, especially after making the initial determination that the object is a legitimate military objective.

The potential for unexpected collateral damage is another issue that appears difficult at first blush. Although the facts may be more complicated, traditional application of LOAC is all that is required. Here, the issue is one of proportionality—an attack is generally prohibited if the damage to noncombatants is excessive in relation to the military advantage gained from the attack. The problem with attacking dual-use cyber infrastructure is that it is difficult, if not impossible, to fully anticipate the extent of the likely collateral damage. Luckily, that is not required. In attempting to predict collateral damage, the commander is "only required to do what is feasible, given the prevailing circumstances, including the time he has to make a decision and the amount of information he has at that time."[9] If anything, the difficulty of precisely determining what collateral damage may be expected benefits commanders by affording them significant latitude in the decision-making process.

The basic legal framework may be summarized as follows:

- States may generally not use force against other states.
- States may use force against other states if
  a. force is authorized by the UN Security Council, or
  b. force is used in self-defense against an armed attack by (1) another state or (2) a nonstate actor if the act can be imputed to a state.
- Force may be used in self-defense directly against nonstate actors if the host state is unable to prevent armed attacks by nonstate actors.
- Use of force is limited by LOAC principles.

Ultimately, determining an appropriate response to a hostile cyber act requires analyzing who the actor is (state, nonstate, unknown) and what the act is (armed attack or not an armed attack). In other words, actor and act attribution.

Actor Attribution

Actor attribution is simply determining who should be held responsible for a hostile cyber act. As noted in the *2011 Department of Defense Strategy for Operating in Cyberspace*, low barriers to entry for hostile cyber acts, coupled with widespread availably of hacking tools, means that small groups, and even individuals, can impact national security.[10] These same characteristics have also made it more difficult to determine whether a hostile act was conducted by rouge individuals or by state actors. The April 2015 *DoD Cyber Strategy* states, "State and non-state threats often also blend together; Patriotic entities often act as cyber surrogates for states, and non-state entities can provide cover for state-based operators."[11] However, whether a specific act of cyber hostility is attributed to a nonstate actor, state actor, or some blend of the two is a significant issue. The distinction helps determine the appropriate response, responder, and rules for engagement.

Hostile cyber acts can be attributed to a state either directly or indirectly.[12] The two methods of state attribution are briefly described as follows:

Direct Attribution. States are responsible for the acts or omissions of individuals exercising the state's machinery of power and authority since these actions are attributed to the state even if the acts exceed the authority granted by the state.

Indirect Attribution. Acts or omissions of nonstate actors are generally not attributable to the state; however, the state may incur responsibility if it fails to exercise due diligence in preventing or reacting to such acts or omissions.[13]

Although not universally accepted in international law, it is generally accepted in practice that a state's right to use force in self-defense is also triggered by armed attacks that cannot be attributed to a state. For example, an armed attack may emanate from a state without that state's knowledge or ability to prevent it. In such circumstances, the armed attack is attributed directly to the attackers, and the victim state may defend with force directly against the nonstate actors despite their being located in a neutral or even allied state. As recently noted in the *Journal of Conflict and Security Law*, it is the nature of the hostile act that triggers the right to self-defense, not the nature of the actor.[14] This simply comports with common sense. A state should not be required to endure an armed attack by nonstate actors when it has the means to defend itself consistent with fundamental LOAC principles. U.S. attacks against terrorists operating within Pakistan are one concrete application of this concept. Once a state has been subjected to an armed attack, it may forcibly defend itself. The decision of whether to do so is a matter of policy, and ultimately the response must satisfy basic LOAC principles including necessity, proportionality, and distinction.

Act Attribution

Act attribution is the process of defining the nature of the hostile cyber act.[15] In other words, what are the attributes of the act? Hostile cyber acts may range from something as benign as attempting to ping a network computer to an attack on the U.S. power grid leaving millions without power for months.[16]

Any response by a victim state must be determined in part by the attributes of the hostile act. A state may passively defend against all hostile actions; however, it may only forcibly retaliate in self-defense against armed attacks. By extension, imminent armed attacks allow states to respond in anticipatory self-defense.[17] International law currently is silent on whether a cyber attack can be considered an armed attack. However, the United States has taken an affirmative position on the issue. The May 2011 *International Strategy for Cyberspace* states, "Right of Self-Defense: Consistent with the United Nations Charter, states have an inherent right to self-defense that may be triggered by certain aggressive acts in cyberspace."[18] This echoes the language of Article 51 of the UN charter, which states that states have the inherent right to engage in individual or collective self-defense in response to an armed attack.[19] More recently, the 2015 *DoD Cyber Strategy* states that cyber attacks pose a significant risk to U.S. interests, including loss of life, significant property damage, damage to U.S. foreign policy, and serious economic consequences. Further, "[t]he United States has been clear that it will respond to a cyberattack on U.S. interests through its defense capabilities."[20] So, clearly the United States has adopted the position that a hostile cyber act may be treated as an armed attack. But given the range of hostile cyber actions, how do we determine whether such an act rises to the level of an armed attack? If the *effects* of a cyber attack are the equivalent of a traditional armed attack, then states should be permitted to respond accordingly. The leading proponent of this effects-based approach is Michael N. Schmitt. His effects-based analysis evaluates hostile cyber acts based on six criteria:

1. Severity: Armed attacks threaten physical injury or destruction of property to a greater degree than other forms of coercion.
2. Immediacy: Armed attacks usually occur with greater immediacy.
3. Directness: Armed attacks have a more direct link to the negative consequences caused.
4. Invasiveness: Armed attacks usually cross into the target state to cause harm.
5. Measurability: The consequences of an armed attack are easier to measure.
6. Presumptive Legitimacy: Because of the general prohibition on the use of armed force between states in international law, an armed attack is presumed illegitimate.[21]

This framework can readily be applied to cyber attacks to determine whether a given hostile act may be considered an armed attack.[22] If so, a forcible response may be appropriate. If not, some lesser form of response may be required.

THE IMPORTANCE OF ATTRIBUTION

An assessment of both act and actor attribution is central in determining the appropriate response to a hostile cyber act. A government may respond in a variety of ways including monitoring, improving passive defenses, applying political pressure, employing active defenses, and counterstriking with both cyber and conventional weapons. *Passive defense* is defined as "measures taken to reduce the probability of and to minimize the effects of damage caused by hostile action without the intention of taking the initiative."[23] Passive defense in the cyber realm includes making systems more difficult to attack through antiviruses and firewalls, educating users to be more security conscious, and reducing post-attack recovery times through redundancy and backup systems.[24] By contrast, *active defense* is "the employment of limited offensive action and counterattacks to deny a contested area or position to the enemy."[25] In the cyber realm, this translates to initiating a cyber counterattack as a defensive response to a hostile cyber attack.[26] Defensive cyber attacks can be broken down into two types. If the goal is to mitigate harm to a targeted system using only the amount of force necessary to protect the system from further damage, it is considered a mitigative counterstrike. The purpose of a mitigative counterstrike must be to mitigate damage from an immediate threat. If the goal of the counterstrike is to punish the attacker, it is considered a retributive counterstrike.[27] Under international law, only the mitigative counterstrike is truly defensive, because its purpose is to defend against an immediate threat.

Actor and act attribution is also critical in determining which government entity should take the lead in responding to a hostile cyber act. Several government agencies are tasked with cyber operations and responsibilities. As summarized by Gen. Keith B. Alexander, commander for U.S. Cyber Command (CYBERCOM), these agencies include the following:

- Department of Defense/Intelligence Community/NSA/CYBERCOM: Responsible for detection, prevention, and defense in foreign space, foreign cyber threat intelligence and attribution, security of national security and military systems, and, in extremis, defense of the homeland if the nation comes under cyber attack from a full scope actor.
- Department of Homeland Security (DHS): Lead for coordinating the overall national effort to enhance the cybersecurity of U.S. critical infrastructure and ensuring protection of the civilian federal government (.gov) networks and systems.
- Federal Bureau of Investigation (FBI): Responsible for detection, investigation, prevention, and response within the domestic arena under their authorities for law enforcement, domestic intelligence, counterintelligence, and counterterrorism. Importantly, when malicious cyber activity is detected in domestic space, the FBI takes the lead to prevent, investigate, and mitigate it.[28]

THE DIFFICULTY OF CONCLUSIVE ATTRIBUTION

Both act and actor attribution are difficult to prove with scientific certainty. Computer networks are not designed to facilitate attribution, and hostile actors exploit this weakness to hide their true identity. For example, the

Internet typically does not use sender identification during the transmission process, so source information can easily be forged. Masking the sender information in this manner is commonly referred to as "spoofing." Hostile cyber actors can also hide their identity and location by employing a system that transforms data in some manner, known as a laundering host. Cyber actors may employ an attack that is complete in milliseconds, or alternatively, is spread out over months. All of these factors make cyber actor attribution difficult.[29] The degree of difficulty is subject to some debate. Former secretary of defense Leon Panetta stated in late 2012 that the DoD had made "significant investments in forensics to address this problem of attribution" and that "potential aggressors should be aware that the United States has the capacity to locate them and to hold them accountable for their actions that may try to harm America."[30] However, such a public declaration raises several issues. First, is the statement an accurate assessment of capabilities or is it more akin to posturing in an attempt to deter potential adversaries? Second, if the statement is technologically accurate, acknowledging this capability and subsequently using it to attribute a hostile act to a specific actor runs the risk of compromising the methods and techniques used in the process. Finally—given the highly adaptive nature of cyber warfare—cyber defenses, including forensics, will inevitably be thwarted by constantly evolving cyber threats. Even if the technical issue of attribution is overcome, what degree of confidence must be achieved to support a finding that a state is responsible under international law? Certain? Very certain? These are subjective political determinations that simply do not lend themselves to precise quantitative analysis.

This same issue exists when trying to assess act attribution. Using the Schmitt model to determine if a hostile cyber act is tantamount to an armed attack requires applying a subjective analysis. How severe is *severe*? What is the definition of *immediate*? What constitutes a *direct link* between a hostile cyber act and the consequences of the act? All of these questions require a subjective, nonscientific assessment.

Fortunately, the legal community has been dealing with the problem of subjective actor and act attribution and has extensively developed the concepts and lexicon related to subjective attribution. This is most evident in the law related to civil and criminal trials. Legal experts refer to these subjective criteria as "standards of proof." A few of the more common ones, in order of the degree of certainty, are the following:

- Scintilla of evidence—the least amount of evidence possible.
- Preponderance of the evidence—In a civil trial, the issue to be decided is often whether or not one party is negligent, and therefore financially responsible for the losses incurred by the other party. The subjective

standard used by courts to assess this question of liability is called the preponderance of the evidence standard. This is simply defined as more probable than not.

- Clear and convincing evidence—creating a firm belief or conviction. It is an intermediate level of proof, being more than a preponderance of the evidence but less than what is required for proof beyond a reasonable doubt.
- Beyond a reasonable doubt—This is the standard used to establish criminal guilt, which is the equivalent of actor attribution, as well as to determine the specific criminal offense committed, which is the equivalent of act attribution. It means entirely convinced and satisfied to a moral certainty. However, it is less than a scientific certainty.[31]

Employing legal subjective criteria is not a new or novel idea. In a 2009 Microsoft white paper, Scott Charney suggested a similar subjective assessment for cyber attribution, noting that

> it [is] important to focus on probability of accurate attribution, as opposed to certainty of attribution. In many areas, of course, absolute certainty is seldom achievable. For this reason, a range of different standards have developed (for example, proof beyond a reasonable doubt, a preponderance of the evidence) and individuals and organizations often have to rely upon probabilities when making critical decisions (such as when opting for one medical treatment over another). Of course, the greater the certainty, the easier it may be to choose a course of action, but that does not mean certainty is required before reasonable action can be taken.[32]

It would be naïve to assume that one could import the whole of court-based attribution concepts to assess cyber attribution. The legal concepts of a scintilla of evidence, preponderance of evidence, and others were never designed to be used in assessing cyber attribution. Indeed, they are well-defined terms that, if applied in a cyber context, may unnecessarily hinder attribution. However, the historical use of subjective attribution illustrates several key points. First, scientific proof is not necessary for attribution. While scientific certainty is the "gold standard" of proof, it is rarely obtainable, and historically has not been necessary to establish attribution. Second, as previously noted, attribution is routinely based on subjective determinations. Third, when using a subjective assessment of attribution, severity of the consequences is linked to the degree of confidence. A court may assess financial responsibility based on a preponderance of the evidence, but it takes a much higher degree of confidence to establish criminal guilt. Finally, although many technical experts may be hesitant or uncomfortable using a subjective assessment, the government, through its legal community, has at its disposal established expertise in subjective attribution.

AN ANALYTIC MODEL FOR ACTOR
AND ACT ATTRIBUTION

Based on the foregoing, the factors included in any proposed analytic model should be based on a subjective assessment of act and actor attribution. An assessment of these factors should indicate who should respond to an act of cyber hostility and what the upper range of appropriate responses should be. Ideally, the responses would incorporate basic LOAC principles. Combining these basic concepts yields the analytic model proposed in figure 9.1.

Several issues are worth noting. First, act and actor attribution are dynamic. Just as in conventional warfare, the preparation for a hostile cyber act may occur in one location, yet the act itself may originate in a different location or, even more likely, be distributed throughout a variety of locations. Further, although an act may appear harmless at first, subsequent information or events may show it to be significantly more harmful than initially believed. Therefore, the appropriate response and responder are likely to be dynamic as well, involving several organizations and a potentially escalating series of responses. Second, the responsive actions in each quadrant represent the upper limits of an appropriate response. For example,

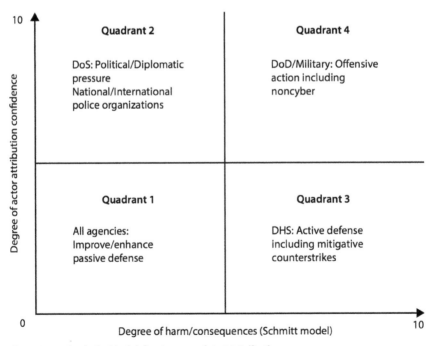

Figure 9.1   Analytic Model for Actor and Act Attribution

the Department of State (DoS) may elect not to apply diplomatic pressure to a state actor for a variety of reasons, even if justified by hostile cyber acts. Further, the various instruments of power described are not equally effective on all hostile actors. For example, it is unlikely that a rogue individual would be greatly deterred by political/diplomatic pressure. Although a military strike against an individual would likely be effective, it is politically untenable. As always, effective application of the instruments of power is an art, and a mechanistic approach will likely fail. Finally, the quadrants do not reflect sole responsibility for responding to hostile cyber acts. However, the framework does help assign primary or lead responsibility, with other agencies in a supporting role.

Quadrant 1: Low Actor Attribution Confidence/Low Degree of Harm

In this common scenario, government agencies are faced with numerous relatively innocuous yet unauthorized cyber acts. For example, on June 3, 2010, General Alexander stated that DoD systems are probed by unauthorized cyber actors approximately 250,000 times per hour, or the equivalent of more than six million times each day.[33] Most cause no damage and do not result in a compromise of data. According to the U.S. Computer Emergency Readiness Team (US-CERT), in 2009, approximately 73.4 percent of all reported cyber incidents were categorized as "Category 5: Scans, Probes, or Attempted Access." This includes "any activity that seeks to access or identify a federal agency computer, open ports, protocols, service, or any combination for later exploit. This activity does not directly result in a compromise or denial of service."[34] For these types of acts, passive defense is an appropriate response. The vast majority of Quadrant 1 actions are easily defeated by encryption, firewalls, antivirus and antimalware programs, or other purely passive measures.

Mitigation of cyber attacks is squarely within the purview of the DHS. *Presidential Policy Directive—Critical Infrastructure Security and Resilience* (PPD 21), a refinement of *Homeland Security Presidential Directive 7*, establishes the national policy for identifying and protecting critical U.S. infrastructure and defines the roles of the various federal and state departments. The Secretary of Homeland Security is directed to "provide strategic guidance, promote a national unity of effort, and coordinate the overall Federal effort to promote the security and resilience of the Nation's critical infrastructure."[35] To help fulfill this responsibility, DHS created the National Cyber Security Division. This organization has, as one of its missions, to "contribute to enhancing the security and resilience of the nation's critical information infrastructure and the Internet by developing and delivering new technologies, tools and techniques to enable DHS and the U.S. to defend, mitigate and secure current and future systems, networks and infrastructure against cyberattacks"[36]

Quadrant 2: High Actor Attribution Confidence/Low Degree of Harm

In this scenario, the government is again faced with acts that cause little harm. However, the acts are still unauthorized and may be the harbinger of more serious, and more harmful, future acts. Unlike the scenario in Quadrant 1, these acts can confidently be attributed to an identified actor. Under these circumstances, passive defensive measures alone may be insufficient. However, because the acts are insufficiently harmful to be considered equivalent to an armed attack, offensive strikes and defensive counterstrikes are not necessary or proportional to the harm being caused. In addition to passive defense, employing appropriate diplomatic pressure may be appropriate for state actors. This approach is consistent with the May 2011 *International Strategy for Cyberspace*. This document states that the United States will combine diplomacy, defense, and development to achieve the national goal of cybersecurity. Diplomatic efforts will be focused on engaging "the international community in frank and urgent dialogue, to build consensus around principles of responsible behavior in cyberspace and the actions necessary, both domestically and as an international community, to build a system of cyberspace stability."[37] Diplomatic efforts to stem the tide of less serious cyber acts are not new. For several years, the United States has been engaged in such efforts to dissuade China from continuing cyber espionage against both the U.S. government and U.S. corporations. Former defense secretary Leon Panetta spent three days in China addressing the issue of its cyber activity. This is an appropriate response to state-attributed cyber acts that fall short of an armed attack. As noted by James Lewis, cybersecurity expert with the Center for Strategic and International Studies, "the damage from Chinese cyber espionage is easy to overstate but that doesn't mean we should accept it."[38] To facilitate diplomatic efforts at cybersecurity, the DoS recently created a new office. The Office of the Coordinator for Cyber Issues is tasked with coordinating DoS global diplomatic engagement on cyber issues, serving as the DoS liaison to the White House and federal departments and agencies on cyber issues, and advising the secretary and deputy secretaries on cyber issues and engagements.[39] If the hostile actor is a nonstate-affiliated individual or group, the FBI, Department of Justice, or analogous international organizations will be primarily responsible for any investigation and prosecution, if appropriate.

Quadrant 3: Low Actor Attribution Confidence/High Degree of Harm

In this scenario, the government is faced with a hostile cyber act capable of causing significant harm. The harm threatened, or caused, may be sufficient to be considered the equivalent of an armed attack. Within the cyber realm, this may involve harming the nation's key resources or critical infrastructure. However, there is insufficient evidence to confidently attribute the act to a specific state or nonstate actor. One potential example of this would be unidentified actors using a state's IT infrastructure to conduct an attack without the consent, or even knowledge, of that state. Retributive strikes require attribution, which is lacking in this scenario. However, the LOAC still permits action in self-defense. When a state is unable to prevent attacks emanating from inside its borders or the attackers operate independently of the state, the victim state may still use force in self-defense, provided it meets the requirements of necessity, proportionality, and distinction.[40] Under these circumstances, active defenses, including mitigative counterstrikes, may be appropriate. The goal of mitigative counterstriking is to "mitigate damage from a current and immediate threat."[41] These active but purely defensive measures can trace an attack back to its source and immediately interrupt the attack. Further, mitigative counterstrikes are relatively precise. This precision limits the risk of excessive collateral damage. Limiting collateral damage helps satisfy the requirement of proportionality and helps reduce the risk of escalating cyber attacks into full-scale kinetic attacks between states.[42] Finally, because of their precision, reduced risk of collateral damage, and purely defensive nature, automated mitigative counterstrikes are less likely to violate international LOAC norms.

In conducting mitigative counterstrikes, the role of the DoD is clearly articulated in *The DoD Cyber Strategy*: "If directed by the President or Secretary of Defense, the U.S. military may conduct cyber operations to counter an imminent or on-going attack against the U.S. homeland or U.S. interests in cyberspace. The purpose of such a defensive measure is to blunt an attack and prevent the destruction of property or loss of life."[43] Here, a defensive strike is contemplated to mitigate a high degree of harm.

Quadrant 4: High Actor Attribution Confidence/High Degree of Harm

In this scenario, the government is faced with a hostile cyber act tantamount to an armed attack. Further, there is a high degree of actor attribution confidence. Conceptually, this is the equivalent of a kinetic attack against the

United States, therefore a DoD response is appropriate. Further, there is no prohibition against responding with kinetic force against a cyber attack provided the response meets traditional LOAC requirements. This, too, is consistent with the 2011 *International Strategy for Cyberspace*, which states, "We fully recognize that cyberspace activities can have effects extending beyond networks; such events may require responses in self-defense. ... When warranted, the United States will respond to hostile acts in cyberspace as we would to any other threat to our country."[44]

There is little disagreement that the DoD should be the lead agency in this scenario. As noted by the U.S. CYBERCOM commander, in extreme situations, it is the role of the DoD to defend "the homeland if the Nation comes under cyber attack from a full scope actor."[45] However, some argue that the DoD should take a more expansive role in cybersecurity, essentially performing the DHS's assigned role. Much of this argument is based on the perceived effectiveness of the DoD, or rather the perceived ineffectiveness of the DHS. However, an expanded role for the DoD in cybersecurity is the wrong approach. First, it unnecessarily expands the role of the military. The military would undoubtedly perform well at securing transportation hubs, power plants, water treatment facilities, critical manufacturing sites, and other critical national infrastructure. However, that is not the mission of the military; the mission of the military is to wage war. Further, effective cyber defense requires a degree of domestic intrusion that should not be conducted by the DoD. As noted by retired major general Charles Dunlap, "The armed forces are the most authoritarian, least democratic, and most powerful institution in American society. The restraint intrinsic to a domestic law enforcement mind-set is not its natural state. ... If nothing else, the fact that the armed forces unapologetically restrict the rights and privileges of their own members should militate toward avoiding their use in civilian settings where the public properly expects those rights and privileges to flourish."[46]

TWO CASES BRIEFLY EXAMINED

Two recent cases of hostile cyber acts and the resulting U.S. responses illustrate the predictive accuracy, and limitations, of the proposed model.

In November of 2014, North Korea conducted an attack against Sony Pictures Entertainment. The attack exfiltrated sensitive corporate data including e-mails and salary information. The hackers also conducted an attack that deleted data and disabled computers. Following this, the hackers began releasing embarrassing e-mails that they had obtained during the hack. It is generally believed that the hack was taken in retaliation for a satirical movie depicting the assassination of North Korean Leader Kim Jong Un.

After extensive investigation, the FBI declared the hack was the work of North Korea. James Comey, then-director of the FBI, stated he had "high confidence" in the conclusion. Further, he provided some detail describing how the attack was attributed to North Korea: "Several times either because they forgot or they had a technical problem they connected directly and we could see them. And we could see that the IP addresses that were being used to post and to send the emails were coming from IPs that were exclusively used by the North Koreans."[47]

Given the high degree of confidence in actor attribution, and relatively low severity of damages, one would expect a Quadrant 2 type response, specifically political and diplomatic pressure against North Korea. Not surprisingly, this is exactly what occurred. In response to the Sony hack, in January 2015, President Obama issued an Executive Order 13687,[48] authorizing financial sanctions against three entities and ten individuals as agencies or officials of the North Korean government. According to a press release by the Treasury Department, the sanctions were imposed to "hold North Korea accountable for its destabilizing, destructive and repressive actions, particularly its efforts to undermine U.S. cyber-security and intimidate U.S. businesses and artists exercising their right of freedom of speech."[49]

Another high-profile hack occurred when the U.S. Office of Personnel Management (OPM) was hacked throughout 2014 and early 2015. During this hack, attackers obtained the personnel files of 4.2 million former and current government employees, security clearance information on 21.5 million individuals, and fingerprint data on another 5.6 million.[50] Joel Brenner, former NSA senior counsel, described the significance of the information obtained: "This is crown jewels material ... a gold mine for foreign intelligence service. This is not the end of American human intelligence, but it's a significant blow."[51]

In contrast to the Sony hack, there was little public actor attribution in the OPM hack. Indeed, although it is generally believed that there is sound evidence that the hack was conducted by China, a conscious decision was made to avoid publicly attributing the attack. A senior official in the Obama administration stated, "We have chosen not to make any official assertions about attribution at this point."[52] In fact, the recently released 231-page report from the Committee on Oversight and Government Reform does not identify the source of the hacks, and instead focuses on how the hacks could have been prevented.[53]

In response to the hack, the U.S. government primarily increased its passive defense against hostile cyber attacks. According to Beth Cobert, the acting director of OPM, cybersecurity has been increased under her watch: "There's a whole series of multi-layer defenses we've put into our systems."[54] However, other than to increase passive defenses, there has been no publicly acknowledged government response against China as a result of the hack.

Given that the OPM hack caused significant harm, and given that, at least privately, the U.S. government has determined with a high degree of confidence that China, a state actor, was responsible, this paper's analytic model would typically predict a Quadrant 4 response—potential military offensive action. Why then was the U.S. government's response so restrained? First, the OPM hack was considered traditional espionage. According to Dave Aitel, cybersecurity expert, in this scenario, U.S. efforts are better spent securing its vulnerable systems rather than retaliation. He stated, "This particular kind of hack is considered normal—nation states spy on each all the time, and we don't sanction them or start cyberwars over it … it was massive, but it was well targeted."[55] Similarly, Michael Hayden, former head of the CIA and National Security Agency (NSA) stated, "This is espionage. I don't blame the Chinese for this at all. If I [as head of the NSA] could have done it, I would have done it in a heartbeat."[56] Further, there are those that posit that the United States was restrained in its response by concern that public attribution and retaliation would have harmed more important U.S. interests, such as securing China's cooperation in limiting Iran's nuclear program or support U.S. efforts to restrain North Korean aggression.[57] Finally, it has also been argued that the United States declined to expose details regarding attribution against China for fear of compromising its own espionage and cyber capabilities.[58] Based on all of these factors, it is likely U.S. officials consciously chose a greatly restrained response than would typically be anticipated.

The multilayered reasons for the United States' greatly attenuated response to the OPM hack reveal the limitation of any mechanistic approach to predicting state behavior—the need to consider the political backdrop against which state action occurs. Despite the undeniable usefulness of an analytic model to determine and predict an appropriate response to cyber hostilities, statecraft remains equal parts art and science.

CONCLUSION AND RECOMMENDATIONS

The cyber community must recognize the critical importance of attribution. It is the basis for effective diplomacy, law enforcement, and a prerequisite for offensive military counterstrikes under the LOAC. The first fundamental question that must be answered after a hostile act is, who committed the act? The second is, how much damage was done? An accurate assessment of actor and act attribution helps define both the proper response to an act of cyber aggression and helps determine the appropriate lead agency to respond to such an act.

Because actor and act attribution fundamentally drive cyber defense, efforts to enhance technical attribution should be given priority. Although assessing attribution is subjective, often the evidence used in such an assessment is technical. Attributing a hostile cyber act is a prerequisite to effective deterrence. No hostile actor, whether nation-state or rogue individual, will ever be deterred from hostile cyber activity if they can effectively deny responsibility. Further, the international community is unlikely to support military action unless a hostile act equivalent to an armed attack can successfully be attributed to an offending party. Because hostile actors will continue to develop new methods to mask their activity, effective deterrence demands that the United States continue to enhance its technical attribution capability.

Legal expertise is critical in assessing attribution and framing an appropriate response. Although the cyber domain is relatively new, the art of actor and act attribution is ancient. Every criminal prosecution that has ever occurred fundamentally required a subjective determination of guilt (actor attribution) and offense (act attribution). Legal practitioners, although often ignorant of the technical aspects of the cyber domain, are well versed in the art of attribution. Cyber experts may be technically adept but are often ignorant of the nuances of subjective attribution. Close integration of both legal experts and technical cyber experts is critical to establishing an appropriate cyber policy and appropriate responses to specific hostile cyber acts.

An analytic framework is an essential tool for cyber practitioners. In a field where significant ambiguity may exist, both as to the nature of the act and the identity of the actor, an analytic construct promotes diagnostic consistency. Additionally, it helps define roles and missions for various responders and provides a common framework and understanding of responsibility. The analytic framework also enhances deterrence by providing notice to hostile cyber actors that the consequences they should expect from committing a hostile cyber act are determined, in part, by the severity of the hostile act and that a severe hostile act will merit a military response.

Finally, those entrusted with recommending and implementing the U.S. response to hostile cyber acts most always consider the political consequences of any response.

NOTES

1. "Hickam Field—Army Air Corp Sergeant," *PearlHarbor.org* (no date), http://www.pearlharbor.org/eyewitness-accounts.asp.

2. David Goldman, "Major Banks Hit with Biggest Cyber Attacks in History," *CNN* (September 28, 2012), http://money.cnn.com/2012/09/27/technology/bank-cyberattacks/index.html.

3. Harold Hongju Koh, "International Law in Cyberspace," remarks to the USCYBERCOM Interagency Legal Conference, Ft. Meade, MD (September 18, 2012), http://www.state.gov/s/l/releases/remarks/197924.htm.

4. *Charter of the United Nations*, chap. I, art. 2(4).

5. *Charter of the United Nations*, chap. VII, art. 51.

6. Jeffrey Carr, *Inside Cyber Warfare* (Sebastopol, CA: O'Reilly Media, 2012), p. 53.

7. Nicholas Tsagourias, "Cyber Attacks, Self-Defence and the Problem of Attribution," *Journal of Conflict and Security Law* 17, no. 2 (Summer 2012), p. 7, http://jcsl.oxfordjournals.org/content/17/2/229.full.pdf+html.

8. "Protocol Additional to the Geneva Conventions of 12 August 1949 and Relating to the Protection of Victims of International Armed Conflicts (Protocol I)," adopted at Geneva on June 8, 1977, http://treaties.un.org/doc/Publication/UNTS/Volume%201125/volume-1125-I-17512-English.pdf.

9. Eric Talbot Jensen, "Unexpected Consequences from Knock-On Effects: A Different Standard for Computer Network Operations?" *American University International Law Review* 18, no. 5 (2003), p. 1186.

10. Department of Defense, *2011 Department of Defense Strategy for Operating in Cyberspace* (Washington, DC: Department of Defense, July 2011), p. 3.

11. United States Department of Defense, *The DoD Cyber Strategy* (Washington, DC: Department of Defense, April 2015), p. 9.

12. Many commentators use the terms *attribution* or *direct responsibility*, and *imputed* or *indirect responsibility*. However, since *imputed responsibility* is functionally the equivalent of attributing the hostile act to the state, the term *indirect attribution* is used to clarify the discussion.

13. Jan Arno Hessbruegge, "The Historical Development of the Doctrines of Attribution and Due Diligence in International Law," *New York University Journal of International Law and Politics* 36 (Winter/Spring 2004), p. 268.

14. Tsagourias, "Cyber Attacks," p. 7.

15. Susan W. Brenner, "'At Light Speed': Attribution and Response to Cybercrime/Terrorism/Warfare," *Journal of Criminal Law & Criminology* 97, no. 2 (2007), p. 379, using the terms *attack* and *attacker* attribution, or *who* and *what* attribution.

16. A *ping* is a test to see if a system on the Internet is working. *Pinging* a server tests and records the response time of the server. http://www.techterms.com/definition/ping.

17. Carr, *Inside Cyber Warfare*, p. 58.

18. *International Strategy for Cyberspace: Prosperity, Security, and Openness in a Networked World* (Washington, DC: White House, May 2011), p. 10.

19. *Charter of the United Nations*, art. 51.

20. United States Department of Defense, *The DoD Cyber Strategy*, pp. 5, 11.

21. Michael N. Schmitt, "Computer Network Attack and the Use of Force in International Law: Thoughts on a Normative Framework," *Columbia Journal of Transnational Law* 37 (1999), pp. 914–15.

22. For an excellent example of an application of the Schmitt analysis, see Andrew C. Fultz, "Stuxnet, Schmitt Analysis, and the Cyber 'Use of Force' Debate," *Joint Force Quarterly* 67 (4th Quarter 2012), pp. 40–48.

23. United States Department of Defense, *Joint Publication 1-02. Department of Defense Dictionary of Military and Associated Terms* (Washington, DC: Department of Defense, November 8, 2010, as amended through August 15, 2012), p. 237.

24. William A. Owens, Kenneth W. Dam, and Herbert S. Lin, *Technology, Policy, Law and Ethics Regarding U.S. Acquisition and Use of Cyberattack Capabilities* (Washington, DC: National Academies Press, 2009), http://www.nap.edu/catalog.php?record_id=12651, p. 13.

25. United States Department of Defense, *Joint Publication 1-02*, p. 2.

26. Owens, Dam, and Lin, *Technology, Policy, Law and Ethics*, p. 134.

27. Jay P. Kesan and Carol M. Hayes, "Mitigative Counterstriking: Self-Defense and Deterrence in Cyberspace," *Harvard Journal of Law and Technology* 25, no. 2 (Spring 2012), pp. 420–21.

28. Gen. Keith B. Alexander, *Statement before the Senate Committee on Armed Services, 27 March 2012* (Washington, DC: United States Congress, 2012), pp. 12–13, http://www.armed-services.senate.gov/statemnt/2012/20March/Alexander-27-12.pdf.

29. Dr. David A. Wheeler, "Planning for the Future of Cyber Attack Attribution," statement before the U.S. House of Representatives Committee on Science and Technology Subcommittee on Technology and Innovation, July 15, 2010, p. 3, http://science.house.gov/sites/republicans.science.house.gov/files/documents/hearings/071510_Wheeler.pdf.

30. Leon E. Panetta, "Secretary of Defense Leon E. Panetta, Remarks to the Business Executives for National Security," New York, October 11, 2012, http://archive.defense.gov/transcripts/transcript.aspx?transcriptid=5136.

31. *Black's Law Dictionary*, 5th edition (St. Paul, MN: West Group, 1979), p. 147.

32. Scott Charney, "Rethinking the Cyber Threat: A Framework and Path Forward," *Microsoft White Paper* (Redmond, WA: Microsoft Corp., 2009), p. 9.

33. Gen. Keith Alexander, "U.S. Cybersecurity Policy and the Role of U.S. Cybercom," address to the Center for Strategic and International Studies, Washington, DC (June 3, 2010).

34. *US CERT Quarterly Trends and Analysis Report* 4, no. 2 (June 16, 2009), p. 2.

35. Barack H. Obama, *Presidential Policy Directive 21. Critical Infrastructure Security and Resilience* (Washington, DC: Office of the President, February 12, 2013).

36. Official Website of the Department of Homeland Security, Cyber Security Division, https://www.dhs.gov/science-and-technology/cyber-security-division.

37. *International Strategy for Cyberspace*, p. 11.

38. "China Stonewalls Panetta on Cyber Attacks," *CBS News* (September 20, 2012), http://www.cbsnews.com/8301-202_162-57516541/china-stonewalls-panetta-on-cyberattacks/.

39. "Office of the Coordinator for Cyber Issues," http://www.state.gov/s/cyberissues/index.htm#.

40. Tsagourias, "Cyber Attacks," p. 7.

41. Kesan and Hayes, "Mitigative Counterstriking," p. 421.

42. Carr, *Inside Cyber Warfare*, p. 72.

43. United States Department of Defense, *The DOD Cyber Strategy*, p. 5.

44. *International Strategy for Cyberspace*, pp. 13–14.

45. Alexander, "Statement before the Senate Committee on Armed Services," p. 13.

46. Charles J. Dunlap Jr., "Perspectives for Cyber Strategists on Law for Cyberwar," *Strategic Studies Quarterly* 5, no. 1 (Spring 2011), pp. 93–94.

47. Kara Scannell, "FBI Details North Korean attack on Sony," (January 7, 2015), https://www.ft.com/content/287beee4-96a2-11e4-a83c-00144feabdc0.

48. Executive Order 13687, 3 C.F.R. 80, January 6, 2015.

49. United States Department of Treasury, Press Center. "Treasury Imposes Sanction against the Government of the Democratic People's Republic of Korea," (January 2, 2015), https://www.treasury.gov/press-center/press-releases/Pages/jl9733.aspx.

50. Committee on Oversight and Government Reform, *The OPM Data Breach: How the Government Jeopardized Our National Security for More than a Generation* (Washington, DC: United States House of Representatives, September 7, 2016).

51. Committee on Oversight and Government Reform, *The OPM Data Breach*, p. iii.

52. Ellen Nakashima, "U.S. Decides against Publicly Blaming China for Data Hack," *Washington Post* (July 21, 2015), https://www.washingtonpost.com/world/national-security/us-avoids-blaming-china-in-data-theft-seen-as-fair-game-in-espionage/2015/07/21/03779096-2eee-11e5-8353-1215475949f4_story.html.

53. Committee on Oversight and Government Reform, *The OPM Data Breach*.

54. Brian Naylor, "One Year after OPM Data Breach, What has the Government Learned?" *National Public Radio* (June 6, 2016), http://www.npr.org/sections/alltechconsidered/2016/06/06/480968999/one-year-after-opm-data-breach-what-has-the-government-learned.

55. Natasha Bertrand, "China Caught the US 'With Our Pants Down'—and the Obama Administration Is Struggling to Respond," *Business Insider* (August 4, 2015), http://www.businessinsider.com/us-retaliation-against-china-for-opm-hacks-2015-8.

56. Nakashima, "U.S. Decides against Publicly Blaming China for Data Hack."

57. Bertrand, "China Caught the US 'With Our Pants Down.'"

58. Nakashima, "U.S. Decides against Publicly Blaming China for Data Hack."

Chapter Ten

Strengthening Private–Public Partnerships in National Cybersecurity

James P. Farwell

The competition between competing demands of economic growth and protecting critical cyber infrastructure (CI) has heightened the need to strengthen partnerships between the U.S. government and private industry. Developing new technologies, strategies, plans, operations, tools, and techniques is essential to protect it. How we meet this challenge has opened up an important philosophical debate in the United States about the role of government and its relationship to private industry.

Former U.S. Cyber Command chief General Keith Alexander had advised Congress that cyber threats to military and commercial sectors are growing and that criminals have exploited 75 percent of our population's computers.[1] The 2017 media reports that loss of hacking tools used by the National Security Agency (NSA) to criminal groups such as Shadow Brokers, which then published them online, has complicated the challenge.[2] Intelligence and criminal threats have spotlighted discussion on how the military protects its assets, networks, and systems. No one disputes the military's pivotal role in cybersecurity.

Yet 90 percent of U.S. critical CI is owned by the private sector.[3] Melissa Hathaway, who served as the cyber coordination executive for the director of national intelligence, has rightly pointed out that corporate and political leaders "appear to be paralyzed about meeting the needs for our cyber infrastructures and enterprises."[4] One recognizes the dilemma. Earning a profit motivates industry while protecting national security motivates the U.S. government. Although often complementary, these agendas can compete—and the current deadlock undercuts American security interests.

While the presidential executive orders and directives are streamlining and making cybersecurity more efficient within the government, the private sector remains in many ways left out, especially as to elements that do not fit into what is deemed critical infrastructure. The United States has an important interest in obtaining access to the most cutting-edge technology but the parties with the most sophisticated knowledge may lack requisite clearance that would allow them to work more closely with the government. That presents a challenge.

From the private side, unclear legal rules and lack of resources limit the ability of many companies to protect themselves against attackers. As cyber attackers generally have an operational edge over those presenting a target's defense, rapid advances in technology will worsen that dilemma. Congress should take action that empowers companies to take more pro-active steps to protect their confidential data and that strikes a balance between encouraging companies to voluntarily strengthen cybersecurity without burdening them with excessive government intrusion or regulation.

THE CURRENT STRATEGY

The U.S. government's current strategy for cybersecurity is articulated in a series of executive orders and presidential directives that have evolved over the last decade. These aim to ensure the security and resiliency of critical infrastructure and government parties through coordination and information sharing and hold relevant department or agency heads more accountable. The strategy aims to

- identify, deter, detect, disrupt, and prepare for threats and hazards to the nation's critical infrastructure;
- reduce vulnerabilities of critical assets, systems, and networks; and
- mitigate the potential consequences to critical infrastructure of incidents or adverse events that do occur.[5]

Presidents Barack Obama and Donald Trump have taken steps to increase coordination, step up information sharing, strengthen risk assessment, ensure that U.S. government agencies adhere to rigorous standards to guard against risks, threats, and vulnerabilities and to protect critical infrastructure. The updates affect primarily the government, despite the official view that voluntary public–private collaboration for collective action is pivotal for security and resilience.

Presidential Policy Directive 21 updated the National Plan issued in 2009 to emphasize the complementary nature of security and resilience for critical infrastructure and integrating assets, systems, and networks into an enterprise approach to risk management.[6] Such integration comports with Executive Order 1636[7] that mandated government parties to coordinate with critical infrastructure owners, improve information sharing with them, and to work with them for risk-based approaches to cybersecurity across five national preparedness mission areas: prevention, protection, mitigation, response, and recovery.[8] An executive order issued on May 11, 2017, holds agency heads accountable for protecting their computer systems and networks and managing risks from cyber attacks.[9] The order mandates agency heads to employ the Commerce Department's National Institutes of Standards and Technology guidelines to manage risk, requires risk assessment reports from more than a dozen agencies, seeks to strengthen cybersecurity protection, and addresses the threat of automated "botnet" attacks over the Internet.[10] The order gives the lead for protecting "national security systems" that operate classified and military networks to the secretary of defense and director of national intelligence. It gives the secretary of Homeland Security the lead for protecting critical private infrastructure. It orders the secretary of the Department of Homeland Security (DHS) to engage with owners and operators of the nation's critical infrastructure and to report back to the president within 180 days on findings and recommendations.

The order focuses on risk analysis of three key areas: (1) critical infrastructure at greater risk whose compromise would "reasonably result in catastrophic regional or national effects on public health or safety, economic security, or national security";[11] (2) the core communications infrastructure; and (3) the electric subsector. It also calls for facilitating the processing of security clearances to appropriate personnel employed by critical infrastructure owners and operators and expanding programs that bring private-sector subject-matter experts into federal service on a temporary basis.[12] These steps reflect a growing concern in Washington and within the private sector over the increasing number of incident breaches caused by cyber attacks.[13]

THE EVOLUTION OF U.S. GOVERNMENT POLICY

More recent actions build upon a 2007 U.S. presidential directive that ordered the Department of Defense (DoD) to protect its critical infrastructure.[14] The order endorsed a collaborative, coordinated effort to identify, assess, and improve critical infrastructure within the Defense Industrial Base (DIB).[15] The DIB includes "the DoD, U.S. Government, and the private sector worldwide industrial complex with capabilities to perform research and develop, produce, deliver, and maintain military weapon systems, subsystems, components or pats to meet military requirements necessary to fulfill the National Military Strategy."[16] Most of the DIB is privately owned. It includes businesses of all sizes.

The DHS holds responsibility for protecting civilian critical infrastructure and key resources (CIKR).[17] It devised the National Infrastructure Protection Plan (NIPP).[18] CIKR includes "assets, systems, networks, and functions that provide vital services to the nation," for which attacks or disruption could produce large-scale human casualties, property destruction, and economic damage as well damage national prestige, morale, and confidence.[19] In concept, NIPP provides a unifying structure to integrate efforts to protect CIKR into a single national program. The plan aims to balance resiliency with focused, risk-informed prevention and preparedness. Eighteen sector-specific plans support NIPP. These address efforts among local, state, and federal officials and agencies, the private sector, and international organizations and allies.[20]

In July 2011, the U.S. DoD released its "Strategy for Operating in Cyberspace."[21] Five precepts guide it. First, treating cyberspace as an operational domain, it sought "increased training, information assurance, greater situational awareness, and creating secure and resilient network environments." Second, calling for "cyber hygiene" in security, it aimed to strengthen the workforce and employ new operating concepts to improve security. Third, it recognized that private–public partnerships form the foundation for an "active, layered defense." Fourth, it embraced international partnerships. Since cyberspace transcends traditional geographic borders, incidents may occur across national jurisdictions, and effective action requires multilateral cooperation among allies. The NATO 2020 report also called for incorporating cyber defense into allied strategic thinking. Finally, the strategy aims to catalyze civilian talent and ingenuity to spur new technology.[22] It recognized that entrepreneurs in small- and medium-sized companies often stand at the cutting edge in moving concepts from innovative idea to reality and scaled adoption.

The advent of networked technology has "spurred innovation, cultivated knowledge, encouraged free expression, and increased the Nation's economic prosperity."[23] Malicious activity, malfunction, human error, and acts of nature challenge this infrastructure.[24] The U.S. government recognizes that these factors define shared challenges in protecting the nation from malicious cyber activity and managing cyber incidents and consequences. That requires greater public–private partnership and cooperation.[25]

In 2016, the White House moved to improve coordination at the federal level. It issued Presidential Policy Directive 41 (PPD-41)[26] to define lines of authority for who's responsible within the federal government for cybersecurity and who in the government to contact in the event of a cyber incident. DHS Secretary Jeh C. Johnson has explained the directive:

> The PPD spells out the lines of responsibility within the federal government for responses to a significant cyber incident, and specifies who to contact in

the government in the event of an incident. The PPD delineates between "threat responses" and "asset responses." A "threat response" essentially involves investigating the crime, so that we can hunt down the bad actor. As the PPD spells out, federal law enforcement is the key point of contact for a threat response. The Department of Homeland Security, through our cybersecurity experts at the National Cybersecurity and Communications Integration Center, will act as the point of contact and lead coordinator for asset response. "Asset response," like a threat response, is crucial. It involves helping the victim find the bad actor on its system, repair its system, patching the vulnerability, reducing the risks of future incidents, and preventing the incident from spreading to others.

Finally, the PPD directs the Department of Homeland Security to lead the effort to write the National Cyber Incident Response Plan. This Plan will set out how the federal government will work with the private sector and state, local, and territorial governments in responding to a significant cyber incident.[27]

PPD-41 speaks as well to intelligence incidents, and to related activities that facilitate building situational threat awareness and intelligence sharing, identification of knowledge gaps, and the ability to degrade or mitigate adversary threat capabilities.[28] The directive sets up an architecture to facilitate National Policy Coordination through the Cyber Response Group that supports the National Security Council. National operational coordination is achieved through relevant sector-specific agencies and a Cyber Unified Coordination Group.[29]

The directive tries to define whether an incident requires a national response. It employs a 0 to 5 scale to characterize incidents. The directive applies only to *significant cyber events*—a category 3 or above—defined as those likely to result in demonstrable harm to the national security interests, foreign relations, or economy of the United States or to the public confidence, civil liberties, or public health and safety of the American people.[30] The directive recognizes that private companies that experience a major incident breach may perceive different priorities than the government. It enjoins the government to take private concerns into account. In concept, the directive encourages private companies to report incidents to the government and seeks to provide reasonable privacy protections to them for such disclosures.[31]

Still, the directive comes up short in failing to provide principles that respect and protect industry.[32] The former director of Information Assurance at the NSA has observed that smaller companies have no idea how to engage with the government and that "many businesses don't see the value in working with the government and sharing information."[33] Partly that stems from executive branch emphasis on sharing information with what it deems critical CI. But many of the most innovative companies are smaller and do not qualify as CI, and so they leave a hole in the policy of protecting private industry. The government is not offering much support and many of smaller companies lack the capacity or resources to take steps that could prove essential in protecting their information. This issue should be addressed. Overall, the policy continues an ongoing debate about the balance of responsibility between the public and private sectors with regard to formulating standards to protect confidential and proprietary data.

THE EMERGING THREAT MATRIX

How acute is the challenge that cybersecurity problems post to public and private parties? The Defense Advanced Research Projects Agency's (DARPA's) deputy director Kaigham J. Gabriel has warned the Subcommittee on Emerging Threats and Capabilities of the House Armed Services Committee that cybersecurity systems take too long to build and may become quickly obsolete in today's threat environment. Once built, they merely set the stage for the next requirement: "Shelf-life of cybersecurity systems and capabilities," he declared, "is sometimes measured in days. Thus, to a greater degree than in other areas of defense, cybersecurity solutions require that we develop the ability to build quickly, at scale, and over a broad range of capabilities. This is true for offensive and defensive capabilities."[34]

The quality and nature of technology for cyber attack or cyber exploitation is expanding. "Computing, imaging, and communications capabilities that, as recently as 15 years ago, were the exclusive domain of military systems, are now in the hands of hundreds of millions of people around the world," Gabriel stated.[35] Nearly a dozen countries are producing electronic warfare systems. Many use mostly commercial, off-the-shelf technology. Decades ago, a new system was produced every ten years. Today, one is produced every year to a year and a half.[36] In testimony before Congress, Dr. James Miller pointed out that DoD acquisition processes require an average of eighty-one months to make new computing systems operational: "That means by the time they are fielded, they are already three to four generations behind the state of the art. We are working to get cycles of 12 to 36 months as opposed to 7 to 8 years."[37]

In the private sector, Century Link's Chief Security Officer David Mahon has well summarized the major cyber threats faced by the public and private sector: (1) nation-state intrusions (also known as "advanced persistent threat"); (2) criminal, which extends to sophisticated organized crime; (3) hacktivism; and (4) insider attacks. One should distinguish between cyber threats and cyber threat indicators. Cyber experts Dan Auerback and Lee Tien suggest that a cybersecurity threat is what we guard against, while a "cyber-security threat indicator" is the activity that allows private or public entities to monitor and execute countermeasures.[38] An indicator triggers what counter measures a company may take to protect against a cyber threat. The Cyber Security Information Sharing Act (CISA) defines a cyber threat indicator as any "information" that would "describe or identify" any "method of causing a user with legitimate access to an information that is stored on, processed by, or transiting an information system to unwittingly enable the defeat of a security control of exploitation of a security vulnerability."[39]

CISA also defines "defensive measure." This is something applied to an information system or to information on that system that "detects, prevents, or mitigates a known or suspected cybersecurity threat or security vulnerability."[40] The Federal Guidance for the Private Sector issued by the DHS and the Department of Justice provides a number of examples that illustrate permissible defensive measures. Significantly, the definition does not embrace "defensive" measures that destroy, render unusable, provide unauthorized access to, or substantially harm third-party information systems. The constraints imposed by statutes such as the Computer Fraud and Abuse Act[41] that make action that damages another party's computer unlawful remain intact.

Fast evolving technology is altering the strategic implications for cyber capabilities. That affects strategic considerations. The global digital infrastructure—"institutions, practices and protocols that together organize and deliver the increasing power of digital technology to business and society"[42]—has reconfigured how business is conducted. Defensive strategies that worked before may prove obsolete. The 2017 hacking threat known as *Wanna Cry*[43] illustrates the emerging sophistication and complexity of new threats. Former Deputy Secretary of Defense William J. Lynn has long worried about the impact of network destruction.[44] The Russian-backed denial of service attacks on Estonia and Georgia[45] and the assault on eBay and PayPal by the hacker group Anonymous[46] illustrate that governments and companies are both vulnerable. The emergence of cyber weapons like Stuxnet opens a window to the future.[47] Stuxnet impeded Iran's nuclear centrifuge program. Initial reports suggested that assets of friendly nations, such as an Indian satellite, also sustained damage,[48] although doubts about that later arose.[49]

Iranian critics cheered Stuxnet I. But Stuxnet II or its successors may target U.S. or allied critical infrastructure. Blended attacks, employing cyber and kinetic weapons in combination, could zero in on military and civilian targets, destroying some, while launching sophisticated penetrations of networks that control critical civilian infrastructure. The emerging political ecosystem from which new weapons are originating from nonstate parties, including criminal enterprises, presages complicated and unpredictable scenarios.[50]

Concerns about Chinese cyber espionage and piracy (or, in obtuse national security jargon, "cyberexploitation") highlight another challenge.

The U.S.–China Economic and Security Review Commission has repeatedly warned that Chinese are guilty of rampant cyber piracy—stealing intellectual property and trade secrets vital to U.S. defense and to keeping the United States technologically competitive.[51] This concern is one element of a broader challenge as rivals or foes employ multiple channels to acquire confidential and proprietary data. What cannot be hacked may yet be obtained through legal acquisition from U.S. companies. A 2012 report to the Commission points to "collaboration between U.S. and Chinese information security firms … over the potential for illicit access to sensitive network vulnerability."[52]

Its 2016 report warned against current Chinese cyber-enabled theft of intellectual property that has "repeatedly infiltrated U.S. national security organizations and extracted information with serious consequences for U.S. national security, including information on the plans and operations of the U.S. military forces and the designs of U.S. weapons and weapons systems."[53] The 2016 recommendations echoed alarms sounded four years earlier in the commercial sector and recommended that Congress "amend the statute authorizing the Committee on Foreign Investment in the United States to bar Chinese state-owned enterprises from acquiring or otherwise gaining effective control of U.S. companies."[54]

Human mistakes or errors in judgment by insider actors challenge our most sensitive networks and systems. Dr. James Peery of the Energy Department's Sandia National Laboratories has warned the U.S. Senate that we must "assume our adversary is in our networks, on our machines." Still, he noted, "We've got to operate anyway."[55] His fears are well founded. In 2008, hackers penetrated the Pentagon's classified Secret Internet Protocol Router Network (SIPRNET) when a flash drive loaded with "Agent.btz," a malicious code devised by a foreign intelligence agency, was left in a Middle East parking lot. Later, someone inserted it into a U.S. CENTCOM laptop.[56] The incident infected computers and even the Joint Worldwide Intelligence Communication System, which carries top-secret information. The damage inflicted remains undisclosed.[57]

Former Deputy Secretary of Defense William J. Lynn acknowledged that other penetrations remain undetected.[58] The Pentagon recognized the problem as early as the 1990s. SOLAR SUNRISE, a series of DoD computer attacks in 1998 that targeted defense networks, led to the installation of intrusion detection systems on key nodes.[59] The incident confirmed findings derived from the 1997 ELIGIBLE RECEIVER exercise series that uncovered vulnerabilities in DoD cyber systems and demonstrated the increasing risks to U.S. interests in cyberspace. Lynn considered the 2008 penetration an "important wake-up call" and a "turning point." [60] The Pentagon took remedial action, launching Operation Buckshot Yankee that led to banning the use of thumb drives[61] and the creation of the U.S. Cyber Command. Still, the incident proved how nettlesome cyber attacks can prove. Cleaning up this single problem took the Pentagon fourteen months.[62]

Individual attackers have underscored the potential for mischief. Over a decade ago, New Jersey programmer David Smith had created "Melissa," a virus that used a Microsoft Word document sent as an e-mail attachment to infect classified U.S. commercial networks, forcing Microsoft and Intel to shut down their e-mail servers.[63] The incident revealed that human beings are often the weak link for cybersecurity—recognition pivotal to the new U.S. strategy.

Corporate vulnerability to outside hackers is growing. A Bloomberg survey of utility, telecommunications, financial services, and health care revealed that technology managers in 124 companies—each with at least ten thousand workers—said they could double the spending on cybersecurity and yet their networks would remain vulnerable.[64] A 2016 study conducted by the Ponemon Institute found that 52 percent of companies surveyed suffered a cyber breach in the preceding year, and 66 percent of those companies suffered from multiple breaches.[65] Hackers who breached Target stores in 2013 cost the company $200 million in losses to credit unions and community banks for reissuing forty million stolen credit cards—of which three million were sold on the black market for a mid-range price of $26.85 per card. Hackers stole seventy million records that contained the name, address, e-mail address, and phone number of Target shoppers. The company was hit with 140 lawsuits. Target experienced a 46 percent drop in profits. The company said it would spend $100 million to upgrade its payment terminals.[66]

Stealthy foes can corrupt hardware and software. Reportedly, Russia and China have probed the U.S. power grid to identify vulnerabilities and left behind software programs that may be deployed for disruption.[67] Concrete evidence of cyber mischief surfaced in Australia, where a disgruntled employee rigged a computerized control system at a water treatment plant and released over two hundred thousand gallons of sewage into parks, rivers, and the grounds of a Hyatt hotel.[68]

Networks or systems can be compromised before they are constructed. Microsoft's Eric Warner has cautioned that foes can "manipulate or sabotage systems during their design, development or delivery to determine or disrupt government functions."[69] Sandia's James Peery has labeled the information technology supply chain "a particularly insidious risk" and of

high consequence national security systems, because of our widespread reliance on commercial-off-the-shelf (COTS) hardware and software technology that is increasingly produced in whole or in part by untrusted, non-US organizations. Unfortunately, the growing complexity of these systems also makes it economically infeasible to verify them thoroughly.

Insufficient attention has been given to technical approaches for mitigating supply chain risks. Counterfeiting and subversion of critical components in high-consequence DoD systems could have a devastating effect on our ability to project military power with confidence around the world. Better methodologies and technologies are needed for assessing and managing supply chain risks."[70]

The official report to the Permanent Select Committee on Intelligence in 2012 that supported Rep. Mike Rogers' cybersecurity bill concluded that "intelligence collection efforts that can and should be provided—in both classified and unclassified form (when possible)—to the private sector in order to help the owners and operators of the vast majority of America's information infrastructure better protect themselves."[71] The committee's observation helped to frame the challenges that the CISA[72] sought to address.

LEGAL HURDLES TO COOPERATION

Information sharing and information protection among companies are vital to identify risks and vulnerabilities, counter cyber threats, and create data banks. Information is power. Companies—and the government—need access to what their partners know or learn. Uncovering errors or problems in software, especially when they may occupy a few lines of code in a product that contains tens of millions of lines, can be difficult. Detection by one party of a vulnerability—a worm, virus, trapdoor, or other risk—as well as countermeasures that a party may develop, should be shared with other potential cyber targets. Viable cybersecurity strategies mandate that parties act on an informed basis. Equally, the government has a strong interest in ensuring that sensitive or classified information is closely held by appropriate parties, but that interest needs to be balanced with the need to provide innovative entrepreneurs who develop cutting-edge technology access to the information needed to provide the products desired. Much debate has centered on whether cyber threats require action mandated by statute or whether voluntary action is more prudent. Prominent issues include (1) U.S. antitrust and unfair business laws[73] and (2) privacy laws such as the Electronic Communications Privacy Act and the Stored Communications Act.[74]

ANTITRUST

Companies fear the antitrust division of the U.S. Department of Justice and the Federal Trade Commission (FTC). Both watch for activity perceived as collusion and that may lead to price fixing, abuse of market power, allocation of customers, and other anticompetitive activity. Their posture underscores another dimension in the tension between public and private interests. No one challenges the conceptual validity of antitrust or unfair business laws. But the public interest in promoting anticompetitive practices embodied in those laws must be balanced against national security interests.

In practice, larger companies—staffed by top-notch attorneys—are able to manage the challenge of sharing relevant information without breaching the Clayton Act, Sherman Act, or unfair business practice laws. A lot of information sharing takes place among companies. For example, Century Link, one of the top Internet service providers (ISPs), advised Congress that when it learns from third-party partners that customer computers are likely infected with malware that makes them part of a botnet, it notifies customers and directs them to resources to help them clean up the malware. It provides educational material, antivirus protection, firewalls, and parental controls. It works with stakeholders and industry partners on Border Gateway Protocol (BGP) security to prevent accidental or malicious Internet route hacking.[75] Other industries engage in comparable information-sharing practices.

Larger companies have the resources and sophistication to avoid illegal collusive activities. Smaller companies may lack that capacity. There is a solution. Narrowly drawn reforms can limit disclosure of risks, threats, vulnerabilities, and approaches to protection of information systems and personally identifiable information. That would enable information sharing[76] and cybersecurity without undercutting a competitive marketplace. Removing antitrust and FTC legal barriers to permit companies to monitor and defend information systems against cyber threats would strengthen their ability to forge defenses that can mitigate or manage risks, threats, and vulnerabilities. Companies should be permitted to freely share cyber threat information among themselves. Reforms should prohibit the use of information shared with the FTC or any other U.S. government party to accord competitors an unfair competitive advantage.

PRIVACY AND CONFIDENTIALITY

Concerns that information sharing or disclosures may create legal liability for claims alleging breach of confidentiality or privacy are acute. These include potential claims for release of confidential information without prior consent. Information security—confidentiality, integrity, availability—is top of mind for many. Governments, the military, hospitals, and companies amass enormous amounts of information about employees, customers, products, and research and wish to protect it.

The case of RSA Security in 2011 illustrates these legal concerns from an industry perspective. RSA manufactures a two-factor authentication token. SecureIDs are widely used electronic keys to computer systems that work using a two-pronged approach to confirming the identity of the person trying to access a computer system. Its system is used by many financial networks and defense contractors. Infiltrators breached and compromised the systems of different U.S. defense contractors. Lockheed Martin fell victim to hackers using duplicates of RSA's SecureID tokens to penetrate internal networks. The event forced Lockheed to shut down all remote access to its intranet for at least a week.[77] The significance of the infiltration is manifest in the fact that Lockheed Martin and RSA supply coded access tokens to millions of corporate users and government officials.[78]

The event cast into high relief the tension between private and public interests. Although RSA eventually disclosed the problem to customers,[79] the company was criticized for putting its interest in earning profits and maintaining the commercial viability of its product ahead of the security concerns of customers.[80] A week passed before RSA disclosed the problem to the press, much more time passed before RSA revealed that the attack had compromised its technology. Critics argue that RSA's behavior cost clients millions of dollars.[81] The company eventually made a formal disclosure on its 8-K filing to the U.S. Securities and Exchange Commission.[82] Experts like Melissa Hathaway argue that the Securities Exchange Commission ought to require companies to make timely disclosures and to take remedial action.[83] The public interest clearly supports Hathaway's position. Why didn't RSA act sooner? The most obvious inference from its actions is that the company perceived its own interests in a different light. RSA has shown little remorse. One wonders whether it worried more about the legal consequences of a problem than its customers. CISA strengthened information-sharing options for critical infrastructure companies, but these should be expanded to include all of the private sector.

CISA attempts to address key issues as to privacy and confidentiality. A detailed analysis of this legislation lies beyond the scope of this paper, but it merits brief comments. Congress designed the law to establish a voluntary cybersecurity information-sharing process that encourages public and private sectors to share cyber threat indicators and defense measures while protecting privacy and civil liberties.[84] The law has two main components. First, it authorizes companies to monitor and implement defensive measures on their own information systems to counter cyber threats. Second, CISA provides certain protections to encourage companies voluntarily to share information about "cyber threat indicators" and "defensive measures" with federal, state, and local governments as well as other companies and private entities.

Protections include protections from liability, nonwaiver of privilege, and protections from Freedom of Information Act disclosure.[85] Securing these protections requires compliance with CISA procedures and removing personal information from data shared or transmitted. One legislative goal was to address fears that companies that shared information might violate the Electronic Communications Privacy Act.[86]

CISA allows companies to "monitor" and "operate defensive measures" on its own information system or with another party's system where written authorization is granted.[87] Broadly, companies can share or receive information as to "cyber threat indicators" and "defensive measures" to achieve a "cyber security purpose" as defined in the Act.[88] One important provision provides an antitrust exemption for such action.[89] Sharing information with the federal government does not waive privileges or protection of trade secrets,[90] and the federal government deems shared information to be proprietary.[91] Importantly, no party is required to share information.[92]

The Federal Guidance is detailed in defining cyber threat indicators. CISA stresses that the only information companies can share with the federal government[93] is that "necessary to describe or identify threats to information and information systems" and that is "directly related to and necessary to identify or describe a cybersecurity threat."[94] It offers example of the types of information a company might share,[95] what it cannot share,[96] and what constitutes a defensive measure as well as examples of such measures.[97]

Although CISA won bipartisan support, opponents were vocal. Apple, Twitter, and Google joined privacy and consumer groups in opposing the language as too broad.[98] Consumer groups argued that the legislation gives tech companies that receive troves of data from Internet users too much legal protection for sharing what they viewed as ill-defined cyber threat indicators.[99] Others contend that as DHS is required to automatically and indiscriminately disseminate to the NSA all indicators received, CISA significantly increases NSA's access to Americans' personal information without proper legal safeguards and would permit law enforcement to use that information to investigate a broad array of crimes, not just cybercrimes. Critics also contend the law authorizes companies to monitor user activities for purposes other than protecting their own networks while according them protection from legal liability.[100]

It makes sense to require federal contractors to inform the government about cyber threats and make it easier for government regulators and corporations to communicate about threats. Facilitating voluntary information sharing between the federal government and private parties, including easing antitrust laws that restrict information sharing between private companies and offering legal protections to companies that act pro-actively to protect their networks, would create a more secure CI and protect consumer privacy without creating a new bureaucracy. While the expertise of our national security entities should be leveraged to promote public–private partnerships, security requirements may limit what can be shared, with whom, or under what circumstances. Close engagement, coordination, and cooperation are required, on a case-by-case basis, to address that issue. While seeking information or intelligence from the government or other parties, companies need to recognize—and take responsibility for—financial and legal risks they incur in operating vulnerable networks.[101]

Robust Private–Public Partnerships

The U.S. government's approach rests upon a risk management framework of cooperation and coordination between the private and public sector. That enables both sectors to set goals and objectives; identify assets, systems, and networks; assess risk based on consequences, vulnerabilities, and threats; establish priorities based on risk assessments and, increasingly, on return-on investment for mitigating risk; implement protective programs and resiliency strategies; and measure effectiveness.[102] Among the key issues that must be addressed in forging robust public–private partnerships are (1) joint planning, (2) creating incentives for innovative public–private partnerships, (3) resolving who defends private industry against cyber attack, (4) balancing cost sharing between public and private sectors, and (5) developing a viable approach that authorizes government to reasonably share classified information on cybersecurity.

JOINT PLANNING

Joint planning between government and industry strengthens the ability of each to counter cyber threats. Advances in technology are accelerating the "network speed" at which incidents occur. That pressures decision makers to act more quickly. Joint planning is vital to anticipate and counter looming threats and risks.

The military equips itself to protect its own assets, systems, and networks. Joint planning can help enable the DIB to leverage that expertise in establishing a cohesive policy framework to forecast and meet challenges. Adopting this approach will force interested parties to focus on key questions: What priorities should govern planning? Where should capital investment be focused? How should industry and the government, each of whom bears responsibility for security, allocate costs and responsibilities? What are actionable requirements to make CI as secure as possible? Where do we acquire the knowledge vital to making informed judgments in answering those questions?

Smart planning for cybersecurity is an iterative process. It entails asking the right questions, developing information needed to ensure the right questions, and conducting progressive analysis through public–private engagement. From a public perspective, government can encourage business to invest in security measures that exceed their narrower business concerns. From a private perspective, industry may gain access to expertise it lacks, along with a greater comprehension of its own responsibilities. Too often, industry expects government to do all of the heavy lifting for cybersecurity. Yet the obligations flow both ways.

Industry is more supple in developing and testing new products. Industry better generates innovative ideas and cutting-edge solutions. Industry owns and operates most of the critical infrastructure, affording it a better understanding of CIKR assets, systems, networks, and facilities. It can move more quickly to reduce risk and respond to incidents. DARPA has recognized that through programs like Cyber Fast Track (CFT), which taps into a pool of nontraditional experts. DARPA recognizes that smaller and medium-sized companies are leaders in innovative technology. It has adjusted its funding accordingly. Kaigham Gabriel noted while he served at the DARPA that it is vital to expand "the number and diversity of talent contributing to the Nation's cybersecurity."[103] The philosophy embraces the far-sighted view of looking to companies that take risks to create new ideas, in comparison to larger organizations that by emphasizing greater adherence to established procedures or protocols may prove less adept at creating new products. DARPA's philosophy smartly stresses collaboration between government and industry.

In the United States, the public and private sectors already work together in many ways. The DHS National Coordinating Center enables operational and collaborative partnerships. The Communications, Security, Reliability and Interoperability Council (CSRIC) provides an effective vehicle for providing recommendations to the Federal Communications Commission.[104] The FBI's Domestic Security Alliance Council (DSAC) is a strategic partnership between the FBI, DHS, and the private sector to ensure effective exchange of information to keep the nation's critical infrastructure safe, secure, and resilient.[105] The National Cyber-Forensics Training Alliance (NCFTA) serves as a conduit between private industry and law enforcement to fight cybercrime.

Malware pandemics such as the Conficker computer worm underscore the need. Conficker targeted Microsoft's Windows Operating System. First detected in November 2008,[106] it exploited flaws in Windows software to co-opt machines and link them to a remotely controlled virtual computer—a botnet. Conficker generated strong cooperation among industry, academia, and government. Collaboration grew to over one hundred level one domain operators and kept Microsoft in daily touch with ICANN and governments.

It also exposed legal challenges. In some countries, contractual barriers and antitrust laws had to be addressed.[107]

Success proved elusive. Conficker's creators have been neither identified nor caught, although in June 2011, Ukraine authorities working with the FBI arrested sixteen hackers in Kiev who used Conficker to seal $72 million from banking accounts.[108] Conficker is a warning to those who flinch from strong public–private collaboration. There was more success in fighting DNS (Domain Name System) Changer Malware, which enables criminals to control user DNS servers and thus what sites the user connects to on the Internet. Criminals could cause an unsuspecting user to connect to a fraudulent website or interfere with a user's online web browsing.[109] Over four million computers were infected. Industry provided critical insights into the information environment, helped identify the infected DNS servers, and helped with remedial action. The FBI is developing evidence and is prosecuting six Estonian nationals arrested and charged after a two-year operation.[110]

The response to these threats underscores that public–private engagement can be effectively achieved. That illuminates the path to addressing defense against cyber attacks. It does so as well for notions of active defense—which remains ill-defined but should include preemptive action, carefully limited and permitted without a structured policy framework—and for offense. Neither the United States nor other nations have released their offensive doctrine and/or descriptions of capability. What's clear is the developing technology is providing the operational flexibility to maneuver in the cyber domain, and to harmonize resources and capabilities within a coherent systematic strategy that permits the achievement of operation aims despite the opposition.

INCENTIVES FOR NEW PARTNERSHIPS

The ability of the private and public sectors to leverage the strengths of one another to create both new spaces for creative thinking and to spur innovation affords a key incentive to promote these relationships. That synergy will produce better strategic thinking and strong policy frameworks. It will also— and this addresses the core of Kaigham Gabriel's concern—increase the rate at which innovation takes place. New knowledge is produced every day. It remakes the world and reshapes the political and information environment and the cyber domain. It accentuates the importance of some things, while rendering others obsolete.[111]

The DARPA has already recognized this challenge and is moving toward providing more grants to small- and medium-sized entrepreneurial companies who can meet that need. The DoD and the NSA need to become more flexible in easing access and clearances to companies and their employees to make possible exchange of information and the symbiotic partnerships that will enable public–private partnerships to flourish.

Yet, we should not rely upon DARPA or other government grants to spur innovation and new technology. Providing tax incentives for new technology, products, and innovation would spur development and make the investment of capital more worthwhile. Defining goals and offering appropriate prizes—financial and other—offers a different approach that could yield tangible results. Engagement between companies and the government, to ascertain what can most strongly encourage companies to act pro-actively, would be productive.

WHO DEFENDS PRIVATE INDUSTRY AGAINST CYBER ATTACK?

A joint policy framework is essential in forging a strategy to protect industry in real time against cyber attack or cyber exploitation. The challenge raises thorny issues. DoD has made clear it will defend against attacks. The issue becomes, "What realistic options does the private sector have that provide practical, effective defenses against cyber attacks?" Major differences exist between the way that the public and private sectors view permissible defenses. Recently, the DoD has embraced the notion of "active defense" to counter asymmetric threats. As William Lynn put it, "In this environment, a fortress mentality will not work. We cannot hide behind a Maginot line of firewalls. ... our defenses must be active."[112] He has noted that in the cyber domain milliseconds can make a difference. In that view, the Pentagon has embraced a defensive system with three overlapping lines of defense. Two, based on commercial best practices, are ordinary hygiene—keeping software up to date and firewalls up to date—and the use of intrusion detection devices and monitoring software to establish a perimeter defense.[113] The third is protecting critical infrastructure, including civilian infrastructure.[114]

The idea that companies should collect evidence and turn it over to proper law enforcement authorities may be useful down the road for prosecutions, but fails to answer the critical question of how, beyond passive defenses like firewalls, one stops an attack or whether preemptive activity is permissible—and if so, under what guidelines? Can the owners of private critical infrastructure engage in "Active defense" as well? If so, does it afford a right of hot pursuit? Does it embrace preemptive action? Who has, or should have, the authority to make decisions in mounting an active defense for national security incidents? The Computer Fraud and Abuse Act[115] makes it a felony to intentionally access a computer without authorization and cause damages of $5,000 or more. A foreign attacker may not be able to capitalize on that to defend itself against privately initiated "active defense," but the Justice Department's responsibility is to enforce the law as written. And what happens if the attack originates in the United States? Does that not compound the problem? Industry currently lacks legal guidance—and recourse—for countering a real-time attack. Thus, one industry leader sees passive defense as reliance upon firewalls, intrusion detection systems, and hygiene, while active defense means working "actively"—in concert—with other private or other parties to identify, intercept, and block attacks. That is a plausible explanation but represents a less aggressive view than that held by many who focus on defending military assets, networks, and systems. The bottom line is that joint planning between government and industry is essential in thinking through who a company—a financial institution, utility, or other private party—summons for help, or what action it may legally or practically take to actively defend itself.

BALANCING PUBLIC AND PRIVATE INTERESTS IN ALLOCATING COST AND SHARING INFORMATION

Who should bear the cost of continuous upgrades to cybersecurity? How should such decisions be reached? Resources and interests vary. A key challenge is that while private business owns 90 percent of critical infrastructure,[116] no U.S. government department possesses the authority to compel companies to meet security performance requirements. The answer lies in balancing regulation and volunteerism. Yet, larger firms can more easily bear costs of protecting physical, human, and cyber assets. Smaller companies face stiff challenges as capital requirements may be steep. No single formula applies across the board. That begs the question of what security standards should be satisfied or who should formulate them—industry or the government?

A second issue pertains to access to cyber expertise and access to classified and/or proprietary information. Demand for cyber expertise greatly exceeds the supply.[117] Top-tier places like Sandia National Laboratory recruit aggressively. It will pay for a master's degree and support new recruits with 75 percent of their salary while they attend school full time, in exchange for two years' service; there is intense competition for their knowledge and skills. Private companies often offer 50 percent higher salaries and benefits. So far, places like Sandia have been able to retain much of their workforce, and thus a reservoir of talent, experience, and unique expertise. Places like Sandia offer innovative hands-on computer security programs, skill refreshing, and continuous learning. The government better understands countermeasures and best practices to address risks and vulnerabilities. The private sector cannot match its intelligence-gathering capacity. All these actions benefit industry—which, for its part, bears the burden of taking active steps to protect its assets, systems, and networks.[118]

But if the government retains a majority of the talent and understanding of cyber countermeasures, then it should more readily share the fruits of its knowledge with private-sector partners to better protect critical infrastructure. Melissa Hathaway offers a practical way forward in addressing this challenge: the DoD and the Department of National Intelligence have the authority to make the policy decision to declassify or "write for release" or create a tear line to release vital information to a broader user community. That will greatly facilitate private–public information sharing and protection of critical infrastructure.[119]

A key challenge is enabling access to classified information among private-sector parties. The prevailing view would limit information sharing to individuals who possess appropriate security clearances, on a basis consistent with protecting national security. Congress is considering ways to enable cybersecurity providers, protected entities, or self-protected entities eligible for a clearance to obtain one if they show they are able to appropriately protect classified cyber threat intelligence. What's needed is for parties like the director of national intelligence or other responsible federal entity to work closely with private parties flexibly and taking into account private-sector innovation, corporate information sharing, and security best practices. Close engagement is required to establish realistic procedures that enable each side to tap into the expertise of the other. One way to achieve that may be to grant temporary clearance for specific projects.[120]

CONCLUSION

The Federal Bureau of Investigation's top cyber cop, Shawn Henry, has minced no words about where we stand in the battle to fend off hackers: "We're not winning," he told the *Wall Street Journal*. In his judgment, the current private and public approach is "unsustainable."[121]

We need to move expeditiously but smartly to minimize cyber risks and vulnerabilities to critical infrastructure for both government and industry. We must strengthen cybersecurity. The government can work with the private sector in ways that offer strong incentives for the private sector to protect its own interest and that of the nation. The challenges state and nonstate actors pose create a real and present danger that must be dealt with. A joint public–private policy framework, augmented by legislative reforms that authorize desired strategies, is vital as this nation forges viable strategies that protect, as much as possible, its critical CI. The sooner the better.

NOTES

1. *Statement of General Keith B. Alexander, Commander, US CYBER COMMAND, Hearing on National Defense Authorization Act for Fiscal Year 2012, Committee on Armed Services, U.S. House of Representatives, March 16, 2011* (Washington, DC: United States House of Representatives, March 16, 2011), p. 4, http://www.fas.org/irp/congress/2011_hr/cybercom.pdf.

2. Dustin Volz, "Ransomware Attack Again Thrusts U.S. Spy Agency into Unwanted Spotlight," *Reuters* (May 16, 2017), http://www.reuters.com/article/us-cyber-attack-blame-idUSKCN18C02D.

3. Chemical, commercial facilities, communications, critical manufacturing, dams, defense industrial base, emergency services, energy, financial services, food and agriculture, government facilities, health care and public health, information technology, nuclear reactors (and materials and waste), transportation systems, and water and wastewater systems. Also see Richard Weitz, "Global Insights: The DHS' Cybersecurity Logjam," *World Politics Review* (April 10, 2012).

4. Telephone interview with Melissa E. Hathaway (August 3, 2012).

5. Department of Homeland Security, *NIPP 2013: Partnering for Critical Infrastructure Security and Resilience* (Washington, DC: Department of Homeland Security, 2013), https://www.dhs.gov/sites/default/files/publications/NIPP%20 2013_Partnering%20for%20Critical%20Infrastructure%20Security%20and%20 Resilience_508_0.pdf.

6. Barack H. Obama, *Presidential Policy Directive 21 (PPD-21): Critical Infrastructure Security and Resilience* (February 12, 2013), https://oba-mawhitehouse.archives.gov/the-press-office/2013/02/12/presidential-policy-directive-critical-infrastructure-security-and-resil.

7. Executive Order 13636, *Improving Critical Infrastructure Cybersecurity* (February 12, 2013), https://obamawhitehouse.archives.gov/the-press-office/2013/ 02/12/executive-order-improving-critical-infrastructure-cybersecurity. The National Plan also aligns with the National Preparedness System called for in Barack H. Obama, *Presidential Policy Directive 8 (PPD-8), National Preparedness* (September 23, 2015), https://www.dhs.gov/presidential-policy-directive-8-national-preparedness.

8. Department of Homeland Security, *NIPP 2013*.

9. Executive Order 13228, "Presidential Executive Order on Strengthening the Cybersecurity of Federal Networks and Critical Infrastructure," (May 11, 2017), https://www.whitehouse.gov/the-press-office/2017/05/11/presidential-executive-order-strengthening-cybersecurity-federal. See also Ellen Nakashima, "Trump Signs Order on Cybersecurity That Holds Agency Heads Accountable for Network Attacks,"

Washington Post (May 12, 2017), https://www.washingtonpost.com/world/national-security/trump-signs-order-on-cybersecurity-that-holds-agency-heads-accountable-for-network-attacks/2017/05/11/4e389522-2b8f-11e7-a616-d7c8a68c1a66_story. html; and "President Issues Executive Order to Strengthen Cybersecurity of Federal Networks and U.S. Critical Infrastructure," *Crowell & Moring* (May 12, 2017), https://www.crowell.com/NewsEvents/AlertsNewsletters/all/President-Issues-Executive-Order-to-Strengthen-Cybersecurity-of-Federal-Networks-and-US-Critical-Infrastructure.

10. National Institute of Standards and Technology, *Security and Privacy Controls for Federal Information Systems and Organizations. NIST Special Publication 800-53 (Revision 4)*, (Washington, DC: United States Department of Commerce, April 2013), http://nvlpubs.nist.gov/nistpubs/SpecialPublications/NIST.SP.800-53r4.pdf.

11. Executive Order 13636, "Improving Critical Infrastructure Cybersecurity," (February 12, 2013), https://obamawhitehouse.archives.gov/the-press-office/2013/02/12/executive-order-improving-critical-infrastructure-cybersecurity.

12. Executive Order 13636, Section 4 (d) and (e).

13. The executive order has a gap that concerned the private sector. It does not give the executive branch authority to indemnify companies that meet certain minimum security standards or to exempt from the Freedom of Information Act any information shared by private entities. See David Bodenheimer and Kate M. Growley, "Cybersecurity Receives Presidential Push with New Cyber Executive Order," *Crowell & Moring* (February 15, 2013), https://www.crowelldatalaw.com/2013/02/cybersecurity-receives-presidential-push-with-new-cyber-executive-order/.

14. George W. Bush, *Homeland Security Presidential Directive 7: Critical Infrastructure Identification, Prioritization, and Protection* (December 17, 2003).

15. Barack H. Obama, *Presidential Policy Directive 20 (PPD-20): U.S. Cyber Operations Policy* (October 2012), https://fas.org/irp/offdocs/ppd/ppd-20.pdf.

16. Michael Chertoff, *National Infrastructure Protection Plan: Partnering to Enhance Protection and Resiliency* (Washington, DC: United States Department of Homeland Security, 2009), p. 4, http://www.dhs.gov/xlibrary/assets/NIPP_Plan.pdf.

17. Chertoff, *National Infrastructure Protection Plan*, p. 2.

18. Chertoff, *National Infrastructure Protection Plan*, pp. 1–6.

19. United States Department of Homeland Security and Department of Defense, *Defense Industrial Base: Critical Infrastructure and Key Resources Sector-Specific Plan as Input to the National Infrastructure Protection Plan* (Washington, DC: Department of Homeland Security and Department of Defense, May 2007), p. 3, http://www.dhs.gov/xlibrary/assets/nipp-ssp-defense-industrial-base.pdf.

20. Chertoff, *National Infrastructure Protection Plan*.

21. United States Department of Defense, *2011 Department of Defense Strategy for Operating in Cyberspace* (Washington, DC: Department of Defense, July 2011), http://www.defense.gov/news/d20110714cyber.pdf.

22. Jamie Shea, chairman, *NATO 2020: Assured Security; Dynamic Engagement: Analysis and Recommendations of the Group of Experts on a New Strategic Concept for NATO* (Brussels: North Atlantic Treaty Organization, May 17, 2010), pp. 11, 14, 20, http://www.nato.int/strategic-concept/expertsreport.pdf.

23. Barak H. Obama, *Presidential Policy* Directive—United *States Cyber Incident Coordination (PPD-41)* (July 26, 2016), https://obamawhitehouse.archives.gov/the-press-office/2016/07/26/presidential-policy-directive-united-states-cyber-incident.

24. Obama, *Presidential Policy Directive—United States Cyber Incident Coordination (PPD-41)*.

25. Obama, *Presidential Policy Directive—United States Cyber Incident Coordination (PPD-41)*.

26. Obama, *Presidential Policy Directive—United States Cyber Incident Coordination (PPD-41)*.

27. Jeh C. Johnson, *Statement by Secretary Jeh C. Johnson Regarding PPD-41, Cyber Incident Coordination* (Washington, DC: Department of Homeland Security, July 26, 2016), https://www.dhs.gov/news/2016/07/26/statement-secretary-jeh-c-johnson-regarding-ppd-41-cyber-incident-coordination.

28. Obama, *Presidential Policy Directive—United States Cyber Incident Coordination (PPD-41)*, C.

29. Obama, *Presidential Policy Directive—United States Cyber Incident Coordination (PPD-41)*, V A and B.

30. Obama, *Presidential Policy Directive—United States Cyber Incident Coordination (PPD-41)*, II B.

31. Obama, *Presidential Policy Directive—United States Cyber Incident Coordination (PPD-41)*, II C.

32. Sean D. Carberry, "Why PPD-41 Is Evolutionary, Not Revolutionary," *FCW. com* (October 24, 2016), https://fcw.com/articles/2016/10/24/ppd41-cyber-carberry.aspx, quoting Lucia Ziobro, section chief of Cyber Operational Engagement at the FBI.

33. Carberry, "Why PPD-41 Is Evolutionary, Not Revolutionary."

34. Kaigham J. Gabriel, "Testimony of Dr. Kaigham J. Gabriel, House Armed Service Committee, Subcommittee on Emerging Threats and Capabilities," (February 29, 2012), p. 8, http://www.darpa.mil/NewsEvents/Releases/2012/02/29a.aspx.

35. Gabriel, "Testimony of Dr. Kaigham J. Gabriel," p. 7.

36. Gabriel, "Testimony of Dr. Kaigham J. Gabriel," p. 6.

37. James N. Miller, "Statement of Dr. James N. Miller, Principal Deputy Under Secretary of Defense for Policy, U.S. Department of Defense, Hearing on National Defense Authorization Act for Fiscal Year 2012, Committee on Armed Services, U.S. House of Representatives," (March 16, 2011), p. 4, http://www.fas.org/irp/congress/2011_hr/cybercom.pdf.

38. Dan Auerbach and Lee Tien, "Dangerously Vague Cybersecurity Legislation Threatens Civil Liberties," *Electronic Frontier Foundation* (March 20, 2012), https://www.eff.org/deeplinks/2012/03/dangerously-vague-cybersecurity-legislation.

39. *Cyber Security Information Sharing Act*, Public Law 114-113 Section 202(6), https://www.federalregister.gov/documents/2016/06/15/2016-13742/cybersecurity-information-sharing-act-of-2015-final-guidance-documents-notice-of-availability.

40. *Cyber Security Information Sharing Act*, Section 102(7).

41. 18 U.S.C. Section 1030.

42. John Hagel III, John Seely Brown, and Lang Davison, *The Power of Pull: How Small Moves, Smartly Made, Can Set Big Things in Motion* (New York: Basic Books, 2010), p. 31.

43. Bruce Y. Lee, "Friday's events Showed How Cyber Attacks May Hurt and Kill People," *Forbes* (May 15, 2017), https://www.forbes.com/sites/brucelee/2017/05/15/fridays-events-showed-how-cyber-attack-may-hurt-and-kill-people/#520689545206.

44. William J. Lynn, III, "Remarks on Cyber at RSA Conference," (February 15, 2011), http://www.defense.gov/speeches/speech.aspx?speechid=1535.

45. The Russian Federation denies state complicity, although many suspect it acted through proxies.

46. Dennis C. Shea and Carolyn Bartholomew, Chairmen, *2016 Report to Congress of the U.S.-China Economic and Security Review Commission* (Washington, DC: U.S.–China Economic and Security Review Commission, November 2016), p. 13, https://www.uscc.gov/sites/default/files/annual_reports/Executive%20Summary%202016.pdf.

47. James P. Farwell and Rafal Rohozinski, "Stuxnet and the Future of Cyberwar," *Survival* 53, no. 1 (2011).

48. Only 60 percent of Stuxnet infections affected Iranian facilities (Farwell and Rohozinski, "Stuxnet and the Future of Cyberwar").

49. James P. Farwell and Rafal Rohozinski, "The New Reality of Cyber War," *Survival* 54, no. 4 (2012).

50. Farwell and Rohozinski, "The New Reality of Cyber War."

51. Bryan Krekel, Patton Adams, and George Bakos, *Occupying the Information High Ground: Chinese Capabilities for Computer Network Operations and Cyber Espionage. Prepared for the U.S.-China Economic and Security Review Commission* (Falls Church, VA: Northrop Grumman Corporation, March 7, 2012).

52. Krekel, Adams, and George Bakos, "Occupying the Information High Ground," p. 13.

53. Krekel, Adams, and George Bakos, "Occupying the Information High Ground," p. 26.

54. Krekel, Adams, and George Bakos, "Occupying the Information High Ground," p. 26.

55. Sydney J. Freedberg, Jr., "They're Here: Cyber Experts Warn Senate That Adversary Is Already Inside U.S. Networks," *Breaking Defense* (March 21, 2012), http://breakingdefense.com/2012/03/they-re-here-cyber-experts-warn-senate-that-adversary-is-alread/.

56. William J. Lynn, III, "Defending a New Domain," *Foreign Affairs* 89, no. 5 (October 2010), https://www.foreignaffairs.com/articles/66552/william-j-lynn-iii/defending-a-new-domain; Sharon Weinberger, "Pentagon Official Says Flash Drive Used in Classified Attack," *AOL News* (August 25, 2010), http://www.aolnews.com/2010/08/25/pentagon-official-says-flash-drive-used-in-classified-cyberattac/; and Kim Zetter, "The Return of the Worm That Ate the Pentagon," *Wired* (December 9, 2011), http://www.wired.com/dangerroom/tag/operation-buckshot-yankee/.

57. Ellen Nakashima, "Cyber-Intruder Sparks Response, Debate," *Washington Post* (December 8, 2011), https://www.washingtonpost.com/national/national-security/cyber-intruder-sparks-response-debate/2011/12/06/gIQAxLuFgO_story.html; and Zetter, "The Return of the Worm."

58. David Alexander, "Pentagon Tries to Lean Forward in Cyberdefense," *Aviation Week* (July 14, 2011).

59. John Pike, "Solar Sunrise," *GlobalSecurity.org* (undated), http://www.globalsecurity.org/military/ops/solar-sunrise.htm.

60. William J. Lynn, III, "Defending a New Domain," p. 1.

61. Ellen Nakashima, "Defense Official Discloses Cyberattack," *Washington Post* (August 24, 2010), http://www.washingtonpost.com/wp-dyn/content/article/2010/08/24/AR2010082406495.html.

62. Rob Rosenberger, "Gov't Hype Surrounds 'Operation Buckshot Yankee,'" *Vmyths.com* (August 26, 2010), http://vmyths.com/2010/08/26/oby/.

63. Smith received a five-year prison sentence and a $5,000 fine. "Melissa Virus Creator Jailed," *BBC News* (May 2, 2002), http://news.bbc.co.uk/2/hi/americas/1963371.stm.

64. "Melissa Virus Creator Jailed."

65. Ponemon Institute, *Fourth Annual Study: Is Your Company Ready for a Big Data Breach?* (Traverse City, MI: Ponemon Institute, September 2016), http://www.experian.com/assets/data-breach/white-papers/2016-experian-data-breach-preparedness-study.pdf.

66. Thu Pham, "After a Data Breach: Who's Liable?" *Duo com* (September 17, 2014), https://duo com/blog/after-a-data- breach-whos-liable; and Brian Krebs, "The Target Breach, by the Numbers," *Krebs on Security* (May 14, 2014), http://krebsonsecurity com/2014/05/the-target-breach-by-the-numbers/. For further discussion, see James P. Farwell, Virginia N. Roddy, Yvonne Chalker, and Gary Elkins, *The Architecture of Cybersecurity* (Lafayette: Sans Souci/University of Louisiana Lafayette Press, 2017).

67. Siobhan Gorman, "Electricity Grid in U.S. Penetrated by Spies," *Wall Street Journal* (April 8, 2009), http://online.wsj.com/article/SB123914805204099085.html. The intrusions were detected by U.S. intelligence agencies, who said water, sewage, and other infrastructure systems were also at risk.

68. Gorman, "Electricity Grid in U.S. Penetrated by Spies."

69. Eric Warner, "Global Cyber Supply Chain Management," *Microsoft Security Blog* (July 26, 2011), http://blogs.technet.com/b/security/archive/2011/07/26/global-cyber-supply-chain-management.aspx.

70. James Peery, "Testimony of Dr. James Peery, Director of the Information Systems and Analysis Center, Sandia National Laboratories, Senate Armed Services Committee, Subcommittee on Emerging Threats and Capabilities," (March 20, 2012), p. 7.

71. Permanent Select Committee on Intelligence, *Cyber Intelligence Sharing and Protection Act. Report together with Minority Views [To Accompany H.R. 3523]* (Washington, DC: United States House of Representatives, April 17, 2012), p. 5, http://intelligence.house.gov/sites/intelligence.house.gov/files/documents/HR3523CommitteeReport.pdf.

72. *Cybersecurity Information Sharing Act of 2015*, Public Law 114-113.

73. See *Sherman Antitrust Act*, 15 U.S.C.A. 1-7, as amended by the Clayton Anti-Trust Act of 1914, 15 U.S.C. 12 et seq, notably Section 1(a); the Federal Trade Commission (FTC) Act of 1914, 15 U.S.C.A. 45 et seq, notably Section 5 that applies

to unfair methods of competition. The Sherman act prohibits business activities that reduce competition in the marketplace and requires the federal government to investigate and pursue trust, companies, and organizations it suspects may violate the Act. It makes illegal contracts, combinations in the form of trust or otherwise, or conspiracy, in restraint of trade or commerce. The FTC Act authorizes the commission to enforce the antitrust laws.

74. 18 U.S.C. 2510, et seq, and 18 USC 2701-12. This legislation deals with protecting the privacy of stored electronic communications. The Uniting and Strengthening America by Promoting Appropriate Tools Required to Intercept and Obstruct Terrorism Act of 2001—the USA PATRIOT Act, 18 USCA 1 (Pub. L. 107-56, 107th Congress) et seq, arguably weakened some provisions of the ECPA.

75. Testimony of Dave Mahon, p. 2.

76. Paul Rosenzweig, *Senate Cybersecurity Bill: Not Ready for PrimeTime* (Washington, DC: Heritage Foundation, March 7, 2012), http://www.heritage.org/research/reports/2012/03/senate-cybersecurity-bill-not-ready-for-prime-time. Though critical of the proposed legislative, in his excellent assessment of Senator Joe Lieberman's bill, Rosenzweig agrees that provisions that enhance information sharing with other private-sector actors without fear of being are a "solid improvement over current law." This author concurs with that view.

77. Jim Finkle and Andrea Shalal-Esa, "Exclusive: Hackers Breached U.S. Defense Contractors," *Reuters* (May 27, 2011), http://www.reuters.com/article/2011/05/27/us-usa-defense-hackers-idUSTRE74Q6VY20110527; and Christopher Drew and John Markoff, "Lockheed Strengthens Network Security after Hacker Attack," *New York Times* (May 29, 2011), http://www.nytimes.com/2011/05/30/business/30hack.html.

78. Drew and Markoff, "Lockheed Strengthens Network Security after Hacker Attack."

79. Art Coviello, "Art Coviello, Executive Chairman, RSA, 'Open Letter to RSA Customers,'" Network Computing Architects, Inc. (June 6, 2011), http://www.ncanet.com/resources/press-releases/91-2011-06-08-art-coviello-rsa-open-letter-customers.html.

80. Jaikumar Vijayan, "Caution Urged in Wake of RSA Security Breach," *Computerworld* (March 19, 2011), http://www.computerworld.com/s/article/9214800/Caution_urged_in_wake_of_RSA_security_breach.html.

81. Andrew Kemshall, "The RSA Security Breach—12 Months Down the Technology Turnpike," *Huffington Post* (March 14, 2012), http://www.huffingtonpost.co.uk/andrew-kemshall/the-rsa-security-breach-1_b_1344643.html.

82. Paul T. Dacier, *EMC Corporation. Form 8-K. Current Report Pursuant to Section 13 or 15 (d) of the Security and Exchange Act of 1934* (Washington, DC: Security and Exchange Commission, March 17, 2011), http://www.sec.gov/Archives/edgar/data/790070/000119312511070159/d8k.htm.

83. Telephone interview with Melissa Hathaway (August 3, 2012).

84. *Federal Guidance on the Cybersecurity Information Sharing Act of 2015* (Washington, DC: Department of Homeland Security and Department of Justice, June 25, 2016), https://www.us-cert.gov/sites/default/files/ais_files/Non-Federal_Entity_Sharing_Guidance_%28Sec%20105%28a%29%29.pdf. See also Brad

S. Karp, "Federal Guidance on the Cybersecurity Information Sharing Act of 2015," *Harvard Law School Forum on Corporate Governance and Financial Regulation* (March 3, 2016), https://corpgov.law.harvard.edu/2016/03/03/federal-guidance-on-the-cybersecurity-information-sharing-act-of-2015/#1.

85. Freedom of Information Act Section 105(d)(3).

86. Electronic Communications Privacy Act of 1986 (ECPA), 18 U.S.C. 2510 et seq. ECPA restricts government wire taps of telephone calls to include transmissions of electronic data by computer, prohibits access to stored electronic communications, and, through pen trap provisions, authorizes the government to trace telephone communications. It protects Internet users' privacy and Internet security by other authorizing companies to monitor their users' activities as necessary to protect their own systems from threats. See Robyn Greene, *Cybersecurity Information Sharing Act of 2015 Is CyberSurveillance, Not Cybersecurity* (Washington, DC: Open Technology Institute–New America, April 9, 2015), https://static. newamerica.org/attachments/2741-cybersecurity-information-sharing-act-of-2015-is-cyber-surveillance-not-cybersecurity/CISA_Cyber-Surveillance.488b3a9d2da64 a27a9f6f53b38beb575.pdf.

87. Public Law No. 114-113, Section 104(a)(1)(A–C), b(1)(A–C).

88. Public Law No. 114-113, Section 104(c)(1).

89. Public Law No. 114-113, Section 104(e)(1), (2).

90. Public Law No. 114-113, Section 105(d)(1).

91. Public Law No. 114-113, Section 105(d)(2).

92. Public Law No. 114-113, Section 106(c)(1)(A), (B).

93. The process included DHS's Automated Indicator Sharing (AIS) initiative. See *Federal Guidance on the Cybersecurity Information Sharing Act of 2015*, p. 13. That includes using a DHS prescribed form, e-mail to DHS's National Cybersecurity and Communications Integration Center, and other prescribed means (*Federal Guidance on the Cybersecurity Information Sharing Act of 2015*, pp. 13–15).

94. "For example, a cyber threat indicator could be centered on a spear phishing email. For a phishing email, personal information about the sender of email ('From'/'Sender' address), a malicious URL in the e-mail, malware files attached to the e-mail, the content of the e-mail, and additional email information related to the malicious email or potential cybersecurity threat actor, such as Subject Line, Message ID, and X-Mailer, could be considered directly related to a cybersecurity threat. The name and e-mail address of the targets of the email (i.e., the 'To' address), however, would be personal information not directly related to a cybersecurity threat and therefore should not typically be included as part of the cyber threat indicator." *Federal Guidance on the Cybersecurity Information Sharing Act of 2015*, p. 5.

95. *Federal Guidance on the Cybersecurity Information Sharing Act of 2015*, p. 6.

96. *Federal Guidance on the Cybersecurity Information Sharing Act of 2015*, pp. 9–10.

97. *Federal Guidance on the Cybersecurity Information Sharing Act of 2015*, pp. 6–7.

98. See Jose Pagliery, "Apple and Other Tech Giants Slam Anti-Hacking Bill for Being Too Creepy," *CNN* (October 26, 2015), http://money.cnn.com/2015/10/26/technology/cisa-cybersecurity-bill-senate/.

99. Mike Godwin "The Many, Many, Many Flaws of CISA," *Slate* (October 26, 2015), http://www.slate.com/articles/technology/future_tense/2015/10/stopcisa_the_cybersecurity_information_sharing_act_is_a_disaster.html.

100. Greene, "Cybersecurity Information Sharing Act of 2015."

101. Devlin Barrett, "U.S. Outgunned in Hacker War," *Wall Street Journal* (March 28, 2012); Greene, "Cybersecurity Information Sharing Act of 2015."

102. Barrett, "U.S. Outgunned in Hacker War," p. 4.

103. Gabriel, "Testimony of Dr. Kaigham J. Gabriel," p. 9.

104. Federal Communications Commission, "Communications Security, Reliability and Interoperability Council III," (no date), http://www.fcc.gov/encyclopedia/communications-security-reliability-and-interoperability-council-iii.

105. "Domestic Security Alliance Council: FBI—Private Industry—DHS—Networking for Security," (no date), http://www.dsac.gov/Pages/index.aspx.

106. John Markoff, "Defying Experts, Rogue Computer Code Still Lurks," *New York Times* (August 26, 2009), http://www.nytimes.com/2009/08/27/technology/27compute.html?_r=1. It could be used to generate spam, steal passwords and logins, deliver fake antivirus warnings, and trick people into paying by credit card to have the infection removed. Id. See also Mark Bowden, *Worm* (Washington, DC: Atlantic Monthly Press, 2011), which takes an in-depth look at the incident.

107. Roger Hurwitz, Camino Kavanagh, Timer Maurer, and Michael Sechrist, rapporteurs, "A Preliminary Report on the Cyber Norms Workshop," sponsored by the Center for Global Security Affairs, University of Toronto, p. 9, http://www.citizenlab.org/cybernorms/preliminary_report.pdf. This discussion of the Conficker challenge and how it was addressed is taken from their report.

108. Bowden, *Worm*, p. 231.

109. Federal Bureau of Investigation, "DNSChanger Malware," (no date), https://www.fbi.gov/file-repository/dns-changer-malware.pdf/view.

110. Melanie Hick, "DNS Changer Virus Spells 'Internet Doomsday'," *Huffington Post UK* (April 25, 2012), http://www.huffingtonpost.co.uk/2012/04/25/dns-changer-virus-internet-doomsday_n_1451606.html.

111. Hagel, Brown, and Davison, *The Power of Pull*, p. 134.

112. William J. Lynn, "Remarks on Cyber at the Council on Foreign Relations. As Delivered by Deputy Secretary of Defense William J. Lynn, III, Council on Foreign Relations, New York City, Thursday, September 30, 2010," http://archive.defense.gov/speeches/speech.aspx?speechid=1509.

113. Lynn, "Remarks on Cyber at the Council on Foreign Relations."

114. Lynn, "Remarks on Cyber at the Council on Foreign Relations." Lynn also noted that collective defense with allies is a fourth strategy.

115. 18 U.S.C. 1030.

116. Richard Weitz, "Global Insights: The DHS' Cybersecurity Logjam," *World Politics Review* (April 10, 2012).

117. Eric Chabrow, "Damn the Economy! IT Employment Rises to New Heights," *CIO Insight* (July 1, 2008), http://www.cioinsight.com/c/a/Trends/Damn-the-Economy-IT-Employment-Rises-to-New-Heights/.

118. Peery, "Testimony of Dr. James Peery," p. 8. Dr. Peery has asked Congress to support a Scholarship for Service program that would strengthen the government's ability to recruit and retain top students.

119. Telephone Interview with Melissa Hathaway (August 3, 2012).

120. Committee Report on H.R. 3523, Permanent Select Committee on Intelligence, *Report 112-445: Cyber Intelligence Sharing and Protection Act*, 112th Congress, 2d Session, (Washington, DC: United States House of Representatives, April 17, 2012), pp. 8–9, https://www.gpo.gov/fdsys/pkg/CRPT-112hrpt445/html/CRPT-112hrpt445.htm.

121. Barrett, "U.S. Outgunned in Hacker War."

Bibliography

Abbott, Kenneth W, and Duncan Snidal. "Hard and Soft Law in International Governance." *International Organization* 54, no. 3 (Summer 2000). http://dx.doi.org/10.1162/002081800551280.

Abbott, Kenneth W., Robert O. Keohane, Andrew Moravcsik, Anne-Marie Slaughter, and Duncan Snidal. "The Concept of Legalization." *International Organization* 54, no. 3 (Summer 2000). http://www.jstor.org/stable/2601339.

Ackerman, Spencer. "Does Obama's 'Net Freedom Agenda' Hurt the U.S.?" *Wired*, January 28, 2011. http://www.wired.com/dangerroom/2011/01/does-obamas-internet-freedom-agenda-hurt-the-u-s-without-helping-dissidents/.

Adler, Emanuel. "Seizing the Middle Ground: Constructivism in World Politics." *European Journal of International Relations* 3, no. 3 (September 1997).

Air Force Doctrine Document (AFDD) 3-12, *Cyberspace Operations*. Maxwell AFB: Curtis E. LeMay Center for Doctrine Development and Education, 2010.

Aldrich, Richard J. *GCHQ: The Uncensored Story of Britain's Most Secret Intelligence Agency*. London: HarperCollins, 2010.

Alexander, David. "Pentagon Tries to Lean Forward in Cyberdefense." *Aviation Week*, July 14, 2011.

Alexander, Keith. "U.S. Cybersecurity Policy and the Role of U.S. Cybercom," address to the Center for Strategic and International Studies, Washington, DC (June 3, 2010).

Alexander, Keith B. "Statement before the Senate Committee on Armed Services, 27 March 2012." Washington, DC: United States Congress, 2012. http://www.armed-services.senate.gov/statemnt/2012/20March/Alexander-27-12.pdf.

Allen, Patrick D., and Chris C. Demchak. "The Palestinian-Israel: Cyberwar." *Military Review* 83, no. 2 (March–April 2003).

Allison, Graham T. *Destined for War: Can America and China Escape Thucydides's Trap?* Boston, MA: Houghton Mifflin Harcourt, 2017.

Alperovitch, Dmitri. *Revealed: Operation Shady RAT. McAfee White Paper.* Santa Clara, CA: McAfee, 2011. http://www.mcafee.com/us/resources/white-papers/wp-operation-shady-rat.pdf.

Anand, Achuthan. *Information Technology: The Future Warfare Weapon.* New Delhi: Ocean Books, 2000.

Anderson, Ross, Rainer Böhme, Richard Clayton, and Tyler Moore. "Security Economics and European Policy." In *Managing Information Risk and the Economics of Security*, edited by Eric Johnson. New York: Springer, 2009. http://weis2008.econinfosec.org/papers/MooreSecurity.pdf.

"Apple iPhone 4S (GSM China/WAPI) 8, 16, 32, 64 GB Specs." *EveryiPhone.com*, July 3, 2017. http://www.everymac.com/systems/apple/iphone/specs/apple-iphone-4s-gsm-china-unicom-a1431-specs.html.

Arquilla, John, and David Ronfeldt. *In Athena's Camp: Preparing for Conflict in the Information Age.* Santa Monica, CA: RAND, 1997.

Auerbach, Dan, and Lee Tien. "Dangerously Vague Cybersecurity Legislation Threatens Civil Liberties." *Electronic Frontier Foundation.* March 20, 2012. https://www.eff.org/deeplinks/2012/03/dangerously-vague-cybersecurity-legislation.

Bamford, James. *The Shadow Factor: The Ultra-Secret NSA from 9/11 to the Eavesdropping on America.* New York: Doubleday, 2009.

Barlow, John Perry. "A Declaration of Independence of Cyberspace" (February 8, 1996).

Barrett, Barrington M. Jr. "Information Warfare: China's Response to U.S. Technological Advantages." *International Journal of Intelligence and Counterintelligence* 18, no. 4 (Winter 2005).

Barrett, Devlin. "U.S. Outgunned in Hacker War." *Wall Street Journal*, March 28, 2012.

Barth, Richard C., and Clint N. Smith. "International Regulation of Encryption: Technology Will Drive Policy." In *Borders in Cyberspace: Information Policy and the Global Information Infrastructure*, edited by Brian Kahin and Charles Nesson, 283–99. Cambridge, MA: MIT Press, 1998.

"Behind the Estonia Cyberattacks." *Radio Free Europe/Radio Liberty* (March 6, 2009). http://www.rferl.org/content/Behind_The_Estonia_Cyberattacks/1505613.html.

Beidleman, Scott W. *GPS versus Galileo: Balancing for Position in Space.* Maxwell AFB: Air University Press, 2006.

Benson, Pam. "Computer Virus Stuxnet a 'Game Changer', DHS Official Tells Senate." *CNN*, November 17, 2010. http://edition.cnn.com/2010/TECH/web/11/17/stuxnet.virus/index.html.

Bertrand, Natasha. "China Caught the US 'With Our Pants Down'—and the Obama Administration is Struggling to Respond." *Business Insider*, August 4, 2015. http://www.businessinsider.com/us-retaliation-against-china-for-opm-hacks-2015-8.

Bhattacharyya, Suman. "Cyberattacks against the US Government Up 1,300% Since 2006." *The Fiscal Times*, June 22, 2016. http://www.thefiscaltimes.com/2016/06/22/Cyberattacks-Against-US-Government-1300-2006.

Black's Law Dictionary, 5th ed. (St. Paul, MN: West Group, 1979).

Bodenheimer, David, and Kate M. Growley. "Cybersecurity Receives Presidential Push with New Cyber Executive Order." *Crowell & Moring*, February 15, 2013. https://www.crowelldatalaw.com/2013/02/cybersecurity-receives-presidential-push-with-new-cyber-executive-order/.

Bohman, James, and William Rehg, eds. *Deliberative Democracy: Essays on Reason and Politics.* Cambridge, MA: MIT Press, 1997.

Bolton, Matthew, and Thomas Nash. "The Role of Middle Power-NGO Coalitions in Global Policy: The Case of the Cluster Munitions Ban." *Global Policy* 1, no. 2 (May 2010).

Bordo, Michael, Alan Taylor, and Jeffrey Williamson, eds. *Globalization in Historical Perspective.* Chicago, IL: University of Chicago Press, 2003.

Borger, Julian. "Pentagon Kept the Lid on Cyberwar in Kosovo." *The Guardian*, November 9, 1999.

Bowden, Mark. *Worm.* Washington, DC: Atlantic Monthly Press, 2011.

Bower, Adam. "Norms without the Great Powers: International Law, Nested Social Structures, and the Ban on Antipersonnel Mines." *International Studies Review* 17, no. 3 (September 2015). http://dx.doi.org/10.1111/misr.12225.

Boyne, Walter. *The Influence of Air Power upon History.* Gretna, LA: Pelican, 2003.

Braden, Bob, David Clark, Jon Crowcroft, Bruce Davie, Steve Deering, Deborah Estrin, Sally Floyd, et al. "Recommendations on Queue Management and Congestion Avoidance in the Internet." *No. RFC 2309, Network Working Group, the Internet Society.* April 1998.

Bradshaw, Samantha, Laura DeNardis, Fen Osler Hampson, Eric Jardine, and Mark Raymond. "The Emergence of Contention in Global Internet Governance." *Global Commission on Internet Governance Paper Series*, no. 17. Waterloo, ON: Centre for International Governance Innovation, 2015. https://www.cigionline.org/publications/emergence-of-contention-global-internet-governance.

Branigan, Tania. "Chinese Army to Target Cyber War Threat." *The Guardian*, July 22, 2010. https://www.theguardian.com/world/2010/jul/22/chinese-army-cyber-war-department.

Brenner, Joel. *America the Vulnerable.* New York: Penguin Press, 2011.

Brenner, Joel F. "Why Isn't Cyberspace More Secure?" *Communications of the ACM* 53, no. 11 (November 2010).

Brenner, Susan W. "'At Light Speed': Attribution and Response to Cybercrime/Terrorism/Warfare." *Journal of Criminal Law & Criminology* 97, no. 2 (2007).

Brenner, Susan W. "Distributed Security: Moving Away from Reactive Law Enforcement." *International Journal of Communications Law & Policy* 9 (December 2004).

Brodkin, Jon. "Tech Giants, Chastened by Heartbleed, Finally Agree to Fund OpenSSL." *ArsTechnica* (April 24, 2014). http://arstechnica.com/information-technology/2014/04/tech-giants-chastened-by-heartbleed-finally-agree-to-fund-openssl/.

Broeders, Dennis. *The Public Core of the Internet: An International Agenda for Internet Governance.* Amsterdam: Amsterdam University Press, 2015. http://www.wrr.nl/fileadmin/en/publicaties/PDF-Rapporten/The_public_core_of_the_internet_Web.pdf.

Brousseau, Eric, Meryem Marzouki, and Cécile Méadel. *Governance, Regulation, and Powers on the Internet.* Cambridge: Cambridge University Press, 2012.

Bus, Jacques. "Societal Dependencies and Trust." In *The Quest for Cyber Peace*, edited by Hamadoun I. Touré and the Permanent Monitoring Panel on Information Security of the World Federation of Scientists. Geneva: International Telecommunications Union, 2011.

Busby, Joshua W. *Moral Movements and Foreign Policy.* Cambridge: Cambridge University Press, 2010.

Bush, George W. *Homeland Security Presidential Directive 7: Critical Infrastructure Identification, Prioritization, and Protection.* December 17, 2003.

Bygrave, Lee A., and John Bing, eds. *Internet Governance: Infrastructure and Institutions.* Oxford, England: Oxford University Press, 2009.

Carberry, Sean D. "Why PPD-41 is Evolutionary, Not Revolutionary." *FCW.com.* October 24, 2016. https://fcw.com/articles/2016/10/24/ppd41-cyber-carberry.aspx.

Carpenter, R. Charli. "Vetting the Advocacy Agenda: Network Centrality and the Paradox of Weapons Norms." *International Organization* 65, no. 1 (January 2011). http://dx.doi.org/10.1017/S0020818310000329.

Carr, Jeffrey. *Inside Cyber Warfare.* Sebastopol, CA: O'Reilly Media, 2012.

Carr, Madeline. "Power Plays in Global Internet Governance." *Millennium: Journal of International Studies* 43, no. 2 (January 2015).

"'Cavalier' GCHQ Online Spy Centre Loses 35 Laptops—Centre Also Struggling To Keep Up With National Cyber Threats." *Computerworld UK.* March 12, 2010. http://archive.is/20120729004038/www.computerworlduk.com/news/it-business/19344/cavalier-gchq-online-spy-centre-loses-35-laptops/.

Cavelty, Myriam Dunn. *Cyber-Security and Threat Politics: US Efforts to Secure the Information Age.* New York: Routledge, 2008.

Cha, Victor D. *Alignment despite Antagonism: The United States-Korea-Japan Security Triangle.* Stanford, CA: Stanford University Press, 1999.

Chabrow, Eric. "Damn the Economy! IT Employment Rises to New Heights." *CIO Insight*, July 1, 2008. http://www.cioinsight.com/c/a/Trends/Damn-the-Economy-IT-Employment-Rises-to-New-Heights/.

Chairman of the Joint Chiefs of Staff. *The National Military Strategy of the United States of America: A Strategy for Today; A Vision for Tomorrow.* Washington, DC: Department of Defense, 2005, 5. http://www.defense.gov/news/mar2005/d20050318nms.pdf.

Charney, Scott. "Rethinking the Cyber Threat: A Framework and Path Forward." *Microsoft White Paper.* Redmond, WA: Microsoft Corp., 2009, 9.

"Chart of Signatures and Ratifications of Treaty 185: Convention on Cybercrime." http://www.coe.int/en/web/conventions/full-list/-conventions/treaty/185/signatures?p_auth=b333kCNV.

Cheong, Ching. "Fighting the Digital War with the Great Firewall." *Straits Times.* April 5, 2010.

Chertoff, Michael. *National Infrastructure Protection Plan: Partnering to Enhance Protection and Resiliency.* Washington, DC: United States Department of Homeland Security, 2009, 4. http://www.dhs.gov/xlibrary/assets/NIPP_Plan.pdf.

Christensen, Thomas J. "Chinese Realpolitik: Reading Beijing's World View." *Foreign Affairs* 75, no. 5 (September/October 1996).

Chung-Min, Lee. "China's Rise, Asia's Dilemma." *The National Interest* 81 (Fall 2005).

Clark, David D., and Susan Landau. "Untangling Attribution." *National Security Journal* 2 (March 16, 2011). http://harvardnsj.org/2011/03/untangling-attribution-2/.

"China Information Technology Security Certification Center Source Code Review Lab Opened." *Microsoft News Center*, September 26, 2003. http://www.microsoft.com/presspass/press/2003/sep03/09-26gspchpr.mspx.

"China Keeping Closer Eye On Phone Text Messages." *New York Times*, December 6, 2005.

"China Mobile Gets Nokia's 5G-Ready Airscale Base Station; Reveals Pre-5G/5G Landmarks With ZTE, Huawei." *Cellular News*, June 14, 2017. https://www.telegeography.com/products/commsupdate/articles/2017/06/14/china-mobile-gets-nokias-5g-ready-airscale-base-station-reveals-pre-5g5g-landmarks-with-zte-huawei/.

"China Stonewalls Panetta on Cyber Attacks." *CBS News*, September 20, 2012. http://www.cbsnews.com/8301-202_162-57516541/china-stonewalls-panetta-on-cyberattacks/.

Clinton, Hillary. "Remarks on Internet Freedom." January 21, 2010. https://www.ft.com/content/f0c3bf8c-06bd-11df-b426-00144feabdc0?mhq5j=e3.

Coker, Christopher. *The Improbable War: China, the United States and the Continuing Logic of Great Power Conflict*. Oxford: Oxford University Press, 2015.

Commission on Cyber Security for the 44th Presidency. *Securing Cyberspace for the 44th Presidency*. Washington, DC: Center for Strategic and International Studies, 2008.

Committee on Oversight and Government Reform. *The OPM Data Breach: How the Government Jeopardized Our National Security for More than a Generation.* Washington, DC: United States House of Representatives, September 7, 2016.

Committee Report on H.R. 3523, Permanent Select Committee on Intelligence, *Report 112-445: Cyber Intelligence Sharing and Protection Act*, 112th Congress, 2nd Session. Washington, DC: United States House of Representatives, April 17, 2012. https://www.gpo.gov/fdsys/pkg/CRPT-112hrpt445/html/CRPT-112hrpt445.htm.

Comor, Edward. "Communication Technology and International Capitalism: The Case of DBS and US Foreign Policy." In *The Global Political Economy of Communication: Hegemony, Telecommunication and the Information Economy*, edited by Edward A. Comor, 83–102. New York: St Martin's Press, 1994.

Constantin, Lucian. "Attack Hits Swedish Signals Intelligence Agency's Website." *Softpedia News*. November 6, 2009.

"Convention on International Information Security," presented to the Second International Meeting of High-Level Officials Responsible for Security Matters, Ekaterinburg, Russia. September 22, 2011. http://2012.infoforum.ru/2012/files/konvencia-mib-en.doc.

Convention Relating to the Regulation of Aerial Navigation (1919).

Corbett, Julian S. *Some Principals of Maritime Strategy*. Annapolis, MD: Naval Institute Press, 1911/1988.

Cornish, Paul, Rex Hughes, and David Livingstone. *Cyberspace and the National Security of the United Kingdom*. London: Chatham House, 2009.

Corrin, Amber. "Dominance in Cyberspace Might not be Possible." *Defense Systems.* January 27, 2011. http://defensesystems.com/articles/2011/01/27/afcea-west-cyber-warfare-panel.aspx.

Council of Europe. Budapest Convention on Cybercrime (2004). http://www.europarl.europa.eu/meetdocs/2014_2019/documents/libe/dv/7_conv_budapest_/7_conv_budapest_en.pdf.

Coviello, Art. "Art Coviello, Executive Chairman, RSA, 'Open Letter to RSA Customers'." *Network Computing Architects*, Inc. June 6, 2011. http://www.ncanet.com/resources/press-releases/91-2011-06-08-art-coviello-rsa-open-letter-customers.html.

Crépeau, Claude, and Alain Slakmon. "Simple Backdoors for RSA Key Generation." In *CT-RSA'03: Proceedings of the 2003 RSA Conference on the Cryptographers' Track*. Berlin: Springer-Verlag, 2003.

Cyber Security Information Sharing Act, Public Law 114-113 Section 202(6). https://www.federalregister.gov/documents/2016/06/15/2016-13742/cybersecurity-information-sharing-act-of-2015-final-guidance-documents-notice-of-availability.

"Cyberwar Also Rages in Mideast." *Associated Press*. October 26, 2000. http://www.wired.com/politics/law/news/2000/10/39766.

Dacier, Paul T. *EMC Corporation. Form 8-K. Current Report Pursuant to Section 13 or 15 (d) of the Security and Exchange Act of 1934*. Washington, DC: Security and Exchange Commission, March 17, 2011. http://www.sec.gov/Archives/edgar/data/790070/000119312511070159/d8k.htm.

de Chardin, Pierre Teilhard. *The Phenomenon of Man*. New York: Harper Perennial, 1955/2002.

Deibert, Ronald. *Black Code: Inside the Battle for Cyberspace*. Toronto: Signal Press, 2013.

Deibert, Ronald, and Rafal Rohozinski, "Contesting Cyberspace and the Coming Crisis of Authority." In *Access Contested: Security, Identity, and Resistance in Asian Cyberspace*, edited by Ronald Deibert, John Palfrey, Rafal Rohozinski, and Jonathan Zittrain, 21–42. Cambridge, MA: MIT Press, 2011.

Deibert, Ronald, and Rafal Rohozinski. "Risking Security: Policies and Paradoxes of Cyberspace Security." *International Political Sociology* 4, no. 1 (March 2010).

Deibert, Ronald, John Palfrey, Rafal Rohozinski, and Jonathan Zittrain, eds. *Access Contested: Security, Identity, and Resistance in Asian Cyberspace*. Cambridge, MA: MIT Press, 2011.

Deibert, Ronald, John Palfrey, Rafal Rohozinski, and Jonathan Zittrain, eds. *Access Controlled: The Shaping of Power, Rights, and Rule in Cyberspace*. Cambridge, MA: MIT Press, 2010.

Deibert, Ronald, John Palfrey, Rafal Rohozinski, and Jonathan Zittrain, eds. *Access Denied: The Practice and Policy of Global Internet Filtering*. Cambridge, MA: MIT Press, 2008.

Delio, Michelle. "A Chinese Call to Hack U.S." *Wired*, April 11, 2001. http://www.wired.com/news/politics/0,1283,42982,00.html.

Demchak, Chris, and Peter Dombrowski. "Cyber Westphalia: Asserting State Prerogatives in Cyberspace." *Georgetown Journal of International Affairs* (2014).

Demchak, Chris, and Peter Dombrowski. "Rise of a Cybered Westphalian Age." *Strategic Studies Quarterly* 5, no. 1 (Spring 2011).

Demchak, Chris C. "Key Trends across a Maturing Cyberspace Affecting US and China Future Influences in a Rising deeply Cybered, Conflictual, and Post-Western

World." Testimony before Hearing on China's Information Controls, Global Media Influence, and Cyber Warfare Strategy, U.S.–China Economic and Security Review Commission, Washington (May 4, 2017). https://www.uscc.gov/sites/default/files/ Chris%20Demchak%20May%204th%202017%20USCC%20testimony.pdf.

Demchak, Chris C. "Testimony, Panel on 'China's Information Controls, Global Media Influence, and Cyber Warfare Strategy.'" *U.S.–China Economic and Security Review Committee Hearing*, Washington, DC, May 4, 2017.

Demchak, Chris C. "Uncivil and Post-Western Cyber Westphalia: Changing Interstate Power Relations of the Cybered Age." *Cyber Defense Review* 1, no. 1 (Spring 2016).

Demchak, Chris C. *Wars of Disruption and Resilience: Cybered Conflict, Power, and National Security*. Athens, GA: University of Georgia Press, 2011.

Demchak, Chris C., and Peter Dombrowski. "Rise of a Cybered Westphalian Age." *Strategic Studies Quarterly* 5, no. 1 (Spring 2011). http://www.au.af.mil/au/ssq/ 2011/spring/demchak-dombrowski.pdf.

Dementis, Georgios, John F. Sarkesain, Thimas C. Wingfield, Goncalo Nuno Baptista Sousa, and James Brett Michael, "Integrating Legal and Policy Factors in Cyberpreparedness." *Computer* 43, no. 4 (2010).

DeNardis, Laura. *Protocol Politics: The Globalization of Internet Governance*. Cambridge, MA: MIT Press 2009.

DeNardis, Laura. *The Global War for Internet Governance*. New Haven, CT: Yale University Press, 2014.

DeNardis, Laura, and Francesca Musiani. "Governance by Infrastructure." In *The Turn to Infrastructure in Internet Governance*, edited by Francesca Musiani, Derrick L. Cogburn, Laura DeNardis, and Nanette S. Levinson, 3–21. New York: Palgrave Macmillan, 2016.

Denmark, Abraham, and James Mulvenon, eds. *Contested Commons: The Future of American Power in a Multipolar World*. Washington, DC: Center for a New American Security, 2010.

Department of Defense Strategy for Operating in Cyberspace. Washington, DC: Department of Defense, July 2011.

Department of Homeland Security. *NIPP 2013: Partnering for Critical Infrastructure Security and Resilience*. Washington, DC: Department of Homeland Security, 2013. https://www.dhs.gov/sites/default/files/publications/NIPP%202013_ Partnering%20for%20Critical%20Infrastructure%20Security%20and%20 Resilience_508_0.pdf.

Di Justo, Patrick. "How Al-Qaida Site Was Hijacked." *Wired*, August 10, 2002. http:// www.wired.com/culture/lifestyle/news/2002/08/54455.

Docherty, Bonnie. "Breaking New Ground: The Convention on Cluster Munitions and the Evolution of International Humanitarian Law." *Human Rights Quarterly* 31, no. 4 (August 2009). http://muse.jhu.edu/article/363660.

Dolman, Everett C. "New Frontiers, Old Realities." *Strategic Studies Quarterly* 6, no. 1 (Spring 2012).

Dolman, Everett C. *Pure Strategy: Power and Principle in the Space and Information Age*. London: Frank Cass, 2005.

Dombrowski, Peter, and Chris Demchak, "Cyber War, Cybered-Conflict and the Maritime Domain." *Naval War College Review* 67 (Spring 2014).

"Domestic Security Alliance Council: FBI—Private Industry—DHS—Networking for Security." (no date). http://www.dsac.gov/Pages/index.aspx.

Douglass, Duncan B. "An Examination of the Fraud Liability Shift in Consumer Card-Based Payment Systems." *Economic Perspectives* 33, no. 1 (1st quarter, 2009).

Douhet, Giulio. *Command of the Air*. Washington, DC: Office of Air Force History, US Government Printing Office, 1983.

Drew, Christopher, and John Markoff. "Lockheed Strengthens Network Security after Hacker Attack." *New York Times*, May 29, 2011. http://www.nytimes.com/2011/05/30/business/30hack.html.

Druzin, Bryan. "Why Does Soft Law Have Any Power Anyway?" *Asian Journal of International Law* 7, no. 2 (July 2017).

Dunlap, Charles J., Jr. "Perspectives for Cyber Strategists on Law for Cyberwar." *Strategic Studies Quarterly* 5, no. 1 (Spring 2011).

Eastlick, Mary Ann, Sherry L. Lotz, and Patricia Warrington. "Understanding Online B-to-C Relationships: An Integrated Model of Privacy Concerns, Trust, and Commitment." *Journal of Business Research* 59, no. 8 (2006).

Electronic Communications Privacy Act of 1986 (ECPA), 18 U.S.C. 2510.

Espiner, Tom. "UK Launches Dedicated Cybersecurity Agency." *ZDNet UK*, June 25, 2009. http://www.zdnet.com/article/uk-launches-dedicated-cybersecurity-agency/.

"EU and US Join NATO Cyber Security Pact." *Computerworld UK*, November 10, 2010. http://www.computerworlduk.com/security/eu-and-us-join-nato-cyber-security-pact-3249914/.

"European Union Considers Stronger Cybersecurity, Stricter Penalties for Hackers." *New New Internet (TNNI)*, October 1, 2010. http://blog.executivebiz.com/2010/10/european-union-considers-stronger-cybersecurity-stricter-penalties-for-hackers/.

Executive Order 13228. *Presidential Executive Order on Strengthening the Cybersecurity of Federal Networks and Critical Infrastructure*. May 11, 2017. https://www.whitehouse.gov/the-press-office/2017/05/11/presidential-executive-order-strengthening-cybersecurity-federal.

Executive Order 13636. *Improving Critical Infrastructure Cybersecurity*. February 12, 2013. https://obamawhitehouse.archives.gov/the-press-office/2013/02/12/executive-order-improving-critical-infrastructure-cybersecurity.

Executive Order 13687. *Imposing Additional Sanctions with Respect to North Korea*. January 6, 2015.

"Expert: Cyber-Attacks on Georgia Websites Tied to Mob, Russian Government." *Los Angeles Times*, August 13, 2008. http://latimesblogs.latimes.com/technology/2008/08/experts-debate.html.

Falliere, Nicolas, Liam O. Murchu, and Eric Chien. "W32.Stuxnet Dossier: Version 1.3." (2010). http://www.symantec.com/content/en/us/enterprise/media/security_response/whitepapers/w32_stuxnet_dossier.pdf.

Farwell, James P., and Rafal Rohozinski. "Stuxnet and the Future of Cyberwar." *Survival* 53, no. 1 (2011).

Farwell, James P., and Rafal Rohozinski. "The New Reality of Cyber War." *Survival* 54, no. 4 (2012).

Farwell, James P., Virginia N. Roddy, Yvonne Chalker, and Gary Elkins. *The Architecture of Cybersecurity*. Lafayette: Sans Souci/University of Louisiana Lafayette Press, 2017.

Fazal, Tanisha M. *State Death: The Politics and Geography of Conquest, Occupation, and Annexation*. Princeton, NJ: Princeton University Press, 2007.

Federal Bureau of Investigation. "DNSChanger Malware." (no date). https://www.fbi.gov/file-repository/dns-changer-malware.pdf/view.

Federal Communications Commission. "Communications Security, Reliability and Interoperability Council III." (no date). http://www.fcc.gov/encyclopedia/communications-security-reliability-and-interoperability-council-iii.

Federal Guidance on the Cybersecurity Information Sharing Act of 2015. Washington, DC: Department of Homeland Security and Department of Justice, June 25, 2016. https://www.us-cert.gov/sites/default/files/ais_files/Non-Federal_Entity_Sharing_Guidance_%28Sec%20105%28a%29%29.pdf.

Finkle, Jim, and Andrea Shalal-Esa. "Exclusive: Hackers Breached U.S. Defense Contractors." *Reuters*, May 27, 2011. http://www.reuters.com/article/2011/05/27/us-usa-defense-hackers-idUSTRE74Q6VY20110527.

Finnemore, Martha, and Kathryn Sikkink. "Taking Stock: The Constructivist Research Program in International Relations and Comparative Politics." *Annual Review of Political Science* 4 (2001).

"FIRST Vision and Mission Statement." Forum of Incident Response and Security Teams (FIRST), accessed September 8, 2016. https://www.first.org/about/mission.

Foley, Conor. "Welcome to Brazil's Version of 'Responsibility to Protect'." *The Guardian*, April 10, 2012. http://www.theguardian.com/commentisfree/cifamerica/2012/apr/10/diplomacy-brazilian-style.

Ford, M., M. Boucadair, A. Durand, P. Levis, and P. Roberts, "Issues with IP Address Sharing." *Internet Engineering Task Force, Request for Comments: 6269* (June 2011). http://www.hjp.at/doc/rfc/rfc6269.html.

Frankel, Sheila, Richard Graveman, John Pearce, and Mark Rooks. *Guidelines for the Secure Deployment of IPv6: Recommendations of the National Institute of Standards and Technology*. Gaithersburg, MD: National Institute of Standards, December 2010.

Freedberg, Sydney J. Jr. "They're Here: Cyber Experts Warn Senate That Adversary Is Already inside U.S. Networks." *Breaking Defense*, March 21, 2012. http://breakingdefense.com/2012/03/they-re-here-cyber-experts-warn-senate-that-adversary-is-alread/.

Fukuyama, Francis. *Trust: The Social Virtues and the Creation of Prosperity*. New York: Free Press, 1995.

Fultz, Andrew C. "Stuxnet, Schmitt Analysis, and the Cyber 'Use of Force' Debate." *Joint Force Quarterly* 67 (4th Quarter 2012).

Fung, Archon. "Varieties of Participation in Complex Governance." *Public Administration Review* 66, no. S1 (2006).

Gabriel, Kaigham J. "Testimony of Dr. Kaigham J. Gabriel, House Armed Service Committee, Subcommittee on Emerging Threats and Capabilities." February 29, 2012. http://www.darpa.mil/NewsEvents/Releases/2012/02/29a.aspx.

Garrity, John. "Getting Connected: The Internet and its Role as a Global Public Good." *Georgetown Journal of International Affairs* 18, no. 1 (Winter/Spring 2017).

Geer, Daniel. "Measuring Security." (undated). http://geer.tinho.net/measuringsecurity.tutorialv2.pdf.

Gertz, Bill. "Inside the Ring: Hacker Training." *Washington Post*, March 4, 2010.

Gibler, Douglas M. "Bordering On Peace: Democracy, Territorial Issues, and Conflict." *International Studies Quarterly* 51, no. 3 (September 2007).

Giles, Keir. "Russia's Public Stance on Cyberspace Issues." In *4th International Conference on Cyber Conflict*, edited by Christian Czosseck, Rain Ottis, and Katharina Ziolkowski, 68, 71–72. Tallinn: NATO Cooperative Cyber Defence Centre of Excellence, 2012.

Gilpin, Robert. *Global Political Economy: Understanding the International Economic Order*. Princeton, NJ: Princeton University Press, 2001.

"Global Internet Governance System is Working But Needs to Be More Inclusive, UN Forum on Internet Governance Told." *UN Press Release*, March 26, 2004. http://www.un.org/News/Press/docs/2004/pi1568.doc.htm.

Godwin, Mike. "The Many, Many, Many Flaws of CISA." *Slate*, October 26, 2015. http://www.slate.com/articles/technology/future_tense/2015/10/stopcisa_the_cybersecurity_information_sharing_act_is_a_disaster.html.

Goldman, David. "Major Banks Hit with Biggest Cyber Attacks in History." *CNN*, September 28, 2012. http://money.cnn.com/2012/09/27/technology/bank-cyberattacks/index.html.

Goldman, Emily, and Leslie Eliason. *The Diffusion of Military Technology and Ideas*. Stanford, CA: Stanford University Press, 2003.

Goldsmith, Jack, and Tim Wu. *Who Controls the Internet? Illusions of a Borderless World*. Oxford: Oxford University Press, 2006.

"Google, Facebook and Yahoo Partner for World IPv6 Day." *Softpedia.com*. January 12, 2011. http://news.softpedia.com/news/Google-Facebook-and-Yahoo-Partner-for-World-IPv6-Day-177852.shtml.

Gorman, Siobhan. "Electricity Grid in U.S. Penetrated by Spies." *Wall Street Journal* April 8, 2009. http://online.wsj.com/article/SB123914805204099085.html.

Govella, Kristi. "Cyber Security: A New Frontier for the U.S.–Japan Alliance." Berkeley APEC Study Center, May 12, 2010. http://bascresearch.blogspot.com/2010/05/cyber-security-new-frontier-for-us.html.

Gray, Colin S. "The Influence of Space Power upon History." *Comparative Strategy* 15, no. 4 (1996).

Greene, Robyn. "Cybersecurity Information Sharing Act of 2015 is Cyber Surveillance, Not Cybersecurity." Washington, DC: Open Technology Institute–New America, April 9, 2015. https://static.newamerica.org/attachments/2741-cybersecurity-information-sharing-act-of-2015-is-cyber-surveillance-not-cybersecurity/CISA_Cyber-Surveillance.488b3a9d2da64a27a9f6f53b38beb575.pdf.

Gross, Grant. "China Agrees to Drop WAPI Standard." *Computer World*, April 22, 2004. http://www.computerworld.com/article/2565021/mobile-wireless/china-agrees-to-drop-wapi-standard.html.

Gross, Judah. "Army Beefs up Cyber-Defense Unit as It Gives up Idea of Unified Cyber Command." *The Times of Israel*, May 14, 2017.

Hagel, John III, John Seely Brown, and Lang Davison. *The Power of Pull: How Small Moves, Smartly Made, Can Set Big Things in Motion.* New York: Basic Books, 2010.

Hague, William. "Security and Freedom in the Cyber Age—Seeking the Rules of the Road." Speech to the Munich Security Conference, February 4, 2011. http://www.fco.gov.uk/en/news/latest-news/?view=Speech&id=544853682.

Halpern, Sue. "US Cyber Weapons: Our 'Demon Pinball'." *The New York Review of Books*, September 29, 2016.

Hammond, Philip. *National Cyber Security Strategy 2016 to 2021.* London: Her Majesty's Government, November 1, 2016.

Hancock, Matt. "The New National Cyber Security Centre Will Be the Authoritative Voice on Information Security in the UK." *Government Communications Headquarters Press Release.* London: Cabinet Office, March 18, 2016.

Hardin, Garrett. "Tragedy of the Commons." *Science* 162, no. 3589 (1968).

Hathaway, Melissa E. Telephone interview, August 3, 2012.

Heller-Roazen, Daniel. *The Enemy of All: Piracy and the Law of Nations.* Cambridge, MA: MIT Press, 2008.

Hess, Charlotte. "Untangling the Web: The Internet as a Commons." *Workshop in Political Theory and Analysis, Indiana University.* March 1996. http://hdl.handle.net/10535/327.

Hessbruegge, Jan Arno. "The Historical Development of the Doctrines of Attribution and Due Diligence in International Law." *New York University Journal of International Law and Politics* 36 (Winter/Spring 2004).

Hick, Melanie. "DNS Changer Virus Spells 'Internet Doomsday'." *Huffington Post UK*, April 25, 2012. http://www.huffingtonpost.co.uk/2012/04/25/dns-changer-virus-internet-doomsday_n_1451606.html.

"Hickam Field—Army Air Corp Sergeant." *PearlHarbor.org.* http://www.pearlharbor.org/eyewitness-accounts.asp.

Hille, Kathrin. "How China Polices the Internet." *Financial Times* online, July 17, 2009. https://www.ft.com/content/e716cfc6-71a1-11de-a821-00144feabdc0?mhq5j=e3.

Hills, Jill. *Telecommunications and Empire.* Champaign: University of Illinois Press, 2007.

Hills, Jill. *The Struggle for Control of Global Communications: The Formative Century.* Champaign: University of Illinois Press, 2002.

Hollis, Duncan. "An e-SOS for Cyberspace." *Harvard International Law Journal* 52, no. 2 (2011). http://www.harvardilj.org/2011/07/issue_52-2_hollis/.

Huberman, Bernado A., and Lada A. Adamic. "Internet: Growth Dynamics of the World-Wide Web." *Nature* 401, no. 131 (September 9, 1999).

Hurwitz, Roger, Camino Kavanagh, Timer Maurer, and Michael Sechrist, rapporteurs. "A Preliminary Report on the Cyber Norms Workshop," sponsored by the Center for Global Security Affairs, University of Toronto, September 12–14, 2012. https://citizenlab.ca/cybernorms2012/introduction.pdf.

Huurdeman, Anton A. *The Worldwide History of Telecommunications.* Hoboken, NJ: John Wiley & Sons, 2003.

Hymans, Jacques E. C. *The Psychology of Nuclear Proliferation: Identity, Emotions and Foreign Policy.* Cambridge: Cambridge University Press, 2006.

IDG. "2016 Global State of the Information Security Survey." *IDG Enterprise*, October 20, 2016. https://www.idgenterprise.com/resource/research/2016-global-state-of-information-security-survey/.

Information Office of the State Council of the People's Republic of China. *The Internet in China*, June 8, 2010. http://www.china.org.cn/government/whitepaper/node_7093508.htm.

International Commission on Intervention and State Sovereignty. *The Responsibility to Protect*. Ottawa: International Development Research Centre, 2001. http://responsibilitytoprotect.org/ICISS%20Report.pdf.

International Law Commission. *Draft Articles on Responsibility of States for Internationally Wrongful Acts*, 2001. http://legal.un.org/ilc/texts/instruments/english/commentaries/9_6_2001.pdf.

International Strategy for Cyberspace: Prosperity, Security, and Openness in a Networked World. Washington, DC: The White House, May 2011. http://www.whitehouse.gov/sites/default/files/rss_viewer/international_strategy_for_cyberspace.pdf.

Internet Corporation for Assigned Names and Numbers. "ICANN Proposal to Perform IANA Functions Now Posted." July 9, 2012. http://www.icann.org/en/news/announcements/announcement-2-09jul12-en.htm.

Internet Corporation for Assigned Names and Numbers. "Memorandum of Understanding Concerning the Technical Work of the Internet Assigned Numbers Authority." March 1, 2000. http://www.icann.org/en/general/ietf-icann-mou-01mar00.htm.

Internet Governance Project. *The Future US Role in Internet Governance: 7 Points in Response to the U.S. Commerce Dept.'s "Statement of Principles."* Atlanta, GA: Georgia Institute of Technology, July 28, 2005.

"Internet Growth Statistics." *Internet World Stats* (updated May 25, 2017). http://www.internetworldstats.com/emarketing.htm.

"ITU Agrees On Key 5G Performance Requirements For IMT-2020." February 23, 2017. http://www.itu.int/en/mediacentre/Pages/2017-PR04.aspx.

Jasper, Scott. *Securing Freedom in the Global Commons*. Stanford, CA: Stanford University Press, 2010.

Jensen, Eric Talbot. "Unexpected Consequences from Knock-On Effects: A Different Standard for Computer Network Operations?" *American University International Law Review* 18, no. 5 (2003).

"Jo Twist, Web Guru Fights Info Pollution." *BBC News*, October 13, 2003. http://news.bbc.co.uk/2/hi/technology/3171376.stm.

Johnson, Jeh C. *Statement by Secretary Jeh C. Johnson Regarding PPD-41, Cyber Incident Coordination*. Washington, DC: Department of Homeland Security, July 26, 2016. https://www.dhs.gov/news/2016/07/26/statement-secretary-jeh-c-johnson-regarding-ppd-41-cyber-incident-coordination.

Kai, Jin. *Rising China in a Changing World: Power Transitions and Global Leadership*. New York: Springer, 2016.

Kaplan, Fred. *Dark Territory: The Secret History of Cyber War*. New York: Simon & Schuster, 2016.

Karp, Brad S. "Federal Guidance on the Cybersecurity Information Sharing Act of 2015." *Harvard Law School Forum on Corporate Governance and Financial Regulation*. March 3, 2016. https://corpgov.law.harvard.edu/2016/03/03/federal-guidance-on-the-cybersecurity-information-sharing-act-of-2015/#1.

Katz, Michael L., and Carl Shapiro. "Systems Competition and Network Effects." *Journal of Economic Perspectives* 8, no. 2 (Spring 1994).

Keck, Alexander, and Patrick Low. "Special and Differential Treatment in the WTO: Why, When and How?" *WTO Staff Working Paper* No. ERSD-2004-03 (2004). http://papers.ssrn.com/sol3/papers.cfm?abstract_id=901629.

Keck, Margaret E., and Kathryn Sikkink. *Activists beyond Borders: Advocacy Networks in International Politics*. Ithaca, NY: Cornell University Press, 1998. 27.

Kello, Lucas. "The Meaning of the Cyber Revolution: Perils to Theory and Statecraft." *International Security* 38, no. 2 (Fall 2013).

Kemshall, Andrew. "The RSA Security Breach–12 Months Down the Technology Turnpike." *Huffington Post*, March 14, 2012. http://www.huffingtonpost.co.uk/andrew-kemshall/the-rsa-security-breach-1_b_1344643.html.

Kendall, Nigel. "Global Cyber Attacks on the Rise: 75 Per Cent of Companies Have Suffered a Cyber Attack, at an Average Cost of $2 Million, Says Symantec Security Survey." *Times* (London), February 22, 2010.

Kennedy, Paul M. *The Rise and Fall of British Naval Mastery*. London: Macmillan, 1983.

Keohane, Robert O. *After Hegemony: Cooperation and Discord in the World Political Economy*. Princeton, NJ: Princeton University Press, 1984.

Kesan, Jay P., and Carol M. Hayes. "Mitigative Counterstriking: Self-Defense and Deterrence in Cyberspace." *Harvard Journal of Law and Technology* 25, no. 2 (Spring 2012).

Klemperer, Paul. "Network Goods (Theory)." In *The New Palgrave Dictionary of Economics, Second Edition*, edited by Steven N. Durlauf and Lawrence E. Blume. Basingstoke: Palgrave, 2008.

Koh, Harold Hongju. "International Law in Cyberspace," remarks to the USCYBERCOM Interagency Legal Conference, Ft. Meade, MD, September 18, 2012. http://www.state.gov/s/l/releases/remarks/197924.htm.

Krasner, Stephen. "Shared Sovereignty: New Institutions for Collapsed and Failing Status." *International Security* 29, no. 2 (Fall 2004).

Krebs, Brian. "The Target Breach, by the Numbers." *Krebs on Security*. May 14, 2014. http://krebsonsecurity.com/2014/05/the-target-breach-by-the-numbers/.

Krekel, Bryan, Patton Adams, and George Bakos. *Occupying the Information High Ground: Chinese Capabilities for Computer Network Operations and Cyber Espionage. Prepared for the U.S.-China Economic and Security Review Commission*. Falls Church, VA: Northrop Grumman Corporation, March 7, 2012.

Kulesza, Joanna. *International Internet Law*. New York: Routledge, 2012.

Kwalwasser, Harold. "Internet Governance." In *Cyber Power and National Security*, edited by Franklin D. Kramer, Stuart H. Starr, and Larry K. Wentz, 491–524. Washington, DC: NDU Press, 2009.

Laberis, Bill. "20 Eye-Opening Cybercrime Statistics." *Security Intelligence*, November 14, 2016.

LaFraniere, Sharon. "China to Scan Text Messages to Spot 'Unhealthy Content'." *New York Times*, January 20, 2010.

Lee, Bruce Y. "Friday's Events Showed How Cyber Attacks May Hurt and Kill People." *Forbes*, May 15, 2017. https://www.forbes.com/sites/brucelee/2017/05/15/fridays-events-showed-how-cyber-attack-may-hurt-and-kill-people/#520689545206.

Lessig, Lawrence. *Code: And Other Laws of Cyberspace*. New York: Basic Books, 1999.

Lessig, Lawrence. *Code: And Other Laws of Cyberspace, Version 2.0.* 2nd Revised Edition. New York: Basic Books, 2006.

Lessig, Lawrence. *The Future of Ideas: The Fate of the Commons in a Connected World*. New York: Vintage, 2002.

Lewis, James A. "Heartbleed and the State of Cybersecurity." *American Foreign Policy Interests* 36, no. 5 (November 2014). http://dx.doi.org/10.1080/10803920.2014.969176.

Li, Han, Rathindra Sarathy, and Heng Xu. "Understanding Situational Online Information Disclosure as a Privacy Calculus." *Journal of Computer Information Systems* 51, no. 1 (2010).

Li, Jinying. "China: The Techno-Politics of the Wall." In *Geoblocking and Global Video Culture*, edited by Ramon Lobato and James Meese, 110–19. Amsterdam: Institute of Network Cultures, 2016.

Li, Xing, and Timothy M Shaw. "'Same Bed, Different Dreams' and 'Riding Tiger' Dilemmas: China's Rise and International Relations/Political Economy." *Journal of Chinese Political Science* 19, no. 1 (2014).

Libicki, Martin C. *Conquest in Cyberspace*. New York: Cambridge University Press, 2007.

Libicki, Martin C. *Cyberdeterrence and Cyberwar*. Santa Monica, CA: RAND Corporation, 2009.

Liebowitz, Stanley J., and Stephen E. Margolis. "Network Effects and Externalities." In *The New Palgrave Dictionary of Economics and the Law*, edited by Peter Newman. London: Palgrave Macmillan, 1998.

Liebowitz, Stanley J., and Stephen E. Margolis. "Network Externality: An Uncommon Tragedy." *Journal of Economic Perspectives* 8, no. 2 (Spring 1994).

Lindsay, David F. "Liability of ISPs for End-User Copyright Infringements." *Telecommunications Journal of Australia* 60, no. 2 (2010).

Lipton, Eric, David E. Sanger, and Scott Shane. "The Perfect Weapon: How Russian Cyberpower Invaded the U.S." *New York Times*, December 13, 2016.

Lloyd, Anthony. "Britain Applies Military Thinking to The Growing Spectre of Cyberwar." *Times* (London), March 8, 2010.

Lonsdale, David J. *The Nature of War in the Information Age*. London: Frank Cass, 2004.

Luttwak, Edward N. *Strategy: The Logic of War and Peace*. Cambridge, MA: Belknap Press, 2003.

Lynn, William J. "Defending a New Domain: The Pentagon's Cyberstrategy." *Foreign Affairs* 89, no. 5 (September/October, 2010).

Lynn, William J. "Remarks on Cyber at the Council on Foreign Relations." As Delivered by Deputy Secretary of Defense William J. Lynn, III, Council on Foreign Relations, New York City, Thursday, September 30, 2010." http://archive.defense.gov/speeches/speech.aspx?speechid=1509.

Lynn, William J. III. "Defending a New Domain." *Foreign Affairs* 89, no. 5 (October 2010). https://www.foreignaffairs.com/articles/66552/william-j-lynn-iii/defending-a-new-domain.

Lynn, William J. III. "Remarks on Cyber at RSA Conference." February 15, 2011. http://www.defense.gov/speeches/speech.aspx?speechid=1535.

Machiavelli, Niccolò. *The Prince*, translated by Peter Bondella. Oxford: Oxford University Press, 2005.

Mackey, Robert. "Irish Flotilla Activists Show Damage to Their Boat." *The Lede: Blogging the News*, July 1, 2011. http://thelede.blogs.nytimes.com/2011/07/01/what-flotilla-activists-videos-look-like/.

MacKinnon, Rebecca. "Commentary: Are China's Demands for Internet 'Self-discipline' Spreading to the West?" *McClatchy Report*, January 18, 2010. http://www.mcclatchydc.com/2010/01/18/82469/commentary-are-chinas-demands.html.

Mahan, Alfred Thayer. *The Influence of Sea Power upon History: 1660-1783.* Twelfth Edition. Boston, MA: Little, Brown, 1890/1918.

Mallery, John C. "Towards a Strategy for Cyber Defense." Presentation at the U.S. Naval War College, Newport, RI, September 17, 2010.

Markoff, John. "Computer Gear May Pose Trojan Horse Threat to Pentagon" *New York Times*, May 10, 2008.

Markoff, John. "Defying Experts, Rogue Computer Code Still Lurks." *New York Times*, August 26, 2009. http://www.nytimes.com/2009/08/27/technology/27compute.html?_r=1. I.

Markoff, John, David E. Sanger, and Thom Shanker, "Cyberwar: In Digital Combat, U.S. Finds No Easy Deterrent." *New York Times*, January 26, 2010.

Markoff, Michele. "Advancing Norms of Responsible State Behavior in Cyberspace." *DipNote: US Department of State Official Blog*, July 9, 2015. https://blogs.state.gov/stories/2015/07/09/advancing-norms-responsible-state-behavior-cyberspace.

Marson, Ingrid. "China Launches Largest Ipv6 Network." *CNET News*, December 29, 2004. http://news.cnet.com/China-launches-largest-IPv6-network/2100-1025_3-5506914.html.

Mathiason, John. *Internet Governance: The New Frontier of Global Institutions*. New York: Routledge, 2008.

Maucione, Scott. "CYBERCOM's New Buying Power Now Closer to Reality." *Federal News Radio*, January 23, 2017. https://federalnewsradio.com/acquisition/2017/01/cybercoms-new-buying-power-now-closer-reality/.

Maurer, Tim. "Cyber Norm Emergence at the United Nations—An Analysis of the Activities at the UN Regarding Cyber-security." Discussion Paper #2011-11. Cambridge, MA: Belfer Center for Science and International Affairs, September 2011. http://belfercenter.ksg.harvard.edu/files/maurer-cyber-norm-dp-2011-11-final.pdf.

McDermott, Roger N. "Does Russia Have a Gerasimov Doctrine?" *Parameters* 46, no. 1 (Spring 2016).

"Melissa Virus Creator Jailed." *BBC News*, May 2, 2002. http://news.bbc.co.uk/2/hi/americas/1963371.stm.

Miller, James N. "Statement of Dr. James N. Miller, Principal Deputy Under Secretary of Defense for Policy, U.S. Department of Defense, Hearing on National Defense Authorization Act for Fiscal Year 2012, Committee on Armed Services, U.S. House of Representatives." March 16, 2011, 4. http://www.fas.org/irp/congress/2011_hr/cybercom.pdf.

Mills, Elinor. "Web Traffic Redirected to China in Mystery Mix-Up." *CNET*, March 25, 2010.

Molyneux, Robert E. *The Internet under the Hood: An Introduction to Network Technologies for Information Professionals.* Westport, CT: Libraries Unlimited, 2003, 86.

Morgan, Forrest E., Karl P. Mueller, Evan S. Medeiros, Kevin L. Pollpeter, and Roger Cliff. *Dangerous Thresholds: Managing Escalation in the 21st Century.* Santa Monica, CA: RAND, 2008.

Mueller, Milton L. *Networks and States: The Global Politics of Internet Governance.* Cambridge, MA: MIT Press, 2010.

Musiani, Francesca, Derrick L. Cogburn, Laura DeNardis, and Nanette S. Levinson, eds. *The Turn to Infrastructure in Internet Governance.* New York: Palgrave, 2015.

Nadelmann, Ethan A. "Global Prohibition Regimes: The Evolution of Norms in International Society." *International Organization* 44, no. 4 (1990).

Nakashima, Ellen. "China Still Trying to Hack U.S. Firms Despite Xi's Vow to Refrain, Analysts Say." *Washington Post*, October 19, 2015. https://www.washingtonpost.com/world/national-security/china-still-trying-to-hack-us-firms-despite-xis-vow-to-refrain-analysts-say/2015/10/18/d9a923fe-75a8-11e5-b9c1-f03c48c96ac2_story.html.

Nakashima, Ellen. "Cyber-intruder Sparks Response, Debate." *Washington Post*, December 8, 2011. https://www.washingtonpost.com/national/national-security/cyber-intruder-sparks-response-debate/2011/12/06/gIQAxLuFgO_story.html.

Nakashima, Ellen. "Defense Official Discloses Cyberattack." *Washington Post*, August 24, 2010. http://www.washingtonpost.com/wp-dyn/content/article/2010/08/24/AR2010082406495.html.

Nakashima, Ellen. "Gen. Keith Alexander Confirmed to Head Cyber-Command." *Washington Post*, May 11, 2010.

Nakashima, Ellen. "Pentagon's Cyber Command Seeks Authority to Expand Its Battlefield." *Washington Post*, November 6, 2010.

Nakashima, Ellen. "Trump Signs Order on Cybersecurity That Holds Agency Heads Accountable for Network Attacks." *Washington Post*, May 12, 2017. https://www.washingtonpost.com/world/national-security/trump-signs-order-on-cybersecurity-that-holds-agency-heads-accountable-for-network-attacks/2017/05/11/4e389522-2b8f-11e7-a616-d7c8a68c1a66_story.html?utm_term=.137f1b6f9a4a&wpisrc=nl_daily202&wpmm=1.

Nakashima, Ellen. "U.S. Decides against Publicly Blaming China for Data Hack." *Washington Post*, July 21, 2015. https://www.washingtonpost.com/world/national-security/us-avoids-blaming-china-in-data-theft-seen-as-fair-game-in-espionage/2015/07/21/03779096-2eee-11e5-8353-1215475949f4_story.html.

Nakashima, Ellen, and Steven Mufson. "U.S., China Vow Not to Engage in Economic Cyberespionage." *Washington Post*, September 25, 2015. https://www.washingtonpost.com/national/us-china-vow-not-to-engage-in-economic-cyberespionage/2015/09/25/90e74b6a-63b9-11e5-8e9e-dce8a2a2a679_story.html.

Nakashima, Ellen, and William Wan. "In China, Business Travelers Take Extreme Precautions to Avoid Cyber-Espionage" *Washington Post*, September 26, 2011.

National Institute of Standards and Technology. *Security and Privacy Controls for Federal Information Systems and Organizations. NIST Special Publication 800-53 (Revision 4)*. Washington, DC: United States Department of Commerce, April 2013. http://nvlpubs.nist.gov/nistpubs/SpecialPublications/NIST.SP.800-53r4.pdf.

National Research Council. *Computers at Risk*. Washington, DC: National Academies Press, 1991.

National Research Council. *Cybersecurity Today and Tomorrow: Pay Now or Pay Later*. Washington, DC: National Academies Press, 2002.

National Research Council. *Information Technology for Counterterrorism*. Washington, DC: National Academies Press, 2003.

National Research Council. *Realizing the Potential of C4I: Fundamental Challenges*. Washington, DC: National Academies Press, 1998.

National Research Council. *Toward a Safer and More Secure Cyberspace*. Washington, DC: National Academies Press, 2007.

National Research Council. *Trust in Cyberspace*. Washington, DC: National Academies Press, 1999.

National Security Strategy. Washington, DC: The White House, May 2010.

National Strategy to Secure Cyberspace (NSSC). Washington, DC: The White House, February 2003.

NATO Cooperative Cyber Defence Centre of Excellence. "Tallinn Manual 2.0 on the International Law Applicable to Cyber Operations." *Fact Sheet*, February 8, 2017. https://ccdcoe.org/sites/default/files/documents/CCDCOE_Tallinn_Manual_Onepager_web.pdf.

Naylor, Brian. "One Year after OPM Data Breach, What Has the Government Learned?" *National Public Radio*, June 6, 2016. http://www.npr.org/sections/alltechconsidered/2016/06/06/480968999/one-year-after-opm-data-breach-what-has-the-government-learned.

Norton-Taylor, Richard. "National Security Strategy Says UK Is under Threat of Cyber Attack." *Guardian*, October 18, 2010. https://www.theguardian.com/politics/2010/oct/18/national-security-strategy-cyber-attacks.

Nye, Joseph S., Jr. *Cyber Power*. Cambridge, MA: Belfer Center for Science and International Affairs, 2010. http://belfercenter.ksg.harvard.edu/files/cyber-power.pdf.

Nye, Joseph S., Jr. "The Regime Complex for Managing Global Cyber Activities." *Global Commission on Internet Governance Paper Series*, no. 1. Waterloo: Centre

for International Governance Innovation, 2014. https://www.cigionline.org/sites/
default/files/gcig_paper_no1.pdf.

O'Connell, Robert L. *Of Arms and Men: A History of War, Weapons, and Aggression.*
London: Oxford University Press, 1989.

Obama, Barack H. *Presidential Policy Directive 8 (PPD-8): National Preparedness.*
September 23, 2015. https://www.dhs.gov/presidential-policy-directive-8-
national-preparedness.

Obama, Barack H. *Presidential Policy Directive 20: U.S. Cyber Operations Policy.*
October 2012. https://fas.org/irp/offdocs/ppd/ppd-20.pdf.

Obama, Barack H. *Presidential Policy Directive 21 (PPD-21): Critical
Infrastructure Security and Resilience.* February 12, 2013. https://obamawhite-
house.archives.gov/the-press-office/2013/02/12/presidential-policy-directive-
critical-infrastructure-security-and-resil.

Obama, Barack H. *Presidential Policy Directive 41: United States Cyber Incident
Coordination.* July 26, 2016. https://obamawhitehouse.archives.gov/the-press-
office/2016/07/26/presidential-policy-directive-united-states-cyber-incident.

Office of the Director of National Intelligence. *Assessing Russian Activities and
Intentions in Recent US Elections. Intelligence Community Assessment 2017-01D.*
Washington, DC: National Intelligence Council, January 6, 2017.

Ostrom, Elinor. "A General Framework for Analyzing Sustainability of Social-
Ecological Systems." *Science* 325, no. 5939 (July 24, 2009).

Ostrom, Elinor. *Governing the Commons: The Evolution of Institutions for Collective
Action.* Cambridge: Cambridge University Press, 1990.

Owens, William A., Kenneth W. Dam, and Herbert S. Lin, eds. *Technology, Policy,
Law, and Ethics Regarding U.S. Acquisition and Use of Cyberattack Capabilities.*
Washington, DC: National Academies Press, 2009.

Owens, William A., Kenneth W. Dam, and Herbert S. Lin. *Technology, Policy, Law
and Ethics Regarding U.S. Acquisition and Use of Cyberattack Capabilities.*
Washington, DC: National Academies Press, 2009. http://www.nap.edu/catalog.
php?record_id=12651.

Padgen, Anthony. "The Destruction of Trust and Its Economic Consequences
in the Case of Eighteenth-Century Naples." In *Trust: Making and Breaking
Cooperative Relations,* edited by Diego Gambetta, 136–38. London: Basil
Blackwell, 1988.

Pagliery, Jose. "Apple and Other Tech Giants Slam Anti-Hacking Bill for Being Too
Creepy." *CNN,* October 26, 2015. http://money.cnn.com/2015/10/26/technology/
cisa-cybersecurity-bill-senate/.

Panetta, Leon E. "Secretary of Defense Leon E. Panetta, Remarks to the Business
Executives for National Security, New York City, October 11, 2012." http://www.
defense.gov/transcripts/transcript.aspx?transcriptid=5136.

Peery, James. "Testimony of Dr. James Peery, Director of the Information Systems and
Analysis Center, Sandia National Laboratories, Senate Armed Services Committee,
Subcommittee on Emerging Threats and Capabilities." March 20, 2012.

Pellerin, Cheryl. "DOD, DHS Join Forces to Promote Cybersecurity." *American
Forces Press Service,* October 13, 2010. http://archive.defense.gov/news/newsar-
ticle.aspx?id=61264.

Permanent Select Committee on Intelligence. *Cyber Intelligence Sharing and Protection Act. Report together with Minority Views [To Accompany H.R. 3523].* Washington, DC: United States House of Representatives, April 17, 2012, 5. http://intelligence.house.gov/sites/intelligence.house.gov/files/documents/HR3523CommitteeReport.pdf.

Pham, Thu. "After a Data Breach: Who's Liable?" *Duo com*, September 17, 2014. https://duocom/blog/after-a-data- breach-whos-liable.

Pike, John. "Solar Sunrise." *GlobalSecurity.org* (undated). http://www.globalsecurity.org/military/ops/solar-sunrise.htm.

Pomerleau, Mark. "Congress Set to Elevate CYBERCOM to Unified Combatant Command." *C4ISRNET*, December 1, 2016. http://www.c4isrnet.com/articles/congress-authorizes-elevating-cybercom-to-unified-combatant-command.

Ponemon Institute. *Fourth Annual Study: Is Your Company Ready for a Big Data Breach?* Traverse City, MI: Ponemon Institute, September 2016. http://www.experian.com/assets/data-breach/white-papers/2016-experian-data-breach-preparedness-study.pdf.

Porche, Isaac. "Stuxnet Is the World's Problem." *Bulletin of the Atomic Scientists* (December 9, 2010).

Posen, Barry R. "Command of the Commons: The Military Foundation of U.S. Hegemony." *International Security* 28, no. 1 (Summer 2003).

"President Issues Executive Order to Strengthen Cybersecurity of Federal Networks and U.S. Critical Infrastructure." *Crowell & Moring*, May 12, 2017. https://www.crowell.com/NewsEvents/AlertsNewsletters/all/President-Issues-Executive-Order-to-Strengthen-Cybersecurity-of-Federal-Networks-and-US-Critical-Infrastructure.

President's Information Technology Advisory Committee. *Cyber Security: A Crisis of Prioritization.* Washington, DC: National Coordination Office for Information Technology Research and Development, February 2005.

Price, Richard. "A Genealogy of the Chemical Weapons Taboo." *International Organization* 49, no. 1 (Winter 1995). http://dx.doi.org/10.1017/S0020818300001582.

Price, Richard. "Reversing the Gun Sights: Transnational Civil Society Targets Land Mines." *International Organization* 52, no. 3 (Summer 1998). http://dx.doi.org/10.1162/002081898550671.

"Prime Minister Vladimir Putin Meets with Secretary General of the International Telecommunication Union Hamadoun Toure." *Working Day*, June 15, 2011. http://premier.gov.ru/eng/events/news/15601/.

"Protocol Additional to the Geneva Conventions of 12 August 1949 and Relating to the Protection of Victims of International Armed Conflicts (Protocol I)," adopted at Geneva on June 8, 1977. http://treaties.un.org/doc/Publication/UNTS/Volume%201125/volume-1125-I-17512-English.pdf.

Putnam, Robert with Robert Leonardi, and Raffaella Y. Nanetti. *Making Democracy Work: Civic Traditions in Modern Italy.* Princeton, NJ: Princeton University Press, 1993.

Raboy, Marc, Normand Landry, and Jeremy Shtern. *Digital Solidarities, Communication Policy and Multi-stakeholder Global Governance: The Legacy of the World Summit on the Information Society.* New York: Peter Lang, 2010.

Rattray, Gregory J. "An Environmental Approach to Understanding Cyberpower." In *Cyberpower and National Security*, edited by Franklin D. Kramer, Stuart H. Starr, and Larry K. Wentz, 253–74. Washington, DC: Potomac Books, 2009.

Rattray, Gregory J. *Strategic Warfare in Cyberspace*. Cambridge, MA: MIT Press, 2001.

Raymond, Mark. "Engaging Security and Intelligence Practitioners in the Emerging Cyber Regime Complex." *Cyber Defense Review* 1, no. 2 (Fall 2016).

Raymond, Mark. "Puncturing the Myth of the Internet as a Commons." *Georgetown Journal of International Affairs* (2013). http://journal.georgetown.edu/wp-content/uploads/2015/07/gjia13005_Raymond-CYBER-III.pdf.

Raymond, Mark. "Renovating the Procedural Architecture of International Law." *Canadian Foreign Policy Journal* 19, no. 3 (2013). http://dx.doi.org/10.1080/11926422.2013.845580.

Raymond, Mark, and Gordon Smith, eds. *Organized Chaos: Reimagining the Internet*. Waterloo: Centre for International Governance Innovation, 2014.

Raymond, Mark, and Laura DeNardis. "Multistakeholderism: Anatomy of an Inchoate Global Institution." *International Theory* 7, no. 3 (2015).

Raymond, Mark, Aaron Shull, and Samantha Bradshaw. "Rule-Making for State Conduct in the Attribution of Cyber-Attacks." In *Mutual Security in the Asia-Pacific: Roles for Australia, Canada and South Korea*, edited by Kang Choi, James Manicom, and Simon Palamar, 153–72. Waterloo: Centre for International Governance Innovation, 2015.

Rayner, Bruce. "Ferreting Out the Fakes." *Electronic Engineering Times*, August 15, 2011.

Reed, Thomas C. *At the Abyss: An Insider's History of the Cold War*. New York: Ballantine Books, 2004.

Reus-Smit, Christian. *The Moral Purpose of the State: Culture, Social Identity, and Institutional Rationality in International Relations*. Princeton, NJ: Princeton University Press, 1999.

Ricks, Thomas. "Ukrainian Elder Statesman: How Russian Hybrid War Is Changing the World Order." *Foreign Policy*, March 21, 2017. http://foreignpolicy.com/2017/03/21/ukrainian-elder-statesman-how-russian-hybrid-war-is-changing-the-world-order/.

Rid, Thomas. *Cyber War Will Not Take Place*. New York: Oxford University Press, 2013.

Risk Steering Committee. *DHS Risk Lexicon: 2010 Edition*. Washington, DC: Department of Homeland Security, September 2010, 26. http://www.dhs.gov/xlibrary/assets/dhs-risk-lexicon-2010.pdf.

Rõigas, Henry, and Tomáš Minárik. "2015 UN GGE Report: Major Players Recommending Norms of Behaviour, Highlighting Aspects of International Law." *Incyder News*, August 31, 2015. https://ccdcoe.org/2015-un-gge-report-major-players-recommending-norms-behaviour-highlighting-aspects-international-l-0.html.

Rollins, John, and Anna C. Henning. *Comprehensive National Cybersecurity Initiative (CNCI)*. Washington, DC: Congressional Research Service, March 10, 2009; declassified in March 2010.

Romano, Benjamin J. "Microsoft Device Helps Police Pluck Evidence from Cyberscene of Crime" *Seattle Times*, April 29, 2008. http://seattletimes.nwsource. com/html/microsoft/2004379751_msftlaw29.html.

Rosenberger, Rob. "Gov't Hype Surrounds 'Operation Buckshot Yankee'." *Vmyths. com*, August 26, 2010. http://vmyths.com/2010/08/26/oby/.

Rosenzweig, Paul. *Cyber Warfare: How Conflicts in Cyberspace Are Challenging America and Changing the World*. Santa Barbara, CA: Praeger, 2013.

Rosenzweig, Paul. *Senate Cybersecurity Bill: Not Ready for PrimeTime*. Washington, DC: Heritage Foundation, March 7, 2012. http://www.heritage.org/research/ reports/2012/03/senate-cybersecurity-bill-not-ready-for-prime-time.

Samuelson, William, and Richard Zeckhauser. "Status Quo Bias in Decision Making." *Journal of Risk and Uncertainty* 1, no. 1 (1988).

Sandholtz, Wayne. *Prohibiting Plunder: How Norms Change*. New York: Oxford University Press, 2007.

Sang-Hun, Choe, Paul Mozure, Nicole Perloth, and David Sanger. "Focus Turns to North Korea Sleeper Cells as Possible Culprits in Cyberattack." *New York Times*, May 16, 2017.

Sanger, David E. *Confront and Conceal: Obama's Secret Wars and Surprising Use of American Power*. New York: Crown, 2012.

Sanger, David E. "Iran Fights Strong Virus Attacking Computers." *New York Times*, September 25, 2010.

Scannell, Kara. "FBI Details North Korean attack on Sony." January 7, 2015. https:// www.ft.com/content/287beee4-96a2-11e4-a83c-00144feabdc0.

Schjølberg, Stein. "Wanted: A United Nations Cyberspace Treaty." In *Global Cyber Deterrence: Views from China, the U.S., Russia, India, and Norway*, edited by Andrew Nagorski, 11–14. New York: EastWest Institute, 2010.

Schmitt, Michael N. "Computer Network Attack and the Use of Force in International Law: Thoughts on a Normative Framework." *Columbia Journal of Transnational Law* 37 (1999).

Schmitt, Michael N., ed. *Tallinn Manual 2.0 on the International Law Applicable to Cyber Operations*, 2nd Edition. Cambridge: Cambridge University Press, 2017. https://ccdcoe.org/tallinn-manual.html.

Schwirtz, Michael, and Joseph Goldstein. "Russian Espionage Piggybacks on a Cybercriminal's Hacking." *New York Times*, March 12, 2017.

Scott, Tony. "Policy to Require Secure Connections across Federal Websites and Web Services." Washington, DC: Executive Office of the President, Office of Management and Budget, June 8, 2015. https://www.whitehouse.gov/sites/default/ files/omb/memoranda/2015/m-15-13.pdf.

Segal, Adam, and Matthew Waxman. "Why a Cybersecurity Treaty Is a Pipe Dream." *Fareed Zakaria GPS*, October 27, 2011. http://globalpublicsquare.blogs.cnn.com/ 2011/10/27/why-a-cybersecurity-treaty-is-a-pipe-dream/.

Seo, Sin-seok, Young J. Won, and James Won-Ki Hong. "Witnessing Distributed Denial-of-Service Traffic from an Attacker's Network." *Proceedings of the 7th International Conference on Network and Services Management* (2011).

Shackelford, Scott J. "From Nuclear War to Net War: Analogizing Cyber Attacks in International Law." *Berkeley Journal of International Law* 25 (May/June 2009).

Shea, Dennis C., and Carolyn Bartholomew (Chairmen). *2016 Report to Congress of the U.S.-China Economic and Security Review Commission.* Washington, DC: U.S.–China Economic and Security Review Commission, November, 2016, 13. https://www.uscc.gov/sites/default/files/annual_reports/Executive%20 Summary%202016.pdf.

Shea, Jamie (Chairman). *NATO 2020: Assured Security; Dynamic Engagement: Analysis and Recommendations of the Group of Experts on a New Strategic Concept for NATO.* Brussels: North Atlantic Treaty Organization, May 17, 2010. http://www. nato.int/strategic-concept/expertsreport.pdf.

Sheldon, John B. "Toward a Theory of Cyber Power: Strategic Purpose in Peace and War." In *Cyberspace and National Security: Threats, Opportunities, and Power in a Virtual World*, edited by Derek S. Reveron, 207–24. Washington, DC: Georgetown University Press, 2012.

Shenkland, Stephen. "Russian Android Malware Tracked Ukrainian Military: Report." *CNET*, December 22, 2016. https://www.cnet.com/news/russian-android-malware-tracked-ukrainian-military-report/.

Shiode, Narushige. "Toward the Construction of Cyber Cities with the Application of Unique Characteristics of Cyberspace." *Online Planning Journal* (1997). http:// www.casa.ucl.ac.uk/planning/articles21/urban.htm.

Singer, Peter W., and Allan Friedman. *Cybersecurity and Cyberwar: What Everyone Needs to Know.* New York: Oxford University Press, 2013.

Singh, Parminder Jeet. "India's Proposal Will Help Take the Web out of U.S. Control." *Hindu Online*, May 17, 2012. http://www.thehindu.com/opinion/op-ed/ article3426292.ece.

Smith, Brad. "The Need for a Digital Geneva Convention—Microsoft on the Issues." *Microsoft*, February 14, 2017. https://blogs.microsoft.com/on-the-issues/2017/02/ 14/need-digital-geneva-convention/.

Smith, Brad. "The Need for Urgent Collective Action to Keep People Safe Online: Lessons from Last Week's Cyberattack." *Microsoft*, May 14, 2017. https:// blogs.microsoft.com/on-the-issues/2017/05/14/need-urgent-collective-action-keep-people-safe-online-lessons-last-weeks-cyberattack/.

"South Korea to Set up Cyber Command against North Korea—Two Years Earlier Than Planned." *Channel News Asia*, July 9, 2009.

Spar, Debora L. "National Policies and Domestic Politics." In *The Oxford Handbook of International Business*, edited by Alan M. Rugman. New York: Oxford University Press, 2008.

Staff, "Foreign Firms Fret as China Implements New Cybersecurity Law." *Bloomberg News*, May 24, 2017.

Staff. "German Army Launches New Cyber Command." *Deutsche Welle*, April 1, 2017. http://www.dw.com/en/german-army-launches-new-cyber-command/ a-38246517.

"Statement by Mr. Dushyant Singh, Member of Parliament, on Agenda Item 16—Information and Communication Technologies for Development, at the 66th Session of the United Nations General Assembly on October 26,

2011." http://content.ibnlive.in.com/article/21-May-2012documents/full-text-indias-un-proposal-to-control-the-internet-259971-53.html.

Statement of General Keith B. Alexander, Commander, US CYBER COMMAND, Hearing on National Defense Authorization Act for Fiscal Year 2012, Committee on Armed Services, U.S. House of Representatives, March 16, 2011. Washington, DC: United States House of Representatives, March 16, 2011. http://www.fas.org/irp/congress/2011_hr/cybercom.pdf.

Stoddart, Kristan. "UK Cyber Security and Critical National Infrastructure Protection." *International Affairs* 92, no. 5 (September 2016).

"Strategic Jousting Between China and America: Testing the Waters." *The Economist*, July 29, 2010).

Tandon, Rajesh, and Ranjita Mohanty. "Civil Society and Governance: A Research Study in India." In *Global Comparative Research Study on Civil Society and Governance.* Sussex: Society for Participatory Research in Asia, 2000.

"The WannaCry Ransomware Attack." *Strategic Comments* 23, no. 16 (May 2017).

"Theft in Molalla [Oregon] Reported to Department of Homeland Security: Computer Controlled Town's Water System." *KPTV Fox News Oregon*, March 26, 2010. http://www.kptv.com/story/14783428/stolen-computer-controlled-towns-water-system-3-26-2010.

Thomas, Daniel C. *The Helsinki Effect: International Norms, Human Rights, and the Demise of Communism.* Princeton, NJ: Princeton University Press, 2001.

Thomas, Ward. "Norms and Security: The Case of International Assassination." *International Security* 25, no. 1 (Summer 2000).

Tian, Ye, Ratan Dey, Yong Lui, and Keith W. Ross. "China's Internet: Topology Mapping and Geolocating." *INFOCOM: The Proceedings of the Institute of Electrical and Electronics Engineers* (2012). http://cis.poly.edu/~ratan/topology-mappingchinainternetshort.pdf.

Tikk-Ringas, Eneken. *Developments in the Field of Information and Telecommunication in the Context of International Security: Work of the UN First Committee, 1998–2012.* Geneva: ICT4Peace, 2012.

Tilly, Charles. "Cities and States in Europe, 1000–1800." *Theory and Society* 18, no. 5 (1989).

Tilly, Charles. *Coercion, Capital, and European States, AD 990–1992.* Malden, MA: Blackwell, 1992.

Treaty on Principles Governing the Activities of States in the Exploration and Use of Outer Space, including the Moon and Other Celestial Bodies (1967).

Tsagourias, Nicholas. "Cyber Attacks, Self-Defence and the Problem of Attribution." *Journal of Conflict and Security Law* 17, no. 2 (Summer 2012). http://jcsl.oxford-journals.org/content/17/2/229.full.pdf+html.

"UN ICT Task Force Global Forum on Internet Governance to be Held in March." *UN press release*, February 13, 2004. http://portal.unesco.org/ci/en/ev.php-URL_ID=14347&URL_DO=DO_PRINTPAGE&URL_SECTION=201.html.

UNGA A/70/174. (2015). https://documents-dds-ny.un.org/doc/UNDOC/GEN/N15/228/35/PDF/N1522835.pdf.

United Nations Convention on the Law of the Sea. 1982.

United Nations General Assembly Economic and Social Council. *Enhanced Cooperation on Public Policy Issues Pertaining to the Internet. Report of the Secretary-General.* New York: United Nations, May 4, 2011. http://unctad.org/meetings/en/SessionalDocuments/a66d77_en.pdf.

United Nations General Assembly Resolution. *Creation of a Global Culture of Cybersecurity and Taking Stock of National Efforts to Protect Critical Information Infrastructures,* 64/211. March 17, 2010. http://www.citizenlab.org/cybernorms/ares64211.pdf.

United Nations General Assembly Resolution. *Group of Governmental Experts on Developments in the Field of Information and Telecommunications in the Context of International Security,* 65/201. November 9, 2010. https://disarmament-library.un.org/UNODA/Library.nsf/1b0b0683e73e6da5852576e40054e901/d9d0a83c0f-2421d6852577e3005c4b5e/%24FILE/A%252065%2520405.pdf.

United Nations General Assembly Resolution. *Report of the Group of Governmental Experts on Developments in the Field of Information and Telecommunications in the Context of International Security,* A/68/98. June 24, 2013. http://www.un.org/ga/search/view_doc.asp?symbol=A/68/98.

United Nations General Assembly Resolution. *Report of the Group of Governmental Experts on Developments in the Field of Information and Telecommunications in the Context of International Security,* A/70/174. July 22, 2015. http://www.un.org/ga/search/view_doc.asp?symbol=A/70/174.

United Nations Office for Disarmament Affairs. The Biological Weapons Convention. April 10, 1972. http://disarmament.un.org/treaties/t/bwc/text.

United States Department of Commerce. *Management of Internet Names and Addresses,* 63 Fed. Reg. 31741. (1998).

United States Department of Defense. *2011 Department of Defense Strategy for Operating in Cyberspace.* Washington, DC: Department of Defense, July 2011. http://www.defense.gov/news/d20110714cyber.pdf.

United States Department of Defense. *Joint Publication 1-02. Department of Defense Dictionary of Military and Associated Terms.* Washington, DC: Department of Defense, November 8, 2010, as amended through August 15, 2012.

United States Department of Defense. *The DoD Cyber Strategy.* Washington, DC: Department of Defense, April 2015. https://www.defense.gov/Portals/1/features/2015/0415_cyber-strategy/Final_2015_DoD_CYBER_STRATEGY_for_web.pdf.

United States Department of Homeland Security and Department of Defense. *Defense Industrial Base: Critical Infrastructure and Key Resources Sector-Specific Plan as Input to the National Infrastructure Protection Plan.* Washington, DC: Department of Homeland Security and Department of Defense, May 2007. http://www.dhs.gov/xlibrary/assets/nipp-ssp-defense-industrial-base.pdf.

United States Department of State. "Internet Freedom Fact Sheet." February 15, 2011. http://www.state.gov/r/pa/prs/ps/2011/02/156623.htm.

United States Department of Treasury, Press Center. "Treasury Imposes Sanction against The Government of the Democratic People's Republic of Korea." January 2, 2015. https://www.treasury.gov/press-center/press-releases/Pages/jl9733.aspx.

US CERT Quarterly Trends and Analysis Report 4, 2 (June 16, 2009).

USCC Research Staff. *The National Security Implication of Investments and Products from the People's Republic of China in the Telecommunications Sector*, U.S.–China Economic and Security Review Commission Staff Report. Washington, DC: U.S.–China Economic and Security Review Commission, January 2011. http://www.uscc.gov/RFP/2011/FINALREPORT_TheNationalSecurityImplicationsof InvestmentsandProductsfromThe PRCintheTelecommunicationsSector.pdf.

Vijayan, Jaikumar. "After Google-China Dust-Up, Cyberwar Emerges as a Threat." *Computerworld*, April 7, 2010. http://www.computerworld.com/s/article/9174558/After_Google_China_dust_up_cyberwar_emerges_as_a_threat.

Vijayan, Jaikumar. "Caution Urged in Wake of RSA Security Breach" *Computerworld*, March 19, 2011. http://www.computerworld.com/s/article/9214800/Caution_urged_in_wake_of_RSA_security_breach.html.

Volz, Dustin. "Ransomware Attack Again Thrusts U.S. Spy Agency into Unwanted Spotlight." *Reuters*, May 16, 2017. http://www.reuters.com/article/us-cyber-attack-blame-idUSKCN18C02D.

Warner, Eric. "Global Cyber Supply Chain Management." *Microsoft Security Blog*, July 26, 2011. http://blogs.technet.com/b/security/archive/2011/07/26/global-cyber-supply-chain-management.aspx.

Weaver, Nicholas. "Thoughts on the NotPetya Ransomware Attack." *Lawfare*, June 28, 2017.

Weber, Rolf H. *Shaping Internet Governance: Regulatory Challenges*. New York: Springer, 2009.

Weedon, Jen, William Nuland, and Alex Stamos. *Information Operations and Facebook*. Menlo Park, CA: Facebook Security, April 27, 2017.

Weinberger, Sharon. "Pentagon Official Says Flash Drive Used in Classified Attack." *AOL News*, August 25, 2010. http://www.aolnews.com/2010/08/25/pentagon-official-says-flash-drive-used-in-classified-cyberattac/.

Weitz, Richard. "Global Insights: The DHS' Cybersecurity Logjam." *World Politics Review* (April 10, 2012).

Wendt, Alexander. *Social Theory of International Politics*. Cambridge: Cambridge University Press, 1999.

Wheeler, David A. "Planning for the Future of Cyber Attack Attribution," statement before the US House of Representatives Committee on Science and Technology Subcommittee on Technology and Innovation, July 15, 2010. http://science.house.gov/sites/republicans.science.house.gov/files/documents/hearings/071510_Wheeler.pdf.

Whitney, Lance. "U.S. Cyber Command Prepped to Launch" *CNET News—Security*, March 23, 2010.

Williams, Brett. "Cyberspace: What is it, Where is it, and Who Cares?" *Armed Forces Journal* (March 13, 2014). http://armedforcesjournal.com/cyberspace-what-is-it-where-is-it-and-who-cares/.

Wilson, Clay. *Avatars, Virtual Reality Technology, and the U.S. Military: Emerging Policy Issues*. Washington, DC: Congressional Research Service, April 2008.

Wines, Michael, Sharon LaFraniere, and Jonathan Ansfield. "China's Censors Tackle and Trip over the Internet." *New York Times*, April 8, 2010.

Wong, Gillian. "Chinese Police Shut Down Hacker Training Business." *Washington Post*, February 8, 2010.

Worthen, Ben. "Internet Strategy: China's Next Generation Internet." *CIO.com*, July 15, 2006. http://www.cio.com/article/22985/Internet_Strategy_China_s_Next_Generation_Internet_.

Wouters, Jan, and Sten Verhoeven. "The Prohibition of Genocide as a Norm of Jus Cogens and its Implications for the Enforcement of the Law of Genocide." *International Criminal Law Review* 5 (2005).

Wu, Tim. *The Master Switch: The Rise and Fall of Information Empires.* New York: Alfred A. Knopf, 2010.

Yannakogeorgos, Panayotis A. "Cyberspace: The New Frontier and the Same Old Multilateralism." In *Global Norms, American Sponsorship, and the Emerging Pattern of World Politics*, edited by Simon Reich, 147–77. New York: Palgrave, 2010.

Yannakogeorgos, Panayotis A. "Internet Governance and National Security." *Strategic Studies Quarterly* 6, no. 3 (Fall 2012).

Yannakogeorgos, Panayotis A. "The Rise of IPv6: Benefits and Costs of Transforming Military Cyberspace." *Air & Space Power Journal* 29, no. 2 (March–April 2015. http://www.afspc.af.mil/news1/story.asp?id=123249968.

Yu, Yang. "Chinese Response to 'Further Notice of Inquiry on the Internet Assigned Numbers Authority Functions.'" China Organizational Name Administration Center (CONAC), July 22, 2011. http://www.ntia.doc.gov/files/ntia/conac_response_to_fnoi.pdf.

Zetter, Kim. "The Return of the Worm that Ate the Pentagon." *Wired*, December 9, 2011. http://www.wired.com/dangerroom/tag/operation-buckshot-yankee/.

Zhao, H. "ITU and Internet Governance—Input to the 7th meeting of the ITU Council Working Group on WSIS," December 12–14, 2004. https://www.itu.int/council/wsis/Geneva3_04/Doc6_Zhao-rev1.doc.

Zimet, Elihu, and Edward Skoudis. "A Graphical Introduction to the Structural Elements of Cyberspace." In *Cyber Power and National Security*, edited by Franklin D. Kramer, Stuart H. Starr, and Larry K. Wentz, 91–112. Washington, DC: NDU Press, 2009.

Index

About the Contributors

Christopher Bronk is an assistant professor of computer and information systems and associate director of the Center for Information Security Research and Education. He holds additional appointments in Rice University's Department of Computer Science and the University of Toronto's Munk School of Global Affairs. He also served as a career diplomat and senior advisor at the U.S. State Department. He earned a PhD from The Maxwell School of Syracuse University, studied international relations at Oxford University, and received a bachelor's degree from the University of Wisconsin-Madison.

Chris C. Demchak is the Grace M. Hopper Professor of Cyber Security and director of the Center for Cyber Conflict Studies (C3S), Strategic and Operational Research Department, U.S. Naval War College. She has also been a LISP programmer, military officer, and tenured University of Arizona professor. She is coeditor of *Designing Resilience* (2010) and author of *Wars of Disruption and Resilience* (2011) and a manuscript in production tentatively entitled *Cyber Westphalia: Redrawing International Economics, Conflict, and Global Structures*. She earned a PhD in political science from the University of California at Berkeley, an MA in economic development from Princeton, an MA in energy engineering from the University of California at Berkeley, and a BA (with high honors) in political science from the University of California, Riverside.

Peter Dombrowski is a professor of strategy in the Strategic and Operational Research Department at the U.S. Naval War College. Previous positions include director of the Naval War College Press, editor of the *Naval War*

College Review, coeditor of *International Studies Quarterly*, associate professor of political science at Iowa State University, and defense analyst at ANSER, Inc. He is the author of over sixty-five books, monographs, articles, book chapters, and government reports and is coauthor with Simon Reich of *The End of Grand Strategy: Maritime Operations in the 21st Century* (2017). He earned a PhD and MA from the University of Maryland and a BA from Williams College.

James P. Farwell is the president and CEO of the Farwell Group. He is also an associate fellow in the Department of War Studies at Kings College, London, and a nonresident senior fellow at the Middle East Institute in Washington, DC. He holds a JD in law from Tulane University and a DCLS in comparative law from the University of Cambridge. He is a certified information privacy professional/United States (CIPP/US) in cybersecurity. He is the author of *Persuasion and Power: The Art of Strategic Communication* (2012) and *The Pakistan Cauldron: Conspiracy, Assassination, and Instability* (2011) and coauthor of *The Architecture of Cybersecurity* (2017) with Virginia Roddy, Geoff Elkins, and Yvonne Chalker.

Michael V. Hayden is the former director of the Central Intelligence Agency, the former director of the National Security Agency, and a retired U.S. Air Force general. He previously served as the first principal deputy director of national intelligence and the highest-ranking military intelligence officer in the United States. He is currently a principal at the Chertoff Group and a distinguished visiting professor at the George Mason University Schar School of Policy and Government. He is the author of *Playing to the Edge: American Intelligence in the Age of Terror* (2016).

Roger Hurwitz was a research scientist at MIT's Computer Science and Artificial Intelligence Laboratory (CSAIL), a senior fellow at the Canada Centre for Global Security Studies at the University of Toronto, and a founder of Explorations in Cyber International Relations (ECIR), a Minerva Research Initiative program at Harvard and MIT. He previously served on the faculties of Northeastern and the Hebrew University and was a codeveloper of the White House Electronics Publication System and the Open Meeting System for Large Scale Collaboration during the Clinton administration. His publications include *Communication Flows: A Census in the United States and Japan* (1984), coauthored with Ithiel de Sola Pool and Hiroshi Inose. He held a PhD in computational social science from MIT. Roger passed away on April 18, 2015.

Martin C. Libicki holds the Keyser Chair of cybersecurity studies at the U.S. Naval Academy and is the author of *Cyberspace in Peace and War*.

He is a former senior scientist at RAND and former senior fellow at the National Defense University. He holds a PhD and MA from the University of California, Berkeley.

Herbert Lin is a senior research scholar for cyber policy and security at the Center for International Security and Cooperation and Hank J. Holland Fellow in Cyber Policy and Security at the Hoover Institution, Stanford University. He is also a chief scientist emeritus at the Computer Science and Telecommunications Board, National Research Council of the National Academies, and recently served on the President's Commission on Enhancing National Cybersecurity. He earned a PhD in physics from MIT.

Eric F. Mejia is a colonel in the U.S. Air Force and is currently assigned as the staff judge advocate for Air University. He holds a JD degree from the University of Arkansas at Little Rock Law School, is a 2004 distinguished graduate of the Air Command and Staff College, and 2013 graduate of Air War College, earning his master of strategic studies degree with highest academic distinction.

Joseph S. Nye Jr. is the University Distinguished Service Professor and former dean of Harvard's Kennedy School of Government. He received his bachelor's degree summa cum laude from Princeton, attended Oxford University as a Rhodes Scholar, and earned a PhD in political science from Harvard. He has served as assistant secretary of defense for international security affairs, chair of the National Intelligence Council, and a deputy undersecretary of state. He is best known for developing and expounding on the term *soft power* in a number of articles and books.

Mark Raymond is the Wick Cary Assistant Professor of International Security at the University of Oklahoma and a fellow at the Center for Democracy and Technology. He is the coeditor, with Gordon Smith, of *Organized Chaos: Reimagining the Internet* (2014). He earned a PhD and MA in political science from the University of Toronto and a BA (with honors) from the University of Western Ontario.

Gary Schaub Jr. is a senior researcher at the Centre for Military Studies, Department of Political Science, University of Copenhagen, and a consultant to the Institute for Defense Analyses. He previously served as assistant professor of strategy at the U.S. Air War College, research fellow at the U.S. Air Force Research Institute, visiting assistant professor at the U.S. Air Force School of Advanced Air and Space Studies, researcher at the Center for International Studies at the University of Pittsburgh, and adjunct assistant professor of history at Chatham College. He earned a PhD from the Graduate School of Public and International Affairs at the University of Pittsburgh, an MA in political science from the University of Illinois at Urbana–Champaign, and a BS (with college and university honors) in applied history and policy and management from Carnegie Mellon University.

Panayotis A. Yannakogeorgos is the dean of the Air Force Cyber College at the Air University. His research interests include the intersection of cyberspace and global security, cyber norms, cyber arms control, violent nonstate actors, and Balkan and Eastern Mediterranean studies. He formerly held appointments as research professor of cyber policy at the Air Force Research Institute, senior program coordinator at the Rutgers University Division of Global Affairs, and was an adviser to the UN Security Council. He holds PhD and MS degrees in global affairs from Rutgers University and an ALB degree in philosophy from Harvard University.

Lightning Source UK Ltd.
Milton Keynes UK
UKHW010610040419
340470UK00001B/73/P